D1459936

EXPLORING ★★ ★★AMERICAN CITIZENSHIP★

John R. O'Connor
Robert M. Goldberg

GLOBE FEARON
EDUCATIONAL PUBLISHER
PARAMUS, NEW JERSEY

Paramount Publishing

John R. O'Connor

John R. O'Connor holds a B.A. from St. Francis College and an M.A. from the University of Pittsburgh. He taught social studies for many years before becoming a principal in the New York City school system. He is widely known for his lectures and articles on reading skills in the social studies. In addition to this book, Mr. O'Connor coauthored other Globe textbooks: *Exploring United States History, Exploring World History, Exploring American History,* and *Unlocking Social Studies Skills.* He edited Globe's *Exploring a Changing World* and *Exploring the Non-Western World.*

Robert M. Goldberg

Robert M. Goldberg holds a B.A. from Brooklyn College, an M.A. from New York University, and a Professional Certificate in administration and supervision from Queens College. He is a social studies specialist and has been active in the fields of urban education, remedial teaching, geography, citizenship education, and also in the development of techniques for teaching social studies skills. He was formerly educational consultant for Diagnostic, Prescriptive, and Remediation Teaching in Oceanside, New York. He was chairman of the social studies department as well as facilitator for the special education teachers, and other teams of teachers interested in interdisciplinary approaches to teaching, at Oceanside Middle School. He is now a consultant for the Oceanside Middle School. In addition to this book, Mr. Goldberg is coauthor of Globe's *Unlocking Geography Skills and Concepts,* and *Unlocking the Constitution and the Declaration of Independence.*

Consultants

Mary Edmond
Director of Multicultural Education/Sex Equity
Grand Rapids Public Schools
Grand Rapids, Michigan

Barry Nelson
Assistant Principal
Supervision, Social Studies
John Dewey High School
Brooklyn, New York

William Marks
Former K-12 Social Studies Coordinator
Dallas Schools
Dallas, Texas

Steven Wolfson
Assistant Principal
Supervision, Social Studies
Fort Hamilton High School
Brooklyn, New York

Helen Richardson
Executive Director for Curriculum
Fulton County Schools
Atlanta, Georgia

Eleanor Smith
Social Studies Teacher
Charlotte-Mecklenburg Public Schools
Charlotte, North Carolina

Illustrations: Duchesne Graphics, Marvin Stein
Photo Research: Lois Safrani
Maps: Function-Thru-Form, Inc., Dyno Lowenstein, York Graphic Services
Cover: photo, Chelsea J. Schrenk; design, Lerner Communications
Text Design: Nancy Dale Muldoon
Acknowledgments for photographs are on pages vi and vii.

ISBN: 0-835-90779-1

Printed in the United States of America   4 5 6 7 8 9 10 99

TABLE OF CONTENTS

Unit 1 AMERICAN CITIZENSHIP AND GOVERNMENT

Unit 2 AMERICAN DEMOCRACY

Unit 3 AMERICAN POLITICAL PARTIES

Unit 4 THE FEDERAL GOVERNMENT

Unit 5   STATE AND LOCAL GOVERNMENTS

Unit 6   OUR SYSTEM OF JUSTICE

Unit 7   OUR ECONOMIC SYSTEM

Unit 8 OUR FOREIGN POLICY

Unit 9 CAREERS IN GOVERNMENT

Appendix

Participation in Government

PHOTO ACKNOWLEDGMENTS

Abbreviations:
F.P.G.: Freelance Photographers Guild
UPI: United Press International
AP: Associated Press

UNIT 1

1: © George Jones/Photo Researchers. 3: (right) Uniphoto. (left) © Stuart Cohen Stock/Boston. 4: Brown Brothers. 11: The Bettmann Archive. 12: (top) Brown Brothers; (bottom) UPI/Bettmann. 13: AP/Wide World Photos. 17: UPI. 18: (top) Museum of the American Indian; (bottom) Brown Brothers. 19: H. Armstrong Roberts. 24: Brown Brothers. 25: Frederic Lewis/Harold Lambert. 26: (top) Brown Brothers; (bottom) Shostal Associates. 30: © Ed Carlin Jr./Frederic Lewis. 31: Brown Brothers. 32: Brown Brothers. 33: (top) The Bettmann Archive/Walker; (bottom) © Paul S. Davis/New England Life.

UNIT 2

39: Bettmann Newsphotos. 40: Bettmann Newsphotos. 41: Brown Brothers. 43: © Eric Carle/Shostal Associates. 47: UPI. 48: Photoworld. 49: UPI. 50: Wide World Photos. 51:(top) © 1978 Betty Medsger; (bottom) Brown Brothers. 56: © Wally MacNee/Woodfin-Camp Associates. 57: (top) Wide World Photos; (bottom) © Jacques M. Chenet/Woodfin-Camp. 58: Brown Brothers. 59: © Bruce Roberts/Photo Researchers. 64: Culver Pictures. 65: (top) Dennis Cook/AP/Wide World Photos; (bottom) © Bob Burroughs/The New York Times. 66: © Michal Heron/Woodfin-Camp Associates. 67: Wide World Photos. 71: Frederic Lewis. 72: UPI. 74: Reuters/Bettmann. 75: © O. Franklin/Sygma.

UNIT 3

79: Reuters/Bettmann. 80: Paul Conklin/Monkmeyer Press. 81: Scott Applegate/AP/Wide World. 83: (left and right) Culver Pictures. 85: Historical Pictures Service. 86: © Mark Reinstein 1990/Uniphoto. 87: © Cindy Charles/Gamma-Liaison. 88: The Boatman's National Bank of St. Louis. 90: Traver/Gamma-Liaison. 95: © Arnold Zann/Black Star. 96: (top) UPI/Bettmann Archive; (bottom) Beryl Goldberg. 99: © Howard Jensen/Scala. 100: Historical Pictures Service.

UNIT 4

107: © Robert Llewellyn. 108: © Costas/Shostal Associates. 109: Wide World Photos. 110: UPI. 111: (right) Monkmeyer Press; (left) UPI. 115: The Bettmann Archive. 117: (top) Gamma-Liaison; (bottom) Terry Ashe/Gamma-Liaison. 121: Library of Congress. 122: B. Markel/Gamma-Liaison. 127: © Frank Fisher/Gamma-Liaison. 128: UPI. 129: Wide World Photos. 130: © Kenny Ashe/Uniphoto. 135: Wide World Photos. 136: UPI/Bettmann Newsphotos. 137: © Dennis Brack/Black Star. 138: UPI. 139: © Dennis Brack/Black Star. 140: (top) UPI; (bottom) © Max Winter/Stock Boston. 143: Shostal Associates. 145: UPI. 146: UPI. 147: UPI/Bettmann Newsphotos. 148: (top and bottom) Wide World Photos. 152: © Terry Arthur/White House Photo. 153: Brown Brothers. 154: EPA/Phototake. 155: Chase Manhattan. 157: © Les Moore/Aging Image/Uniphoto. 162: Reuters/Bettmann. 163: UPI. 164: Wide World Photos. 165: Mike Yamshita/Woodfin-Camp. 166: Library of Congress. 171: Dennis Cook/AP/Wide World Photos. 172: Wide World Photos. 175: (top) © Katrina Thomas/Photo Researchers; (bottom) © Randy Taylor/Sygma. 176: © Beryl Goldberg 1979.

UNIT 5

181: © Anne Heimann/Stock Market. 182: Photoworld. 183: © Beryl Goldberg 1979. 184: Wide World Photos. 185: Bob Daemmrich/The Image Works. 188: Craig Hammell/Stock Market. 189: © Mike Keating/Photo Researchers. 191: Suzanne Szasz/Photo Researchers. 196: Lawrence Migdale/Photo Researchers. 197: © Yvonne Freund, Rapho/Photo Researchers. 199: (top) Farrell Grehan/Photo Researchers; (bottom) Dade County Manager's Office. 200: Photoworld. 205: © Marc Romanelli/Image Bank. 206: H. Armstrong Roberts. 207: Harold M. Lambert. 211: Office of Public Information Houston Police Department. 214: © Martin M. Rotker/Taurus Photos. 215: Will McIntyre/Photo Researchers. 216: (top right and left) © Beryl Goldberg; (bottom) © Jim Pozanik/Gamma-Liaison.

UNIT 6

221: Shostal Associates. 223: Photoworld. 225: (top) UPI; (bottom) © John Running/Stock Photo. 226: Wide World Photos. 227: © Paul Conklin/Monkmeyer Press. 233: (top) ©

Chas. Gatewood; (bottom) UPI. 234: Photoworld. 235: © Beryl Goldberg. 236: © Stacy Pick/Uniphoto. 239: (top right and left) Spring 3100, NYPD Magazine; (bottom) Photoworld. 240: (top) The Bettmann Archive; (bottom) © Bryan Allen/Shostal Associates. 241: © 1985 John Ashe/Stock Market. 242: Shostal Associates. 244:Georg Gester/Photo Researchers. 249: (top and bottom) UPI. 250: (top) Bureau of Public Information, NYPD, City of New York; (bottom) Bob Daemmrich/The Image Works. 251: Bureau of Public Information, NYPD, City of New York. 252: (top) © Stacy Pick/Uniphoto; (bottom) Photoworld. 257: © Bob Daemmrich/The Image Works. 258: (top) Brooks, The Birmingham News; (bottom) © Gail Greeg/Shostal Associates. 259: © Beryl Goldberg 1979.

UNIT 7

267: © Catherine Ursillo/Photo Researchers. 269: Shostal Associates. 270: Henry Monroe. 271: Doria Steedman/Stock Market. 272: Frederic Lewis Photographs. 276: © Betty Medsger. 277: American Stock Exchange. 278: (top) © Shelley Katz/Black Star; (bottom) U.S. Information Agency. 279: The Bettmann Archive. 285: The Bettmann Archive. 286: (top and bottom) Brown Brothers. 287: UPI. 288: © Ellis Herwig/Picture Cube. 293: Frederic Lewis/Cezus. 296: The Bettmann Archive. 297: © Tony Hollyman/Photo Researchers. 301: Frederic Lewis. 302: H. Armstrong Roberts. 303: Bob Daemmrich/The Image Works. 304: Beryl Goldberg. 310: USDA. 311: © Beryl Goldberg. 312: (top) © Dennis Brack/Black Star; (bottom) © Beryl Goldberg. 317: The Bettmann Archive. 318: © Jeff Albertson/Picture Cube. 320: ©

Mary Kay Keegan. 322: Alan Carey/The Image Works. 329: The Bettmann Archive. 330: © Julie Houdon/Stock Boston. 331: Culver Pictures. 332: Frederic Lewis Photographs. 333: (top) © Stacy Pick/Stock Boston; (bottom) Tass/Sovofoto.

UNIT 8

339: The Photo Source Ltd./Shostal Associates. 341: (top) Historical Pictures Service; (bottom) Library of Congress. 342: UPI. 343: Wide World Photos. 347: © 1990 Dennis Brack/Black Star. 348: UPI. 349: UPI. 350: © Peter L. Gould/F.P.G. 351: Wide World Photos. 352: © 1990 Black Star Pool/P. Huber. 356: Halstead/Gamma-Liaison. 357: United States Senate. 358: Photoworld. 359: Joe Marquette/UPI/Bettmann Newsphotos. 360: Bill Gentile/Sipa Press. 366: © O. Franklin/Sygma. 367: The United Nations. 368: (top and bottom) The United Nations. 369: UPI/Bettmann. 370: (top and bottom) UPI. 374: © Tom Mihalek/Sygma. 375: (top) The United Nations; (bottom) B. Sumner/Stock Market. 376: Wide World Photos. 377: Jeremy Bigwood/Gamma-Liaison.

UNIT 9

381: Dammerich. 383: U.S. Civil Service Commission. 384: UPI. 385: U.S. Civil Service Commission. 386: © Beryl Goldberg. 390: Gabe Palmer/Stock Market. 391: The National Education Association. 392: (top) © Mary Randlett; (bottom) © Larry Downing/Woodfin-Camp. 393: © Beryl Goldberg. 394: Reuters/Bettmann.

Unit 1 ★

AMERICAN CITIZENSHIP AND GOVERNMENT

The final step in becoming a citizen of the United States—taking the oath of allegiance.

1

THE AMERICAN CITIZEN

PURPOSES FOR READING

1. To learn why great value is placed on United States citizenship
2. To learn who citizens of the United States are, and how a person can become a citizen

KNOWING NEW WORDS

Constitution
   (kon stih TOO shun) paragraph 3—the plan of government for the United States
   EXAMPLE: Students read the **Constitution** to learn the rights that all citizens have.

personal
   (PUR suh nul) paragraph 5—of or coming from a particular person; private
   EXAMPLE: How I voted is a **personal** matter.

liberty
   (LIB ur tee) paragraph 5—the freedom to act as one chooses
   EXAMPLE: Her parents gave her the **liberty** to choose whether or not she wanted to go with them.

security
   (sih KYOOR ih tee) paragraph 5—freedom from danger or risk
   EXAMPLE: The armed forces provide us with **security** from enemy attack.

Few people anywhere have as many rights, freedoms, and powers as the citizens of the United States.

1▶ Who is this United States citizen who has the rights and powers shown in the pictures on page 2? If you are born in the United States, you are an American citizen—as soon as you are born. Persons born in the United States are members of the United States family at once. Sometimes persons are citizens at birth even if they were born outside the country. This is so when one or both of their parents are citizens. But such citizen-parents must have lived a certain period of time in the United States or its possessions.

2▶ However, you may be an **alien,** that is, a person who lives in the United States but who is not a citizen. You may want to join the United States family. You can become a **naturalized** citizen. This is the legal way by which a person gets new **citizenship.** Sometimes, a law is passed to naturalize a group of people all at once. In 1868, after the Civil War, African Americans were given citizenship by the Fourteenth Amendment. In 1900 Congress passed a law giving citizenship to the people of Hawaii. Puerto Ricans became citizens in 1917. American Indians, the people of Guam, and those of the Virgin Islands were granted citizenship in the same way—by an act of Congress.

3▶ Suppose you want to become a citizen on your own. Most aliens do. Read the information in the following box. Learn the steps you would have to take.

How an Alien Becomes an American Citizen

· **Petition**
You can petition for citizenship if you have lived in the United States for at least five years (three if married to an American citizen and even less if you have served in the armed forces). You must agree to be loyal to the government of the United States and give up loyalty to the country you are currently a citizen of. You must also prove that you have only one husband or wife.

· **Examination**
You will be tested to show that you can read, write, and speak English. But if you have been living in the United States for 20 or more years and are at least 50 years old, the rule is different. You can be tested in your native language or any other language. You must also prove that you know and understand the main ideas and events in the history of the United States government.

· **Citizenship Granted**
If you pass the test, you will be asked to swear to obey the laws of the United States. This is what is meant by **pledging your allegiance.**

From 1892 to 1943 millions of immigrants entered the United States through Ellis Island—located in the harbor of New York. Why did so many people want to come to the United States?

4► Nations and bosses are sometimes much alike. Bosses may not care much about the persons they select for jobs if there are many jobs to be filled. However, if there are only a few jobs open, they are likely to select those people with the most needed skills. So it is with nations. The United States is a nation made up of many individuals. Some of these people have come from other countries. They are **immigrants.** Others are children, grandchildren, great-grandchildren, and so forth, of these immigrants. At first, because there was so much open land and many jobs to fill, almost everybody was welcome as an immigrant. After a while, however, there was less land for newcomers and fewer jobs. Sometimes the rules for admitting immigrants were not equal for all groups. Some people were not allowed to become citizens of the United States. Chinese and Japanese were among the first to be forbidden citizenship. Although this has been changed, limits have been placed on the number of people who may enter the United States in any year. About 675,000 people are allowed to enter the country each year.

Also, the president can admit refugees. These are people who are forced to leave their own country for fear of being persecuted. There are over 14 million refugees in the world today.

5► If something has great worth, many people want it. Millions of people all over the world want to be citizens of the United States because United States citizenship is worth so much. Each United States citizen has rights that many other governments will not give to their people. These rights are written down for all to know. There can be no mistake about what they are. They do not depend upon the wishes of a single ruler or group. Rights of United States citizens are of three kinds: personal liberty, personal security, and personal property.

6► **Personal liberties** are special freedoms given to every citizen. Freedom of speech, freedom of religious beliefs, and freedom of the press are examples. Americans can also gather together in groups peacefully. They are used to these freedoms. Often, Americans do not realize that in many countries of the world, citizens have never enjoyed these liberties.

7▶ **Personal security** means that every citizen has the right to enjoy life in safety and to be given the chance to build a good name. These rights extend to people who are accused of a crime. Under the laws of the United States government, persons are to be treated as innocent until they are proven guilty. Every citizen has **property rights.** Each can own property. There are few limits placed on the use of personal property. No one can take a person's property without following the laws that protect property rights. Even the government cannot take a person's property for its own use without paying the owner what the property is worth.

8▶ Yes, American citizens have many freedoms. But that does not mean that everyone can do whatever he or she pleases without respect for others. For every right that a citizen has, there is also a duty. The right to have a jury trial carries with it the duty of the citizen to serve on a jury when asked. The right to vote should carry with it the citizen's responsibility to know about the candidates for office and to vote wisely. A citizen should not use property to harm others. A citizen should not set fire to his or her property and endanger the property of others nearby. A citizen may speak freely on any subject. Yet, a person should not abuse this right by shouting "Fire!" in a crowded theater. That would place the lives of others in danger. Being a citizen is a special privilege. Good citizens know their rights and use their rights. At the same time, they respect the rights of others.

9▶ The rights of United States citizens are very dear to them. They would never want them taken away. Millions of people have come to the United States because they wanted to enjoy the freedom of this country. There are millions more who would come if they had the chance to do so. They would be happy to take the responsibilities that go along with each right protected by the United States government.

10▶ In this book we will study how that government works—how we rule ourselves. We will learn how we protect our personal liberty, our safety, our property. We will learn how we act as responsible citizens. We will learn the dangers we face if we do not.

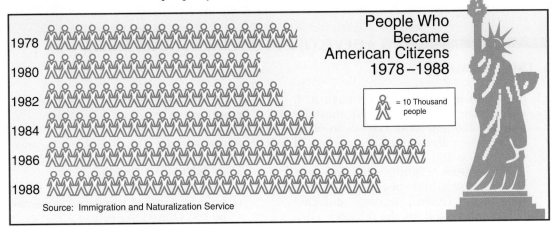

People Who Became American Citizens 1978–1988

= 10 Thousand people

1978
1980
1982
1984
1986
1988

Source: Immigration and Naturalization Service

CHAPTER 1 REVIEW

★ UNDERSTANDING WHAT YOU HAVE READ

1. Another title for this chapter might be
   a. "How a Person Becomes a Citizen"
   b. "Why People Come to America"
   c. "The Rights of Citizens"

2. How persons may get United States citizenship is told in paragraphs
   a. 2 and 4
   b. 3 and 6
   c. 2 and 3

3. Paragraph 1 tells us that to be born a United States citizen, a person must be
   a. born in the United States or have a parent who is a United States citizen
   b. born only to a United States citizen who has lived at least 20 years within the country
   c. naturalized

4. Paragraph 5 tells us that
   a. United States citizens are immigrants
   b. United States citizens have three kinds of rights
   c. United States citizens are leaving the country

5. In paragraph 2, we learn that all of these groups were made citizens by laws passed by Congress EXCEPT
   a. American Indians
   b. Puerto Ricans
   c. Japanese Americans

6. United States citizens are sure of the rights they have because
   a. our judges have often told them of their rights
   b. they are written down for all to read
   c. England granted rights to its settlers in America

7. For every right a citizen has, there is also a
   a. duty
   b. liberty
   c. privilege

8. There are limits on the rights of citizens in that
   a. a state may take away any right by passing a law
   b. one person's rights should not take away the rights of another person
   c. new citizens of the United States do not have all the rights of other citizens

★ DEVELOPING SOCIAL STUDIES SKILLS

A. Using a Chart

1. Read part II of the chart on page 3. It states that people under 50 must be able to read and write English in order to become citizens. Yet the people in Puerto Rico and Guam, some of whom do not speak English, are American citizens. How did people in Puerto Rico and Guam become citizens? Which paragraph of the chapter contains the information to answer the question?

2. According to the chart on page 7, American citizens could be people born
   a. in the United States only
   b. anywhere in the world
   c. only in parts of the world governed by the United States

HOW A PERSON BECOMES A CITIZEN BY BIRTH
A Person Becomes a Citizen by Being:

Born Under American Authority in:	Born Outside American Authority
The United States	To Parents:
Puerto Rico	Both of whom are American citizens
Guam	One of whom is an American citizen
Virgin Islands	
United States ships anywhere	
Any United States embassy or legation (offices of the United States in another country)	

B. Using the Parts of a Book

Knowing the parts of a book will be useful to you. First, look at the **title page.** It is at the front of the book. On this page, you find the name or title of the book, the names of the persons who wrote it, and the company that published it.

Following the title page is a **table of contents.** This is a list of the book's units and chapters. The list shows the page numbers on which the units and chapters begin. Sometimes a book has lists of maps and special features and their page numbers. The table of contents gives you an idea of the kinds of information you will find in the book.

Near the end of the book are the **glossary** and **index.** A glossary is a list of words and terms and their meanings. The index is a list of important names, places, and topics. The index is arranged in alphabetical order. Next to each item in the index are the numbers of the pages where the item is mentioned. The index helps you locate all the important topics in the book.

Use what you have learned about the parts of the book to answer the following questions. Write your answers on a separate sheet of paper.

1. Who are the authors of this book?

2. What kind of book is suggested by the title?

3. Where can you find a list of the titles of units and chapters?

4. On what page of the book does the list of many words and their meanings begin?

5. How many units are there in this book?

6. In which unit can you find out how political parties are organized?

7. In which unit can you learn how a bill becomes a law?

8. On what page or pages is county government mentioned?

9. On what page might you find out what a party platform is?

C. Using Word Clues

A good detective uses clues in order to solve a crime. A good student uses clues to figure out the meaning of unknown or difficult words. These clues are called context clues. They help us learn new words because they point out the meaning. All of the following are context or word clues:

a comma, the word *or,* parentheses, a dash, the words *that is* following the new word, the sentence following the new word, the sentence before the new word

In chapter 1, the following words have clues that tell you their meaning. The clues are described for you. Locate each of the words and clues in the chapter.

• paragraph 2   **alien.** The meaning of the word alien is in the part of the sentence that follows the words, "that is."

• paragraph 2   **in the same way.** The dash (—) after these words tells that the words in the same way mean "by an act of Congress."

• chart, page 3   **pledging allegiance.** The sentence before the words pledging your allegiance tells the meaning of the term.

• paragraph 4   **immigrants.** The sentence before the sentence "They are immigrants" gives the meaning of the word immigrants.

• chart, page 7   **embassy** or **legation.** The words embassy or legation are followed by parentheses ( ). The words in parentheses explain the meaning of embassy or legation.

Throughout this book, there will be such clues for words that may not be familiar to you. Look for them. From time to time, you will be given an opportunity to review these clues.

★DEVELOPING CRITICAL THINKING SKILLS

A. Interpreting a Poem

The following is part of a poem written by Emma Lazarus. It was placed on a tablet at the main entrance to the Statue of Liberty. (The French people had given the statue to the United States as a gift. It was raised in New York harbor in 1886.) The words on the tablet tell a great deal about the millions of immigrants who have come to the United States. Before reading the poem be sure you understand the following words:

huddled   (HUD uld)—crowded closely together
EXAMPLE: The lost children **huddled** together in the woods.

refuse   (REF yoos)—trash, something no one wants
EXAMPLE: The people thought to be **refuse** by some Europeans helped to make America great.

In Emma Lazarus's poem, the statue is saying:

> *. . . Give me your tired, your poor,*
> *Your huddled masses yearning to breathe free,*
> *The wretched refuse of your teeming shore.*
> *Send these, the homeless, tempest-tost, to me.*
> *I lift my lamp beside the golden door!*

1. We call this statue the Statue of Liberty because
   a. the statue can be visited for free
   b. it represents a spirit of freedom and welcome
   c. it was placed in the harbor when the United States became free from England

2. Who are the "huddled masses yearning to breathe free"?
   a. The immigrants who were slaves
   b. The immigrants who were Christians
   c. Immigrants who wanted to come to America

3. Who is speaking in the poem?
   a. The Statue of Liberty
   b. The New York State government
   c. The people of the United States

4. Why might New York harbor be considered the "golden door"?
   a. It was the entrance to a better life for most immigrants.
   b. The Golden Gate Bridge is in the harbor.
   c. The Statue of Liberty is made mostly of gold.

5. An immigrant is one who
   a. has left one country to visit a new country
   b. has left one country to live in another country
   c. has become a citizen of the United States

6. The poem says that most of the immigrants were
   a. poor
   b. rich
   c. farmers

B. Writing About Citizenship

Imagine you are a citizen of a country other than the United States. Write an essay describing reasons why you might want to become a United States citizen.

2

THE NEED FOR GOVERNMENT

PURPOSES FOR READING

1. To understand why we need government
2. To understand a few of the different types of governments
3. To understand why governments cost money
4. To understand about the citizens' responsibilities to their government

KNOWING NEW WORDS

conditions
    (kun DISH uns) paragraph 5—the ways people or things are
    EXAMPLE: Some people live under poor **conditions.** Others may live under very good **conditions.**

inherit
    (in HEH rits) paragraph 4—to receive a gift from someone who has died

EXAMPLE: The prince **inherits** his father's kingdom. He then becomes the king.

regulate
    (REG yuh layt) paragraph 2—to control by use of rules
    EXAMPLE: The queen passed laws in order to **regulate** the lives of her people.

Here are people living without any kind of government. Name some ways they could help themselves by forming a government.

1 ► It would be nice to be free to do as one pleases. So some people may think. However, imagine the disorder if everyone did as he or she pleased. Even people who care about others' rights do not always agree on everything. Furthermore, there are people who don't seem to care whether they respect the rights and property of others. To prevent the kind of disorder shown in the cartoon on page 10, peoples all over the world have formed governments.

2 ► Government is the authority that makes and enforces laws and looks after the public (people's) interests. A government is more than just persons who hold public office. It is the combination of all the laws and customs of a country together with the public officials who carry out those laws. A law, of course, is a rule made by the government. It is made for people. Laws regulate people's lives. Governments are not always the same. They differ from place to place and from country to country. Still, the goals of governments are often the same.

3 ► Governments try to make known the rights and duties of all their people. They help to keep order and protect lives and property. They have ways of making people perform their duties. Governments can punish those who are not willing to perform them. Governments often take over jobs that private citizens would have difficulty doing. Such jobs might include taking care of streets, establishing schools, preventing crime, guarding public health, and settling arguments among citizens.

4 ► There are many kinds of governments that try to carry out these goals. In some of them, one person is the ruler. This

Louis XIV was the absolute monarch of France three hundred years ago. Are there any absolute monarchs in power today?

ruler has great control over the lives of the people. One such kind of government is a **monarchy** (MON ur kee). The ruling person who inherits his or her title and position is called a monarch. Very often the monarch is a king or queen. Sometimes the monarch is called a shah or sheik. If the monarch has a great deal of power, the government is called an **absolute monarchy**. The people have little to say about what kind of laws there should be. If the country limits the powers of the monarch, the government is called a **limited monarchy**.

5 ► If a person gains control of a government without inheriting the title of monarch, we call the ruler a **dictator.** Such a government is called a **dictatorship.** Few dare oppose the dictator. A person's rights are those the dictator allows. There are dictatorships today in Africa, South America, Asia, and Europe. In this century sev-

Hitler, dictator of Germany, and Franco, dictator of Spain, inspect troops in the late 1930s. Why do dictators often depend upon troops to keep themselves in power?

eral dictators gained total control over the countries they ruled. These governments are called **totalitarian.** In such totalitarian governments the ruler or rulers control the daily life of all the citizens. Totalitarian governments try to control not only economic and political conditions but also what people think, believe, and value. The government uses terror to force the people to do what the ruler wants them to do. Adolf Hitler of Nazi Germany and Joseph

From 1929 to 1953, Joseph Stalin ruled the Soviet Union as a brutal totalitarian dictator. He executed millions who opposed him.

Stalin of the Soviet Union were totalitarian dictators.

6 ▶ If a country is ruled by a small group of people, we call it an **oligarchy** (OL uh gar kee). Sometimes the small group is made up of wealthy people who have inherited their titles (such as dukes, countesses, barons). This kind of government is called an **aristocracy** (ar ih STOK ruh see). Hundreds of years ago many governments were of this kind. Present-day oligarchies in some countries really run totalitarian governments. These governments use force to control the people. There is no system by which the people are able to change their condition in an orderly manner. This is the case in some Communist countries.

7 ▶ A democratic government is different from an absolute monarchy, a dictatorship, or an oligarchy. In a democracy, the people as a whole decide how they will be ruled. No present-day government is a *pure,* or direct, democracy. In a pure democracy, all the people vote on every problem that comes before them. Imagine if all the people had to vote on every local and national issue. People would have to spend all their time every day voting. Pure democracy

isn't possible when there are large numbers of people.

8▶ Is the United States government a democracy? Yes. But the United States has a democratic government that is not a pure, or direct, democracy. The form of our government is called **representative democracy.** Because there are so many people, groups of people elect one of their number to represent them. The people vote through their representatives. The representatives of the people make the laws of the country. There is no monarch. This kind of government is called a **republic.** The United States is a republic, and it is a **democratic republic.**

9▶ Of course not all republics are democratic. Nor are all democracies republics. How can this be? In some republics the representatives can be chosen only from the rich or from those who inherit a position in the social life of the country. In other republics not all the adults can vote. In still others there is only one choice when it comes to selecting representatives. These are **undemocratic** republics. Some countries such as the United Kingdom (of which present-day England is a part) are democratic. Yet they have a ruling monarch. The people choose representatives to make the laws. The monarch has very limited real power.

10▶ All governments cost money. The old saying, "You can't get something for nothing," is true of governments. Governments are expected to provide services for their people. Our national government alone spends over a trillion dollars a year to provide the services people want or need. Most citizens want a strong military defense, good health care for all, help for

Elizabeth II of England. How can a country have a monarchy and yet be a democracy?

the poor, speedy transportation, and other benefits. But they must be willing to pay for them. People pay for government services through taxes on income, property, and the goods and services they buy. Most people pay taxes willingly. They do so because they know the tax money is used to provide benefits for most people.

11▶ Governments make laws or rules. We cannot get along without rules. Think how impossible it would be to play games or get along in school or even at home without rules. The rules of government are laws. These laws tell people what they may do or may not do to keep order in their society. Laws make it easier for people to do what is considered the right thing. Laws make it uncomfortable for those who are not willing to do what is considered the right thing. Laws help good citizens. Laws can punish citizens who are not obeying the laws.

12► A citizen has the responsibility to obey the law. Laws are usually not made for the benefit of only a few. In a democracy, laws benefit most people. We may not steal because by doing so we deny our neighbor the right to own property. We obey traffic laws so we do not endanger the lives of others. We pay taxes because the money is used to provide for the good of all. Under our system of government, we have the right to change laws that we think are unwise or unfair. The ways we can change our laws will be studied in later chapters.

CHAPTER 2 REVIEW

★ UNDERSTANDING WHAT YOU HAVE READ

The Main Idea

We cannot remember everything we read, see, or hear. But there are important ideas that ought to remain with us.

In reading this book, you will see that each chapter has a title. The title, or name, of the chapter tells us what the chapter is about. Sometimes it may ask a question that we know will be answered in the chapter. There is a main idea, or purpose, for each chapter.

In the chapter, each paragraph contains an important thought. We call this the main idea of the paragraph. It might be a sentence in the paragraph that tells us what the paragraph is about. Or it might be a thought we get that summarizes the thoughts in the paragraph. Check yourself. See if you can tell which of these are main ideas of paragraphs. The first two are done for you.

1. The main idea of paragraph 2 is that:
   a. laws are made by the people
   b. officials carry out laws
   c. the government looks after the interests of the people

Choice c is the main idea. Look at the facts in the paragraph. Laws are made by the government. Laws are made for people. Governments are not the same, but they may have the same goals. Government is more than officials. Put all these ideas together. The thought they all try to bring to us is that governments look after people in one way or another. That is the main idea.

2. The main idea of paragraph 4 is that:
   a. in a monarchy, the people are ruled by a person who has inherited his or her power
   b. a dictator rules with complete power
   c. in a totalitarian government, people have only the rights their ruler gives them

Choice a is the main idea. The paragraph tells about monarchy, both absolute and limited. Monarchs may be called kings or queens. A monarchy has one ruler. The monarch may be absolute or limited in power.

Now try it on your own.

3. The main idea of paragraph 10 is that:
   a. citizens want their country to have a strong military defense
   b. government services cost money

c. most people pay taxes

4. The main idea of paragraph 11 is that:
   a. laws are needed for order in our lives
   b. lawbreakers are always punished
   c. games need a set of rules

5. The main idea of paragraph 12 is that:
   a. in our system of government, we can change unfair laws
   b. our laws are made for the benefit of most people
   c. tax money is used for many services

★DEVELOPING CRITICAL THINKING SKILLS

A. Interpreting Cartoons

Study the cartoon at the beginning of the chapter. The cartoon shows disorder. To get order from a situation such as the cartoon shows, a government would have to provide some services, or make certain laws. The cartoon shows that collecting and getting rid of garbage is one service that is needed. Can you name some others?

B. Comparing

For each quotation in Column A, choose from Column B the letter of the kind of government that best matches it. Write the answers in your notebook. Letters may be used more than once.

Column A	Column B
1. "Taxes will be collected by the queen's army."	a. Democracy
2. "This is government of the people and by the people and for the people."	b. Absolute monarchy
3. "I accept the crown worn by my father and his father before him."	c. Oligarchy
4. "I have taken over. I am your ruler. I am the state."	d. Dictatorship
5. "We shall elect representatives to govern, one for each 100,000 people."	
6. "The party shall rule, and you shall obey the party."	
7. "There is no power in the country but me. The monarchy is dead."	

3 OUR AMERICAN WAY OF GOVERNMENT GROWS

PURPOSES FOR READING

To learn about the ideas that led to our present laws

KNOWING NEW WORDS

charter
(CHAR tur) paragraph 6—written laws under which people live—a constitution
EXAMPLE: The king signed a **charter** that listed the rules of the colony.

monarch
(MON ark) paragraph 10—a royal ruler such as a king or queen
EXAMPLE: King George was the **monarch** of England and all its colonies.

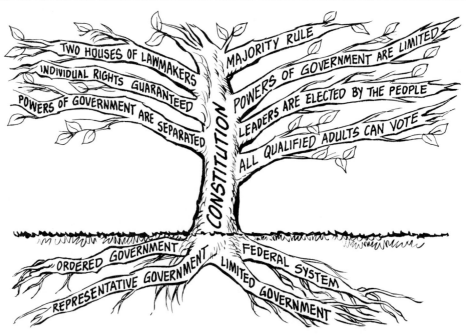

Our American system of government has grown from our roots through our Constitution.

1▶ In the American form of government, the powers of leaders are granted to them by a majority of the people. The way we govern ourselves is the result of the Constitution. The Constitution is the set of written rules by which the people of our nation live and work together.

2▶ The comparison of the American system of government with a tree is a good one. (See diagram on page 16.) The tree is the largest and longest living of all plants. Like a tree, our democratic system, now more than 200 years old, is the longest lasting of its kind. A healthy tree grows and makes a place for itself in nature. Like a tree, our democratic system has grown. It has become stronger with the passing years. It has added many freedoms for its citizens. It has been able to withstand the storms of wars both from within and outside the country. Like a strong tree, our democracy has been able to bend and spring back from the storms that threaten it. It has continued to grow strong, even when it faced new challenges.

3▶ The American way of government did not come about by luck. A fairy godmother did not grant to the writers of the Constitution ''three wishes'' for this great government. Nor was our Constitution an entirely new idea. The men who wrote the Constitution were well educated. They knew the writings of the great minds of Europe and of the early settlers in the colonies. They knew those ideas that served the people and those that did not. They used their knowledge and their skills to draw up a plan of government that has lasted with few **changes** to the present day.

4▶ Many of the roots of our democracy came from England. Although there were many settlers from Holland, Germany, Ireland, France, and Sweden, most early settlers came from England. It was England that ruled the 13 colonies that became the United States. Many of the English settlers came here knowing about their own government. They knew what was good about their government and what things they wanted to change. Three ideas from English government were used in planning the new United States government. These ideas were **ordered** government, **limited** government, and **representative** government.

5▶ **Ordered government.** The settlers knew the importance of order in their new home in America. They quickly set up smaller governments similar to those they knew in England. Many of the things they did are still with us today. They divided their land into smaller parts. Each part was called a county. It was easier to govern

Signing the Magna Carta. Why is this considered a first step in bringing about democracy?

Iroquois objects. Top: A Mohawk pipe. Bottom left: Carved comb made of bone. Right: Pottery jar. In what important way were the settlers influenced by the Iroquois system of government?

smaller sections of land than one large one. The sheriff became the chief law officer. The justice of the peace was the judge in smaller settlements. A **grand jury**—a chosen group of settlers—decided if a person should have a trial. A trial was conducted by a jury of other settlers.

6 ▶ **Limited government.** The settlers thought that governments should not be all-powerful. They believed that government powers should have limits. Each person was thought to have certain God-given rights that a government could not take away. These ideas came from the settlers' past. It was in 1215 that English nobles forced the king to sign the **Magna Carta,** or "Great Charter." This limited the **power** of the English king. Since that time, English people have limited the powers of their rulers more and more. The writers of the Constitution learned from many famous documents—the Magna Carta, the Petition of Right, and the English Bill of Rights.

7 ▶ English settlers brought with them the idea of **representative** government. In England, the governing body is called the **Parliament.** It is made up of two houses, or lawmaking bodies. Most members of one house inherit their position. The people elect the members of the other house. The settlers felt that people should be able to vote and elect all the leaders and representatives. Those who are elected would probably act as their voters wished. The English idea of representative government grew strong in America.

8 ▶ The settlers were also influenced by the system of government among the Native Americans. The Iroquois lived in New York and the Ohio Valley. Each of the six tribal nations of the Iroquois had its own tribal council. In addition, each nation sent representatives to a lawmaking body that governed all six nations. Their government was the first **federal** system in America.

9 ▶ The period of English colonies in

The House of Commons of the British Parliament. Only people who owned property could vote for members of the 18th-century House of Commons.

America lasted for 168 years (1607–1775). This was a growing period for governments in America. During these years, several plans of government were tried. The 13 colonies became like 13 schools of government. Through these years and these trials, Americans learned to master the art of ruling themselves. By the year 1750, there were three main types of government in the colonies. They were different chiefly through the manner in which the governor of the colony was chosen.

10▶ In most colonies there was a governor and two lawmaking bodies or houses. In the **royal** colony, the monarch named the governor and one of the houses that made the laws. The other house had representatives elected by the people in the colony. In the **proprietary** colony, the governor, law-

making bodies, court system, and local governments were set up by the proprietor. This was a person who was given land in America by the monarch. The proprietors were allowed to rule as they wished. A **charter** colony governed itself. The charter was given by the English monarch. It granted land to settlers in America. The governor was elected by the voters of the colony. In the royal and proprietary colonies the governor had the most power. In those two kinds of colonies, he could veto or turn down laws that the lawmakers may have passed. But in the self-governing colonies, the governor had no such power. Gradually the colonists began to dislike those plans that allowed England to control the governments of the colonies.

11▶ When the colonies began having

Many colonial leaders believed that governments should get their powers from the consent of the governed. In 1776 they met to sign the Declaration of Independence.

trouble with the English monarch, they gained new experience in self-government. The First Continental Congress was held in 1774. Twelve colonies sent delegates to try to find ways to end the troubles with England. A year later they met again. This Second Continental Congress was the start of our national government; all 13 colonies sent delegates.

12▶ On July 4, 1776, the colonies declared themselves free from English rule. The Declaration of Independence was signed. The world was told the reasons why the colonies declared themselves a new nation, the United States of America. In that declaration are the words that make this document special to all Americans. The words sum up many ideas of government that led to our Constitution. All people are equal under the law. Everyone has God-given rights of life, liberty, and the right to work for the things that bring happiness. To make sure that these rights are safe, governments are given power by the people. Just before and shortly after the Declaration of Independence each of the 13 states wrote a constitution for itself. These state constitutions used many of the ideas stated in the Declaration of Independence.

13▶ We can see that the tree of American government has grown strong with several roots. There were the ideas from England of ordered, limited, and representative government. There were the writings and documents of thinkers of government in Europe and America. There was the practice in government in the colonies for almost 170 years. In addition, there was the influence of the Native Americans. Finally, these roots were planted in the lives of citizens of the United States with the Declaration of Independence.

CHAPTER 3 REVIEW

★ UNDERSTANDING WHAT YOU HAVE READ

1. Which statement best expresses the main idea of paragraph 2?
   a. A healthy tree grows and makes a place for itself.
   b. Our Constitution is like a strong tree that bends and springs back when storms threaten it.
   c. Our government has granted many freedoms to its citizens.

2. Which sentence best expresses the main idea of paragraph 3?
   a. Our Constitution was an entirely new idea.

   b. The men who wrote our Constitution were not sure of those things that make a good government.
   c. The writers of the Constitution were educated men who knew much about governments and how they served the people.

3. Which is the main idea of paragraph 6?
   a. No one had limited the power of the English king.
   b. People in the English colonies felt that there should be a limit on the power of governments.

c. The past tells us much about the present.

4. Which is the main idea of paragraph 10?
   a. For almost 370 years the English colonies gained experience in governing themselves.
   b. England ruled the colonies for almost 270 years.
   c. There were three types of government in the English colonies.

5. According to paragraph 2, how has our democratic government grown stronger with the passing years?
   a. It has added many freedoms.
   b. It has many more generals.
   c. It has made use of the atomic bomb.

6. In paragraph 4, the word roots means

a. seeds for trees
b. kinds of governments
c. ideas

7. According to paragraph 12, what is it that the Declaration of Independence does NOT say?
   a. The colonies want to be free from England.
   b. All people are equal under the law.
   c. There will be a president to rule the colonies.

8. This chapter tells us that the Constitution came from
   a. luck
   b. several ideas that the colonists thought up
   c. many ideas from England, the colonies, and elsewhere

★DEVELOPING SOCIAL STUDIES SKILLS

A. Using an Index

Use the index in this book to answer the following questions. Remember that there are times when the facts you are looking for may be listed under several headings. For example: To find out facts about the House of Representatives, you might look under **federal government** or **Congress** or **House of Representatives.**

1. On which page(s) would you find facts about the Constitution?

2. On which page(s) would you find facts about lobbyists?

3. On how many pages is crime mentioned?

4. On how many pages would you find mention of political parties?

5. Which page(s) would tell you something about the Supreme Court?

6. Which page(s) would tell you about careers in government?

7. Which page(s) would tell you about police departments?

8. Which page(s) would tell you about how a bill becomes a law?

9. Which page(s) would tell you about the president's cabinet?

10. Which page(s) would tell you about qualifications for the presidency?

★DEVELOPING CRITICAL THINKING SKILLS

A. Finding Support for Statements

It often happens that you will hear or read a statement with which you agree or disagree. But can you find support to back up the truth of such a statement?

The following are several statements that call for support. Each statement is followed by the number of the paragraph in which the topic of the statement is discussed. Read each statement. Write S in your notebook if it is supported by what you have read in the paragraph. Write N if the statement is not supported. Explain why. The first one has been done for you.

1. All the ideas in our Constitution were new to the people of the world. (paragraph 3)

N—They knew about the writings of the great thinkers of Europe and the colonies.

2. English settlers in America thought that governments should not have too much power. (paragraph 6)

3. Some of the roots of our democracy came from English government. (paragraph 4)

4. Nothing of the governments of the colonies is part of our government today. (paragraph 5)

5. All the English colonies had the same kind of government. (paragraph 10)

6. The English colonies were never able to get together to try to solve their problems. (paragraph 11)

B. Writing About Citizenship

Using the cartoon on page 16 as reference, list any four ideas about government that influenced the writers of our Constitution. Next, list any six freedoms that Americans are given by our Constitution. Then, using your lists, write an essay proving how any *one* of the ideas about government led to freedoms for Americans. Make sure that your essay is well–organized.

4

THE FIRST GOVERNMENT OF THE UNITED STATES

PURPOSES FOR READING

1. To learn the strengths and weaknesses of the young United States government, 1783 to 1789
2. To learn what steps were taken to overcome the weaknesses of the new government
3. To understand how the Constitution came to be written

KNOWING NEW WORDS

historians
(his STOR ee uns) paragraph 1—those who write or make a study of history
EXAMPLE: **Historians** have tried to explain why there are troubles in the Middle East.

interfere
(in tur FEER) paragraph 8—to meddle in the affairs of others
EXAMPLE: Mary asked her brother not to **interfere** with the discussion she was having on the telephone.

critical
(KRIT ih kul) paragraph 1—dangerous; with great risk
EXAMPLE: The victim of the auto accident was in **critical** condition.

1▶ When a person is listed on the "critical list" by a hospital, we know that the person's life is in danger. We call such a time a period of crisis. If the doctor says, "The patient is passing through the crisis," he or she means that within the next few hours the patient might die. Historians speak of the years after the colonies became independent from England in the same way. The years from 1781 to 1789 are called "The Critical Period" in American history.

2▶ The young nation had many troubles during those years. The life of the new government was in danger. One of its greatest problems was that it was poor. During the war against England, the United States had borrowed large sums of money from France, Spain, and the Netherlands. These nations refused to make any more loans after the fighting ended. The United States could not support the army and navy and pay its workers.

3▶ There were other money problems, too. Gold and silver coins were rare in the early United States. Both the Congress and the state governments printed their own money. People usually take paper money at its full value only if it is backed by precious metals or by a government they can trust. The young nation's money did not meet either condition. The money fell rapidly in value. Soon a hundred dollars would not even buy a barrel of flour or a pair of shoes. Before the fighting for freedom ended, Congress stopped printing money. This was because the money cost more to print than the value of the goods it would buy.

4▶ Another problem following the war was that many people had no jobs. During

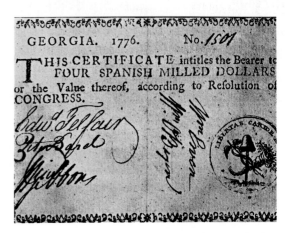

Both Congress and the states printed money in the late 1770s. What gives paper money its value?

the Revolution, many Americans had worked at making arms and other goods they once got from England. At the end of the war, these goods were no longer needed.

5▶ If the **Articles of Confederation,** the plan for the new government, was examined, it would seem that the national government had many powers. After all, Congress could make war. It could borrow money and raise and equip an army and navy. It had the power to coin money. It could establish post offices and make treaties with Native American peoples. There are some historians who think that the new government might have continued despite all its weaknesses if times had not been so bad.

6▶ It is important to understand that the people who wrote the Articles of Confederation did not want a strong central government. There were two reasons for their feelings. First, these were people who were more loyal to their own states than to the national government. They wanted their states to have the most power. Second, many Americans had led an unhappy life under the English government. The English government had tried to make rules for all the colonies. These rules had often proved harmful to the interests of the people in the colonies. When England tried to enforce these rules, the fight for freedom began. Americans had just become independent of a strong central government—England's government. They did not want to repeat the mistakes the English government had made.

7▶ Because of these feelings, the Articles of Confederation did not give Congress some powers it might have been able to use. Congress could not tax people. It had to ask the states for money or borrow it. Congress had no say about trade between one state and another. It had no say about trade between any state and a foreign country. The Articles did not provide for a president or courts to carry out the laws. The government could only beg the states to do what it asked. Nine of the thirteen states had to agree on each idea before it became a law. Therefore, the central government could take no quick actions. And all the states had to agree if there was to be a change in the Articles of Confederation.

8▶ Since the new nation had many weaknesses, it was treated badly by other countries. The Spanish held Florida and the city of New Orleans. The Spanish interfered with the trade of our farmers on the Mississippi River. England refused to leave fur-trading posts in the Northwest. Our ships were stopped and searched by pirates off the coast of Africa. Congress was helpless. If the nation were a person, it would have been sent to the hospital and placed on "the critical list."

9▶ Leaders in several states saw that changes had to be made in the Articles of Confederation. One of the leaders was George Washington. At first, these leaders tried to **amend,** or make changes, in the Articles. This did not work because any change had to have the agreement of all the states. One state or another always stood in the way. Finally, in 1787, most of the states agreed to send representatives to a convention (meeting) to change the Articles of Confederation. The convention met in

George Washington leading his troops in the Battle of Princeton during the Revolutionary War. The new flag flies in the background. Washington's leadership won him support of the people. In the late 1780s he worked to change the Articles of Confederation. What do you think people look for in the leadership in a democracy?

Thirty-nine people at the 1787 Constitutional Convention signed the Constitution. In what city was the convention held?

Philadelphia in the summer of 1787. The representatives soon learned that so many changes had to be made in their government that an entirely new plan for the government had to be written. As a result, the Articles of Confederation was replaced. Out of this meeting came the Constitution of the United States. The meeting, therefore, has been called the Constitutional Convention.

10 ▶ Many wise men attended the convention. George Washington was elected the president of the convention. Benjamin Franklin, more than 80 years of age, was the oldest person present. Franklin has been praised for his part in the meeting. Whenever there were sharp arguments about the wording of the new plan for government, Franklin's common sense won out. Two of the representatives at the convention later became presidents of the United States. One was to become a vice-president. Seventeen later served in the Senate and eleven in the House of Representatives. Twenty-nine of the delegates had college educations. This was at a time when a college education was rare.

11 ▶ James Madison of Virginia became one of the most important men at the convention. Madison had spent a great deal of his time studying law. Because of his learning, he was named a delegate by his state.

Madison became a leader of the group that thought the national government should have greater powers. Although the meetings were held in secret, we know much about them through James Madison. He kept a private record of all that happened at the convention. Many years later, his notes were made public. Because of his work in writing the new plan of government, he is often called "The Father of the Constitution."

At the age of 36, James Madison was a leader at the Constitutional Convention. Twenty-two years later he became the nation's president.

26

CHAPTER 4 REVIEW

★ **UNDERSTANDING WHAT YOU HAVE READ**

1. The main idea of paragraph 3 is that
   a. prices of goods were high when the United States began
   b. the new United States government had money problems
   c. state governments printed their own money

2. The main idea of paragraph 7 is that
   a. Congress had little power to enforce laws
   b. Congress did not use its power to tax often
   c. the states could make treaties with foreign countries

3. The main idea of paragraph 10 is that
   a. George Washington was the leader of the convention that wrote the Constitution
   b. the people who wrote the Constitution were wise and educated men
   c. there were many times when the leaders of the convention could not agree

4. An important idea of this chapter is that
   a. the young United States had a weak central government
   b. each state gave powers to the national government
   c. Congress had the power to raise an army and navy

5. A cause of the money problems of the new nation was that
   a. Congress could not print money
   b. Congress could not borrow money
   c. states and Congress both printed money

6. A record of the Constitutional Convention was kept by
   a. George Washington
   b. Benjamin Franklin
   c. James Madison

7. The years 1781–1789 were called critical for the United States because
   a. the new nation was so weak it might not last
   b. some leaders thought there should be changes in the new government
   c. England had tried to enforce laws the colonies disliked

8. Under the Articles of Confederation, Congress had the power to
   a. tax the states
   b. make treaties with Native American peoples
   c. elect a president

9. The Articles of Confederation could be changed if
   a. all the states agreed to a change
   b. Congress made the changes
   c. seven of the thirteen states agreed to a change

10. The leaders of the convention in Philadelphia decided to write an entirely new plan for the United States government because
    a. George Washington thought a complete change was needed
    b. the states felt Congress had too much power
    c. there were too many changes that had to be made in the Articles of Confederation

★ DEVELOPING CRITICAL THINKING SKILLS

A. Separating Facts From Opinions

Citizens must learn to make decisions on the basis of facts. Some people don't take the time to do this. Instead, they make decisions before they have enough facts. Or they state their own ideas or opinions as if they were facts. To think clearly and to make proper decisions, we must learn the difference between FACTS and OPINIONS.

Facts can be proved. Opinions cannot be proved. Is your classroom painted? This is a question that can be answered in fact. Either the room is painted or it is not. Is the color of the classroom walls prettier than the color of your living-room walls at home? This is harder to prove. People have their own ideas of what is pretty. Whether the classroom is prettier is a matter of personal opinion.

An *opinion* is what a person or group *thinks* about a subject. An opinion can tell the following:

a. What a person *thinks* will happen

b. What a person thinks *should* happen

c. The *feeling* a person has about a subject

d. What a person *believes* about a subject

Note the difference in these examples:

FACT: Millions of people have come to the United States from other countries. (It can be proved.)

OPINION: The United States should limit the number of people who can become citizens. (Some may agree; some may not. Some think this *should* be United States policy. It is an opinion.)

FACT: There are women in the United States armed forces. (It can be proved. They are there.)

OPINION: Women should not take part in real fighting against an enemy. (This is a judgment of what some people think *should* be done, not what is being done. Any question that involves people's values and feelings about what should be done is an opinion.)

FACT: In some English colonies, the governor was named by the king or queen. (It can be proved. It did take place.)

OPINION: Governors of English colonies were happy people. (Not everyone will agree on what happiness is. It cannot be proved.)

In your notebook write "Fact" for each statement that can be proved by getting the necessary information. Write "Opinion" if you think the answer depends on values, beliefs, or feelings about what should be done.

1. The people of the United States had more troubles after independence than they had under the English king.

2. The young United States would have lasted even if the Constitution were not written.

3. The money of the young United States had little value.

4. The Constitution would have been easier to write if the delegates had been more cooperative.

5. Leaders among the English settlers in America did not think the English monarch ruled in their interest.

6. If the young United States government had a president, it could have taken care of its troubles.

7. Many foreign countries treated the United States as if it were a weak nation.

8. Many leaders of the United States did not want a government like the English government.

9. The work of Benjamin Franklin at the convention in Philadelphia was more important than that of any other person.

10. Several of the men who helped to write the Constitution later held high offices in the government.

B. Knowing Word Meanings Through Context Clues

See if you know the meaning of the words from chapter 4 that are listed below. In your notebook, write the clues that helped you to know the meaning of each word.

1. **crisis,** paragraph 1

2. **Articles of Confederation,** paragraph 5

3. **amend,** paragraph 9

4. **convention,** paragraph 9

PARTICIPATION IN GOVERNMENT

KNOW YOUR REPRESENTATIVES

Do you know the names of your representatives in the U.S. Congress or state government? You should know who they are. These representatives are your agents, acting for you in the creation of laws that affect your life.

A good way to get to know your representative is to work up a profile of each. First, call or write a local government office to get a list of your representatives. Then, gather information about them one at a time. In gathering available information, you should learn something about their backgrounds, their previous occupations, and the areas in which they have the greatest knowledge and interest.

It is important to know that no member of Congress has enough time to learn all there is to know about each and every issue. Every legislator has a staff to assist in carrying out legislative duties. They compile facts for the legislator and keep him or her informed on important issues. They run a home office as well as one in Washington, D.C. You can contact the local office to find out the information you need.

Here is an outline of information you might use for a profile of your representative:

· Name and political party
· Previous occupation
· Congressional district
· First year elected
· Next election

· Office address and phone number in Washington, D.C. and nearest district office
· Committee assignments
· Major bills sponsored this session

5 HOW WAS THE CONSTITUTION CREATED?

PURPOSES FOR READING

1. To understand the problems that faced the leaders of the United States in writing a plan of government
2. To learn how difficult problems are settled through compromise

KNOWING NEW WORDS

majority
> (muh JOR ih tee) paragraph 5—a number greater than half the total
> EXAMPLE: A **majority** of voters voted for the school bond issue.

minority
> (muh NOR ih tee) paragraph 5—a number less than half the total
> EXAMPLE: Spanish-speaking Americans are a **minority.**

federal
> (FED ur ul) paragraph 3—of or concerning a plan of government in which states recognize the power of a central government, but have powers of their own
> EXAMPLE: To coin money is a power of the **federal** government, but to establish schools is a power of the state governments.

The Constitutional Convention met in Independence Hall in Philadelphia, Pennsylvania, in 1787. This building was also the site of the signing of the Declaration of Independence in 1776.

1► Have you ever created something that no one else had made before? It may have been a picture, a story, even a game. Imagine how good you would feel if you knew that your creation would last for hundreds of years! Happily for us, our Founding Fathers had this kind of success. These were the men who created our present **political system.**

2► You read in chapter 4 that delegates from the states met in Philadelphia in 1787. All the states sent delegates to the meeting except for Rhode Island. George Washington and Benjamin Franklin were there. So was James Madison, who later said, "I was not absent for a single day." Alexander Hamilton, who wanted the country to have a strong national government and a president for life, was there. Patrick Henry refused to attend. He did not want a strong national government. In all, there were 55 delegates from 12 states. They argued over a plan of government through the summer of 1787. Some delegates were so upset over not getting their way that they left and went home. Only 39 stayed to finish the writing of the new plan of government. Their creation, the Constitution of the United States, has been in effect since the states accepted it in 1789. It is the oldest written constitution in the world.

3► The Founding Fathers were trying to do something that seemed to be impossible. They wanted to make the national government stronger. But, they did not want to make the states weaker. Impossible? The delegates at Philadelphia created a **federal** system of government.

4► Under the **federal** system, Americans would be citizens of *two* governments: the

Benjamin Franklin has been called the "wisest American." Can you support that statement?

national government (the government of the United States of America) and a state government. The national government would be known as the federal government. It would have the powers it needed to make and enforce laws for the people of *all* the states. One person would head the government. He was to be called the president. The people in each state would elect others to represent them in the national or federal government. These people would form the Congress of the United States and make laws for the nation. The state governments would be given the control of matters within their own states. Both governments would be able to deal directly with the people.

5► Many tough questions faced the members of the convention. How could the government gain the respect of foreign nations? Should states with large populations

Did Alexander Hamilton propose a plan for a strong or a weak national government?

have more power than states with fewer people? How could the government please the people of different parts of the country when their ways of earning a living were so different? How could the government care for the wishes of the most people (the **majority**), yet take care of the rights of the **minority?** How much power should be given to the average citizen? One might think that the delegates could not agree on any ways of answering these questions. But they did finally agree after four months of heated arguments.

6► How were agreements reached? We can examine several examples. Two sides may have different ideas on how to solve a problem. If they want to work out an agreement, the chances are that they will **compromise** (KOM pruh miz). Each side will give in a little, and if necessary, a little more. Their final agreement will combine some of the ideas of both sides. Neither side will get all that it wanted. It was through compromises that the problems

facing the convention were solved. Perhaps, the Constitution did not fully please anyone. Yet, very few of the delegates were completely displeased. Most of them felt they had done the best job possible. Let us see how some of these compromises were made.

7► Under the Articles of Confederation, each state had one representative in Congress. The population of the state did not matter. Each state had but one vote. Those states with the greatest number of people did not want to continue this system. They argued that a state with a few people should not have the same voice in making laws as a state with a large population. The smaller states protested. They were afraid that if the larger states had more votes, the larger states could pass whatever laws they wished.

8► The large and small states reached a compromise. Congress would be made up of two groups called **houses.** In one house, the number of representatives would depend on the population of the state. This was to be called the **House of Representatives.** This pleased the larger states. In the other house of Congress, each state would have the same number of representatives. This house was called the **Senate.** Since all states, no matter what their population, would have equal representation in the Senate, the smaller states were pleased as well.

9► Six states made up "the South" at the time of the convention. Farming was the chief way of making a living in the South. The other seven states were considered "the North." Most northerners were also farmers. But many northerners made a liv-

32

ing through business and trade. The northern states wanted Congress to control trade among the states and with foreign countries. In this way, their business would be protected.

10► The South did not agree with the wishes of the North. Congress would have more representatives from the North (seven states in the North, but six states in the South). If Congress had the power to control trade, Congress could pass laws favoring business people and shippers. The South knew that the North favored a **tariff.** A tariff is a tax on goods coming into the country. This would protect business. With a tax on goods coming into the country,

business people could sell their products at lower prices than foreign-made goods. The people of the South bought many goods from England. They would have to pay higher prices for foreign goods. The South feared Congress's control of trade for another reason. Southerners thought the North would forbid the slave trade.

Top: A southern plantation. Bottom: The northern port of Boston. Why didn't the South want taxes on goods going out of the country? Why did the North want laws to protect their trade and their shipping?

11► The South also worried that Congress would favor tariffs on goods and materials going out of the country. This would raise the prices of their farm products sold abroad. Then people outside the country might not buy southern tobacco and cotton because of the high prices. The convention reached a compromise. The federal government was given the power to control trade. Congress was given the power to put tariffs on goods and materials coming into the country. This favored businesses and the North. But Congress was forbidden to put tariffs on goods and materials going out of the country. This benefited southern planters. It was also agreed that Congress would not stop anyone from bringing slaves into the country until 1808.

12 ▶ The southern states wanted something else. Slaves were becoming the chief source of labor in the South. The South wanted to count slaves in deciding how many representatives a state would have in Congress. However, they did not want to count slaves in deciding how much tax a state should pay. The North said that the South treated slaves as property, not as people. So, they should not count slaves in deciding the population of a state. But the North did want the slaves counted in deciding how much tax the states should pay. Again a compromise was reached. It was called the three-fifths compromise. It was agreed that five slaves would count as three people in deciding the number of representatives in Congress from each state. It was also agreed that Congress would count every five slaves as three people when it came time to figure out taxes for the states. So, a slave, a black person, was not considered a "full person" under the Constitution as it was first written. The new Constitution allowed slavery to exist. The Constitution did not consider black slaves as full human beings until 1865.

13 ▶ There were people who feared the Constitution gave too much power to the federal government. How were the people's rights to be protected? Thomas Jefferson of Virginia suggested that a Bill of Rights be added to the document. (Jefferson was in Europe when the convention was held.) Jefferson wanted a clear statement of people's rights. The Constitution had to be approved by 9 of the 13 states before it could become the law of the land. All winter and into the spring, people in the states argued about the strengths and weaknesses of the Constitution. By June 1788, 9 states had voted to approve the document. Many people voted for the new plan of government with the understanding that a Bill of Rights would be added later. The Constitution became the law of the land. The new government began its work in the spring of 1789. The first 10 amendments, the Bill of Rights, were added in 1791.

CHAPTER 5 REVIEW

★ UNDERSTANDING WHAT YOU HAVE READ

1. The main idea of paragraph 5 is that
   a. the wishes of the majority must be respected
   b. there were arguments among large and small states
   c. several tough questions faced those who wrote the Constitution
2. A reason why there are two houses in Congress is
   a. it settled an argument between large and small states
   b. there were two houses under the Articles of Confederation
   c. one house is for the federal government; the other is for state governments

3. The Bill of Rights was
   a. demanded by southern planters
   b. the first thing agreed upon by the leaders of the convention
   c. added to the Constitution after it was approved
4. The house of Congress that has two representatives from each state is the
   a. House of Representatives
   b. Assembly
   c. Senate

5. Under the Constitution, the government is headed by the
   a. Congress
   b. president
   c. Senate
6. The northern states wanted
   a. to tax goods coming into the country
   b. slaves to be counted as one person
   c. states to control foriegn trade

★ **DEVELOPING CRITICAL THINKING SKILLS**

A. Making Comparisons

Compare the Articles of Confederation and the Constitution. In your notebook, complete the following chart, "Improving Our National Government," showing the differences between the Articles of Confederation and the Constitution.

IMPROVING OUR NATIONAL GOVERNMENT

Articles of Confederation	The United States Constitution
1. There was no president or single leader of the national government.	1.
2. Congress could not raise money.	2.
3. Each state was able to trade with foreign countries.	3.
4. All states had one representative in Congress.	4.
5. States taxed goods from other states.	5.
6. Congress had to ask the states for needed money.	6.

B. Writing About Citizenship

Use any two of the above facts to write a paragraph explaining why the Constitution is a better set of rules than the Articles of Confederation.

C. Interpreting Cartoons

1. In scene 1, who do the people seated at the table represent?

2. In what city is this important meeting taking place?

3. What is the purpose of their meeting?

4. What is it that the different groups want?

5. What would be the title of scene 2?

6. What happened between scene 1 and scene 2?

7. What would you put in the picture if you were making the movie?

8. What would go into the last scene that is labeled the "Constitution"?

D. Interpreting Primary Sources

In September 1787, Benjamin Franklin made a speech to the members of the convention writing the Constitution. He was then so feeble that his words had to be read for him. But his words tell us something about our Constitution.

I confess that there are several parts of this Constitution which I do not at present approve, but I am not sure I shall never approve them. . . . The older I get, the more apt I am to doubt my own judgment, and to pay more respect to the judgment of others. . . .

I agreed to this Constitution, with all its faults, if they are such, because I think a general government is necessary for us. . . . [Otherwise we] can only end in Despotism [rule by absolute power]. . . .

I doubt, too, whether any other Convention we can obtain may be able to make a better Constitution. For when you assemble a number of men to have the advantage of their joint wisdom, you . . . assemble . . . all their prejudices, their passions, their errors of opinion, their local interests, and their selfish views. . . . Thus, I consent, Sir, to this Constitution because I expect no better.

1. How do the words of Benjamin Franklin show that the Constitution was, in many ways, a compromise?

2. What do you think is the meaning of despotism?

3. Which paragraph in this chapter has the same thought as that offered by Benjamin Franklin?

4. Could Franklin's words be used as advice to any groups or nations today?

E. Questions for Thought and Discussion

1. Alexander Hamilton wanted a plan for the new government in which a leader, the president, would be elected for a life term. Why do you think this idea was turned down by the convention?

2. Patrick Henry had made some of the strongest speeches against rule by the king of England. Yet, when the time came to form a new government for the United States, he refused to attend the Constitutional Convention. Why might this have been so?

3. Why do you think the head of the new government of the United States was called a president, instead of a king or an emperor?

4. Under the Articles of Confederation, it was possible that less than half the people could have great power in Congress. How was this so?

5. Why is it difficult, even today, for a new nation to have the respect of older nations?

6. What were some good reasons why the convention at Philadelphia met in secret? Should conferences among nations today be held in secret?

Unit 2

AMERICAN DEMOCRACY

These Americans, mostly Hispanic, celebrate their new citizenship at a rally in Miami, Florida.

6 RIGHTS AND POWERS OF THE PEOPLE

PURPOSES FOR READING

1. To discover the origin (beginnings) of our rights
2. To understand the rights and powers "we the people" have
3. To understand that along with our rights, there are responsibilities
4. To understand how our rights are protected

KNOWING NEW WORDS

authority
(uh THOR ih tee) paragraph 1—the right to make the final decisions; the right to have the final say
EXAMPLE: A dictator has total **authority** to decide whether people live or die.

petition
(puh TISH un) paragraph 3—a formal way (usually written) of asking a government official for something
EXAMPLE: Our block sent a **petition** to the school board asking for a bus to pick up our children.

sovereignty
(SOV rin tee) paragraph 1—the highest power of or over a nation
EXAMPLE: Our system of government places **sovereignty** in the hands of the voters.

FREEDOM OF SPEECH

FREEDOM OF RELIGION

NO CRUEL OR UNUSUAL PUNISHMENTS

RIGHT TO COUNSEL

FREEDOM OF THE PRESS

RIGHT TO TRIAL BY JURY

FREEDOM FROM UNREASONABLE SEARCH

RIGHT TO ASSEMBLE

"We the people of the United States . . . do ordain and establish [create] this Constitution for the United States of America."

These words are from the Preamble, or introduction, to our Constitution. According to these words:

a. Who created the rules of the United States government?

b. Who has the power in our country — heads of government or the people?

1▶ Suppose you plan to marry and have children. Will you and your partner share authority as equals? Will your children have a say in making decisions? In some homes decision making is shared. There are also nations that are run this way. The United States is one such country. We have much to say about the decisions our government makes. Once more, read the quote at the beginning of the chapter. The people are said to have made the Constitution. These rules for our government place power in the hands of the people. That is what we mean by **popular sovereignty.** All authority for government action must come from the people. In a democracy such as ours, the rights of the people are **purposely** protected and improved.

2▶ The Constitution sets the rules for national, state, and local governments. Each government has only the powers given to it by the people. It cannot do anything it pleases. All American citizens have many rights. They have not given the government the power to take these rights away. For example, no one can legally be kept from voting because of race or sex. Congress can make no law to take away the right of free speech. It cannot take away

Thomas Jefferson wrote much of the Declaration of Independence. Fifteen years later he favored adding the Bill of Rights to the Constitution.

freedom of the press, religion, or assembly.

3▶ The 1st Amendment of the Bill of Rights (1791) states our civil liberties. They are freedom of religion, speech, press, assembly, and petition. There are also civil rights people have. Civil rights are those that protect us from discrimination. This means that one must not be treated differently from others. The 5th and 14th Amendments tell us that all citizens have equal rights before the law.

4▶ The Constitution, however, does not name every right we have. The 9th Amendment states that people have other rights besides those listed. Each state also has a Bill of Rights. No state may deny its citizens rights that are granted in the federal Constitution. When citizens think that they have been denied their rights, courts must decide whether or not this is so. Read the pictograph on page 40 to learn what your rights are. In the Declaration of Independence (1776), Thomas Jefferson wrote that all people "are endowed [given] by their Creator with certain unalienable [not able to be taken away] rights." (See page 400.)

1. Which rights might Jefferson have meant to be God-given to all people?

2. Which rights, it might be said, were created for us by our government?

3. For each right, can you name a responsibility each citizen has?

5▶ You know that there are rights that our government cannot take away. However, how do we keep some bully from taking over the government? How would we keep such a person from taking away our rights? The Founders of our government thought of this problem. They set up safety rules. These rules can prevent a bully from taking over. That is why our plan of government has a **separation of powers.**

Lawmakers make the laws. They do not enforce them. Those who enforce laws cannot make them. Courts neither make laws nor enforce them. Courts decide whether our laws agree with the rules laid down in the Constitution. More about the way each part of our government checks the other parts will be found in chapter 16.

6▶ Citizens have responsibilities, too. Many are not demanded by law. Citizens may choose to help their community. Laws do not force them to do so. Citizens serve on boards of education without pay. Some work to improve schools, hospitals, and playgrounds. Others work for a better understanding among people. They want to make their communities better places for all people. As a responsible citizen you not only live in your community. You also work to make it a better place in which to live.

7▶ Citizens who are able to vote have the duty to do so. Many citizens, however, don't seem to value their right to vote. (The right to vote is called **suffrage.**) Yet without this right, few Americans could have in-

Separation of Powers

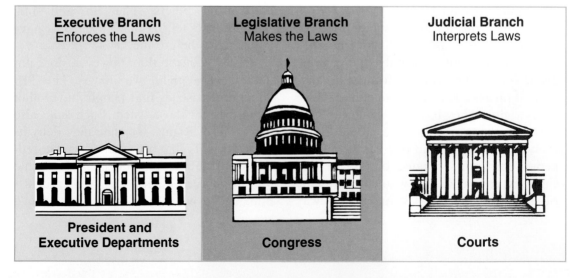

Executive Branch	Legislative Branch	Judicial Branch
Enforces the Laws	Makes the Laws	Interprets Laws
President and Executive Departments	Congress	Courts

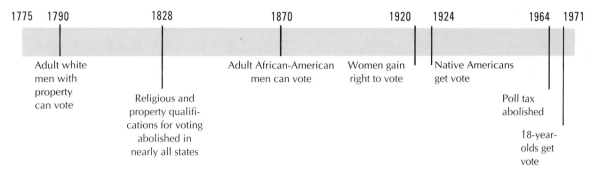

1775 1790 | 1828 | 1870 | 1920 | 1924 | 1964 | 1971

Adult white men with property can vote

Religious and property qualifications for voting abolished in nearly all states

Adult African-American men can vote

Women gain right to vote

Native Americans get vote

Poll tax abolished

18-year-olds get vote

creased their rights and liberties. Democracy as we know it did not happen at once. It has grown and improved over the years. Rights have increased as people have used their right to vote. The right to vote does not belong to all persons. It is a civil right. It is given to those who meet the terms of the law. States control this right so long as they do not act against federal rules.

8 ▶ When our country was young, people had fewer civil rights than they have today. Only a few had the right to vote. Study the time line above.

Tell whether these statements are *true* or *false*.

1. Before 1828, all American adult men could vote.

2. Before 1828, people could vote if they owned property.

3. After 1828, anyone could vote.

4. Women could not vote until 1920.

5. Most American Indians could not vote until 1924.

6. Since the start of the American Revolution in 1776, more than 140 years passed before all men and women in this country could vote.

7. All African-American men gained the right to vote by 1870.

8. Eighteen-year-old Americans were given the vote in 1971.

9 ▶ Some people still cannot vote in our elections. No state has given anyone under the age of 18 the right to vote. Those who are not citizens may not vote. Many states have **residency** laws. This means that a person must live in the state a certain number

Volunteers help a group of citizens register to vote. Can a democratic government exist without elections?

of days before voting. This keeps persons from going from one state to another just to vote for a particular person. In most states, a person must register before voting.

10 ▶ Our leaders are elected to carry out the wishes of the people. Still, great numbers of Americans are not voting. Leaders in government believe this is a serious problem. If large numbers of people do not vote, a small number can decide who our leaders will be. There is a greater chance that a dictator might be elected. Nonvoters helped to bring the Nazi party to power in Germany. Our leaders are asking, "Do nonvoters believe in our system of government?" The next chapter will help you to understand what we believe about our system of government.

CHAPTER 6 REVIEW

★ UNDERSTANDING WHAT YOU HAVE READ

1. The main idea of paragraph 5 is that by separating the powers of the government we have
   a. kept a bully from taking over the country
   b. given more power to the president
   c. given more power to the people

2. According to paragraph 10, a great problem facing Americans is that many people do not
   a. believe in God
   b. spend enough money
   c. vote

3. According to paragraph 5, which illustration shows how our rights are protected?
   a. The person who enforces the laws cannot make them also.
   b. People must be educated.
   c. People must vote.

4. What has the same meaning as the word **sovereignty** in paragraph 1?
   a. Power
   b. Right to vote
   c. Popular person

5. The national, state, and local governments all have to follow the rules set down by
   a. the Constitution
   b. the people of the states
   c. the president of the United States

6. Which is not an example of a citizen being responsible?
   a. Voting
   b. Not paying taxes
   c. Volunteering as a firefighter

7. The document that first mentioned the rights of the American people is the
   a. Pledge of Allegiance
   b. Bill of Rights
   c. Declaration of Independence

A. Fact or Opinion

Review the differences between facts and opinions on page 28. Then tell whether these statements are facts or someone's opinion.

1. People who don't vote don't believe in our system of government.

2. One person, a dictator, could never take over the government of the United States.

3. No one can legally be kept from voting because of his or her sex.

4. Our courts should be able to make laws.

5. Voting laws should be the same in all states.

6. If George Washington were not present at the Constitutional Convention, our Constitution would never be what it is.

7. When our country was young, some groups had fewer civil rights than they have today.

8. Much of the talk about the duties of citizens is foolish.

B. Decision Making

All over the United States people are making decisions. Every day people make **choices**—both good and bad. In this book you will learn how to prepare yourself to make important decisions. Good decision making depends on a number of skills. Before you make important decisions, you should figure out what are your own and others' needs. You will have to base your decisions on accurate information. You will have to learn about the many choices open to you. You will have to learn to weigh your decisions carefully. At times it might seem difficult to select the best from several choices. So you will give careful thought about which actions might bring the best results.

THE BILL OF RIGHTS IN ACTION

In this chapter you learned about some of the rights we have as citizens. Suppose you were on a jury deciding the following five cases. Use the information you have gained from this chapter. In each case, what decisions would you make about the rights of citizens? What reasons can you give to support your decisions?

A city has an ordinance (law) forbidding parades without a permit.

1. A group of people demanding civil rights march down the main street of the city. They do not disrupt traffic, because they walk only on the sidewalk. They claim the law against parades is unconstitutional. Are they right?

The 1st Amendment to the Constitution says that Congress shall make no law abridging freedom of speech. This means that Americans have the right to free speech.

2. A person who does not like the city's mayor makes a speech in a public park. She attacks all his programs. The police arrest her because she needs a permit to speak in a public park. She is also charged with disturbing the peace. Is she guilty of one or both of the charges placed against her?

The 8th Amendment to the Constitution says that "cruel and unusual" punishments shall not be given.

3. In some states prisoners are whipped as punishment. One prisoner appealed to the court on the grounds that whipping was a cruel and unusual punishment. Should he win damages?

The 8th Amendment to the Constitution states that excessive bail shall not be re-

quired. Bail is money deposited with a court as a guarantee that the defendant will appear for trial.

4. A poor woman was arrested and accused of stealing a car. She remained in jail for several months because she could not raise bail. Bail was set at $10,000. The time she spent in jail would be deducted from her sentence, if she was found guilty. Her lawyer argued that bail was too high and that she should be set free. Do you agree?

The 6th Amendment to the Constitution states that in all criminal cases, the accused must be informed of the nature and cause of the charges. This means that a person cannot just be arrested. He or she must be charged with a crime.

5. After a series of fires, the police arrested a man who had been in jail three times for setting fires. The police held the man in jail for some time, stating that they were protecting the public from this man. The prisoner appealed (asked a higher authority) to be set free. Should he win?

C. Writing About Citizenship

1. Using the time line on page 43, list who could vote in 1790. Then list any events and their dates that show when other Americans received the right to vote.

2. Using the list that you have prepared, write a well–organized essay that proves that voting rights in the United States have grown since 1790.

7

OUR DEMOCRACY: WHAT WE BELIEVE

PURPOSES FOR READING

1. To understand the meaning of consent of the governed
2. To understand the meaning of majority rule and minority rights
3. To understand that democracy and dictatorship do not look at human freedom in the same way
4. To understand why compromise is important in our system of government

Herbert Hoover presents the Republican party's program to people gathered at Madison Square Garden in 1928. Hoover was running for president. How can voters show that they agree or disagree with a political party's program?

1 ▶ Something new was begun in 1776. It was the government of the United States. The idea behind our government was not new. But never had such a government as this been tried before. It was truly an experiment. There is a phrase in the Declaration of Independence that best states the basis of our government: "Governments . . . deriving their just powers from the consent of the governed." Ours is government by the **consent** of the people. The people have agreed to give powers or authority to their government. In turn, those same people have agreed to **accept** the authority of their government.

2 ▶ How do officials govern people? There are two ways. (1) The ruler or ruling party can tell people what to do. The rulers can use threats or force to see that the people obey. (2) The other way is for the people to tell their chosen leaders what has to be done. The first way is that of a dictatorship. The Communist party in China does not ask the people what they believe should be done. Yet there is a written constitution in China. It says there should be freedom of speech and the press. But in reality no party except the Communist party is allowed to hold any power. If the Communist party leaders give an order, it is carried out. The people are not asked to agree or disagree with it.

3 ▶ In our democracy, the people have established laws to govern themselves. They have agreed (given their consent) to obey those laws. The people have agreed to accept the rulings of our courts. Even our highest officials must agree to obey the laws of the nation. For example, during the Korean War, steel workers announced they were going on strike. Steel was needed to supply our troops in battle. President Truman "took over" the steel mills. They were run by the federal government until the strike was settled. The Supreme Court ruled that the president had no power to take such action. The president accepted the ruling. This is an example of the "consent of the governed." We have agreed to run our nation in an orderly manner under laws made by the people.

4 ▶ All people do not have to agree about what our government does or should do. But, when we disagree, we have orderly ways of showing our dislike. We can bring about change in peaceful, lawful ways.

Franklin D. Roosevelt, the Democratic party's candidate for president in 1932, greets farmers in Georgia. Why do those who want to be leaders in a democracy go out to meet the people?

Unemployed workers and government workers protest President Roosevelt's plans to cut some government job programs in 1939. In a dictatorship do government leaders allow people to protest against the government?

Such is not the case in undemocratic countries where people have very few rights. Dictators do not allow the people to decide on their government's actions. Many nations do not have our form of government. In many countries the people are not allowed to decide how their rulers should govern them. In dictatorships there is no free consent of the governed.

5▶ A rule of our democracy is that a **majority** must agree. A majority is at least one more than half a given number. For example, there are 100 United States senators. Fifty-one senators are a majority. So 51 senators may vote for a bill to become a law. Forty-nine senators may not want such a law. The law will be passed by the Senate. The 51 senators are a majority.

6▶ Where there is a majority, there must be a **minority.** A minority is less than half of a given number. In a democracy, the minority accepts the laws passed by the majority. The minority has a right to disagree, however. Those in the minority may try to get others to agree with their point of view. They will try to make that minority grow until it becomes a majority. The rights of the minority are protected by law. They may speak openly about their reasons for disliking a law or an act of government. They may try to elect people who will change laws. Their rights are protected by the Bill of Rights.

7▶ Rule by the majority is important in our democracy. Without it, our system could not work. Those who did not like a law would simply disobey it. When people agree to accept the will of the majority, they have protection against two evils. They are protected against the disorder that would come from no government at all. They are also protected against too strong a government as in a dictatorship.

8▶ The majority is not always the same. Nor is the minority always the same. People may change their views over a period of time. For years most people in our country thought that the government should not protect workers who wanted to join unions. Now our laws protect unions. Workers cannot lose their jobs by joining a union. The majority also agrees that workers should be paid at least a certain minimum wage. Nor do the same people always make up the majority. Fifty-one senators may want to raise taxes. Among that 51, there may be some who want to control gas prices. There may be others who do not.

9 ► "All men are created equal." This is a truth stated in the Declaration of Independence. But what does it mean to say that people are created equal? We know that all people do not have the same weight, height, strength, or talents. But all persons are to be treated in the same manner. Each person is to be respected because each is a human being. Each has a value that cannot be measured. The law should treat everyone equally. All persons should have the same opportunity to make use of their talents. Our schools are provided to give all people an equal chance to learn. You may become a lawyer, a doctor, a teacher, or a carpenter if you have the ability. You will not be told that you must work in a mine or on a farm far from home. Governments in some countries (such as China) do tell people where they must work and live.

10 ► Our government does not guarantee that all persons will be what they wish to be. It does not make certain that everyone will be successful or rich. But it does guarantee that all should have the same chance for success. This is a goal. It isn't always reached. Some people in minority groups have not had equality of opportunity. To these, "all people are created equal" has not been a "truth." It is up to Americans to make it so.

11 ► Our democracy is not perfect. We are always trying to make it better. For most of us, our government will sometimes act in ways that we dislike. But we cannot demand that our government must always do what we want it to do. Others may not

In the 1970s China's leaders forced students to leave the cities to work on farms. Should governments tell people where to work? Why? Why not?

Why is it important for all people to have an equal chance to make use of their abilities?

pay. Not everyone is satisfied with the compromise. But it must be accepted. Otherwise, the strongest will take all they want. The strong will take the place of the majority. There will be no rights for a minority. There will be no democracy. Under a dictatorship, the ruler is always right. No other voice is heard.

13▶ To some, our democracy has some weaknesses. Perhaps there is no perfect kind of government. But our system of government is the best one that people have made so far. It is the job of our people to make it as nearly perfect as a government can be. If the people do govern, then a government is only as good as the people make it.

Mussolini, dictator of Italy, 1922–1943. Do dictators allow others to speak out in public?

agree with us. Both sides cannot have their own way. Like a family, we will settle differences by compromise. Jim wants Dad to drive him to basketball practice. Liz wants Dad to drive her to volleyball. Dad can't do both. He'll drive Jim this week. He'll drive Liz the next. Our democracy works in the same way.

12▶ Making compromises is important in a democracy. Farmers want higher prices for milk. City people want lower milk prices. The price will fall somewhere between the two wishes. Landlords want higher rents. Tenants want lower rents. The government may step in to control rents. No doubt, the rent will be lower than landlords want, higher than tenants want to

CHAPTER 7 REVIEW

★ UNDERSTANDING WHAT YOU HAVE READ

1. The main idea of paragraphs 5 and 6 is that
   a. a minority group has few rights
   b. people in a democracy must always agree
   c. majority rule is a basis for our democracy
   d. people's rights are protected by the Bill of Rights

2. "In our democracy, people agree to obey laws passed by the majority." This is the main idea of paragraph
   a. 7
   b. 8
   c. 9

3. A **minority** is
   a. no one in the group
   b. half the group
   c. less than half the group

4. The Declaration of Independence states that
   a. citizens can do what they want to do
   b. the minority must agree with the majority
   c. governments rule by the consent of the people
   d. governments should always hold free elections

5. In this chapter you learned that in democratic governments
   a. the power to govern belongs to the majority of the people
   b. the goal is to rule large countries
   c. equal treatment of minorities is not allowed

6. All people are created equal. **Equal** in our government means
   a. everyone has the same ability or talent
   b. our laws are to treat everyone in the same way
   c. only the rights of majorities are protected

7. Compromises in a democracy are important because
   a. without them, the strong would always win over the weak
   b. not all rights are protected by law
   c. then everyone is completely satisfied

8. The "consent of the governed" means that
   a. there is equal opportunity for all
   b. the dignity of each citizen is respected
   c. the will of the people is carried out in an orderly way

9. President Nixon resigned from office. Vice-President Ford became president. President Ford appointed Nelson Rockefeller as vice-president. There was no argument, no violence. None was expected. This is an example of
   a. government by consent of the people and according to law
   b. the rights of a minority
   c. compromise

10. Our government guarantees that
    a. all persons will be whatever the government wants them to be
    b. everyone will be either successful or rich
    c. all persons should have the same chance for success

★ DEVELOPING CRITICAL THINKING SKILLS

A. Who Is the Majority?

Our government leaders and lawmakers are elected by voters. Who can vote? When our country began, only those who owned land could vote. So in the 18th century, the majority was not really a majority of all the people. The majority was not made up of more than half of all the people. The majority in those years was not even more than half of all white people, nor even more than half of all white males. The majority was only more than half of those who were allowed to vote. During most of the 19th century, African Americans did not have the right to vote. Only in the 20th century did women gain the right to vote and have the chance to become part of the majority. At the same time, those in power found ways to keep many African Americans and others from being a part of the voting majority.

Read what three early American thinkers had to say about the rule of the majority. Then answer the questions that follow.

a. "The best government rests on the people, and not on the few, on persons and not on property. . . . A government of equal rights must, therefore, rest upon mind, not upon wealth or brute force."

George Bancroft, 1835

b. "It is the people that rule; it is not a mere fraction of them that [takes] authority. The success of the American experiment depended, as it still does, upon the character of the people."

Alexander Mackay, 1847

c. "The government of the people is too often the power of some. . . . . The weak find their liberty . . . from the power of law and justice over all."

Fisher Ames, 1805

1. Have our laws always been made by a majority of the people?

2. What people in our country may not be able to vote today?

3. What does George Bancroft mean by "a government of equal rights must rest . . . upon mind, not upon wealth or . . . force."? Do you agree or disagree?

4. Over 100 years ago, Alexander Mackay said that "it is the people that rule." Was that true in 1847? Who did not share in the rule by majority then? What might blacks or women have said about this statement? Which paragraph in the chapter supports his statement that the "success of the American experiment" depends on the character of the people?

5. Explain the statement of Fisher Ames that the "weak find their liberty . . . from the power of law." How are the weak protected by law? How do our laws protect us from "the power of some"?

B. Drawing Conclusions

1. You are a certain number of years old. Suppose you go to a recreation center where most people are two years older than you. Are you in the majority or the minority?

2. People you know may belong to a political party. Are they members of the party that is in the majority or minority in your town or city? in your state?

3. You may live in a village, on a farm, in a small town, or in a large city. Do most people in your state live in villages, on farms, in small towns, or in cities? Are you in the majority based upon the place where you live?

4. Your parents, grandparents, or their parents may have come to the United States from some other country. Is this true of most people in your neighborhood? Are you a majority member in your neighborhood based upon your background?

5. Do you like to dance? Do the majority of people your age like dancing? Are you in the minority?

6. CONCLUSIONS: Are you always in the majority? Are you always in the minority? Are you in the majority in some cases and in the minority in others? What generalization can you make about the grouping of people?

C. Writing About Citizenship

Write an essay on one of these two topics:

1. Describe a time when you had an opinion that was held by a minority of people. What was the opinion? How did you feel about being in the minority? What did you learn from being in the minority?

2. Do you believe that certain laws in the United States should be changed so that minority groups are treated more fairly? If so, which laws do you think should be changed? What should the new laws say?

8

THE STRUGGLE FOR DEMOCRACY GOES ON

PURPOSES FOR READING

1. To understand that minority groups in the United States have had to struggle for their civil rights
2. To understand how the Constitution helps minorities
3. To understand how African Americans and women have won their civil rights

KNOWING NEW WORDS

discrimination
(dih skrim uh NAY shun) paragraph 1—unfair treatment of a class, person, or group
EXAMPLE: When only one race is given jobs, there is **discrimination** in hiring.

boycott
(BOI kot) paragraph 6—the withholding of business in order to win a point of view
EXAMPLE: The **boycott** of the store lasted until its prices were lowered.

THE GOALS OF A FREE SOCIETY ARE THE GOALS OF ALL AMERICANS

1▶ Millions of Americans have suffered from discrimination. Many suffer from it today. These people are members of minority groups. They could be in a minority because of their religion or their language. It could be because of their race or sex. It might be that they are old or poor. Yet, they deserve all their democratic rights. The Constitution has given them the tools to open the treasure chest of democracy.

2▶ The freedoms of speech and press are basic tools of democracy. All Americans have the right to write or say almost whatever they please. People can give their opinions even when most Americans may not agree with them. However, a person may not make false charges against another. Nor may a person make false statements that endanger the life of another. The guilty person may be sued by the one who has been harmed.

3▶ The right of assembly means that people can come together for any lawful purpose. They may even come together to criticize their government. Through the right of **petition,** people can complain to their government. They may do so without fear of being punished. They may hold meetings or march in parades for many causes. There are limits on this right, too. An assembly may not interfere with traffic. It may not block sidewalks and doorways to buildings. It may not interfere with the rights of other citizens. Let us see how two groups have used these rights, these tools, with success.

4▶ African Americans gained freedom (1865) and citizenship (1868) only after the Civil War. Another step in the movement to freedom was the 15th Amendment (1870). It states that a person cannot be denied the right to vote because of skin color or race. But, in many southern states laws were passed to "get around" the words of the amendment. These laws denied voting rights and the rights of citizenship to African Americans. In many northern states, discrimination continued in customs and traditions. In 1896, the Supreme Court ruled in the case of *Plessy* vs. *Ferguson* that the Constitution did not guarantee social equality of the races. Therefore, separation of the races could continue if all separate facilities were "equal."

5▶ In World War II, the federal govern-

A citizen protest in the shadow of the Capitol. What privilege of Americans are these people enjoying? How has the right of assembly been used in the past?

Sugar, ketchup, and mustard are poured over the heads of those sitting-in at a lunch counter in 1963. What was the purpose of sitting-in and trying to get served at the lunch counter?

ment began to do away with **segregation** (separation) of blacks and whites in the armed forces. A short time later, many states set up human rights commissions. In 1954, the Supreme Court ordered an end to "separate schools" throughout the land. A new civil rights act followed. As a result, the Justice Department gained the power to look into practices of discrimination. It could act to enforce federal laws. But passing a law does not mean an end to discrimination.

6► In many cases, laws were passed only after demonstrations showed lawmakers the need to act. "Sit-ins" helped to end separation of races in stores and eating places. The Reverend Dr. Martin Luther King, Jr., led a boycott of buses in Montgomery, Alabama, in 1955. A local law forced African Americans to sit in the rear of public buses. For more than a year, Dr. King and his followers refused to ride buses in Montgomery. The boycott was a success. Bus companies lost business. Buses were taken out of service. Stores lost business because African Americans did not go downtown to shop. The Supreme

Court then ruled again for minority rights. It ruled that separate seating on buses was against the law.

7► In 1963, several hundred thousand people marched in Washington, D.C. They demanded equal treatment for all Ameri-

Jesse Jackson. Jackson, a civil rights leader, ran for president in 1984 and 1988.

BOLD

57

cans. Afterward, leaders of the march met with President Kennedy in the White House. A later march on Montgomery, Alabama, demanded voting rights for African American citizens. This march was supported by people of all races from all parts of the country.

8▶ Progress was made. The Civil Rights Act of 1964 guaranteed many rights. Full and equal use of public parks, restaurants, hotels, and the like became the law of the land. The act gave power to the Civil Rights Commission to investigate when people were denied equal protection of the laws. The act was aimed at stopping discrimination and segregation. It protects people of whatever "race, color, religion, or national origin." In the same year, the 24th Amendment to the Constitution outlawed the poll tax. This tax had been used to keep poor blacks from voting in some states. Other laws followed. The Voting Rights Act of 1965 was very important. With the help of federal officers, thousands of black voters took part in the election of 1966. Today many blacks are officials in federal, state, and city governments. The number is small, however, when compared with the number of blacks in our nation.

9▶ There has been discrimination against women, too. There are more women than men in the United States. There are more women than men of voting age. Women live longer than men. Therefore, the difference is likely to become even greater. The problem, then, is a serious one. Women now have almost the same rights as men. Still, women have been shut out of some occupations. Even today, in general, women receive much less pay than do men for the same work.

10▶ The demand for complete equality for women grew in the 19th century. Not until 1920 did women gain the right to vote. Some women had jobs that paid well in business and industry during World War II. By the 1960s more and more women were demanding equality. American families had become smaller in size. Women did not have to spend as much time at home as was expected in years before. Inventions have made work at home easier than fifty years ago. Women have gained more education in professions outside the home.

Why is Carrie Chapman Catt proudly smiling? It is probably because she successfully led the campaign to win the vote for women. She is about to vote for the first time. What is the year in which this picture was taken?

Surveying at a building site. Why are more women training for professional jobs today?

11▶ In 1966, the National Organization for Women (NOW) was formed to fight for equal treatment. NOW was under the leadership of Betty Friedan. NOW and other groups formed to promote "women's liberation." They have worked to convince Americans of a number of things. Women are individuals, important in themselves. Women have their own talents and goals. They do not have to accept direction from men. Both men and women make up the society in which we live.

12▶ The women's movement seeks to change old ideas about "a woman's place." The movement points out how women have been treated differently from men. In the past, books and magazines often described women as homemakers, nurses, or typists. They rarely showed women as professional people. The English language has been geared to men in certain jobs. Some examples are firemen, chairmen, and Congressmen. It is as if women were not expected to hold such positions. Women still earn only about 70 percent of what men do for the same work. They are seldom chosen over men in certain jobs. They have difficulty getting jobs in police and fire departments. Women are often made to feel that only some careers are "for them."

13▶ Women are a majority of the voters. But they still are not well repre-sented in national government. Women account for less than 6 percent of national representation. In 1972 Congress proposed the Equal Rights Amendment (ERA). It would have assured complete equality under the law for women. It was not approved by the required 38 states.

14▶ Women are, however, making gains. In 1984 Geraldine Ferraro made history by being the first woman nominated by a major political party for vice-president. Four times as many women are serving in state legislatures in the early 1990s as in 1969. Women now hold more than 17 percent of state legislative seats. Women also hold more than 13 percent of the elected executive positions in state government. There have been women governors in Kansas, Oregon, South Carolina, and Texas. In many states, women are secretaries of state and state treasurers. Women have successfully run for mayor of some of our largest cities, including Houston, Hartford, and Washington, D.C. There is an increase in women lawyers, dentists, doctors, and pharmacists. More and more women are becoming accountants and college professors. The army, navy, and air force train women as officers. By 1990 women made up about half the working force of the nation. There is little doubt that ideas are changing about "a women's place" in government and business.

CHAPTER 8 REVIEW

★UNDERSTANDING WHAT YOU HAVE READ

1. An example of the meaning of the word *discrimination* as used in this chapter would be which of the following?
   a. Let me separate my school books from my other books.
   b. Hundreds of people suffer from back pain every day.
   c. Only men could join the club.

2. Which shows the main idea of paragraph 2?
   a. A woman yells "fire" in a crowded theater when there is a fire.
   b. A woman yells "fire" in a crowded theater. There is no fire. She is arrested.
   c. A woman sues the theater owner for showing poor pictures.

3. It is possible for the Supreme Court to change a decision. This is discussed in
   a. paragraphs 4 and 6
   b. paragraphs 5 and 6
   c. paragraphs 4 and 5.

4. A method used to keep poor African Americans from voting was
   a. the poll tax
   b. the Civil Rights Act of 1964
   c. the 24th Amendment.

5. The best example showing that African Americans are gaining political power is
   a. more and more African Americans have been appointed to high offices
   b. many African Americans voting
   c. African Americans boycotted the buses in Alabama in 1955.

6. The organization formed to help women is called
   a. WUN (Women United Now)
   b. NOW (National Organization for Women)
   c. WRO (Women's Rights Organization).

7. An important leader in the civil rights movement for African Americans was
   a. Dr. Martin Luther King, Jr.
   b. Dr. Timothy King, Jr.
   c. Dr. Martin Holliday.

8. Which is true of the civil rights acts?
   a. They only benefit blacks.
   b. Only blacks and women benefit.
   c. All Americans benefit.

9. Proof that women are making economic gains is the increase of women who are
   a. typists
   b. waitresses
   c. doctors.

★ DEVELOPING CRITICAL THINKING SKILLS

A. Decision Making

The following two articles are reprinted from the Board of Education minutes of a school district in New York State. Read them and answer the decision-making questions.

If you were a school board member would you make the same decisions today? Why? Why not? Support your decision.

APRIL 8, 1925: It was voted that the Superintendent should not appoint any new women teachers who were married. Married teachers already on the staff would be allowed to continue, but all single female teachers who married would not have their contracts renewed.

MAY 7, 1929: The primary purpose of education in our public schools or higher institutions of learning is to equip the boy or man to make a living and the girl or woman to make a home.

B. Interpreting Primary Sources

We learn a great deal about our past by reading what people wrote. We can learn how they lived, worked, and what they thought. These are original or first sources.

The following statements were made by Susan B. Anthony, one of the leaders for women's rights in the 1850s until her death in the early 1900s.

Alfred F. Puffer

Deputy Collector of Internal Revenue

Dear Sir:

I have your polite note informing me that as publisher of *The Revolution* I am indebted to the United States government in the sum of $14.10 for the tax on monthly sales of that journal.

Enclosed you will find the amount—fourteen dollars ten cents—but you will please understand that I pay it under protest.

The Revolution, you are aware, is a journal, the main object of which is to apply to these degenerate [degrading] times the great principles on which our ancestors fought the battles of the Revolution. . . . To inflict taxation upon any class of the people, without at the same time conferring upon them the right of representation, is tyranny.

I am not represented in the United States government, and yet that government taxes me; and it taxes me, too, for publishing a paper the chief purpose of which is to point out and rebuke [scold] the glaring and oppressive inconsistency between its professions [beliefs] and its practices [what it does].

> Under the circumstances, the Federal government ought to be ashamed to exact [ask for] this tax of me. However, as there is such pressing need of money to supply a treasury . . . . I consent to contribute to its necessities this large sum [$14.10], assuring you that when the women get the ballot and become their own representatives, as they surely will and that very soon, they will conduct themselves more generously and equitably toward the men than men now do toward them; for we shall then not only permit you to pay taxes, but compel you to vote also. . . .
>
> I am, dear Mr. Puffer, very respectfully yours,
>
> Susan B. Anthony

Source: *The Revolution*, No. 49 East 23rd St. (Woman's Bureau), New York City, June 4th, 1869.

1. Write in your notebook the letters of the statements you believe Susan Anthony would make.

   a. Women are being taxed but have no representation in government.

   b. Women should be treated equally with men.

   c. Women don't have the legal right to vote.

   d. Women should receive the same pay as men for the same job.

   e. Only women can run our country properly.

   f. The government has no right to tax anyone.

   g. The United States government does not practice what it preaches.

   h. The founders of our country fought England for the same rights that women don't have.

2. After studying Anthony's letter, answer these questions.

   a. How does Susan Anthony describe tyranny?

   b. From the statement, what is the meaning of inconsistency between beliefs and practices?

   c. Do people like Susan Anthony help or harm the improvement of democracy?

C. Writing About Citizenship

Choose an issue that is important to you. For example, the issue may concern school policy with which you disagree, or it may concern something in your community. Write a letter to the editor of your school paper about the issue you have chosen. Make your letter persuasive by clearly stating your opinions and telling what led you to those opinions. Be sure that your letter is in the right form.

OTHERS SEEK
THEIR CIVIL RIGHTS

PURPOSES FOR READING

1. To learn how there has been discrimination against American Hispanics, Asians, and Indians
2. To understand how different groups are trying to gain their civil rights

KNOWING NEW WORDS

theory
(THEE uh ree) paragraph 1—an idea used to explain an event, something that is happening

EXAMPLE: The scientist had to test his **theory** before he could tell anybody about it.

DISCRIMINATION AGAINST MINORITIES

1. Which people are being discriminated against?

2. Why are they being discriminated against?

3. What can they do to gain their civil rights?

4. Who slammed the doors?

1► Salad is a popular American dish. It is made up of more than one kind of food. Different dressings give it different flavors. Yet, we can clearly see each vegetable when the salad is served. Some think that America is much like a bowl of salad. They call it the salad bowl theory. Many peoples make up the country (the salad bowl). The theory is a way of describing the **diversity** of Americans. There are people of different races and languages. Each has likes and dislikes. Each has customs and beliefs. Each has an **identity** of his or

In the late 19th century there were many anti-Chinese riots. From 1882 until 1943 federal laws prevented further Chinese immigration.

her own. Yet, each gives something in making our country what it is.

2► Each group in America that has been a minority has known some discrimination. Prejudice against Asians was strong in California and other western states. The Chinese had problems getting an education. They could not get many kinds of jobs. They were not rented rooms or sold housing. In the 19th century, Congress even forbade Chinese to enter the country or become citizens. Later, it limited Japanese and other Asian people from coming to America.

3► Language and **cultural** differences made it hard for the Chinese to get along in America. It is hard to succeed in school when the language in use is strange. In 1974, the Supreme Court ruled that young Chinese Americans had been discriminated against in public schools. The court ordered that Chinese students receive bilingual instruction in San Francisco schools. Chinese Americans have suffered for a very common reason. Their ways of life were different from those of the majority. They were not understood. Today many Chinese Americans are business people, doctors, and lawyers. Others are factory workers, teachers, and scientists.

4► A shocking case of discrimination against Asians took place in World War II. The United States was at war with Japan. But loyal Americans of Japanese descent were not trusted. More than 100,000 of these Americans lived on the West Coast. Our government forced them to move into special camps. Those who owned homes had to sell them. They had to take the little money they were offered for their homes

Japanese–Americans receive compensation checks from Attorney General Dick Thornburgh.

and property. The camps were guarded with barbed wire. Families were not allowed to leave the camps. In October 1990 an estimated 60,000 Japanese Americans who were in the camps received checks for $20,000 each. In this way the country apologized to Japanese Americans. The government said that internment "was caused by racial prejudice, war hysteria, and a failure of political leadership."

5▶ Another Asian Group, the Filipinos, settled mainly on the West Coast. Many Filipinos, recruited by businesses, began to arrive from the Philippines in the early 1900s. Many worked in low-paying jobs. There was much housing and job discrimination against them. In 1934, Congress was pressured to pass a law limiting Filipino immigration to 50 persons a year. New laws passed in 1965 and in 1990 eased immigration. Thousands of Filipinos again are coming to the United States. Many are college-educated professionals and middle-class business people.

6▶ Another large minority speaks Spanish. From 1975 to 1990, the Hispanic population in the United States has increased to 20 million people. The largest number have come into the country from Mexico. Today, two-thirds of Mexican Americans live in cities. Many live in southwestern states such as California and Texas. As the Spanish-American population has grown so has their voting power. More than 3,000 Spanish Americans have been elected to federal and state governments. Still, most Mexican Americans have suffered from discrimination in housing and jobs. During the Civil Rights Movement of the 1960s, Mexican Americans organized to fight against such discrimination. They called themselves Chicanos to express pride in their dual heritage. This struggle to gain equal rights continues today.

7▶ Cesar Chavez was an important Chicano leader who fought against injustice. His group, called the United Farm Workers, wanted better pay and working conditions for farm workers. Chavez believed in reaching these goals through peaceful protests.

Cesar Chavez organized Mexican-American and other farm workers. What are the UFW's goals?

Xavier Suarez, the mayor of Miami, Florida. Born in Cuba, Suarez is a leader of one of the largest Hispanic groups in the United States. Many Americans are bilingual (by LING gwul). That means they can speak two languages.

But he had to call many strikes to reach his goals. He was put in jail several times for refusing to end his protests. The Farm Workers were able to win some victories for better wages and working conditions. Other Hispanics have followed the lead of Chavez. They are working hard to improve their living conditions, too.

8 ▶ Puerto Ricans are another large Spanish-speaking group. They have come from the Commonwealth of Puerto Rico. Many lived in poverty on their small island. They came to many East Coast cities looking for jobs and a better life. Unlike other immigrants entering the United States, Puerto Ricans are already American citizens. As citizens they have the right to vote. They also face a language problem in public schools. Puerto Rican leaders were able to convince Congress that Puerto Ricans should not be kept from voting because they did not speak English. In some states and cities, Spanish has become almost an official second language.

9 ▶ Large numbers of Cubans began to arrive in the United States in the early 1960s. They came here in search of free-dom. Fidel Castro, a Communist dictator, had taken over Cuba in 1959. Since that time, Cubans have come to make up more than half the population of Miami, Florida. In 1985, Xavier Suarez, a Cuban, was elected mayor of Miami.

10 ▶ Almost all Spanish-speaking people have suffered from prejudice. Mexicans and Puerto Ricans have been the worst victims. Some have been well educated with special skills. Most, however, have been poor. They have had to take low-paying jobs that require little skill. They have lived in the poorest sections of cities. The Cubans probably suffered less than others. Many of them were already middle class and well educated.

11 ▶ Spanish Americans have been improving their position in life. Laws to fight discrimination and poverty have helped them. Many have become middle class. The Census Bureau reports income levels of groups of people. Several hundred thousand Hispanic people have raised their incomes above the poverty level. Yet, success has been slow for many. There are not enough jobs. Many Puerto Ricans have left

East Coast cities in the past ten years. They returned to the island of Puerto Rico.

12▶ American Indians are often called the First or Native Americans. Unjust treatment of them began in colonial days. Only in the colonies of Rhode Island and Pennsylvania were there serious attempts to treat them as equals. The government made many treaties with Indian peoples and tribes. Still their lands were taken away from them. New lands would then be promised them. They were told these lands were theirs forever. Each time, however, the treaty was broken by the government. Indians were driven off their lands again and again. Most other Americans did not seem to care. Indians fought hard to preserve their customs and ways of living.

13▶ It was not until 1924 that Indians born in the United States were given citizenship. Yet, some states held back rights enjoyed by other Americans. Not until 1948 did all states allow Indians to vote. The problem is not solved. Indians are the poorest Americans. Their white neighbors still look down on them. But some are helping themselves. Many young Indians have received an education and found work in the cities. Some have gotten skilled jobs. A group of Indian leaders has developed. They are educated. Many have staged boycotts and demonstrations to bring attention to the problems. They have gone to court to recover land lost because of broken promises. They will not allow other Americans to forget the white people's treatment of Native Americans.

14▶ Some groups have suffered because of their religion. Catholics, Jews, Mormons, Protestants, and others have been attacked at some time or other. The election of a Catholic president, John F. Kennedy, was a sign of progress. Religious prejudice seems to have declined in our nation. There is trouble now and then. But it is not thought to be a serious problem today.

15▶ Progress has been made in the civil rights movement. Americans seem to be more aware of how their fellow citizens should be treated. The struggle for civil rights has cost many lives. Homes and churches have been bombed. Adults and

The Wampanoag Indian Tribal Council meets in Massachusetts. They lost a court case to try to recover land taken from them in the 19th century. In what year did most Indians gain American citizenship?

children have been killed. But, the movement has continued. Equal treatment of all people is not yet complete. Laws do not always bring about changes in the thinking and behavior of people. The citizen who believes that all people are created equal has a duty. That duty is to make sure that no person is denied human rights at any time. Agencies have been set up by federal and local governments. Their duty is to enforce civil rights laws. Persons who are denied their rights have the law on their side.

CHAPTER 9 REVIEW

★ UNDERSTANDING WHAT YOU HAVE READ

1. An idea of paragraph 12 is that
   a. Indians are going to court to get payment for land taken from them
   b. many young Indians are helping themselves
   c. the U.S. government has broken many treaties with the Indians

2. An important idea in paragraph 15 is that the civil rights movement has
   a. gone along very smoothly
   b. been a hard struggle
   c. been completed

3. Which statement would be the main idea of the chapter?
   a. Nearly all Americans have been discriminated against at one time or another.
   b. Only Asian, Spanish, African, and female Americans have been discriminated against in the United States.
   c. Only religious groups like Jews, Mormons, and Catholics have been discriminated against in the United States.

4. Many people have overcome discrimination by

   a. ability and hard work
   b. using force
   c. escaping from communism

5. Members of which group of Americans were forced into guarded camps in the United States during World War II?
   a. Mexican Americans
   b. Japanese Americans
   c. Chinese Americans

6. Chicano is a name given to themselves by some
   a. Puerto Rican Americans
   b. Mexican Americans
   c. Cuban Americans

7. Many Spanish-speaking people came to the United States to escape from a Communist dictatorship in
   a. the Philippines
   b. Cuba
   c. Mexico

8. Immigration laws discriminated against which group until 1965?
   a. Canadians
   b. Filipinos
   c. Puerto Ricans

★ DEVELOPING CRITICAL THINKING SKILLS

A. Making Inferences

Read this 19th-century folksong and answer the questions that follow.

Help Wanted
No Irish Need Apply

I'm a decent boy just landed	(1)
From the town of Balyfad:	(2)
I want a situation yes,	(3)
And want it very bad.	(4)
I seen employment advertised	(5)
Tis just the thing says I:	(6)
But the dirty Spalpeen ended with	(7)
No Irish need apply.	(8)
Well, I gets my dander rising,	(9)
I'd like to black his eye;	(10)
To tell an Irish gentleman	(11)
No Irish need apply.	(12)
Some do think it a misfortune	(13)
To be christened Pat or Dan:	(14)
But to me it is an honor	(15)
To be born an Irishman.	(16)

1. Which lines tell you that the songwriter is an immigrant?

2. Which lines tell you he wants a job?

3. Which lines tell you that the songwriter is proud of his background?

4. What does this song tell you about the problems faced by some immigrant groups?

5. If you were the songwriter what would you do?

6. Do you know of any situation today similar to this one?

7. Which group(s) learned about in this unit had similar problems?

8. What did the other groups of people faced with this situation do to help themselves?

9. Is it now against the law to be refused a job because of background, race, language, or religion? Explain your answer.

B. Writing About Citizenship

1. Someone has said, "People from many different backgrounds make a better country than one in which people have the same background." Do you agree or disagree? Explain.

2. In the civil rights struggle, many methods or techniques have been used to change people's minds—or to get governments to act. Think of the groups you have read about in chapters 8 and 9. How did they try to change their conditions through peaceful means? One way is through parades that draw attention to their cause. What were some others? Which is the best way, in your opinion? Why?

10

OUR FLEXIBLE CONSTITUTION

PURPOSES FOR READING

1. To understand the meaning of amendments to the Constitution
2. To understand how our Constitution has been able to meet changes in our nation as it has grown
3. To understand how amendments are made
4. To understand that many practices of government are customs developed over a long period of time

KNOWING NEW WORDS

proposed
(pruh POZD) paragraph 5—to suggest; offer
EXAMPLE: The student council **proposed** a change in the school dress code.

ratify
(RAT uh fy) paragraph 6—to approve
EXAMPLE: Several classes would not **ratify** the action of the student council.

convention
(kon VEN shun) paragraph 6—a formal meeting of members or delegates
EXAMPLE: The **convention** of lawyers offered ideas they hoped Congress would approve.

repealed
(rih PEELD) paragraph 8—done away with; withdrawn
EXAMPLE: There were so many complaints about the town parking rules that the council **repealed** them.

electors
(ih LEK turs) paragraph 11—people who elect
EXAMPLE: The people chose **electors** who would pick members of the school board.

1 ▶ Frank and Jane Homer bought a house soon after they were married. It was a small house, only four rooms. But there was room to expand, to enlarge the house if they needed more space. They didn't know what changes the passing years might bring. But this house was to be their future.

2 ▶ Frank and Jane, when they were married, did not know they would have four children. Later two rooms had to be made upstairs. They could not have known that Frank would find a better job as a salesperson, or that Jane would handle a travel service. One room had to be changed into an office. They did not know that more closets would be needed. Frank built them in two rooms of the house. As the children grew, the basement had to be changed into a recreation room. After many years, it is still the same house. But it has been changed, **amended,** to meet the needs of the family.

3 ▶ Our Constitution is like the house of the Homers. It was built in 1789. Our system of government is the same as it was then. But the writers of the Constitution could not have known the future any more than the Homers could. They could not have known that the United States would become a country of more than 240 million people. They could not have pictured our cities and highways. They could not have known of the telephone, radio, and TV. They could not have known of the motor car, the airplane, and trips to the moon. But they allowed for changes in the "house of government," the Constitution. They set up a way that our Constitution could be changed, **amended,** to meet changing times.

4 ▶ Changes in our "house of government" are called **amendments.** These are like adding a closet or room to a house. An amendment may try to correct an error in the Constitution. Or, it may make a change because of a new condition. These changes or amendments are not made easily. In our country's history, there have been only 27 amendments. The first ten were the Bill of Rights. They were added only two years after our government began. The next two

were needed to correct weaknesses in the Constitution. This means that since the year 1804, our Constitution has been added to only 15 times. As a comparison, during the same period, France has changed its entire form of government five times.

5► There are two parts to the way that amendments are made. First, a change has to be **proposed.** This can be done by a two-thirds vote of both houses of Congress. Or lawmakers in two-thirds of the states may ask for an amendment. Congress will then call for a convention to decide whether changes should be made. So far, every amendment has been proposed first by Congress.

6► Second, the states must **ratify,** or approve, the suggested change. When Congress votes in favor of an amendment, it is then sent to the states. State lawmakers vote on the proposed change. If three-fourths of the states vote yes, the amendment is added to the Constitution. Every amendment but one has been approved in this way. Another method could be used. It has been used only once. States can vote on a proposed amendment in a convention

called to do only that. State lawmakers would have no part in deciding on a proposed change. Note also that the president has no role at all in the plan for amendment.

7► Americans are always trying to make their government better. They want "a more perfect union." In the history of our country, over 3,000 amendments have been suggested. Only 27 have been approved. Sixty years passed between the 12th and 13th Amendments. Then, within five years after the Civil War, three were added. These are known as the Civil War Amendments. They made our nation more democratic. The first (the 13th) put an end to slavery. The next (the 14th) stated that all persons born in the country are citizens. It also said that states cannot take away the rights citizens hold under the Constitution. Under the 15th Amendment, a person cannot be denied the right to vote because of race or color.

8► The last 12 amendments have been added since 1900. Some of these have corrected weaknesses in our democracy. Study the list of amendments on the next page.

After serving two terms as president, Dwight D. Eisenhower meets with the nation's youngest elected president, John F. Kennedy, on inauguration day in 1961. Would the 22nd Amendment have allowed Eisenhower to serve a third term?

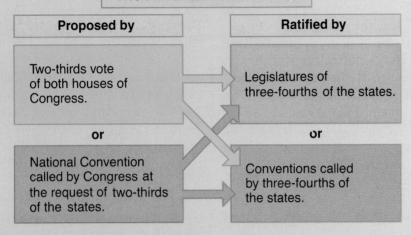

The Amendment Process

Proposed by	Ratified by
Two-thirds vote of both houses of Congress.	Legislatures of three-fourths of the states.
or	or
National Convention called by Congress at the request of two-thirds of the states.	Conventions called by three-fourths of the states.

16th Amendment (1913)— Congress has the power to tax incomes and collect income taxes.

17th Amendment (1913)— United States senators shall be elected by the voters of their state.

18th Amendment (1919)— The making or selling of alcoholic beverages is forbidden.

19th Amendment (1920)— No person can be denied the right to vote because of sex.

20th Amendment (1933)— Congress must start its session on January 3. The president takes office on January 20.

21st Amendment (1933)— The 18th Amendment is repealed.

22nd Amendment (1951)— The president can be elected only twice.

23rd Amendment (1961)— Citizens in Washington, D.C., have the right to vote.

24th Amendment (1964)— A citizen can vote for candidates for office in the national government without paying a poll tax or any other kind of tax.

25th Amendment (1967)— The vice-president becomes the acting president when the president is disabled.

26th Amendment (1971)— Citizens 18 years of age or older may vote.

27th Amendment (1991)— A session of Congress cannot vote itself a pay increase. It can only pass a law which changes pay after the next election of Representatives.

9 ▶ There are other practices of our government that are customs or habits. They are not law. But, we often think of them as laws. The reason is that they have been practiced for so many years. We have become used to them. They are much like our own habits. We start to do things in a certain way. Then, we seem to go on doing the same thing over and over again. Often we cannot tell how the habit began. It is the same with government. We often call these customs and habits of government our "unwritten Constitution."

10 ▶ Political parties are an example of the unwritten Constitution. Those who wrote the Constitution said nothing about them. Parties didn't exist. The truth is that some of our Founding Fathers didn't want political parties. Yet political parties began. They have grown to play an important part in the workings of government. (See Unit 3.) Another example is that no law says that the president must go before Congress each January and tell them about the "State of the Union." The Constitution simply mentions that the president should from time to time give Congress information about the state of the union. But presidents have been going before Congress in January for more than 50 years.

President Bill Clinton gives his State of the Union address to Congress. What does the Constitution say about the president giving this address?

Walter Mondale of Minnesota campaigning for president in 1984. Which amendment gave citizens 18 years of age or older the right to vote?

11▶ There is nothing in the Constitution that says a president must name a cabinet. Yet, every president has had one. Moreover, the Constitution also says that "electors" shall choose the president. (See page 147.) This has not been changed. But, in practice, the people choose the president. Electors only serve to approve the choice the people make. None of these customs goes against the Constitution. They only show how the ideas of government have changed over a period of time. In some ways, they are like amendments to the Constitution.

CHAPTER 10 REVIEW

★ UNDERSTANDING WHAT YOU HAVE READ

1. The main idea of paragraph 3 is that
   a. the Constitution allows for changes to be made when they are needed
   b. the Constitution has been changed so often that it is not the same document it was in 1789
   c. there is no way that a weakness in the Constitution can be corrected

2. An **amendment** to the Constitution might be compared with
   a. selling a used refrigerator
   b. adding a room to a house
   c. buying a new car

3. In the Bill of Rights, there are
   a. 5 amendments
   b. 10 amendments
   c. 12 amendments

4. Which is the most common way that an amendment is **proposed?**
   a. Conventions in two-thirds of the states
   b. A vote of the majority of the Senate
   c. A two-thirds vote in both houses of Congress

5. Which of these has no part in amending the Constitution?

a. The House of Representatives
b. The states
c. The president

6. The Civil War Amendments dealt chiefly with the
   a. rights of accused persons
   b. rights of African Americans
   c. duties of the president

7. Eighteen-year-olds have the right to vote according to which amendment?
   a. The Bill of Rights
   b. The 13th Amendment
   c. The 26th Amendment

8. According to the Constitution, which of these statements is true?
   a. A president may not be elected more than twice.
   b. A person must pay taxes in order to vote.

c. United States senators are now elected by the lawmakers of each state.

9. One can infer from chapter 10 that
   a. the way of amending the Constitution was written in the original Constitution
   b. Congress has always had the power to tax incomes
   c. every way for amending the Constitution has been tried many times

10. From this chapter, one learns that
    a. customs have an important place in our system of government
    b. rules for political parties are stated in the Constitution
    c. the Constitution tells us which officials can be members of the president's cabinet

★ DEVELOPING CRITICAL THINKING SKILLS

Making Generalizations

It is important that we know facts about our government. But we cannot remember all the facts we read about. We remember them for a while. But, if we do not refer to them often, we forget them. Facts are useful to us. They are more useful if we can put facts together and draw conclusions from them.

We give a name to these conclusions. They are **general** statements. They tell what has taken place most often or will most likely take place. We call them generalizations (jen ur uh lih ZAY shuns). We can make generalizations after finding out many facts about a topic.

A. example:

There are 30 students in your class. In a normal month the following is true.

FACTS: Twelve students are present every day.

Eight students are absent 1 day this month.

Six students are absent 2 days this month.

Four students are absent 3 days this month.

What general statement can be made about the attendance of your class? You cannot say, "We have 100-percent attendance all the time." You cannot say, "Our class has the best attendance record in school." You don't have the facts for all the other classes. But you can make this generalization: *"In this month, our class had a high percentage of attendance."* This generalization or conclusion is based on the facts you have.

B. example:

FACTS: George Washington, the first president, came from Virginia.

Thomas Jefferson, the third president, came from Virginia.

James Madison, the fourth president, came from Virginia.

James Monroe, the fifth president, came from Virginia.

GENERALIZATION: Most of our early presidents came from the state of Virginia.

NOTE: We cannot say that all early presidents came from Virginia. John Adams, the second president, came from Massachusetts. Nor can we say "most of our presidents." We did not look at all presidents. We have not considered facts about all presidents.

What generalization can you make about the following facts? Write the generalization in your notebook.

FACTS: There have been 27 amendments to the Constitution.

Eleven amendments were made before 1800.

Four amendments were passed between 1800 and 1900

There have been 12 amendments since 1900.

What generalization or conclusion might you make from these facts in chapter 10?

FACTS: Two-thirds of both houses of Congress must approve an amendment.

Three-fourths of the states must approve an amendment.

Only 27 amendments have been made in over 200 years of our history.

Write the generalization for the above facts in your notebook.

PARTICIPATION IN GOVERNMENT

VOTING

Today, it seems that many Americans are taking our system of government for granted. Few Americans vote in local and national elections. The Congressional Research Service recently gathered statistics on voter participation in 26 countries, including many European countries, Israel, Canada, Japan, and India. While the average voter participation in those countries was around 85 percent, participation in the United States was only 49 percent.

There are many reasons that someone may choose not to vote. Some people think that government has become so big that their one vote does not make any difference in the outcome of an election. Some people do not believe that big-party politics allows the people to have enough choice in whom they vote for. They think that the major parties have too much control over what the candidates think and say. Therefore, they may choose to vote for a candidate of a small party or they may choose simply not to vote.

What do you think about voting? How do you think that the voting system might be changed so that more people in the United States would participate?

Unit
3

AMERICAN POLITICAL PARTIES

emocratic and Republican party candidates for presidency are elected at national conventions.

11

HOW POLITICAL PARTIES ARE FORMED

PURPOSES FOR READING

1. To understand what politics is
2. To understand what a political party is
3. To know how political parties began in the United States
4. To learn some of the things political parties do for Americans

---

KNOWING NEW WORDS

influence
(IN floo uns) paragraph 9—to use power to get others to agree with you; to have power over
EXAMPLE: Jerry tried to **influence** his friend's choice of a new tape recorder.

campaign
(kam PAYN) paragraph 2—to take part in a plan or method used to win an election or reach a goal
EXAMPLE: Many political candidates use television to **campaign** for office.

MY PARTY WANTS TO CALL THE WHITE HOUSE HOME

1▶ Suppose you are in a school where money is cut from the budget. The principal must spend less for student activities. This means that certain activities will have to be cut. Which will be cut? Will it be football and basketball? Will it be photography, the newspaper club, or social activities? The principal may let the student government decide how student-activity money will be spent. In order to do this a special election needs to be held. Students will have to elect their own representatives.

2▶ Some students will want to be representatives. They wish to have the power to decide how the money will be spent. They may join with others who have the same point of view. Students will begin taking sides. They must select the best possible person who will win for them. They will decide on a popular name for their group. They will want your vote. They need votes to win the election. Therefore, they will campaign for the students they want as representatives. They will make posters and speeches. They will speak to you in the halls. They will make promises of what their candidates will do if they are elected.

They spend time and energy to win their point of view. They will have formed **parties.**

3▶ Real political parties are like the ones found in many schools. A **political party** is made up of a group of people. They join together because they have the same ideas. They want to put their ideas into action. To do this they must control the government. In democracies parties gain control of the government by winning elections.

4▶ Members of political parties are in politics. Politics is usually thought to be the seeking, getting, and using of power. However, it has other meanings as well. **Politics** is the word to describe everything about governments. The making of laws is politics. How the laws are carried out is politics. How lawmakers are selected is politics. How people who enforce laws are selected is politics. You see, therefore, that the word politics covers many things. It covers the everyday routines. It covers the great decisions in government. It would cover whether or not new schools will be built. It would cover an amendment to the Constitution of the United States.

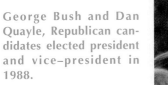

George Bush and Dan Quayle, Republican candidates elected president and vice-president in 1988.

John F. Kennedy with Lyndon Johnson and other members of the Democratic party in 1960. Why do political leaders stay in touch with other members of their party?

5▶ Political parties are very important in our democracy. The party is like the link in a chain. It connects the government to the people. It tells the government what the people want (the will of the people). It helps to hold the government responsible for its actions. We can see this by learning what political parties do.

6▶ Think back to the school elections mentioned in paragraph 2. The parties **nominate,** or choose, the **candidates.** These are the people who will run for office. They then want your vote. To get votes they have to tell people what is going on. They do this in two ways. First, they tell their opinion on certain issues or ideas. Second, they criticize, that is, they tell what is wrong with the people and ideas of the other party or parties. Thus they educate the public. They use signs, advertisements, and speeches. They communicate in any way they can think of.

7▶ Parties try to nominate good candidates. They do this because they want to win the election. They want to get and stay in power. They serve as **watchdogs** over all public business. This means that they guard against waste and illegal practices. This is often done by the party out of power. Why? They do this to convince the vot-

ers to change their government leaders.

8▶ Citizens as voters play the most important part. They must try to keep the people in political parties honest. Sometimes members of parties don't seem to care about the things the party stands for. They may only be seeking to make money. They might take bribes or use other dishonest means to gain their goals. A few times in our history a small number of people have gotten control of a party. They used it for their own self-interests. At times even one person has controlled a party in a city or state. This person is called a ''political boss.'' Honest citizens should try to stop dishonesty in politics. They do this by becoming active. They join with others against dishonest politicians. They educate other citizens. Then it is up to citizens to be responsible. Citizens must learn who is honest and who is not—who does a good job and who does not. Then they must vote for the people of their choice.

9▶ To most American voters politics means choosing between two parties. The two large parties are the Democratic party and the Republican party. Having a two-party system started before the Democrats or Republicans ever came into being. It goes back to the beginning of our nation's

A Republican campaign poster. Many Federalists had supported a meeting at Hartford in 1814. The meeting had demanded changes in the Constitution.

A Federalist and Republican attacking each other during a debate in Congress in 1798. How are the cartoons on this page like political cartoons of today?

history. You may be surprised to learn that our Founding Fathers did not like political parties. Parties were not even mentioned in the Constitution. George Washington warned about the dangers of political parties. But not everyone agreed with our early leaders. Few people in politics agree on every idea. Therefore, Americans formed parties. Why? They do this to win elections and to influence what the government does.

10 ▶ The first two political parties in the United States were formed because of an argument. The argument was over how strong the national government should be. Two sides formed. One was led by Thomas Jefferson. The other was led by Alexander Hamilton. Though both were members of George Washington's cabinet they often disagreed. Groups formed to support the idea and person of their choice. American

political parties had begun. American voters now had a choice.

11 ▶ Hamilton's party, called the Federalists, ended after the War of 1812. Jefferson's followers called themselves Republicans. Later they called themselves Democratic-Republicans. Later still, in 1832, they named themselves Democrats. The Republican party as we know it today started during the 1850s. Abraham Lincoln was the first president from the new Republican party.

12 ▶ Each party stands for more than one issue. Over the years each party has changed its ideas. More important for us, however, are the ideas they have in common. Both political parties agree on our civil liberties. Neither wants to change the form of government. Both cooperate in times of crises. Both parties do their part to help democracy in our country work.

CHAPTER 11 REVIEW

1. The main idea of paragraph 12 is that
   a. parties always stand for the same ideas
   b. the Republicans and Democrats both want to change our form of government
   c. the people in both parties believe in helping our government work

2. The main idea of paragraph 8 is that
   a. there is dishonesty in politics
   b. there are many political bosses
   c. voters need to keep politicians honest

3. Political parties are groups
   a. of countries joined together to increase armed forces
   b. of families who want to control their lives better
   c. of people who want to control the government

4. Which of the following is NOT politics?
   a. Passing a law
   b. Getting a parking ticket
   c. Listening to the radio

5. What does "will of the people" mean?
   a. The written message people fill out before they die
   b. A famous candidate
   c. What the people want

6. The person who runs for office is the
   a. campaign
   b. watchdog
   c. candidate

7. The word **watchdogs** in paragraph 7 means

   a. politicians are like animals
   b. protectors
   c. the pets that represent each political party

8. In democracies parties get control of governments by
   a. winning elections
   b. becoming politicians
   c. gaining control of the army or police

9. Political parties began in the United States because
   a. not all the leaders agreed on how to run the government
   b. not all the leaders liked each other
   c. George Washington wanted them

10. Which is true of today's political parties?
    a. Both the Democratic and Republican parties started at the same time.
    b. The Democratic party was formed after the Republicans had been created.
    c. The Democratic party is older than the Republican party.

11. The party that is not in power
    a. has nothing to do until the next election
    b. keeps watch over the party that is in power
    c. breaks up after each election it loses

12. Which part of the Constitution guarantees the right to form political parties?
    a. The Preamble
    b. The 14th Amendment
    c. Political parties are not mentioned.

★ **DEVELOPING CRITICAL THINKING SKILLS**

A. Interpreting Pictures

Study the picture. Then answer the questions.

1. How is this picture of a political campaign in 1881 similar to the photo on page 96?

2. Why do you think the candidate is paying attention to the baby?

3. Is there anything in the picture that indicates that the family may be poor?

4. Why is the candidate visiting a low-income family?

B. Interpreting a Cartoon

Study the cartoon. Then answer the questions.

1. What does the turning door mean in the cartoon?

2. What are some things that the "outs" will do in order to get into power?

3. In real life, which party is now in power in our national government?

C. Writing About Citizenship

Answer the following question in a brief essay: Do you think that the two-party system is a good system? Why or why not? What might be a better system?

12

HOW AN ELECTION IS WON

PURPOSES FOR READING

1. To understand why people work for a political party
2. To learn how people become candidates

KNOWING NEW WORDS

qualified
> (KWOL uh fyd) paragraph 5— permitted by law or rules
> EXAMPLE: At age 18 most people are **qualified** to vote.

volunteers
> (vol un TEERS) paragraph 10— those who do something by their own free will
> EXAMPLE: Today many young people are **volunteers** in the military service.

primary
> (PRY mer ee) paragraph 5—a special election to choose a political party's candidates, who will later run in a regular election
> EXAMPLE: Last week the Republicans in Florida held their **primary** for a candidate for president.

How does each level of a political party help win elections? In 1990, Sharon Pratt-Dixon won election as Mayor of Washington, D.C.

1▶ A political election is like a game. The goal of the election game is to win. To win a pennant in baseball one must have a good team. This is so for political parties also. A party that expects to take part in many elections must have a well-organized team. A political team is called an organization. Some call it a **political machine.** The people in political organizations have many positions or jobs to play. They plan conventions and other meetings. They raise money to pay bills. They carry on campaigns. They speak to the voters. They are on the party team.

2▶ Our big parties have big organizations. See the chart on page 89. A party organization has many parts. It may begin in your neighborhood at the voting **precinct** (PREE singkt). Every county or city is divided into precincts. Each precinct has a place to vote (a polling place). The precinct usually contains between 500 and 1,000 voters. The party members of a precinct elect a **captain.** The captains are responsible for ''getting out'' the vote. This means getting voters to the polls on election day.

3▶ Some persons from a precinct may be members of a **ward committee.** (See the chart.) Leaders of wards are selected by voters or precinct captains. Some members of a ward committee may also have other jobs. Some may also belong to the city or county committee. State committees, too, are made up of persons who are party members. They are chosen by the party from different districts in the state. There is also a **national committee.** This committee is most active in the years when a president is to be chosen. The people on the committees work toward the goal of winning.

4▶ There may be many candidates for an office. Some may simply announce their desire to run for office. In such cases we say, "This hat is thrown into the ring." Several who want to be candidates might be from one party. A few different ways are used to choose the "one" candidate from a party. At some local levels party members have a **caucus** (KAW kus). This is a meeting of party leaders. These party members choose the candidate. Party bosses often control a caucus.

5▶ Most states now use **direct primary elections.** This is usually the first step in our way of filling an office. When only members of a party can vote in a primary election, it is called a closed primary. Sometimes any qualified voter, even a member of another party, is permitted to vote. This is called an open primary. Primary elections are held on whatever date a state sees fit. The winner becomes the party's nominated candidate. Political bosses sometimes also control primaries. If they do, it is the fault of the voters.

Campaign workers planning strategy in a county race. How might strategy for a county race differ from strategy in a national race?

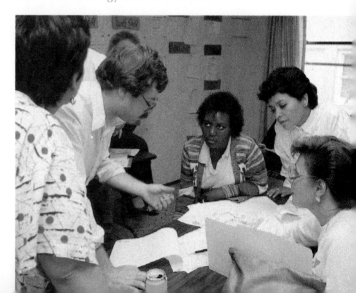

Study the party organization chart on the next page. Then answer the following questions. The answers are to be found by reading the chart and paragraphs 1, 2, and 3.

1. Which committee is the most numerous throughout the country?

2. Which leader is most likely to live in your neighborhood?

3. Which committee has the most to do with selecting a presidential candidate?

4. Which person would you go to if you wanted to get started in politics?

5. Why is the title of the chart "Party Organization"?

6. In your opinion which part of the organization is the most important for winning an election?

6▶ Voters can also choose candidates outside of the regular parties. They may sign a petition, a written request. The petition asks to have a person's name put on the official list of candidates. Candidates nominated in this way have little chance for election. However, sometimes they do win.

7▶ Weeks, sometimes months, pass between nomination and election day. During this time the campaign is carried on. The party leaders write up the **party platform.** This is an official statement of party ideas. It is with this platform that the candidate seeks to get votes. Other campaigning is done by workers. Some are professional politicians. Most are people who willingly give their time. They work to give their candidate a "winning image." People want their candidate to be good at everything. They want a leader with a sense of humor. An honest person with a family gets votes. Their candidate should be intelligent, love animals, the outdoors, and children. This kind of person appeals to many voters.

8▶ The Tuesday after the first Monday in November is the big day. This is the day on which most general elections take place. Some few states have chosen other days for local elections. Maine chooses its governor and members of Congress in September. Elections are carried out in a much better way than years ago. Once votes were announced out loud. Then ballots—written or

County Election, painting by George Caleb Bingham. How does this painting support the statement that "political leaders are elected by the people"?

Party Organization

NATIONAL COMMITTEE

Advises and helps. Supervises the national convention, which selects the party's candidates for president and vice-president.

STATE COMMITTEE

Plans and directs ways to improve the party in the state. Selects delegates for the national convention.

COUNTY OR CITY COMMITTEE

Appoints and oversees committees to work with precinct leaders.

Finance Committee
Gets donations. Plans how to spend the money.

Registration Committee
Helps to get voters registered.

Speakers Committee
Provides speakers and helps to make large meetings.

Information Committee
Gathers facts on issues and candidates.

Publicity Committee
Gets publicity for candidates.

Ward or District Leader

Precinct Captain
Appoints and guides precinct workers. Gets voters to the polls.

Ward or District Leader

Possible Election Day Precinct Committees

1. Poll Committee—Members stay at polls to see who has voted.
2. Telephone Committee—Calls voters to remind them to vote.
3. Poll Watching Committee.
4. Others as needed.

Precinct Worker
Visits voters at home and gets them to vote.

Walter Mondale and Geraldine Ferraro at the Democratic National Convention in San Francisco in 1984. Ferraro was the first woman chosen to run on a major party's presidential ticket.

printed sheets of paper—were used. This secret ballot prevented others from knowing how a citizen voted. But it was easy to cheat. Some people stuffed extra votes in the ballot box. Today more than half of the votes are cast in secret with voting machines. Regardless of the method used, political parties play their part. They send **poll watchers** to see that all is honest.

9 ▶ Unfortunately, there is still some dishonesty in elections. Extra names might be added to the list of voters. This means that some people use two or more names. They try to vote two or more times. To prevent this, many states ask that a voter register. Dishonest people may even be on an election board.

10 ▶ Members of the political team get very excited about the outcome of an election. They are the people without whom a candidate cannot win. Who are these people who give up so much of their time? Some are professional politicians of course. Others are often volunteers. Many of the volunteers are upper-middle-class homemakers and college students. Very few of these people ever get paid. Why do they do it? Many believe in what the party stands

for. They want to see that the party's plans and ideas are put into action. Candidates, of course, win a job when the election is won. Others may receive jobs also. The candidate may appoint them. Party leaders may get them a job. (This is called **political patronage.**) Other supporters may get government contracts.

11 ▶ American politics has been led to a large degree by lawyers. They can arrange their own working hours. They can often benefit from the time spent in politics. Still others may want to be elected to office in the future. They learn how elections are won and lost. Special studies, however, have shown that many people working for a party do so for a "feeling." Party workers have a chance to mix with famous people. They form friendships with other politically active persons. They feel that they belong. They want to have the excitement of the contest. They have the chance to put their own ideas into action. All these people are members of a team. They have one goal: To win the election for the candidate of their choice.

12 ▶ We expect candidates or those promoting products on television and radio or

in newspapers to present strong points of view. Often, however, the entire truth is not told and statements are not backed by proof. Information passed to the public may contain ''trick'' phrases or expressions. This is called propaganda.

13► Propaganda is the spreading of an idea in order to shape people's opinions. There are two types. Concealed propaganda occurs when ideas are passed off as facts, and their sources are kept hidden. In an election campaign this can be harmful when one candidate is made to look bad. Revealed propaganda is the other type. Most advertising is revealed propaganda. Products are advertised in order to get people to buy them. During an election campaign candidates use the media to get votes.

14► Citizens should be able to distinguish between fact and opinion (page 28). They must be able to recognize the methods that are used to influence them. Listed below are some forms of propaganda.

1. **Name calling.** Name calling is giving people or things a bad label so that they will be rejected. In politics, this can cause a candidate to lose an election. For example, one candidate may call another candidate dishonest.

2. **Glittering Generalities.** Glittering generalities is the technique of using vague words or ideas to get people to accept an idea or a person. Usually the words deal with ideas that stand for something most people favor. For example, Candidate X says in a speech that she is for the flag, peace, and the American way. She does not, however, specify what she means.

3. **Transfer.** Transfer is associating a person or idea with something everyone thinks is good. In politics this might be a senator having her picture taken kissing a smiling baby. The idea is to link the senator with the baby and transfer the good feelings associated with the baby to the senator.

4. **Testimonial.** Testimonial is getting a well-known person to endorse (back up) a person, product, or idea. An athlete endorses running shoes to convince people to buy the shoes.

5. **Plain Folks.** Plain folks is the technique used when candidates go out of their way to appear to be just like us — average American people. A candidate might have his picture taken while shopping in a supermarket. Another might tell about her poor childhood when there was little money for food and clothing.

6. **Card stacking.** Card stacking refers to a game of cards where a dealer fixes or ''stacks'' the deck to get the hand she wants. Persons talk about the facts that show only their good side. For example, the president might tell the nation that he has decreased taxes. He doesn't mention that to do this he had to cut spending for such things as education.

7. **Bandwagon.** Bandwagon is the method of convincing people that everyone else is doing the same thing. A politician may tell voters that everyone in their neighborhood is voting for her and they should, too.

CHAPTER 12 REVIEW

★ UNDERSTANDING WHAT YOU HAVE READ

1. The main idea of paragraphs 4, 5, and 6 is that
   a. there are many ways that a person can become a candidate
   b. party bosses choose the candidates
   c. primary elections since 1975 have been held every year

2. The main idea of paragraph 7 is what
   a. politicians do for a living
   b. happens during campaigns
   c. people do to get nominated

3. The main idea of paragraphs 10 and 11 is that
   a. lawyers spend a lot of time in politics
   b. people work for political parties to get favors
   c. there are many reasons why people work for political parties

4. A polling place is a place where
   a. people vote
   b. party members meet
   c. speeches are made

5. "Getting out" the vote in paragraph 2 means
   a. getting people to vote
   b. counting the votes

   c. making sure the voting is done honestly

6. Members of a political party are all
   a. equal in importance
   b. working at different levels of an organization
   c. mechanics working on some political machines

7. To "throw a hat into the ring" means to
   a. go to a political fund-raising party
   b. announce the desire to be a candidate
   c. choose a candidate

8. One thing that all party volunteer workers have in common is
   a. money
   b. health
   c. time

9. The people most responsible to see that there is honesty in elections are
   a. the poll watchers
   b. the voters
   c. the party in power

10. The giving of jobs as political favors is called
    a. poll watching
    b. political patronage
    c. political machinery

★ DEVELOPING CRITICAL THINKING SKILLS

A. Interpreting a Cartoon

Draw and explain your own political cartoon showing a candidate and party platform.

B. Reading Graphs

Study the graph "Who Turns Out to Vote" on page 93. Then answer the questions that follow.

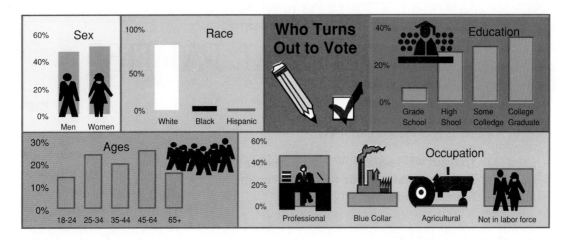

Note: Bars within each category (sex, race, etc.) compare the number of people voting within that category.

Source: U.S. Bureau of the Census.

1. According to the graph, were there more men or more women who actually voted?

2. According to the graph, which age group had the most voters?

3. According to the graph, what is a description of the typical, or average, voter?

4. Suppose you were a candidate for president with very little campaign money. Who would you try to reach and influence to vote for you? Why?

C. Identifying Propaganda Techniques

The following speech might have been made by a candidate for city council. The speech contains ten numbered examples of propaganda. In your notebook, identify which of the seven techniques of propaganda—name calling, glittering generalities, transfer, testimonial, plain folks, card stacking, and bandwagon—the speaker is using in each example. In many cases, more than one technique is used in a single statement.

(1) "I'm running for city council because I believe this city needs a new council that is honest and will keep the best interests of the people in mind. (2) I told the governor at dinner last night that I have the cooperation of many groups in this city. (3) With the support of those groups, the governor, and all of you, we can reach our goals. (4) I was born in this community and my entire family has lived here for many years. (5) I didn't leave town to get my education. (6) Unlike my opponent, I stayed right here and went to school with the rest of you. (7) I am strictly for the flag and peace and am proud to say I fought side by side with my fellow Americans in World War II. (8) I have not come this far by passing the buck and letting others do my work for me. (9) You want a representative to be a leader and not a follower like my opponent. (10) I am the man for the job and together we will make our community a better place by using the ideas that made America great."

FUNDING POLITICAL PARTIES

13

PURPOSES FOR READING

1. To learn where and how candidates get their campaign money
2. To understand why the federal government helps candidates to finance campaigns

KNOWING NEW WORDS

deduct
(dih DUKT) paragraph 3—to take away
EXAMPLE: The cashier will **deduct** the discount from the ticket price.

1. Why is money needed for political campaigns?

2. Where do you think the money is coming from?

3. What are some other titles for the cartoon?

President Jimmy Carter at a Democratic fund-raising dinner. With him is then Chicago mayor Jane Byrne.

1 ▶ Getting money for campaigns and spending it wisely are very important. Money can often mean the difference between winning and losing an election. Election costs have skyrocketed. One historian figured out the costs of Lincoln's presidential campaign of 1860. It was about $100,000. President Nixon spent about $60 million while winning in 1972. In 1992, all candidates for the presidency spent over $3 billion.

2 ▶ There are many ways to raise money for political campaigns. Party members may go to people's homes to ask for contributions. Requests for money are sent through the mails. People may pay as much as $1,000 a plate for a fund-raising dinner. Political action committees (PACs) raise money for specific candidates.

3 ▶ Still, most Americans give little or nothing to pay the expenses of their party. Therefore parties turn to special people or groups to raise money. Money is often contributed by candidates' friends and families. Businesses, labor unions, landlords, and bankers give large amounts of money. Those who give to political campaigns can deduct money from their income tax.

4 ▶ People and groups contribute money to politics for many reasons. Some want to get favors from the winner. Others want to put their ideas into the platform. Still others give because they feel it is their duty as citizens.

5 ▶ Costs of campaigns continue to go up. See the chart on this page. The greatest expense is the media. The costs are high for TV commercials, and ads in newspapers and magazines. A single half hour on TV can cost over $200,000. In the early 1970s Congress tried to reduce these huge expenses. Laws placed limits on contributions and spending. But these laws are only for

Presidential Campaign Spending			
Year	Estimated Spending	Votes Cast for President	Cost per Voter
1984	1.8 billion	92,653,000	$19.42
1988	2.7 billion	91,595,000	$29.47
1992	3.25 billion	101,017,000	$32.17

Source: Herbert E. Alexander, Citizens' Research Foundation.

The Kennedy–Nixon debate was the first televised presidential debate. Televised debates are important to campaigns.

federal elections. The laws also permit public funds for people running for president. Several states have passed the same kinds of laws for local and state elections.

6▶ The candidate may contribute any amount to his or her own race. Each federal candidate must form a finance committee. The committee must report what is spent. In 1980, both major candidates for president went over their spending limits in some primary elections. They had to repay.

7▶ There is a worry about some people or groups "buying an election." Large contributors often expect favors if the candidate is elected. To stop some of this, other laws have been passed. A person may not give more than $1,000 to a candidate. No one may donate more than $25,000 a year. Groups may donate up to $5,000 to a candidate. These laws, too, are for federal elections only.

8▶ The laws also permit a presidential candidate to use federal funds. This is called public funding. The money comes from taxpayers. If taxpayers wish to contribute, they may add one dollar to their federal income tax. In 1988 over $90 million of public funds was spent. More than half the states are helping candidates with public funds.

9▶ Look again at the cartoon at the be-

Cartoon of trusts in 1889. What would be the advantages of candidates getting support from large trusts? What would be the disadvantages?

ginning of this chapter. Can you now answer all the questions that follow it? Even with public financing, things have not changed much. To win an election two things are absolutely necessary. One is to have a good candidate. The second is to have the money to pay the campaign expenses.

CHAPTER 13 REVIEW

★ UNDERSTANDING WHAT YOU HAVE READ

1. The main idea of paragraph 6 is that the government
   a. is enforcing the rules on campaign financing
   b. does little about financing
   c. sets up finance committees to help candidates

2. How much can one person give to campaigns in one year?
   a. no limit
   b. $1,000
   c. $25,000

3. What did the 1992 presidential campaign cost taxpayers?
   a. over $3 billion
   b. almost $1 billion
   c. about $50 million

4. The federal government has limited the amount of money one can give to a candidate in order to
   a. prevent citizens from being embarrassed
   b. lessen the influence of wealthy people
   c. form finance committees

5. There are many reasons why people contribute to politics. This is the main idea of
   a. paragraph 2
   b. paragraph 3
   c. paragraph 4

6. The federal government has helped presidential candidates by letting them
   a. pay campaign workers below the minimum wage
   b. have free time on TV for the campaign
   c. use public funds for the campaign

7. A reason why political parties must spend time and energy to raise money is that
   a. most Americans give little or nothing to political parties
   b. most people want to be asked to give
   c. most Americans distrust political parties

8. Labor unions and businesses contribute money to political parties because
   a. they want the party to support their ideas and plans
   b. they can deduct the money from income taxes
   c. the federal law requires that they give money

9. The biggest campaign cost is for
   a. ads on TV
   b. transportation around the country
   c. speakers

10. The figures in the chart on page 95 show that campaign spending is
   a. going up but the cost per voter is less
   b. going down but the cost per voter is more
   c. going up and the cost per voter is more

★ **DEVELOPING CRITICAL THINKING SKILLS**

A. Considering Points of View

On this page are different points of view about the use of public funds (tax money) to finance campaigns in federal elections. Read each of the speaker's comments. Tell whether Speaker A, Speaker B, or both speakers would agree with the following statements. Write your answer next to the number of each question in your notebook.

1. Campaign costs are too high.

2. If tax money is used to finance a campaign, voters are involved and that's good.

3. Trust the voters. Give them the facts. That will ensure honest elections.

4. A candidate has no right to expect to have his or her campaign financed by tax money. He or she must earn the support received.

5. A candidate must meet every voter possible. That's where the expense comes in.

SPEAKER A:

Political parties spend millions of dollars to elect their candidate for president. Half of this money is donated [given] by a few hundred people. The average voter has not contributed to political campaigns. But using public funds paints a different picture. With the $1 checkoff on a tax return, everyone can become involved, not only the wealthy and those with special interests. In the 1988 campaign for president, over $195 million in public funds was made available to both major political parties for their campaign.

A candidate for president cannot meet everyone in person. If I were running for president, I'd have to use TV and radio. I'd have to use newspapers and the mail. These things cost money. If public funds are used, no candidate would have to think of "paying back" special donors if he or she is elected.

SPEAKER B:

When you ask the public to finance a campaign, you are asking people to use their tax money to help some people who are not very good candidates. A person running for office should earn the support of the people. If the people want the candidate, they will put up the money to get him or her elected. Few people are going to donate to the campaign of a candidate who is not a good one.

We can stop people from "buying elections" in another way. Put a limit on how much can be given to a campaign. Sure, the costs of campaigns have gone up. But that's because the campaigns are too long. Spending starts months ahead of the election and grows and grows. People don't need all that time to decide whom they want.

B. Writing About Citizenship

Write a brief essay on this topic: Would you ever consider donating money to a political candidate? Why or why not? Under what circumstances, if any, would you do so?

14

THIRD PARTIES IN OUR HISTORY

PURPOSES FOR READING

1. To understand why people will form new political parties
2. To learn the successes and failures of new or third parties
3. To understand the role of third parties in some national elections

KNOWING NEW WORDS

electoral votes
(ih LEK tuh rul VOHTS) paragraph 4—votes cast by electors, who are those elected to choose a president
EXAMPLE: A majority of **electoral** votes will decide who is president.

Progressives
(pruh GRES ivs) paragraph 7—people favoring progress; members of the Progressive party
EXAMPLE: The **Progressives** thought

they were making some gains in removing what they said were the evils of big business.

reforms
(rih FORMS) paragraph 6—improvements; removal of evils or defects
EXAMPLE: Dorothea Dix fought for **reforms** in the treatment of the mentally ill.

Theodore Roosevelt, who ran for president on the Progressive party ticket in 1912. His candidacy split the Republican vote and enabled the Democrat, Woodrow Wilson, to win the election. What chance does a third-party presidential candidate have?

Tammany Hall cartoon. How does this cartoon illustrate the misuse of political party practices?

1▶ Supertown's election day is a few months away. This year, a mayor and members of council are being chosen. The Democratic and Republican parties have named people to fill these offices. One party promises to keep spending in the town government just as it is for another year. The other party wants to cut taxes by a large amount. Neither party wants to spend money for a new school. Nor do they plan to repair other schools. You want better schools in Supertown. You want this more than anything else. What can you do?

2▶ Suppose you and a group of people who believe as you do have spoken with the leaders of both parties. They listen, but they do not agree with you. You think there are many others who want better schools, too. You call a meeting of all who are interested in your ideas. A hundred people come to the meeting. The group agrees that it should put up its own candidates for town offices. Several people say they are willing to run. They will run on the platform of the Better Schools party. Your group takes care of all the details needed to have your party on the ballot for the election. A third party has been formed. It was formed because neither of the major parties favored what a group of voters felt was needed. It is a small party. It is in only one town. It has one issue.

3▶ Third parties have been formed on a national scale, too. Many have put up candidates for Congress and for president. Some still do. Some have one issue they favor and want our government to adopt. Others have a whole program to offer the voters. What success have third parties had in our history?

4▶ Abraham Lincoln was elected president in 1860. In that election, there were four candidates for president. The Republican party had chosen Lincoln. The Democratic party chose Stephen Douglas. Members of the major parties who did not agree with their party's stand on slavery formed two other parties. The election results are in the chart on page 101. Neither of the minor, or third, parties lasted after the election. All of their **electoral votes** came from border and southern states. (A complete discussion of the electoral system appears in Unit 4.) The Civil War ended the argument over the question of slavery.

5▶ In the 1880s, farmers decided to do something about their problems. They felt they were treated unfairly by railroad com-

ELECTION OF 1860		
Candidate	**Votes**	**Electoral Votes**
Lincoln	1,866,352	180
Douglas	1,375,157	12
Breckinridge	847,953	72
Bell	589,581	39

1. Which candidate was elected president?

2. Which candidate was second in electoral votes?

3. How many electoral votes did third-party candidates win?

4. Combine the number of votes received by the two new parties. Compare with the votes for Douglas.

5. Did more voters vote for Lincoln or for the other candidates?

panies. They also felt that the federal government favored eastern businesses. Farmers in western states united to try to get help from state governments. When this plan failed, they formed their own political party. It was called the People's party, or **Populist** party. They named a candidate for president in 1892. In the election, the People's party received over a million votes. The party sent 15 members to Congress. Five of them were in the United States Senate.

6► Did the People's party succeed? It never again made such a showing in a national election. But many parts of its platform were taken on by both major parties. Through them, many of the **reforms** the Populists wanted were made into law. The party had asked for primary elections. It wanted a secret ballot, too. It wanted a graduated income tax. This is a tax based on the ability of people to pay it. This be-

came part of the Constitution in 1913. They also favored the election of United States senators directly by the people. This, too, was added to the Constitution, as the 17th Amendment.

7► From 1900 to 1920, a spirit of reform in government swept across the nation. People wanted to make changes. They wanted to get rid of some bad practices in government and business. They called themselves **Progressives**—people making progress. Progressives wanted many of the things for which the People's party had stood. They also wanted to get rid of dishonesty in city governments. They favored pure food laws and an end to child labor. They supported the right of women to vote. Most of these reforms were made into law by 1920.

8► The election of 1912 showed the strength of the Progressives. In that election, Theodore Roosevelt ran for president on the Progressive party ticket. (Roosevelt had been president from 1901 to 1909. He ran again because he did not think that President Taft had followed the Progressive's programs.) The results for the 1912 election are shown on the chart on this page. The Progressives were not able to win the election. But they did receive more public support than one of the major parties.

9▶ The Progressives returned once more to run a strong candidate in 1924. They were supported chiefly by farmers and workers. These people disliked the platforms of the major parties. Their candidate, Robert La Follette of Wisconsin, received about five million votes. But the party won electoral votes only in Wisconsin.

10▶ The election of 1968 was another one in which a third party made a strong showing. The country was then involved in the war in Vietnam. There had been protests against the war throughout the country. Some young men had refused to be drafted to fight in Vietnam. The American Independent party was formed. George C. Wallace of Alabama ran as its candidate. Wallace called for "law and order" in our nation. Many thought he hoped that neither major party would receive enough electoral votes to elect its candidate. Then, the House of Representatives would have to

ELECTION OF 1912			
Candidate	Party	Vote	Electoral Vote
Wilson	Democrat	6,286,214	435
T. Roosevelt	Progressive	4,126,020	88
Taft	Republican	3,483,922	8
Debs	Socialist	897,011	0

1. Who was elected president?

2. Who was the second in the electoral votes? In popular votes?

3. How many electoral votes did third-party candidates receive?

4. Combine the number of votes of the two new parties. Compare with the votes for Taft.

5. Did more voters vote for Wilson or for other candidates?

ELECTION OF 1968

Candidate	Party	Votes	Electoral Votes
Nixon	Republican	31,785,480	301
Humphrey	Democrat	31,275,166	191
Wallace	American Independent	9,906,473	46

1. Who was elected president?

2. Who was second in electoral votes? In popular votes?

3. How many electoral votes did the third-party candidate receive?

4. Combine the votes for Wallace and Humphrey. Compare with the votes for Nixon.

5. Did more voters vote for Nixon or for other candidates?

elect the president. The results of the 1968 elections are shown in the chart on this page. Wallace came in third place.

11 ► The third-party candidate in the 1992 election had the strongest showing since Roosevelt in 1912. Ross Perot, a successful businessman, ran as an independent. He called for major economic reforms. He wanted to reduce drastically the federal deficit by increasing taxes and cutting government spending. Although Perot failed to win any electoral votes, he received almost 19 percent of the popular vote. He probably did not change the election outcome, since half of Perot voters said they would have voted for Clinton and half for Bush. However, Perot's popularity showed that many voters were very concerned about the economy.

12 ► None of the third or minor parties you have read about have won national elections. Yet, in many cases, they have gained support for their programs. Major parties have taken over their ideas. Their ideas often become the law of the land. Were they successful after all?

13 ► There are many small parties in our nation. Some exist only in a town or city. Others are statewide. Some will not name their own candidates in elections. They will ask party members to vote for the candidate of a major party who supports their views. In this way, they can influence elections. Others will name their own candidates. Some have elected governors, senators, and mayors. Successful third parties usually support more than one issue. They appeal to a wider range of voters.

CHAPTER 14 REVIEW

★ **UNDERSTANDING WHAT YOU HAVE READ**

1. A good title for paragraph 2 might be
   a. Running for Public Office
   b. How a Third Party Is Formed
   c. Repairing Our Schools

2. The results of the 1860 election (see chart on page 101) tell us that
   a. no candidate received a majority (more than half) of electoral votes
   b. Lincoln did not receive a majority of the popular vote
   c. small parties received more electoral votes than Lincoln

3. The People's party began with
   a. the presidential election of 1896
   b. poorly paid workers in eastern factories
   c. meetings of dissatisfied farmers

4. Third parties have had success in
   a. electing Abraham Lincoln in 1860
   b. having their ideas accepted by major parties
   c. having the Bill of Rights added to the Constitution

5. When did a third party gain more votes than a major party in a national election?
   a. 1860
   b. 1912
   c. 1968

6. Third or smaller parties have been most successful in electing
   a. members of Congress
   b. vice-presidents
   c. presidents

7. Which of these third parties received the greatest number of electoral votes in the election of 1912?
   a. Progressive party
   b. Socialist party
   c. American Independent party

8. Third parties have had success in the adoption of the
   a. 13th Amendment
   b. 17th Amendment
   c. 21st Amendment

9. Which third party received more than four million votes in two presidential elections?
   a. People's party
   b. Socialist party
   c. Progressive party

10. In the election of 1968, Richard Nixon received
    a. more than half the popular vote
    b. less than half the electoral vote
    c. less than half the popular vote

★ **DEVELOPING CRITICAL THINKING SKILLS**

Fact or Opinion

Tell whether the following are facts or merely someone's opinion. Write the word fact or opinion next to the number of each statement in your notebook.

1. There is little use in forming a third party in a state election.

2. The chief purpose of the Populist party

(People's party) was to gain benefits for farmers.

3. The Progressive party will never again reach the success it had in the early 1900s.

4. Third parties have made a very small contribution to the success of our form of government.

5. Third parties have never elected their own candidate as president.

6. The Democratic party has done more for the country than the Republican party has.

7. Some third parties have elected governors of states.

8. It is better to support the candidate of a major party than to vote for the candidate of a third party.

9. Major parties have sometimes taken over ideas of smaller parties.

PARTICIPATION IN GOVERNMENT

REGISTERING TO VOTE

Each year at election time, you will see and hear pleas to "get out and vote." Leaders want everyone who is registered to vote in every election. Americans, however, have a poor voting record when compared with other democratic nations, such as Canada, England, or West Germany. A heavy turnout of voters in the United States usually means that six out of ten eligible voters actually exercised their right in the election. In recent elections for president, the percentage of voters has been even lower.

Unfortunately, young people are among the poorest groups in exercising their right to vote. The 26th Amendment to the Constitution, passed in 1971, gave 18-year-olds the right to vote. It is a right that young people had sought for many years. Yet, even in national elections since that time, less than half of the eligible 18-year-olds have voted. In local elections, the percentage is a great deal less.

Why is this so? Is it because voting in a democracy is not required? Should it be required of people who enjoy greater freedoms than any other people in the world? What could be more important in a democracy than voting? If you are not eligible to vote now, you will be at age 18. At that time, in order to vote you must *register*.

There is a good reason why you must register. If it were not required, there would be no way of telling whether a person voted more than once. When registering, you fill out a form giving your date of birth and citizenship. You also list your present address and how long you've lived there. You cannot vote in a state or local election if you do not actually live in that state or town. Most states will not allow you to vote if you have not lived there for a certain amount of time. The amount will vary from state to state.

When and where to register will also differ from place to place. In most instances places where you can register are open at certain times over a set period. You can inquire about the time and place from your local government.

Unit 4

THE FEDERAL GOVERNMENT

Fourth of July fireworks in Washington, D.C., the U.S. capital and center of our federal government.

15

THE FEDERAL GOVERNMENT

PURPOSES FOR READING

1. To understand the meaning of a federal government
2. To learn the duties and powers of the national and state governments
3. To learn where the federal and state governments get their powers

KNOWING NEW WORDS

national government
  (NASH uh nul GUV urn munt)
  paragraph 2—the government of
  the whole nation; sometimes called
  the federal government.
  EXAMPLE: The **national government**
  pays social security benefits to
  retired workers.

welfare
  (WEL fair) paragraph 7—the
  condition of happiness, success,
  and comfort
  EXAMPLE: The government has
  passed laws to improve the **welfare**
  of working people.

The Capitol Building in Washington, D.C. Many Americans each year visit Washington to observe the federal government in action.

United States postal workers. The federal government provides many different kinds of jobs. What other kinds of federal jobs can you name?

1▶ "The government should do something about our problems." "The government doesn't seem to care whether or not we have jobs." "Does the government know how much it costs to live today?" We often hear such comments from Americans. Some people seem to feel that all problems should be blamed on "the government." But, in a way, this "government" that receives so much blame is really us, the citizens of the United States. We the people have chosen our lawmakers and high officials. The people have a right to tell government officials what they want and what their problems are. They also have to accept the blame if government officials continue to carry out actions of which they disapprove.

2▶ The word government is not always a clear term. When there is praise for government or a complaint against government, people should know of which government they are speaking. There are many governments in the United States. There is the national or federal government, the United States of America. There are 50 different state governments. There are also county, city, and town governments. All these governments have some powers. All people in the 50 states live according to the laws and rules of several governments.

3▶ The United States has a **federal** system of government. This means that the Constitution, the basis for all our governments, has divided powers between the federal government and the state governments. The powers of our federal or national government are set down in the Constitution. The Constitution lists many of the powers of the federal government. In general, these are powers needed to make the country run smoothly. The Constitution also lists some of the things the federal government cannot do.

4▶ The federal (national) government has the power to make laws and enforce them. It can carry on business with other countries. It can make sure that our nation is defended against all enemies. The federal government has the power to collect taxes, coin and borrow money, and establish post offices. It can also declare war and raise armed forces. The national government, but not the state governments, can regulate trade with other countries. The federal government also has the power to regulate commerce or business between the states.

5▶ The federal government has other powers that are not expressed (written down) in the Constitution. These are **implied** powers. Article I of the Constitution says that Congress can "make all laws which shall be necessary and proper" to carry out the powers it has been given. This has been called the **elastic clause.** As elastic stretches, so the meaning of this clause has been stretched to give the federal government power to pass many kinds of laws.

6▶ The **implied,** or unstated, powers of the federal government cover many topics. The Constitution says that the national government has the power to make laws concerning trade between the states. The meaning of this has been stretched to include things not mentioned in the Constitution. Today the national government regulates many things besides trade. It regulates air, rail, bus, and truck transportation from one state to another. Radio and TV are also regulated by the federal government.

7▶ Article I, Section 8, of the Constitution also gives the lawmakers of the federal government power to "provide for the . . . general welfare of the United States." Under this power, the federal government has done many things that were not thought of when the Constitution was first written. Through this welfare clause, the federal government has built dams and flood-control projects, established national parks, and provided social security benefits for aged and disabled citizens.

8▶ The Constitution has **reserved,** or saved, powers only for the states. The powers not given to the federal government are "reserved to the states or to the people." As a result, states can decide who should be allowed to vote in each state. States carry out their own elections. They establish schools and colleges. They have their own police, build highways, and license drivers. States grant licenses to storekeepers, barbers, teachers, doctors, and nurses. States, in fact, have the power to make any kind of

Dallas–Fort Worth airport. Airports serving large cities are becoming bigger and bigger. Why is it important for the federal government to regulate air transportation?

State police can enforce the law. Is the power to enforce the law reserved to the states, or is it shared by both the federal government and the states?

laws except those that have been denied by the Constitution.

9▶ There are some powers that are held by both the federal government and the states. Both can tax people and businesses. Both can borrow money. Both can enforce their laws. Also, each state has its own courts to take care of cases within that state. Each state can also provide for the general welfare of people in the state, as the federal government does for the entire country.

10▶ When the state and federal governments have the same powers, such powers are called **concurrent** powers. These are shared powers. It is possible for both state and federal laws to be applied at the same time or for the same event. For example, both state and federal governments have passed laws concerning the inspection of food. In many places, a third government, the city, also inspects food. Both the federal government and the states have standards for clean water. There are times when federal officials investigate a crime that has

been committed. They are helped in getting their work done by state, county, and city police as well.

11▶ The Constitution also states some things that federal and state governments cannot do. States cannot coin money. States cannot make treaties with foreign governments. They cannot tax goods leaving the country. The federal government cannot tax goods leaving the country. But it can tax goods coming into the country from other countries. The federal government cannot interfere with the personal liberties of its citizens.

12▶ The Constitution protects our liberties and gives us certain rights. The right to a trial by jury is a civil right. The right to vote is a civil right. Because of laws passed by the federal government, every American now has the right to rent an apartment or house, regardless of race, religious beliefs, or national origin. Freedom of speech, press, religion, and assembly are civil liberties. No government, state or federal, can take away these liberties. In addition, no American can be imprisoned, except after a

Honor America Day, Lincoln Memorial, Washington, D.C. Freedom of assembly is guaranteed by the Constitution. Why is it important?

fair trial. No person's property can be taken by the government unless she or he receives just pay for it.

13▶ The Constitution forbids some laws from being passed. A law cannot be passed making an act a crime after the act has been committed. For example, suppose a city decides today to make it a crime to sing loudly on the street after midnight. The city cannot arrest Mr. Jones because he sang loudly on the street last month. It has to wait until he does it again. The Constitution states what laws may or may not be passed. It also prevents too much power

from getting into the hands of any group. In a dictatorship, the government can make people "disappear." They can be thrown into prison and never be heard from again. This cannot happen in the United States. Every person who is arrested must be charged with a crime and given a trial. If the jury finds that the person is guilty, then a prison sentence may follow. If the jury finds the person innocent, there cannot be another trial for the same crime. This prevents the government from bringing a person to trial over and over again until he or she is found guilty.

CHAPTER 15 REVIEW

★ UNDERSTANDING WHAT YOU HAVE READ

1. The main idea of paragraphs 5, 6, and 7 is that
   a. the federal government has powers that are not written down in the Constitution
   b. the federal government has built dams and flood-control projects
   c. there are powers that only the states can use

2. The idea that federal, state, and city officials cooperate in enforcing laws is found in
   a. paragraph 7
   b. paragraph 8
   c. paragraph 10

3. An **implied** power (paragraph 5) is one that
   a. is not stated
   b. can easily be changed
   c. is given to the states

4. **Concurrent** powers (paragraph 10) are those that
   a. safeguard the powers of the federal government
   b. can be used by both federal and state governments
   c. cannot be used by the states

5. One of the reasons why ours is called a **federal** government is because
   a. the people choose their lawmakers
   b. foreign affairs are handled by the federal government
   c. there are federal and state governments, each with certain powers

6. States can decide their own voting laws because
   a. this power was saved for them in the Constitution

b. states have to elect many officials

c. states have the power to tax property

7. A state may not make a treaty with a foreign country because

a. this power is shared with the federal government

b. this power is part of the elastic clause

c. it is forbidden to do so by the Constitution

★ DEVELOPING SOCIAL STUDIES SKILLS

A. Finding Information

For each of the cases below, tell whether you would go to the state or federal government to find the information. Give reasons for your answer.

1. You wish to take an examination to become a lawyer.

2. You wish to learn what is required to obtain a license to drive a car.

3. You wish to complain about a new highway that is to run from your state into several others.

4. You wish to turn in some old coins.

5. You want to know what powers your city government has.

6. You want to know if you are able to vote in the next election.

7. You want to find out the skills you must have to become an officer in the navy, army, or air force.

B. Interpreting a Chart

Study the chart on this page and page 114. Then answer the questions on page 114.

POWERS GRANTED BY THE CONSTITUTION		
Federal Government Only (Delegated)	**State and Federal Government** (Concurrent)	**State Government Only** (Reserved)
Regulate interstate commerce	Levy and collect taxes	Conduct elections
Coin money	Borrow money	License professionals
Establish post offices	Establish courts	Establish schools
Declare war	Provide for general welfare	Set up local governments
Govern territories		Regulate trade within the state
Conduct foreign affairs		
Raise an army, navy, air force		

POWERS DENIED BY THE CONSTITUTION		
Federal Government Only	**State and Federal Government**	**State Government Only**
Tax on exports	Deprive a person of life, liberty, or property without due process of law	Coin money
Grant titles of nobility		Make treaties with foreign countries
Deny rights stated in the Constitution	Pass laws making an act a crime after it has been committed	All powers granted to the federal government only
	Punish a person without a trial	Tax imports and exports

Tell whether the following statements are true (T), false (F), or there is not enough information in the charts upon which to base a judgment of the statement (N).

1. Both the states and the federal government can coin money.

2. Only the federal government can make a trade agreement with another country.

3. The power of the federal government has grown since the Constitution was written.

4. The states may not establish their own post offices.

5. Neither the states nor the federal government may tax goods leaving the country.

6. The federal government sets up city governments.

C. Writing About Citizenship

Using the chart above, write an essay explaining why the three types of governments must work together to make the country run smoothly.

16

SAFEGUARDS OF THE FEDERAL SYSTEM

PURPOSES FOR READING

1. To understand why the leaders who formed our government divided the powers of government
2. To understand how each branch of government checks the power of the other branches

KNOWING NEW WORDS

ambassadors
(am BAS uh durs) paragraph 5—representatives from one government to another
EXAMPLE: The **ambassadors** from India and Pakistan arrived for the meeting with the president.

vacancy
(VAY kun see) paragraph 7—an empty space; a position with no one to fill it
EXAMPLE: When a member of the council died, there was a **vacancy** on the council.

American colonists pulling down a statue of George III. What does this picture tell you about the colonists' feeling toward dividing the powers of government?

Checks and Balances.

	Checks president	Checks Congress	Checks Supreme Court
CONGRESS	• Congress must approve treaties. • Congress must approve president's appointments. • Can remove president from office. • Can pass laws by a 2/3 vote in spite of president's veto.		• Congress must approve judges that are appointed. • Can remove judges from office. • Can propose amendments to the Constitution.
PRESIDENT		• Can veto bills (proposed laws). • Can call special sessions of Congress.	• Appoints judges.
SUPREME COURT	• Can declare president's actions unconstitutional. • Interprets treaties.	• Can declare laws unconstitutional. • Interprets treaties/laws.	

1▶ The American colonies fought their way to freedom from Great Britain and rule by the English monarch. Although King George did not rule alone, English rulers had more power than the lawmakers of the English government. The leaders of the United States in 1787 did not want their government to be like England's. They took great care to avoid setting up a government in which one person or one group had too much power. They did not want to be victims of one-person rule again. As a result, they established our national government under the Constitution. In this government, there were and still are three parts or branches. The framers of the Constitution made sure that none of these branches had more power than the others.

2▶ In chapter 1, you learned that the Constitution stated that the federal government—the national government—had certain powers. In addition, the powers given to it are divided among its three branches. The **legislative** branch (Congress) makes the laws. The **executive** branch (headed by the president) enforces the laws, or puts them into effect. The **judicial** branch (headed by the Supreme Court) decides whether Congress has the power to pass the laws it does pass. It interprets, or tells, what the laws mean. This system is called **separation of powers.**

3▶ Each of the branches of government has its own job to do. Yet, the branches are not completely independent of each other. Each branch can check, or limit, the power of the other branches. Each branch is about equal in its ability to check the other two branches. So, there is a **balance** in the powers of the three branches. This system keeps one branch of the national government from being more powerful than the other branches. It is called the system of **checks and balances.** Let us see how this system works.

4▶ The chief job of Congress is to pass laws for the nation. The president can approve these laws by signing them. But the president can check the power of Congress by refusing to sign them. This is called a **veto.** Generally, a law does not go into effect unless the president signs it. But, Congress has a check on the veto of the president. It can consider the same bill again and approve it by a two-thirds vote. If it does, the bill becomes a law despite the president's veto.

5▶ The president has the power to ap-

During his presidency, Richard M. Nixon appointed four justices to the Supreme Court including the chief justice. These justices shared many of Nixon's views.

point top government officials. The president names judges to federal courts and to the Supreme Court. The president appoints ambassadors to foreign countries. The president has the power to make treaties with foreign countries. But all of these powers are limited. Congress must approve these appointments and treaties. If Congress does not give its approval to these actions of the president, they cannot go into effect. Thus, Congress has another check on the power of the president.

6▶ The Supreme Court has a check on Congress, and even on the president. The Court decides what our laws really mean. It can decide that Congress has passed a law that it does not have the power to pass. In such a case, the Court declares that such a law is **unconstitutional.** This means that the Constitution does not allow such a law. The Court, too, may make such a ruling about the actions of the president.

7▶ It might seem that the Supreme Court has the final power over the actions of both Congress and the president. How can the power of the Court be checked? How can Congress overcome a Court ruling that a law is unconstitutional? Congress can vote a change in the Constitution—**amend** it. If three-fourths of the states approve the change Congress suggests, the change becomes part of the Constitution. Congress is then free to pass laws that agree with the change that has been approved. How can the president check the power of the Supreme Court? The president can wait for a vacancy on the Supreme Court. Then the president can appoint a judge or judges who agree with his or her ideas concerning the Constitution.

8▶ There is another way that citizens are protected from government officials who abuse their power. Through the method called **impeachment,** a president, a judge, or other high officials can be removed from office. The method called impeachment will be discussed in more detail in chapter 20.

Opening of the 102nd Congress. Members are sworn in by the Speaker of the House at the opening of Congress. What other duties does the Speaker of the House perform?

CHAPTER 16 REVIEW

1. The main idea of paragraph 1 is that
   a. American colonies gained their freedom from England
   b. the leaders of the United States formed a government in which no person or group has the greatest power
   c. the powers of the three branches of government come from the Constitution

2. The chief way that the Supreme Court checks Congress is by
   a. refusing to approve treaties
   b. declaring laws unconstitutional
   c. changing the Constitution

3. One way that Congress checks the president is that it can
   a. pass an amendment to the Constitution
   b. approve decisions by the Supreme Court
   c. pass a bill by a two-thirds vote after the president vetoes it

4. The president's chief way of checking the power of Congress is by
   a. making treaties with foreign countries
   b. refusing to sign bills passed by Congress
   c. refusing to appoint federal judges

5. When the president appoints an ambassador to a foreign country
   a. that appointment must be approved by Congress
   b. that appointment must be approved by the Supreme Court
   c. the president has used a power not granted in the Constitution

6. The purpose of the system of checks and balances is to make sure that the
   a. powers of the three branches of government are nearly equal
   b. branches of government use the powers granted them by the Constitution
   c. states check the powers of the president

7. The president appoints a judge to the Supreme Court. Who can stop that appointment if the person is unfit?
   a. The Congress
   b. The Supreme Court
   c. The states

8. Which of these statements are true? Which are false?
   a. The president cannot stop laws passed by Congress from going into effect.
   b. The president's chief job is to enforce laws passed by Congress.
   c. The leaders of the United States in 1787 wanted a government like that of England.

★ DEVELOPING SOCIAL STUDIES SKILLS

A. Using Word Clues

Look in the following paragraphs for the terms listed below. What are the meanings of these terms? What clues helped you to know their meanings?

Paragraph 2—federal government

Paragraph 2—interprets

Paragraph 4—veto

Paragraph 6—unconstitutional

Paragraph 7—amend

B. Knowing New Terms

Match each term in Column A with the best description in Column B. There is one EXTRA item in Column B. Write the letters of your answers in your notebook.

Column A	Column B
1. veto	a. Each branch of government can limit the power of other branches.
2. checks and balances	b. The lawmaking body of the national government.
3. separation of powers	c. Telling what our laws mean.
4. impeachment	d. A method for removing high officials from office.
5. amend	e. The president does not sign a bill passed by Congress.
6. legislative	f. The branches of the national government have different powers.
	g. A change, as in the Constitution.

C. Using Checks and Balances

Complete these sentences about checks and balances by writing the answers in your notebook.

1. If the president does not sign a bill passed by Congress, Congress can _____.

2. If the president appoints a high official who seems to be unfit for that office, Congress can _____.

3. If Congress passes a law the president does not like, the president can _____.

4. If Congress passes a law that the Constitution forbids, the Supreme Court can _____.

5. If the Supreme Court decides that a law is unconstitutional, Congress can _____.

D. Writing About Citizenship

Write one or two well-organized paragraphs answering the following question: How do the systems of separation of powers and checks and balances work to prevent one person from running the United States?

HOW CONGRESS IS ORGANIZED

PURPOSES FOR READING

1. To learn the make-up of the Congress of the United States
2. To learn the powers and duties of the House of Representatives and the Senate

KNOWING NEW WORDS

session
(SESH un) paragraph 3—the period of time during which sittings or meetings of a court, council, or lawmaking body take place
EXAMPLE: The council met in a long **session.**

The Congress

Senate

100 members
2 from Each State
Term–6 yrs.

House of Representatives

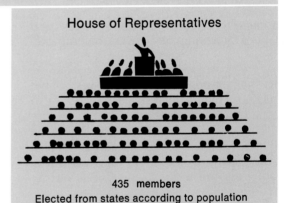

435 members
Elected from states according to population
Term–2 yrs.

In making laws, Congress acts for the people. In fact, it is the people. Lawmakers represent people, not trees or acres.—**Supreme Court of the United States, 1964**

1 ▶ Our government is a government of laws. Laws protect all of us from those who would take all power for themselves. Laws limit the number of years that our officials may hold office. Officials who represent the people must face re-election. This gives the people a chance to show if they approve of the way their representatives have carried out the trust placed in them.

2 ▶ The laws of our nation are made by Congress—the national legislature. Congress is made up of two lawmaking bodies called houses. The two houses are the **Senate** and the **House of Representatives.** Those who wrote the Constitution had good reasons for forming two houses of Congress. They had lived under the English government. The Parliament, the lawmaking body of that government, was made up of two houses. Then, too, the Founders settled the argument between the large and small states by setting up the two-house system. (See page 32.) One house, the House of Representatives, has 435 members chosen according to the population of the state that elects them. The House of Representatives is often referred to simply as "the House." The more people living in a state, the more members that state can have. The other house, the Senate, has two members from each state. Some experts think that the two-house system is a good one for another reason. If a bill has to pass both houses before it becomes a law, there is less chance that Congress might pass unwise laws.

3 ▶ We refer to the House of Representatives and the Senate working together as the Congress. Members of the House of Representatives are elected for terms of two years. An election is held every two years. This means that all 435 members are elected at one time. With each election, therefore, there is a "new" House of Representatives. Thus, a Congress lasts two years. The members of Congress who were elected to begin their meetings in 1991 were called the 102nd Congress. This was the 102nd election of members of the House of Representatives. The first Congress under the Constitution met in 1789. Congress meets, or is in session, each year. So, there are two years of meetings of Congress for each numbered Congress. Since senators serve six-year terms, one-third of the senators are elected every two years.

4 ▶ The Senate is one of the most important lawmaking bodies in the world. It is

The Senate in 1850. Why are there no women senators in this picture? In what other ways do today's members of both the Senate and the House differ from these 19th-century members of Congress?

The Senate and the House meet together to hear the president's State of the Union address. The vice-president (Dan Quayle, top left) runs meetings of the Senate. The Speaker of the House (Tom Foley, top right) runs meetings of the House.

made up of 100 senators, two from each state. Senators must live in the state that elects them. For example, a senator from Ohio must live in Ohio. A senator must be at least 30 years of age. In addition, a senator must have been a citizen of the United States for nine years. The vice-president **presides** over, or runs, the meetings of the Senate. The vice-president is not a senator. So the vice-president does not take part in Senate debates and votes on bills only in case of a tie. When the vice-president is absent from Senate meetings, the president *pro tempore* ("for the time") presides over the Senate. This officer is elected by the Senate and is usually a member of the party with the most senators.

5▶ The Constitution gives the Senate special powers. The Senate must approve all treaties (agreements) with foreign countries by a two-thirds vote. It approves ambassadors, judges, and cabinet members named by the president. If the president or other high officer of government is accused of "treason, bribery, or other high crimes," the trial is held in the Senate. (This is called an impeachment trial. No president has ever been found guilty and only one trial has ever been held.)

6▶ The House of Representatives is the lower house of Congress. There are 435 members of the House. A member of the House of Representatives must be at least 25 years old and a citizen of the country for seven years. Members of the House of Representatives usually live in the district that elects them. The number of representatives from each state depends upon the number of people in that state. As the number of people in a state grows that state will have more representatives. If a state loses population, it may lose representatives.

7▶ All states are divided into districts or parts. Each state legislature decides how to divide the state into districts. For example, five districts in a state would mean there were five representatives. Districts are supposed to be equal or nearly equal in population. The average number of people in a district in 1991 was 570,000. No matter the population of a state, it must have at least one representative in Congress.

8▶ For some years, some states had been divided into districts with great differences in population. Some city districts had as many as 900,000 people. In rural areas, some members of Congress represented only 200,000 people. Some citizens in cities believed that this was not fair representation. They thought the interests of people in cities were not being heard in Washington. They argued that 900,000 people should have more representatives than a district of 200,000 people. It was the number of people not the size of the district that mattered. They took the case to the United States Supreme Court. In 1964, the Court ruled that district lines had to be changed to make the population of each district as nearly equal as possible. This is called the "one person–one vote" ruling. This is the meaning of the quotation at the beginning of the chapter. The Supreme Court said Congress represents the people, not the size of a piece of land.

9▶ The House of Representatives has special powers, too. All bills for raising money for the national government (reve-nue bills) must be introduced in the House of Representatives. The House also has the power to elect the president if no candidate has received a majority of the **electoral** votes. (See page 147.) Also, it is the House that impeaches federal officials when they have done something wrong. To impeach means to charge, or accuse, a person of wrongdoing in office. If the House of Representatives agrees on charges against an official, the trial is held before the Senate. The Senate acts as the jury in the case.

10▶ The Speaker of the House presides over meetings of the House of Representatives. The Speaker is a member of the majority party. The Speaker is an important official of the government. If both the president and vice-president should die while in office, the Speaker would become president. The Speaker also helps to select the members who will head House committees.

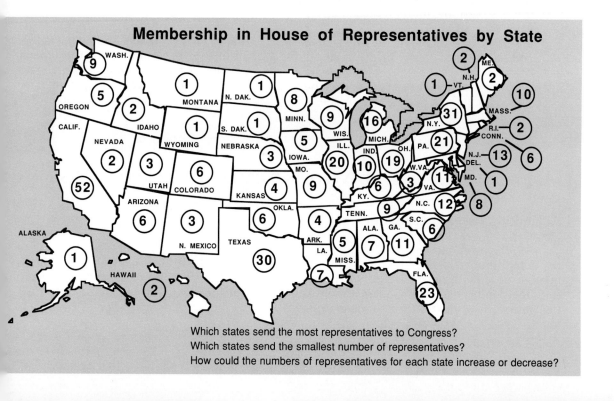

Membership in House of Representatives by State

Which states send the most representatives to Congress?
Which states send the smallest number of representatives?
How could the numbers of representatives for each state increase or decrease?

CHAPTER 17 REVIEW

1. A good title for paragraph 4 is
   a. How the Senate Is Organized
   b. Leaders of the Senate
   c. Voting in the Senate

2. An important idea of this chapter is that
   a. there is a strong movement to change Congress from two houses to one house
   b. the vice-president has a great deal to say when the Senate meets
   c. members of the House of Representatives are elected from districts that should have about the same number of people

3. One who presides over a meeting
   a. is the first speaker in the meeting
   b. runs the meeting as its chairperson
   c. counts the votes of members

4. One reason why the writers of the Constitution provided for a Congress of two houses was
   a. one house would always be in session
   b. there would be more representatives from each state
   c. it settled the argument between large and small states

5. The vice-president may not take part in the Senate's discussions because he or she
   a. is not elected by the people
   b. does not have the qualifications to be a senator
   c. is not a member of the Senate

6. The Speaker of the House of Representatives is a very important official in the federal government because the Speaker
   a. is elected to that office by the people
   b. would become president if the president and vice-president both died in office
   c. is a member of the president's cabinet and the National Security Council

7. The Supreme Court has ruled that
   a. all states should have the same number of representatives
   b. cities should have more representatives than rural areas
   c. districts electing representatives should have about the same number of people

8. The Senate holds back the power of the president in that
   a. it approves or does not approve appointments of judges and ambassadors
   b. all bills to raise money for the federal government must begin in the Senate
   c. it elects the president if no candidate receives a majority of the electoral votes

★ **DEVELOPING CRITICAL THINKING SKILLS**

A. Limiting Terms of Legislators

In 1990, voters in many parts of the country considered passing laws limiting the number of terms a person could serve in a state legislature, or in the Congress. Across the nation, it appeared that once people were elected to a legislature, they were successful in election after election in keeping their seat in government. These are some of the arguments in the debate over limiting the terms of lawmakers.

I favor limiting the terms of legislators because:

- Current members of legislatures have been in office so long, they have become professional lawmakers.

- The founders of our nation believed in "citizen" lawmakers instead of lifetime politicians.

- Political Action Committees (PACs) and powerful interest groups finance campaigns of those already in office. One who wishes to oppose them does not have the money to win an election.

- In the Congress and in many states, 90 percent of the members of those in office are re-elected.

- There is a limit on the terms a president can serve. Why shouldn't there be one on lawmakers as well?

- Fresh members of legislatures and Congress every few years would mean lobbyists would not have as much influence on them.

I oppose limiting the terms of legislators because:

- Voters should be allowed to choose whom they want to represent them without any restrictions.

- A limit on the number of terms of office would deprive the country of its most experienced lawmakers.

- It takes time to learn the rules and traditions of a legislature and experience counts.

- Lobbyists and special interests would have an easier time influencing a new legislator than one who is experienced.

- Forcing members of Congress to retire at an early age is a temptation for them to make as much money as they can during their few years in office.

1. What is meant by "citizen" lawmakers rather than "professional" lawmakers?

2. Why has it been difficult for challengers in an election to defeat those in office for many years?

3. What do you think is meant by "it takes time to learn the rules and traditions" of a legislature?

4. Which argument for limiting terms impresses you the most? The least? Why?

5. Which argument against a limit on terms of office impresses you the most? The least? Why?

6. In your opinion, should the terms of legislators be limited or not? Support your opinion with reasons.

■■■■■■■■■■■■■■■■ ★ DEVELOPING SOCIAL STUDIES SKILLS

A. Reviewing Basic Facts

In your notebook, write true if the statement is true. If it is not true, change the underlined word or words to make the statement true.

1. Each session of Congress lasts for only <u>four</u> years.

2. The first Congress under the Constitution met in <u>1789</u>.

3. The vice-president votes on issues before the Senate only <u>in case of a tie vote.</u>

4. The Senate approves treaties with foreign countries by a <u>majority</u> vote.

5. All bills for raising money for the national government must be introduced in the <u>Senate</u>.

6. In the House of Representatives the number of members from each state <u>depends on the population of the state.</u>

B. Thinking It Through

1. What is the meaning of the quotation at the beginning of the chapter, "Lawmakers represent people, not trees or acres"?

2. Why do you think the House of Representatives and not the Senate was given the power of introducing bills for raising money for the federal government?

3. An old saying is, "Memories are short." Voters sometimes quickly forget an act of their representatives that they may not like. Which will the voters have more time to forget—an action by a senator or a representative of Congress?

PARTICIPATION IN GOVERNMENT

TALKING TO YOUR REPRESENTATIVES

Members of Congress spend a great deal of time doing favors for and helping the folks back home. They may search for solutions to problems, find jobs, get information, guide visitors around the Capitol, and even run errands. Voters welcome this help because often in a large government it is hard to get answers to questions. Below are tips that members of Congress have given to people in their districts on the best way to contact their representatives and get help from them.

- Visit state or district offices of your representative.
- Write a short letter that includes your name, address, and telephone number.
- Be fair in presenting your problem. It is your opinion that is wanted.

- Don't criticize the representative for a past voting record without giving reasonable and fair evidence to support your opinion.
- Don't wait until the last minute to ask for help in solving a problem.

18

THE HARD ROAD FROM BILL TO LAW

PURPOSES FOR READING

1. To learn how laws of our federal government are made
2. To understand the special care taken to make sure that unwise laws are not passed
3. To understand the nature of the job of a member of Congress

KNOWING NEW WORDS

conference
(KON fur uns) paragraph 5—of or concerning a meeting of people or committees to settle differences

EXAMPLE: Since both sides could not agree, they had a **conference** to decide the matter.

Senator Claiborne Pell of Rhode Island is chairman of the Senate Foreign Relations Committee. The work of congressional committees is an important part of lawmaking.

1▶ Thousands of bills are introduced in an average session of Congress. Suppose you were a United States senator. How many of these bills do you think you would have time to read and study? On how many bills would you be able to cast a wise vote? Not many, you can be sure. It would be impossible for every member of Congress to read and study each of the thousands of bills offered during each session.

2▶ It would be impossible for each representative and senator to read every bill. The House of Representatives and Senate have formed smaller groups, therefore, to study these bills. These groups are called **committees.** There are 16 committees in the Senate and 22 in the House. Congress can change the number of committees whenever it wishes to. Each committee deals with one area of law, such as foreign affairs, education, labor, banking, or agriculture. Special committees are formed to handle special problems as they arise. Usually only bills approved by the committees reach Congress for a vote.

President Lyndon Johnson and Dr. Martin Luther King, Jr., at the signing of the Civil Rights Act in 1964.

3▶ Passing the committee is the first step a bill must take on its way to becoming a law. A bill may be **introduced** (step 1) in either the House of Representatives or the Senate. Many laws are introduced in both houses. Then, the bill is sent to the proper **committee** for study (step 2). The committee members spend some time deciding if the bill is worthwhile. They may ask experts and other people what they think of the bill. These meetings are called **hearings** (step 3). After the hearings, the committee votes to decide whether the bill should be brought before the full Senate or House of Representatives.

4▶ If a bill is approved by the House of Representatives (step 4), it is sent to the Senate for its approval. A bill approved by the Senate is sent to the House of Representatives for its vote. A bill must **pass both houses of Congress** before it is sent to the president (step 5). If the **president signs** the bill (step 6), it becomes law. A bill could be stopped at any of these stages on its way to becoming a law. Only a few of the bills introduced ever become laws.

5▶ There are times when a **conference committee** of House and Senate members is needed to decide the final wording of a bill. For example, suppose a bill passes the House that is nearly the same as a bill passed by the Senate. There is no reason to have both bills become law. The conference committee meets and irons out the differences in the bills. The result is one bill, which is given again to the House and the Senate for a vote. The conference committee is also called together in another case. A bill, for example, passes the House. The Senate approves the bill, but makes a

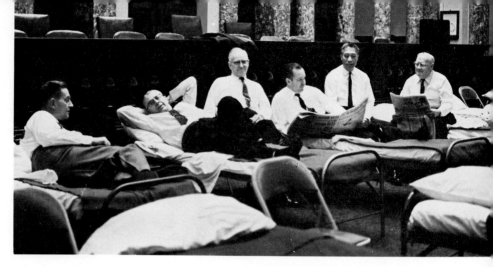

Senators during a long filibuster. Do you think the filibuster hurts or helps the legislative process?

few changes in it. Now, it is not the same bill as the House had passed. The conference committee meets and agrees on a compromise bill. The two houses then vote on the wording agreed to by the conference committee.

6▶ The Senate has a way of stopping or delaying the passage of a bill that the House does not have. Senators may speak for as long as they wish on any subject. There have been times when senators have spoken for days on subjects that have nothing to do with the bill before them. The idea is to "talk a bill to death." This is called a **filibuster.** This is one way that a small number of senators may delay a vote for such a long time that the vote is finally put off entirely. Of course, the Senate can set a time limit on the debate any time 60 percent of the senators vote to do so. If agreed to, no senator may speak for more than one hour. This is called **cloture.** Then the Senate can vote on the bill being considered. But rarely does the Senate agree to cloture. Senators place great value on their right to speak for as long as they wish.

7▶ The work of the committees of Congress is an important part of the procedure for passing laws. The chairperson of the committee is usually the member of the majority party who has served the longest time on that committee. The practice of choosing chairpersons is called **seniority.** The chairperson is the senior member of the committee. There is much argument over the seniority system of choosing the head of the committee. Some say it makes the chairpersons those with the most experience in Congress. Others believe that it keeps younger lawmakers from becoming leaders in Congress.

8▶ Committees often have to study hundreds of bills. Within a committee, a **subcommittee** or smaller group is formed to look carefully at a few bills. Such groups try to find out if there is a need for the law that has been suggested. Subcommittees carry out hearings or collect information about the subject in which they are interested.

9▶ The work of subcommittees is often front-page news in our newspapers. Some people have refused to answer questions before the committees of Congress. They argue that some subcommittees have acted like courts: the committee members treat some witnesses as though they were on trial for some misdeed. Committees of Congress are not courts. They try to get as much information about a proposed law as possible. Special committees make reports of their findings to Congress and the country.

Budget Conference Committee of the House and Senate. When is a conference committee needed?

Some of these reports have been very helpful in preparing new laws. For example, the findings of a subcommittee about conditions in the manufacture of drugs led to a new and stronger food and drug law.

10▶ Members of Congress receive advice about bills before them from people in their district and state. Records of the meetings of the House and Senate have always been kept. Every speech and every vote is recorded. A hundred years ago, news traveled more slowly than it does now. Voters did not know of the actions of Congress until weeks after a vote had taken place. Now the work of Congress is reported daily in newspapers, radio, and TV. You can learn how your representative or senators voted on a bill by reading your daily newspaper. TV cameras follow hearings of subcommittees of Congress. Members of the House and Senate are guests on radio and TV programs. Telegrams and letters by the thousands reach members of Congress each day. All citizens can write their representative and senators to let them know how they feel about an issue.

11▶ A member of Congress does more than make speeches and vote on bills. Much study and preparation is done before voting takes place. Congressmen and Congresswomen spend time on matters not directly related to voting on bills. Their mail is heavy. They have to read their mail or have someone read it for them. They must know what the people at home are thinking. Those who write members of Congress expect an answer to their letters. There is a staff to help representatives and senators with this task. Letters may suggest how members of Congress should vote on a bill. They may ask their representative or senators to speak at an important event. Others may ask advice on business matters.

12▶ Members of Congress have to attend committee hearings. They may be members of more than one committee. Experts who come from all over the country to give information to committees deserve to have members listen to them when they come to Washington. Representatives and senators must read. Not only must they read bills, they must read newspapers, magazines, and reports of all kinds. They must know what is going on in the nation and the world. Lobbyists and members of Congress meet to talk over bills. (See chapter 19.) When visitors from their home state come to Washington, members of Congress meet with them. Representatives and senators do not end their day until late in the evening. Then, there is more reading if there is time. Often they are invited to social or government events at night. They are busy people. Most citizens would be surprised how many events members of Congress can crowd into a single day.

CHAPTER 18 REVIEW

★ UNDERSTANDING WHAT YOU HAVE READ

1. The main idea of paragraph 7 is that
   a. a system of seniority is used to choose chairpersons of committees in Congress
   b. the majority party wants younger members of Congress to become committee chairpersons
   c. all members of Congress like the seniority system

2. A subcommittee is
   a. a smaller group within a committee
   b. the lowest ranking committee in the House
   c. made up of oider senior members of the Senate

3. When the Senate has a hearing on a bill, it
   a. argues over the bill before the entire Senate
   b. asks the advice of experts about the merits of the bill
   c. asks the people at home to vote on the merits of the bill

4. "Members of Congress cannot hide what they do in Congress from the voters in their districts." This statement is an important idea of
   a. paragraph 5
   b. paragraph 9
   c. paragraph 10

5. Committees are formed in each house of Congress so that
   a. older members may have more power
   b. visitors to Congress may find out about bills in which they are interested

c. a small group of representatives or senators can study a bill, rather than allow every bill to be debated on the floor, that is, in front of the full house

6. Few bills introduced in Congress become laws because
   a. few bills are important
   b. presidents veto most bills that Congress passes
   c. before it becomes a law, a bill must be approved by committees, both houses of Congress, and the president

7. Some people refuse to answer questions before committees of Congress because they
   a. feel they are facing a court rather than a body trying to find how good a bill is
   b. don't care to have the whole country know their opinion of a bill
   c. are not paid for their expert information

8. Members of Congress make a point of seeing visitors from their home districts because
   a. visitors need the help of their representatives in seeing the sights of the capital
   b. they are experts on the bills they will be asked to vote on
   c. they want to know the opinions of the people they represent, and they want the people to know the kind of job they are doing as elected lawmakers

★ **DEVELOPING SOCIAL STUDIES SKILLS**

How a Bill Becomes a Law

Study the chart at the bottom of the page. Then answer these qustions. Next to the number in your notebook, if the statement is true, write T; if it is false, write F; if there is no information in the chart to make a judgement, write N.

1. The Senate and House of Representatives could be considering bills that are almost alike at the same time.

2. If bills that are almost alike pass both houses of Congress, a committee from both houses meets to agree on the wording of the bill.

3. A bill may pass the Senate only and go to the president for his signature.

4. The president has nothing to do with a bill until it has passed both houses of Congress.

5. The House and Senate vote on a bill before committees hold hearings on it.

6. All bills must pass both houses of Congress by a two-thirds vote.

7. A bill may be introduced in either the House of Representatives or the Senate.

8. The president has 30 days after a bill passes Congress to decide whether or not to sign it.

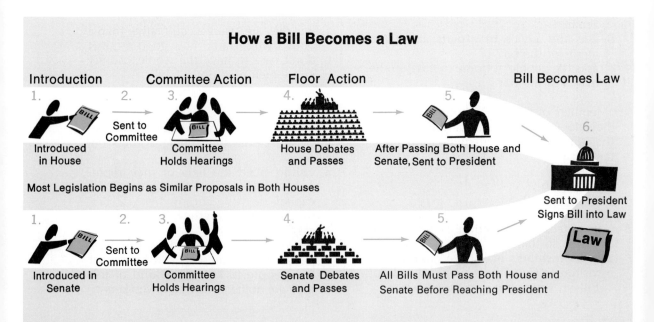

How a Bill Becomes a Law

A. Which Statement Is Hardest to Prove Correct?

From each group, choose the statement that is more difficult to prove correct than the others in the group. Write the reasons for your choice in your notebook.

1. a. The work of Congress is reported to the country faster than it was a hundred years ago.
   b. Members of the Rules Committee are often the members of the House with the longest service in the House.
   c. A senator who answers very little mail from his or her home state cannot be re-elected.

2. a. Congress forms special committees for special kinds of bills.
   b. A senator reads more books and papers than other government officials.
   c. Most senators do not read thousands of bills each session of Congress.

3. a. A member of Congress does more than speak and vote on bills.
   b. It is expected that Congress will change its rules for committee hearings at a future session.
   c. More than one-third of the members of Congress are lawyers.

B. The Seniority System

Below are statements by two representatives, as they speak about the seniority system in selection of chairpersons of committees in the House of Representatives. Read these statements, then answer the questions that follow.

Representative A—a senior member of the Committee on Education and Labor:

I've been in Congress for 24 years. I've been a member of the Education Committee for every one of those years. In that time I have studied hundreds of bills about education. As a committee member, I have met hundreds of experts in this field. I know what the House can and cannot do to help education in our country. My experience and the experience of others who have served a long time on this committee should mean something. The chairperson of the committee should be the senior member.

Representative B—a new member of Congress serving her first term:

I represent a state with several large cities. This is my first year in the House. I want to be put on a committee that deals with the problems of the people who elected me. The needs of education in our large cities are great. I want to be on the committee that considers those needs. There are other members of Congress who represent large cities on that committee, too. Although some have not been in the House as long as other representatives, they deserve to be heard, too. They are young and have new ideas. The chairperson should be the best person on the committee, no matter how long that person has been in the House.

1. Which representative would probably support a change in the rules by which the committee works? Why?

2. Which representative probably has the greatest number of friends in the House? Why?

3. Which representative would probably get older members of the House to support his or her views? Why?

4. Which representative would probably want the federal government to give more aid to schools in large cities? Why?

5. Which representative would probably want large cities to find ways to solve their own problems? Why?

6. As a new member of the House, is Representative B sure to be placed on the Education Committee? Why?

7. With which representative do you agree? Why?

C. Making Decisions

Suppose you are a member of Congress. You are a member of a committee with hundreds of bills to study. From among the bills listed below, which would you want the whole Congress to consider first? Next? Put all the bills in order of their importance to you. On which bills would you want experts to give you advice?

In making your decisions regarding the importance of bills, consider the cost of the bill (Is it worth the expense?); whom it may benefit or harm; and whether it can be put into effect without difficulty.

1. Suppose a president of the United States was born in your town. A bill to spend $200,000 has been proposed. The bill would have the federal government take over and maintain as a national park or monument the house in which the president was born.

2. A bill to increase the salaries of United States senators from $85,000 a year to $96,000 a year.

3. A bill providing for the federal government to give $1 million to each state for every $1 million the state spends on low-rent housing for the poor.

4. A bill to reduce to 14 the age at which youngsters in all states may end their schooling.

5. A bill providing for the federal government to spend $250,000 for a study of ways of improving safety in elevators in office buildings.

D. Writing About Citizenship

Write one or two well-organized paragraphs about the following questions: Do you believe that senators should be allowed to filibuster? Or do you believe that filibustering blocks the lawmaking process? Give reasons for your opinions.

19

VOTING PRESSURES ON CONGRESS

PURPOSES FOR READING

1. To understand the kinds of pressure faced by Congress in making decisions on proposed laws
2. To learn about the work of lobbyists and how they attempt to get votes from members of Congress
3. To understand about pressure groups and how they attempt to win votes in Congress

KNOWING NEW WORDS

candidates
    (KAN dih dayts) paragraph 9—the people who seek public office
    EXAMPLE: The Republican party chose George Bush and Dan Quayle as their **candidates.**

registered
    (REJ ih sturd) paragraph 4—enrolled; entered; signed in

EXAMPLE: He **registered** for school before the new year began.

lobbyists
    (LOB ee ists) paragraph 4—trained experts who try to influence members of Congress
    EXAMPLE: The **lobbyists** worked hard to get the eduction bill passed.

George Bush with members of Congress. Why was it important for a Republican president to gain the support of the Democratic leaders of Congress?

1▶ The coach says you must attend the team meeting tonight or you can't play on the team this year. You have an important test tomorrow and your teacher tells you that you had better study for it. Your mother says you have to get Aunt Letty's birthday gift tonight because her birthday is tomorrow. A friend calls and says this is the last night for that movie you wanted to see. It seems that there are demands on you from all sides. Everyone has something for you to do—all at once. How do you feel? Sometimes, members of Congress have the same feeling. There are pressures on them to vote one way or another from many sources.

2▶ The president is the leader of his party in the nation. The president suggests to Congress bills that he would like to pass into law. He expects the support and votes of members of his own party in Congress,

Senators John Kerry and Edward Kennedy of Massachusetts discuss a bill. Senators sometimes lobby each other to get bills passed.

along with others. He may call members about a bill or invite them to meet with him to talk over how they plan to vote. Since representatives and senators hope to be elected to Congress again, they listen carefully to their party leader. At election time, it may help if the president agrees to come to a member's district and campaign for that member.

3▶ Members of Congress pressure each other. Suppose you are a member of the House of Representatives. You will introduce some bills you want Congress to pass. Other members will do the same. You want the support and vote of other members. They will look forward to your vote for their bills. Some of these bills may call for the federal government to spend money to build sewage plants, roads, or dams in your home district. Such spending will mean jobs and money "back home." You may not approve of some bills that others introduce. But in order to get votes for the bills you want, you may have to vote for the other members' bills. Such "trading" of votes often takes place.

4▶ All kinds of organizations are interested in the work of Congress. Businesses, labor unions, teachers, doctors, farmers, state and city governments, and others have special interests they want laws to protect. These groups let Congress know their feelings by sending trained experts, **lobbyists,** to Washington. This name, lobbyist, is given to them because in the past such people used to talk to members of Congress in the lobby of the House or Senate. Today, they are not allowed on the floor (the meeting room) of the House or Senate during a session. They must be registered. This is

James Brady and Senator Howard Metzenbaum of Ohio. Brady was wounded by a gunman who was trying to assassinate President Ronald Reagan. Now he lobbies for gun control.

done so that Congress knows who the lobbyists are and whom they represent. It also protects members of Congress from being offered bribes for their votes.

5 ▶ Lobbyists are highly trained for their jobs. They work hard for the organization they represent. Perhaps as many as 15,000 lobbyists work in Washington. Over a billion dollars is spent by lobbyists each year to influence votes in Congress. A few individual lobbyist groups spend almost $3 million a year. Members of Congress seem to find that many lobbyists are helpful. They provide information that members of Congress want in order to make judgments on bills before them. In general, lobbyists will not deceive members of Congress. In order for them to do their work well, lobbyists must be trusted. Whatever lobbyists do to help members of Congress, however, they are doing it to get votes for their company, their union, or their organization.

"Everybody in America has a lobby."

Thomas P. O'Neill, former Speaker of the House of Representatives

"Without lobbying, Government could not function. The flow of information to Congress and to every federal agency is a vital part of our democratic system."

Senator Edward M. Kennedy and former Senators Dick Clark and Robert Stafford

"The Congress and the public should be aware of who's trying to influence whom and why and for what."

Former Senator Abraham Ribicoff

6 ▶ You can tell from the statements of these members of Congress that they expect lobbying. They also think lobbyists serve a useful purpose. But there are some dangers in lobbying, too. Lobbyists are pleased when they can help a lawmaker in some way. Members of Congress need money to get reelected to office. Lobbyists are happy to buy tickets for fund-raising events for individual members of Congress. Many times, conferences with lawmakers are held over a dinner paid for by the lobby. Lawmakers, lobbyists believe, might show their gratitude for the favors they

have received by a favorable vote on a bill before Congress.

7 ▶ There is probably no way that lobbying can be stopped. The laws and rules of the federal government affect the lives of all Americans in some way. As the number of federal laws grows with each meeting of Congress, so the number of lobbyists grows. More than 500 businesses have lobbyists in Washington. States and cities, hoping to get funds for their use from Congress, have their own lobbies. There are lobbies for auto companies, airlines, elderly people, workers, milk producers, manufacturers of medicine, among hundreds of others. Are the votes of Congress influenced by lobbyists? In some cases, they probably are. But, members of Congress will tell you the best way to get their vote is by presenting a good, sound argument for a bill.

8 ▶ Groups that are organized to try to win votes from Congress are called **pressure groups.** There are pressure groups for almost every topic of public interest: for control of firearms, against control of firearms, for women's rights, for lower taxes, for the protection of natural resources, to guard national health, and others. Pressure groups use lobbyists to educate members of Congress about their causes. Another method is the use of large letter-writing campaigns. In some cases, thousands of sample letters are sent to members of the group. Members need only sign the letter and mail it to their representative or senators in Congress. The idea is to flood Congress with thousands of letters for or against a bill. Still another method is to present members of Congress with a petition, a list of written demands or requests. Each petition is signed by hundreds or thousands of people who agree with the demands or requests.

Senior citizens presenting petitions for a social security increase. Identify the pressure groups pictured on pages 139–140. Describe the kind of pressure each group is using to win support for its cause.

Thousands of people attend an Earth Day Rally in Washington, D.C. The right to assemble peacefully is protected by the 1st Amendment of the Constitution.

9► Money is also a form of pressure on Congress. Members of Congress want to be re-elected. An election campaign for Congress or governor may cost millions of dollars. Two members of Congress running for re-election raised a total of $3 million dollars. That amount was more than the total raised by 300 challengers for seats in the House of Representatives. Campaign expenses are far above the salaries of members of either the House or Senate. Candidates depend on contributions (gifts) from individuals and groups. Federal laws do not allow business firms and labor unions to send money directly to a candidate. However, political action committees (PACs) are often formed. These committees of citizens who have the same beliefs raise money for a candidate's campaign fund. PACs can give money to help re-elect those members of Congress who have voted in their interests.

10►When a group of people feel that their interests are not receiving the attention they deserve, often they will demonstrate. This may be in the form of a public meeting or a march of thousands to show lawmakers their deep concern for an issue. The demonstration is another way of putting pressure on Congress. The greatest kind of demonstration is a march on Washington, the nation's capital. This has been a custom in America for many years. But, with the ease of communication and transportation, marches before Congress and the president seem to have taken place more often in recent years.

11►Most marches on Washington are in the form of protest—against something the federal government hasn't done, is delaying doing, or plans to do. During one summer, hundreds of Native Americans walked 2,700 miles across the country in six weeks to protest a bill to end their treaties with the national government. Shortly before their arrival in Washington, thousands demonstrated in favor of a proposed Equal Rights Amendment. In 1989 and 1990, thousands of people came to Washington demonstrating for or against abortion. In 1991, many people held demonstrations for peace in the Middle East.

139

Martin Luther King, Jr., leads the civil rights Freedom March on Washington in 1963. Below, an American Indian protest march.

12 ▶ There have been marches of many kinds: "For Peace," "For the Earth," "For the Homeless," "Hunger Marches," "Honor America Day." Do these demonstrations influence the way members of Congress vote? No one can tell for sure. Demonstrators feel that they do, or marches would not continue. Members of Congress can be impressed by the number of people who come to show how strongly they feel about certain issues. One of the greatest demonstrations of all was the "Freedom March" in 1963. Over 200,000 people demonstrated for civil rights for African Americans. Many feel that the "Freedom March" was one reason for the passage of the Civil Rights Act of 1964.

Right is a Farm Aid concert in 1986 that raised money to help American farmers.

CHAPTER 19 REVIEW

★ **UNDERSTANDING WHAT YOU HAVE READ**

1. The main idea of paragraph 9 is that
   a. members of Congress want to be re-elected
   b. business firms form committees to raise money to support candidates of their choice
   c. most people who wish to be elected to Congress need a great deal of money for their campaigns

2. An important idea of paragraph 8 is that
   a. pressure groups try to influence the votes of members of Congress
   b. members of Congress often receive thousands of letters about a bill they are debating
   c. lobbyists meet members of Congress outside the sessions of Congress

3. Which statement best explains how members of Congress feel about lobbyists?
   a. If they are trustworthy, they are helpful.
   b. Lobbyists are an evil that must be done away with.
   c. There are too many lobbyists who are not trained for the work they do.

4. In Washington, there are lobbyists for
   a. business firms
   b. labor unions
   c. farmers
   d. all of these

5. Lobbyists are chiefly interested in having laws passed that
   a. benefit the entire nation
   b. benefit the most people in the country
   c. favor their group or organization

6. A danger that may be a result of lobbying is that
   a. members of Congress may receive gifts from groups when they wish to be re-elected

   b. members of Congress may vote for a bill a lobbyist wants because of favors received
   c. lobbyists usually have incorrect information about the bill they are interested in

7. Marches on Washington usually are
   a. gestures of thanks for something the federal government has done
   b. protests against some action or planned action by the federal government
   c. a way people have of celebrating national holidays

8. Marches on Washington have been held to support all of these EXCEPT
   a. increases in the prices of farm products
   b. an end to war
   c. space exploration
   d. civil rights

9. Senator Kennedy (in the quotation before paragraph 6) believes lobbying is important because it
   a. provides important information to Congress and government agencies
   b. places pressure on Congress to vote for or against a bill
   c. helps members of Congress get re-elected to office

10. Which is the best judgment of the effect of marches on votes in Congress?
    a. Nearly every march has won its point by getting a favorable vote from Congress.
    b. No one can be sure if demonstrations in Washington change votes in Congress.
    c. Most marches are ignored by members of Congress.

★ **DEVELOPING CRITICAL THINKING SKILLS**

A. Interpreting a Cartoon

1. What would be a good title for this cartoon?

2. How does each character influence the member of Congress?

3. Which characters do you think should have the most influence on Congress?

4. How would you describe the expression on the face of the member of Congress?

B. Writing About Citizenship

Write an essay on one of the following topics:

1. Discuss reasons why lobbying of Congress should be allowed. Then discuss reasons why lobbying of Congress should not be allowed. Which side seems to have more reasonable arguments? Why? Do you think that lobbying is generally a good or a bad practice?

2. Members of Congress have to make some difficult decisions. They may feel strongly in their own minds that a certain law is needed, and that it is right. Yet, as far as they can tell, the voters who elected them feel the opposite way. How should they vote—according to what they believe to be right, or according to what the majority of voters believe? Support your opinion.

THE PRESIDENT: NATIONAL AND WORLD LEADER

PURPOSES FOR READING

1. To know who can become president of the United States
2. To understand the powers and duties of the chief executive

KNOWING NEW WORDS

qualifications
(kwol uh fuh KAY shuns)
paragraph 2—those things needed to make a person fit to hold an office
EXAMPLE: One of the **qualifications** for judges is that they must know the law.

agencies
(AY jun sees) paragraph 3—groups that have power to act for others, as committees acting for the president or Congress

EXAMPLE: The Central Intelligence Agency is one of the **agencies** that gather information needed to prevent a surprise attack on the nation.

budget
(BUJ it) paragraph 5—a listing of expected income and expenses
EXAMPLE: The family did not plan for a new car in their **budget** for this year.

Former presidents Ronald Reagan, Gerald Ford, Jimmy Carter, and Richard Nixon (left to right). What are the qualities of leadership needed in a president?

143

Powers of the President

- Approves or Vetoes Bills
- Commander in Chief of the Armed Forces
- Appoints Cabinet Members, Ambassadors, and Federal Judges
- Proposes Laws and Programs to Congress
- Reports to Congress on the State of the Nation
- Prepares the Federal Budget
- May Pardon Those Guilty of Federal Crimes

1▶ President Harry S Truman called the job of president of the United States "a man-killer, five or six full-time jobs, all different, all difficult." Yet few presidents have wanted to give up their jobs. Most have wanted to be reelected president a second time. One reason may be that the job of president of the United States is probably the most important job in the world—and the most powerful one. It has been said that "no king or emperor ever had the power of a modern president of the United States." The president has more buttons to push, more gadgets, more billions of dollars to spend and more ways to spend it than any other person in history. What are the powers and duties of the person who holds such a powerful yet difficult job?

2▶ The qualifications for president of the United States are stated in Article II of the Constitution. The president must be a citizen by birth of the United States. Also, the president must be at least 35 years old and must have lived in the United States for 14 years. The term of office is four years. A person may not be elected to the office more than twice. There are no other

limits on who may become president. (The president may be referred to as "he" from time to time. This is because all our presidents so far have been men. There is no reason, however, why a woman cannot be elected president.) A person's race or religion cannot keep him or her from being elected. The president, to carry out his duties well, needs good health and a strong character. Probably no other office in the world places such pressures on a person as that of president of the United States.

3▶ The president has many duties. First, the president is the **chief executive**—the head of the executive branch of government. As such, he has the duty of enforcing our laws, that is, seeing that they are put into effect. He has no choice in carrying out this duty. He must enforce the laws even though there may be laws he does not like. In carrying out his duties, the president has help. He appoints members of the cabinet and the heads of many federal agencies and commissions. In addition, he has his own staff of advisers. (See chapter 22.)

4▶ A second duty of the president is that of **commander in chief of the armed forces.** Presidents in modern times have com-

President Nixon viewing the Great Wall of China. Visiting foreign nations is another duty of the president.

manded the greatest armed force in the world. Presidents may not declare war. That is a duty given to Congress. But presidents may send armed forces anywhere in the world to protect American interests. In the past, presidents have sent armed forces to Latin America, Lebanon, and Vietnam. Because there is always the danger of war in such a move, Congress limited this power in 1973. Now, forces sent to foreign lands by the president can be kept there only for 90 days. If there is to be a longer stay, it must be approved by Congress. In 1990, however, Secretary of State James Baker told leaders of Congress that the president could not promise to consult them before taking armed action in the Persian Gulf. Debate over the limits Congress can place on actions by armed forces was increased by this statement.

5► The president is not a member of Congress. But he does have something to say about how laws are made. This can be called a legislative duty. The president has the power to sign bills passed by Congress.

If he does not like a bill, he may veto or disapprove it. Also, he may suggest to Congress that certain laws should or should not be passed. The president sends a message to Congress each year telling them of the "State of the Union" and what he believes are the needs of the country. He also holds meetings with important members of Congress. The president prepares the budget for the nation, which Congress must approve. In the budget, the president decides how much money he feels should be spent on foreign aid, help to farmers, education, and how much should be given to states and cities. In this way, he really decides, with the help of Congress, matters that affect the entire nation and the world.

6► The president has a fourth duty. Our **relations with other countries** are a duty of the president. Treaties with other nations are made through the office of the president. The secretary of state usually represents the president in carrying out this duty. The president also appoints ambassadors and other representatives of the nation to foreign countries. Presidents since Franklin D. Roosevelt have traveled to many places in the world to improve our relations with other nations.

7► President Truman believed that presidents have a fifth duty. The president represents the nation before the world. As such, he has many social duties to perform and ceremonies to attend. We call these **ceremonial** duties. For example, the president receives heads of other nations when they visit the United States. In carrying out ceremonial duties, the president is acting as the head of the nation, the symbol of unity of the American people.

145

President Roosevelt (center) meeting with Churchill of Great Britain (left) and Stalin of the Soviet Union (right).

8▶ The president is also the **leader of his political party.** He is elected as a member of a political party. When he ran for the office of president, he placed before the voters the program of his party. When he was elected, it meant that the voters chose his party's plans for the country above those of any other party. In office, the president must do what he can to get Congress to put through the program of his party. Members of Congress from the president's party want his support, too. Often, the support of the president may mean that a member of Congress will be re-elected. The president is often guided by the wishes of members of his political party when he decides to sign or veto a bill.

9▶ The president is a **world leader.** People look for help and guidance from the leaders of their social group, or city. So do the people of the world look to the leaders of powerful nations for guidance. Because the president is the head of the strongest nation in the world, what he does is watched carefully by people throughout the world. An American president was a leader in the forming of the United Nations in 1945. Our armed forces are located in other countries. Our country spends billions of dollars to help foreign nations solve their problems. Trouble in any part of the world may call for some action by the president of the United States. Presidents, too, act as peacemakers. One of the best examples is the role played by President Carter in bringing together the heads of Israel and Egypt to work out a peace plan in 1978.

10▶ The president must know about hundreds of different events and ideas. A president may read about events that have taken place during the night, even before he leaves his bedroom in the morning. Then, he gets the *Congressional Record.* Parts of the *Record* are marked showing him the speeches he should read. Then, as many as eight papers from all over the world are given to him. He reads news events and comments from many different people. Other staff members tell him of matters on which they have been working. By eight or nine o'clock, he gets to his office. He is already prepared to meet heads of foreign governments, members of Congress, ambassadors with reports, and other visitors. He is also ready to carry on the other business of the day.

11▶ The burdens of the office of president have made our people concerned with the office of vice-president. Under the Constitution, the only duty of the vice-president is to preside over meetings of the Senate. The last several presidents have given vice-presidents other important work to do. The choice of the vice-president is important to the nation. Since 1900, four vice-presidents have become president upon the death of the president. The 25th Amendment to the Constitution allows the vice-president to act as president when the president becomes disabled or ill. It also allows the president to appoint a vice-president if there is no vice-president. This has happened twice in the nation's history.

Nelson A. Rockefeller takes the oath as vice-president of the United States in 1974.

President Nixon named Gerald R. Ford as vice-president when Vice-President Spiro Agnew resigned in 1973. In August of 1974, Gerald Ford became president when President Nixon resigned. A short time later, President Ford appointed Nelson Rockefeller vice-president. This was the first time in our history when both the president and the vice-president had not been elected to those offices.

12▶ The president is chosen for office by electors. The voters in each state really vote for electors who represent them in choosing a president. Each state has as many electors as it has members in Congress. (Example: North Carolina has 11 representatives and 2 senators in Congress. It has 13 electors, or 13 electoral votes. When voters in a state vote for someone for president, they are really telling the electors to vote for that person. The electors are called the **electoral college.** However, they never meet together. Instead, their votes are sent to the U.S. Senate. There the electoral votes are counted a few weeks after the election. The person getting more than half the electoral votes wins. We know who has been elected even before the electoral votes are counted. Each elector, by custom, will vote for the person who received the most popular votes in his or her state.

13▶ The president may not be elected more than twice. This was not always so. The limit on the number of terms was set by the 22nd Amendment to the Constitution, approved in 1951. Before the 22nd Amendment was passed, President Franklin D. Roosevelt had been elected four times, beginning in 1932. No other president has been elected more than twice.

House Judiciary Committee meeting to draw up impeachment charges against Nixon.

14 ▶ The president can be removed from office during his term only if he is found guilty of wrongdoing. The method by which the president or other high government officials are removed is called **impeachment.** The first step in impeachment calls for charges to be made by a majority of the House of Representatives. The trial on the impeachment charges is held in the Senate. The chief justice of the Supreme Court presides at the trial. A vote by two-thirds of the Senate is needed for removal from office.

15 ▶ No president has been found guilty of impeachment charges. One president, Andrew Johnson, was impeached; that is, a trial on charges of wrongdoing was held in the Senate. The vote to remove him from office fell one vote short of the needed two-thirds. A committee in the House of Representatives prepared impeachment charges in the case of President Richard Nixon. But President Nixon resigned before the charges were approved by the House of Representatives. Later, President Gerald Ford pardoned Richard Nixon for all federal crimes he "committed or may have committed" while serving as president. (Under the Constitution, the president has the power to grant pardons for offenses against the national government.)

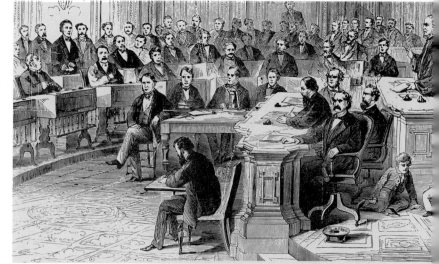

The Senate impeachment trial of Andrew Johnson, 1868. Compare the impeachment proceedings of Johnson and Nixon. How were they similar? How were they different?

CHAPTER 20 REVIEW

1. The main idea of paragraph 5 is that
   a. the president is not a member of Congress
   b. the president rarely speaks with members of Congress
   c. the president has something to say about the work of Congress

2. The main idea of paragraph 10 is that
   a. the president's day starts at a late hour
   b. the staff of the president prepares work for him
   c. the president must have a knowledge of events taking place all over the world

3. An important idea of this chapter is that
   a. the office of president is respected throughout the world
   b. most of the president's work is done by the people around him
   c. the president's powers are limited by the Constitution

4. The president has all of these powers EXCEPT the power to
   a. declare war
   b. name judges to the Supreme Court
   c. grant pardons to those found guilty of federal crimes

5. According to the Constitution, the president of the United States
   a. cannot be elected more than twice
   b. must be at least 50 years old
   c. must be a male

6. In trying to get Congress to pass certain laws, the president does all of these EXCEPT
   a. sends messages to Congress telling them of the laws he wishes them to pass
   b. serves on committees of Congress
   c. holds meetings with members of Congress

7. The president is called the leader of his party for all these reasons EXCEPT:
   a. The president ran for the office on the program prepared by the party.
   b. The president has the title of chairman of the party.
   c. Members of Congress of the president's party want his support when they run for reelection.

8. The president tells Congress of the "State of the Union." (See paragraph 5.) This means that the president explains
   a. the condition of the country
   b. how states can be created
   c. the results of the last election

9. According to the 25th Amendment to the Constitution
   a. the number of terms of the president is limited
   b. the vice-president may act as president when the president is too ill to do so
   c. the term of the vice-president is set at four years

10. In case of impeachment, the duty of the House of Representatives is to
    a. act as the jury in the trial
    b. consider a pardon for those found guilty
    c. prepare the charges of wrongdoing

11. The best definition of **impeachment** is
    a. charges of wrongdoing are prepared against a government official
    b. a government official is removed from office
    c. the president grants a pardon to a person found guilty of a crime against the national government

★ DEVELOPING CRITICAL THINKING SKILLS

A. Interpreting a Cartoon

Study the cartoon. Then answer the questions that follow it.

THE MANY ROLES OF THE PRESIDENT

1. Why does the president see himself differently in each mirror?

2. Which roles of the president are shown in the cartoon?

3. Which role would the president play at a political fund raiser?

4. What would be a good title for this cartoon?

B. Writing About Citizenship

Write one or two well-organized paragraphs on this topic: Which do you think is the most important duty of the president? Give reasons for your choice.

C. Using Source Materials

Read the following account of the traveling arrangements of the president. Then answer the questions.

The Traveling White House

Dwight Eisenhower was the first president to travel to a great many foreign countries while in office. The presidents who followed him continued the practice of foreign visits. Ronald Reagan traveled a great deal during his presidential terms. George Bush also was a global traveler. In one eight-day period in 1990, Bush visited Saudi Arabia, Egypt, and four countries in Europe. Several days later, Bush flew to South America for talks in five more countries. Before Bill Clinton traveled to an economic summit in Japan in July 1993, there were many months of careful planning.

The planning for each foreign visit involves hundreds of people. Most of what presidents need for their safety is sent ahead of their arrival date. This includes armored limousines and metal detectors to screen crowds for weapons. An ambulance is provided to travel along with the motorcade. Fire trucks are placed near the landing zones at airports. A bullet-proof platform must be available wherever the president will speak.

Presidents must always remain in close contact with Washington. Special telephones and switchboards are set up to connect the president to any place in the world.

Planners think of and prepare for every possible emergency in advance. Military aides follow the president on every visit. They carry secret codes in the event of an emergency and armed forces must be called into action.

For the health and safety of the president, at least two doctors are always available. Hospital arrangements are made in advance. White House personnel prepare meals and take care of clothing needs. In some instances, food and water will even be flown from Washington. These are only some of the many security measures when a president travels.

Tell whether these statements are true (T), false (F), or there is not enough information to make a judgment (N). Write the correct answer in your notebook.

1. When a president visits a foreign country, a limousine is flown there for his use.

2. Those who guard the president probably feel more secure when the president is surrounded by many people.

3. When a president prepares to make a trip outside Washington, the police in that city are responsible for the safety of the president.

4. In foreign countries, a president may have to wait several hours before receiving important news from Washington.

5. Presidents of the last 20 years are making fewer trips to foreign countries.

6. Limousines used by traveling presidents are filled with secret devices that no spectator could possibly see.

21

EXECUTIVE DEPARTMENTS AND AGENCIES

PURPOSES FOR READING

1. To understand how advisers help the president carry out the duties of the office
2. To learn of the work of government departments and agencies
3. To understand the results of government regulation of many activities in the lives of its citizens

KNOWING NEW WORDS

cabinet
(KAB in nit) paragraph 2—the group of persons appointed by the heads of governments to advise them
EXAMPLE: The president met with members of the **cabinet** to learn their views on new kinds of energy.

President Reagan meeting with his cabinet. How does the cabinet help the president carry out his duties?

1▶ Spring is the time when gardeners plant their flowers. The gardens are bare and empty. The young plants are very tiny when they are first put into the earth. There seems to be room for so many. So more plants are added to fill up the empty spaces. But as summer comes and the plants develop full bloom, there are no empty spaces. Flowers are crowded together, almost overflowing the gardens. To some, the mass of flowers is beautiful. To others, there are just too many plants for beauty. The agencies of the federal government have grown in much the same way. There were only a few at first. Then more were added until the number of such departments and agencies, to many, seemed to be overflowing Washington.

2▶ In 1789, President George Washington appointed four assistants to help him. They were called the secretary of state, the secretary of the treasury, the secretary of war, and the attorney general. These advisers were the first president's cabinet. From 1798 to 1965, six other departments were created: Navy, Agriculture, Labor, Interior, Commerce, and Health, Education, and Welfare (HEW). Shortly after World War II, the departments of War and Navy were combined into the Defense Department. In 1965, the Department of Housing and Urban Development (HUD) was created. A year later, the Department of Transportation was added to the government. Education was created as a separate department in 1979. Education had been part of HEW, which is now called the Department of Health and Human Services. The Department of Energy was created in 1977. The latest department is

George Washington's first cabinet. It included a secretary of state, secretary of treasury, secretary of war, and an attorney general.

that of Veterans Affairs. It became a cabinet post in 1989. Cabinet members must know almost everything there is to know about the departments they head. They also need people to assist them.

3▶ The president meets with the cabinet regularly. From the secretaries (the heads of each of the 13 departments), the president seeks advice on a number of matters. Secretaries, on the other hand, may suggest to the president actions he might take or laws they wish him to suggest to Congress. The heads of the National Security Council and the Office of Management and Budget also attend these sessions. They are not cabinet members, but their advice is important to the president. At these meetings, important decisions are made. Although all present are invited to give their opinions, the final decisions are made by the president.

4 ▶ The president also has a White House staff. Some handle the daily routines of the president's office. They arrange appointments with members of Congress and other visitors, take phone calls, see that the president has the time to perform his duties. Others prepare ceremonies for visits from heads of other countries. Still others deal with news people. They speak with reporters almost daily about White House events that are of public interest. The president can also have any other special advisers he chooses. These are not members of the cabinet.

5 ▶ The interests of the federal government in the welfare of the people have grown as the country has grown. (See page 174.) The federal government is now involved in many kinds of activities that were once thought not to be the business of government. As the interests and powers of the federal government have increased, agencies have been set up to decide the rules for many activities. A government agency is a group of people whose top officials are appointed by the president to do a special kind of job.

6 ▶ Congress first decides what agencies the federal government needs. It then passes a law creating the agency or commission. Top officials of the agency or commission are appointed by the president, but the agency reports to Congress on the work it does. The appointed members of an agency serve from five to seven years. They are members of both political parties. For the most part, the agencies work independently of both the president and Congress.

Agencies set up rules to protect all the people. Many agencies are **regulatory**—they regulate or control some part of American life.

7 ▶ The oldest agency of this kind is the Interstate Commerce Commission (ICC). It was created in 1887. In the last half of the 19th century, state laws could not stop unfair practices of railroads operating in more than one state. The ICC was set up to regulate railroad traffic between states. Now the ICC regulates all land transportation—railroad, bus, and truck. Like other commissions, the ICC tries to see that no group harms others. It has the job of protecting the rights of business people and those who use railroads, trucks, and other forms of public transportation.

8 ▶ The number of agencies of the federal government has grown steadily since 1887. The Federal Aviation Administration (FAA) now makes rules that govern air travel in the United States. The selection of

Environmental Protection Agency laboratory. Why has this agency become so important?

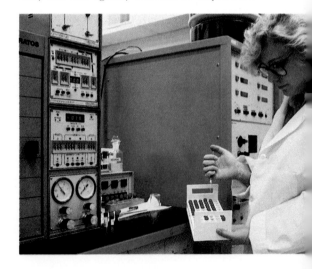

places to which aircraft should fly, the air lanes they use, the safety rules they must obey—these are all under the control of the FAA. The Commission on Civil Rights has an important job. It makes sure that citizens are not deprived of their right to vote. The Food and Drug Administration (FDA) protects consumers against impure and unsafe foods. All of these agencies have authority only if what they are trying to control is carried on in more than one state (interstate commerce).

9▶ The Federal Trade Commission (FTC) protects citizens against false advertising of products of many kinds. The Federal Communications Commission (FCC) regulates telegraph, telephone, radio, and TV. The FCC grants licenses to broadcasting stations. It also decides how much time TV and radio stations must use in presenting news programs. It encourages broadcasters to set up codes (rules of behavior) for the kinds of programs that are offered to the public. Another agency was created when Congress recognized the problem of pollution. The Environmental Protection Agency was set up in 1970. The EPA has the power to enforce standards for all kinds of pollution control. And in 1977, Congress passed a law placing the purity of drinking water under the supervision of the federal government for the first time.

10▶ Some people believe that the federal government should act as the parent of the family—the nation. All problems are to be solved by the national government. The government should provide clean air, pure food and water, good pensions, decent pay, and low medical bills, and ensure less crime. Congress has listened to some of

Federal insurance on money in the bank. During the Great Depression of the 1930s many banks failed. Depositors lost their savings. Why did the government then set up the Federal Deposit Insurance Corporation?

these claims and has created agencies and **bureaus** to carry out these demands. (A bureau is an office that carries out a special duty. The growth of the number of these offices has led to our calling the national government a **bureaucracy,** that is, a government through offices.) One study found that there are nearly 400 agencies and bureaus of the national government. Almost 250 have been added in the last 50 years. Nearly 3.5 million people work for the executive department and the independent agencies of government.

11▶ Each established agency must have a head with assistants, office space, and hundreds of workers. Most government workers are called civil service employees. Most federal workers have passed tests to fill the positions they hold. For years, these tests were given by the Civil Service Commission, set up by Congress in 1883. In 1978, Congress replaced the commission

SOME IMPORTANT AGENCIES OF THE NATIONAL GOVERNMENT

Central Intelligence Agency	Federal Trade Commission
Commission on Civil Rights	General Accounting Office
Consumer Product Safety Commission	Interstate Commerce Commission
Environmental Protection Agency	National Aeronautics and Space Administration
Equal Employment Opportunity Commission	National Foundation on the Arts and the Humanities
Farm Credit Administration	National Labor Relations Board
Federal Communications Commission	National Transportation Safety Board
	Nuclear Regulatory Commission
Federal Deposit Insurance Corporation	Securities and Exchange Commission
Federal Election Commission	Small Business Administration
Federal Maritime Commission	Tennessee Valley Authority
Federal Reserve System	U.S. Postal Service

Which of the Purposes for Reading mentioned at the beginning of the chapter does this list help you to understand?

with the Office of Personnel Management. The records of the largest government agencies in each year require the services of over 200,000 secretaries, typists, and file clerks.

12► From these offices come rules and regulations of many kinds. In addition to those mentioned earlier in this chapter, the government sets minimum wages (the lowest wage that can be paid) for work, pro-tects against false advertising and danger-ous drugs, and rules for the rates charged for power for homes and industry. It sets rules for the hiring of workers and activities of banks.

13► The growing interests of the national government cost money. Agencies must have funds to carry out their work. Before rules are made for business or individuals, an agency must investigate the

Workers at the FBI building in Washington, D.C. Almost 3 million people work for the executive branch of the federal government.

problem. It must inform those concerned what the rules are. It must be able to enforce the rules. The payroll for civilian workers of the federal government is now over $8 billion a year. There are those who say that the government is too big. They believe that the government has its hand in too many activities. They point to the increasing costs of what they call "big government." Others think that the national government must do things to provide for the welfare of its people. They point out that state and local governments cannot protect citizens as well as the national government can. Nor do local governments have the funds needed to do so.

CHAPTER 21 REVIEW

★ UNDERSTANDING WHAT YOU HAVE READ

1. The main idea of paragraph 2 is that
   a. the growth of the nation has caused the president to have greater responsibilities
   b. Congress has given more responsibilities to the president
   c. the power of Congress has weakened with the passing years

2. The main idea of paragraph 6 is to describe
   a. why people want federal agencies

   b. why people oppose federal agencies
   c. how federal agencies are established

3. An important idea of this chapter is that the federal government has spread its power into many activities because
   a. it is concerned with the welfare of all of the people
   b. it had to show that it had more power than the states
   c. the president wishes to work independently of Congress

4. All the heads of these departments are members of the president's cabinet EXCEPT
   a. the Department of Energy
   b. the Department of Investigation
   c. the Department of Housing and Urban Development

5. If you were a reporter trying to write a story about the president's plans for a trip across the country, you would most likely talk with
   a. a member of the cabinet
   b. a member of the president's personal staff
   c. a member of the Interstate Commerce Commission

6. The Interstate Commerce Commission (ICC) was created because
   a. states did not care about unfair railroad practices
   b. railroad companies asked the government for help
   c. states could not stop unfair practices of railroads doing business in more than one state

7. An advantage of federal laws and rules over laws and rules for each state is that
   a. standards are then the same for all states
   b. federal laws are easier to enforce
   c. the power of the federal government is increased

8. If persons argue against the growing number of government agencies, they would point out the
   a. high costs of paying government employees
   b. fact that broadcasters have to obey standards for their programs
   c. rules that improve the safety of air travel

9. To **regulate** an activity is to
   a. trade with it
   b. set rules for it
   c. point out its dangers

10. Which statement below best describes the meaning of **bureaucracy**?
    a. "There are too many people at cabinet meetings."
    b. "I shouldn't have to take a test to get a government job."
    c. "We're not governed by people; we're governed by offices."

★ DEVELOPING CRITICAL THINKING SKILLS

A. Using Original Sources

The following article appeared in newspapers across the country. After you read it, see if you can answer the questions that follow it.

At 7:45 A.M. Nancy Ruddell sits down for her first cup of morning coffee, adding an artificial sweetener containing saccharin. "Contains no cyclamate" reads the little packet. Cyclamate cannot be sold for use by humans because of a **Food and Drug Administration** ruling in 1969.

This day that started at 6:15 A.M. is an ordinary one for the Ruddells. But throughout this day, and every other day, the Ruddell's lives—and those of every American—are shaped by federal regulations.

This, then, is a look at the regulations in a day in the life of one American family in this city of 109,000.

6:15 A.M. A burst on the alarm clock arouses the family. The clock reads the particular time because **Congress** decreed Daylight Savings Time ended when October did.

6:25 A.M. Jeffrey, age 5, slips out of his pajamas that are flame retardant because the **Consumer Product Safety Commission** requires sleepwear for children to be so treated.

6:50 A.M. Three quarts of milk are deposited at the back door and brought into the kitchen by Jeffrey. Nancy mixes the milk with Non-Fat Dry Milk she bought at the supermarket. This cuts the drink's calories and cholesterol. It is also cheaper than ordinary skim milk because the **U.S. Department of Agriculture** sets a higher support price for skim milk than for whole milk.

7:37 A.M. Jennifer, age 10, and Jeffrey take fruit-flavored chewable vitamins. . . . The manufacture and labeling of vitamins are now regulated by the **Food and Drug Administration.**

7:55 A.M. Driving to work, Tom recalls how a **federal safety** inspector ordered the wearing of hard hats at the workshop of the Trolley Museum in Maine where he worked during summer vacations.

8:19 A.M. Jennifer carries her homemade lunch to school. . . . Many other students at Jennifer's school will eat a lunch prepared by the school cafeteria—a lunch whose contents are required by the **Department of Agriculture.**

8:35 A.M. Nancy picks up a jar of peanut butter at the supermarket. The **Food and Drug Administration** says this can be called peanut butter because it is 90 percent peanuts. Any less, and it must be called "peanut spread."

1:10 P.M. Tom goes over a report at his office. It shows that 23 federal bodies either receive reports from Pennsylvania Power and Light Company or affect its business in some way. (The **Agriculture Department** lends money for rural electrical service. The **Environmental Protection Agency** controls smokestack pollution. The **Federal Power Commission** controls prices of interstate sales of electricity. The **Equal Employment Opportunity Commission** wants to know about minority-group employees.)

> 1:25 P.M.   Nancy sits in the family living room talking to a visitor about the **Environmental Protection Agency** ban on the insecticide DDT, which she blames for the bands of mosquitos at their rented vacation home the last two summers.
>
> 8:30 P.M.   Friends arrive for a holiday gathering. The children watch a special on TV, the ads for which have been screened for misleading statements under the **Federal Trade Commission** regulations.
>
> Brooks Jackson and Evans Witt
> Associated Press
> *St. Louis Post Dispatch*

1. Make a listing of agencies or bodies of the federal government that are mentioned in this article. Next to each, briefly state how it affects our lives, as you read or might conclude from this article.

2. Where do government agencies get the power to make such regulations as are described in the article?

3. With which regulations that are mentioned in the article do you agree? Are there any with which you disagree? Why?

4. Why do you think there is more government regulation than ever before in our history?

5. What do you think was the authors' purpose in writing this article? What do you think their opinions are about all or some of the regulations?

B. Writing About Citizenship

Write an essay on one of the following topics:

1. Which government agency do you think has the most influence on your daily life? Do you think it affects you in a positive or a negative way? Give some examples of ways in which the agency affects you.

2. Do you think that there are too many federal government agencies? Do you think that there are too few? Do you think that the federal government should play a large role in American life, or should the states play the larger role? Why do you think so? What would happen if there were no government agencies?

3. Think about making a career in the federal government. Of the agencies that you have read about in this chapter, which do you think you would most like to work for? Write a paper explaining why you think that agency's work might be interesting. Then tell what additional information you would like to have about the agency.

★ SUMMARIZING THE CHAPTER

A. Building Your Skills

Match the items in the Regulations column with the government agency in the Agency column that carries out the regulations mentioned. Write the letters of your choices next to the numbers in your notebook. There is one EXTRA item in the Regulations column.

Agency

1. Consumer Product Safety Commission

2. Commission on Civil Rights

3. Environmental Protection Agency

4. Federal Communications Commission

5. Federal Deposit Insurance Commission

6. Interstate Commerce Commission

7. National Aeronautics and Space Administration

Regulations

a. establishes rules for clean air

b. regulates what can be shown on TV programs

c. establishes rules for trucks carrying goods from one state to another

d. listens to complaints about race discrimination

e. sets standards for the employment of government workers

f. checks to make sure electrical appliances are safe for use in the home

g. guarantees the safety of your bank account

h. researches activities beyond the earth

B. Making Decisions—Using a Balance Sheet

Some people believe that there are too many ways that the federal government regulates our lives. Others believe that government rules are necessary. Divide your paper into two headings—What Is Good About Government Regulation; What Is Bad About Government Regulation. List the arguments supporting each side.

After completing both lists, decide which list presents the better support for its view. What conclusion did you reach?

22

THE SUPREME COURT: UMPIRE FOR THE NATION

PURPOSES FOR READING

1. To learn the make-up of the Supreme Court
2. To understand the great powers of the Supreme Court
3. To understand how decisions of the Court affect the lives of Americans

KNOWING NEW WORDS

unconstitutional
(un kon stih TOO shuh nul) paragraph 5—not allowed by the Constitution
EXAMPLE: The Court ruled that it was **unconstitutional** for Congress to pass a law taxing exports.

interprets
(in TUR prits) paragraph 9— explains

EXAMPLE: The aide **interprets** the remarks of the Russian ambassador for the president.

void
(VOID) paragraph 9—having no legal force or effect
EXAMPLE: The check was declared **void** because there was no date on it.

Ruth Bader Ginsburg being sworn in as Supreme Court associate justice by Chief Justice William Rehnquist.

Supreme Court entrance. What is the importance of the words above the entrance?

1 ▶ If you are interested in sports, you may have noticed the work of referees and umpires. They are like judges. They make sure that games are played according to the rules. They don't tell players what to do. They merely judge whether the actions of players are within the rules. In the government of the United States, the Constitution states the "rules for the game." The Supreme Court is the "umpire" of government. It decides when the rules have been broken—when there are laws or actions that do not agree with the Constitution.

2 ▶ Among all the courts in this country, only one is named in the Constitution. That is the Supreme Court. The Constitution does not state the number of judges on the Supreme Court. It does not state the quali-

fications for judges. (On the Supreme Court, they are called **justices.**) It does state, however, that the judges of the Supreme Court and federal courts shall serve during "good behavior." The justices of the Supreme Court serve for life, or as long as they desire. The justices, therefore, do not have to account to the president, the Congress, or even to the people of the United States for their decisions. They are supposed to be free from politics and other pressures. Justices may be of any race. They may be either male or female.

3 ▶ A justice of the Supreme Court could serve through the terms of any number of presidents. For example, Oliver Wendell Holmes was appointed a justice by President Theodore Roosevelt in 1902. He served through the terms of Presidents Taft, Wilson, Harding, Coolidge, and Hoover. Thurgood Marshall was appointed a justice by President Lyndon Johnson in 1967. Justice Marshall was the first African American to be appointed to the Supreme Court. In 1981, Sandra Day O'Connor was appointed by Ronald Reagan to serve on the Supreme Court. She became the first woman justice. In 1986, Antonin Scalia became the first Italian-American justice.

4 ▶ Congress has established the number of justices of the Supreme Court at nine. There is a chief justice and eight associate justices. The president appoints the members of the Supreme Court. The Senate must approve these appointments. Senators do not always agree with the appointment the president wants to make. Robert Bork, nominated by President Reagan, was not confirmed by the Senate after a long and dramatic hearing. Congress

has also established lower courts called federal or district courts. These courts handle disputes about federal laws. They also hear cases in which a federal crime has been committed. Other cases are heard by courts of the 50 states.

5▶ The Supreme Court is one of the most powerful courts in the world. It can rule that federal and state laws are unconstitutional. This means that it can decide that Congress and state legislatures cannot pass certain laws. (It acts as if it were the umpire stating that players have violated the rules of the game.) Chief Justice John Marshall first stated this power of the Court in 1803. From time to time since then, his ruling has caused arguments about the power of the Court. However, most citizens have been willing to have the Supreme Court decide what our laws mean.

6▶ One of the deep disagreements with the rulings of the Supreme Court took place during the second term of President Franklin Roosevelt. The Supreme Court had declared unconstitutional seven of nine of the most important laws the president had asked Congress to pass. The president felt that the people supported these laws. He believed the Court should consider whether these laws were needed for the "welfare of the country." (See chapter 15, page 110.)

7▶ The president asked Congress to change laws about the make-up of the Court. Six of the nine justices were then over 70 years old. President Roosevelt suggested that he be allowed to appoint one more justice for each justice over 70 who would not retire. His plan ran into protests from Congress and across the nation. Con-

gress did not approve it. Yet, in a short time, some of the justices did retire. Also, the Court began to make rulings in favor of the president's proposals. Before President Roosevelt died in 1945, he had appointed nine new justices to the Supreme Court. These events give a picture of how the president, the Supreme Court, and Congress can check each other's powers.

8▶ The sessions, or meetings, of the Supreme Court are carried on in a very serious manner. All justices sit on the bench to hear a case. The chief justice sits in the center. Lawyers who have come to argue their cases sit in front of the bench. They are given one hour to present their arguments. Any justice may break in with questions at any time. The Court hears cases of

John Marshall, third chief justice of the Supreme Court. Who is chief justice now?

As the result of the Supreme Court ruling in 1954, schools such as this high school are no longer segregated.

many kinds for a few weeks. Then the justices study these cases and past ones that seem to be like the one they just heard. They look over the records of these cases, talk over their ideas, and vote. All justices do not have to agree in coming to a decision. Many cases are decided by a 5 to 4 or a 6 to 3 vote. This is chiefly because cases before the court cover difficult questions of law.

9 ▶ The Supreme Court enjoys great respect from the American people. Settling disputes through courts is an important part of our democracy. Many laws are written in broad language. There can be honest disagreements about what laws mean. The Supreme Court interprets laws and tells what they mean. When the Supreme Court makes a decision, it is of great importance to the country. New laws are often passed to take the place of the laws that are declared void.

10 ▶ Because of its decisions over the years, some have said that the Supreme Court is really making laws. Some of its rulings have changed practices all over the nation. One of these important rulings was made in 1954. After hearing a case brought before it, all nine justices agreed that separate schools for white and black students were unconstitutional. This did away with a ruling by another Supreme Court in 1896 that "separate but equal" schools were legal. As a result of this ruling, many states were forced to make changes to bring an end to segregated or separate schools.

11 ▶ In 1962, the Court made another decision that had far-reaching effects. A voter in Memphis, Tennessee, argued before the Court that representatives in his state were not chosen fairly. One farming county in the state had one representative in the state legislature. Yet it had only 3,000 people. In Memphis, there was one representative for 78,000 people. The Court ruled that the voter's claim was correct. The Court said, in effect, that state legislatures must represent the voters of the state

in an equal manner. In 1964, the Court made the same ruling about representatives in Congress. This is known as the "one person–one vote" ruling.

12▶ Other decisions of the Court have laid down rules that protect people accused of crimes. The Court has ruled that a state must provide a lawyer for an accused person who is too poor to have a lawyer. The Court has said that confessions of guilt cannot be used in a federal court unless accused persons have been told of their rights. In police stations today, there are signs that tell persons accused of crimes that they have the right to say nothing or have a lawyer present before they make a statement. According to the Court, juveniles must be given the same protection as adults when they are accused.

13▶ There is a great deal of discussion across the nation over a Court ruling that outlaws the death penalty for some crimes.

Many states had laws that required a sentence of death for particular crimes. Several states have changed their laws as a result. Some have done away with the death sentence completely. Others have made new laws allowing the death sentence for some crimes. However, such sentences are allowed only under conditions that agree with the Court's ruling.

14▶ Laws may not be applied in the same way if situations are different. New laws may be made after a Supreme Court ruling. There are those who say that the Court should interpret the Constitution exactly as it is written, or follow the ruling in previous cases. Others believe that the Constitution should be interpreted according to changes in society and the public's view of what is right today. There is no doubt, however, that the power of the Supreme Court has an effect on our social and political life today.

President Roosevelt's action in 1937 was called "packing the court."

CHAPTER 22 REVIEW

★ UNDERSTANDING WHAT YOU HAVE READ

1. A good title for paragraph 8 is
   a. The Job of Chief Justice
   b. How the Supreme Court Hears a Case
   c. The Most Difficult Cases

2. In paragraph 2, "free from politics" means that
   a. there is no limit on how long a justice may serve
   b. judges do not have to worry about being reappointed to their positions
   c. only the Senate and the president have the right to appoint justices

3. An important idea of this chapter is that the Supreme Court
   a. has made rulings that have protected the civil rights of many people
   b. is not concerned with representatives in state legislatures
   c. does not change decisions of other federal courts

4. Some decisions of the Supreme Court are by a 5 to 4 vote because
   a. the vice-president can vote to break a Supreme Court tie
   b. justices usually vote according to the wishes of the political party to which they belong
   c. cases heard by the Court often cover difficult points of law

5. The power of the Supreme Court to explain laws is necessary because
   a. many laws are written in such language that it is difficult to tell what the law means in every case
   b. Congress passes laws knowing that the Supreme Court will decide what the laws mean
   c. the writers of the Constitution were not able to agree on what their words meant

6. Some say that the Supreme Court is really making laws because
   a. the Court has too many 5-to-4 decisions
   b. some of the Court's decisions have changed longstanding customs or practices in this country
   c. the thinking of the Court has changed in the last 100 years

7. The "one person–one vote" ruling of 1964 is important because it
   a. showed that the Court has the power to declare laws passed by Congress unconstitutional
   b. made sure that all people were equally represented in Congress
   c. forbade segregation of races in public schools

8. The Constitution says that justices of the Supreme Court will serve "during good behavior." This means that they
   a. must be members of the same party as the president
   b. must examine all laws passed by Congress
   c. can be removed if they break a federal law

9. The Supreme Court may be called the "umpire of the nation" because
   a. it decides whether government actions fit the rules stated in the Constitution
   b. justices are named by the president
   c. their work is carried out in a very serious manner

10. The president may, in time, change decisions of the Supreme Court by
    a. the impeachment of justices
    b. appointing justices who agree with the president's thinking
    c. increasing the number of justices on the Court

★**DEVELOPING CRITICAL THINKING SKILLS**

A. Applying Supreme Court Decisions

In social studies, there are terms that you will see again and again. Three of these important terms are the following:

political—Is about the way people are governed. Political conditions, then, refer to the workings of government, how people govern themselves, and how they are governed.

economic—Is about the way people earn a living. Economic conditions refer to the wages people are paid, the goods they make and sell, and what they are able to buy and trade.

social—Is about the way people live together. Social conditions refer to the customs people have, their clothes, use of leisure time, their interests, etc.

The decisions of the Supreme Court cover many sides of American life. Some deal with political matters; others deal with economic and social matters. Tell whether these decisions or actions of the Court deal with political, economic, or social matters, or with a combination of these three. Support your view.

1. Separate schools for black and white children are forbidden.

2. Congress may pass laws setting the wage that workers must be paid if they are making goods in more than one state.

3. A person does not have to pay a poll tax in order to vote.

4. Congress can pass laws forbidding businesses from joining together to control trade.

5. Members of a state legislature must represent an equal number of people.

6. States may have different laws concerning marriage and divorce.

7. Congress may pass laws forbidding children under 14 years of age to work.

8. Congress may fix the time for national elections.

9. Congress may forbid a strike in some factories until employers and employees have a period of time to "cool off."

10. People cannot be denied service in public places because of the color of their skin.

B. How the Supreme Court Interprets the Law

In paragraph 9, you read that many laws and statements in the Constitution are written in broad language. The Supreme Court interprets this broad language and decides what laws mean in our nation at the time the Court hears a case. What does fair trial mean? Or equal representation, peaceful assembly, cruel punishment, unreasonable search? The Court has to make decisions in these and hundreds of other questions. Here are three cases in which the Supreme Court has interpreted the meaning of words in the Constitution.

Case 1

MARCH 2, 1961. About 200 people marched in Columbia, South Carolina, to protest segregation. The march took place early in the afternoon. Police thought they knew some people in the crowd who might cause trouble. They told the crowd to break up and move away. They gave 15 minutes to have their orders carried out. At the end of 15 minutes 187 people were arrested. They received fines and some were put in jail for a period of 5 to 30 days.

Those arrested appealed to the Supreme Court. In 1963, by a vote of eight to one, the Supreme Court decided that the marchers did not do anything against the law. They had assembled (gathered together) peaceably. The Court said they did not disturb the peace since they did not stop traffic, march in secret, or harm any person.

How did the Court, in this case, help to explain the meaning of "peaceably to assemble" as written in the Constitution?

Case 2

Mr. G. was accused of breaking into a poolroom in Florida in 1961. He asked the judge to name a lawyer to defend him since he did not have a lawyer. The judge said that under the laws of Florida, he could not name a lawyer unless the crime was a more serious one, such as murder. Mr. G. defended himself. He was found guilty and sentenced to five years in jail. He appealed to the Florida Supreme Court. The state court agreed with the judge at his trial. He then wrote to the United States Supreme Court.

In 1963, the Supreme Court of the United States ruled that Mr. G. had not had a fair trial. In this case, all the justices of the Court agreed. The Court ruled that a person must have a lawyer, if he wants one, in order to have a fair trial. (More than 20 years before this case, the Supreme Court had said that a person did not have to have a lawyer for a fair trial.) Mr. G. was given a second trial and found not guilty.

Case 3

Two men loaded a trunk on a train in California, bound for Boston. Railroad officials thought the trunk was very heavy for its size. It was also leaking powder, often used to cover the odor of illegal drugs. Federal agents in Boston met the train. Police dogs trained to detect drugs smelled the trunk and gave signs that there were drugs in them. The two men were arrested. Ninety minutes later, and without a search warrant, the agents opened the trunk. They found the illegal drugs. At their trial, the evidence obtained from the trunk was not allowed to be used against the two men. The government appealed the judge's decision in this case through the courts and finally to the Supreme Court.

In June 1977, the Supreme Court ruled, by a vote of seven to two, that the evidence could not be used in the trial of the two men. The Court ruled that arresting officers could not search without a warrant at the time of arrest in this case. Officers may search without a warrant at the time of arrest if it's necessary to protect themselves against hidden weapons or to prevent evidence from being destroyed. Since 90 minutes had passed, neither of these conditions was present.

How did the Court interpret the meaning of "people to be secure . . . against unreasonable searches," as written in the Constitution? Why do you think the Court ruled against the arresting officers even though it was clear the two men were guilty of transporting drugs?

CONCLUSIONS:

1. Do the justices of the Supreme Court agree on all decisions made by the Court?

2. Do any of these rulings affect the lives of individual people or groups?

3. Why is it necessary for the Supreme Court to decide what the language of the Constitution means?

4. How can a ruling of the Supreme Court be changed?

C. Writing About Citizenship

Write a brief essay on the following topic: How do you think the Supreme Court should interpret laws? Do you think that they should interpret the Constitution exactly as it is written? Or should they interpret the Constitution according to changes in society? Give reasons for your opinion.

BALANCING FEDERAL INCOME AND EXPENSES

23

PURPOSES FOR READING

1. To learn the sources of income of the federal government
2. To learn where the federal government spends its income
3. To understand the problems in trying to make expenses meet income

KNOWING NEW WORDS

corporation
   (kor puh RAY shun) paragraph 3—a group of people given a charter from the state or federal government allowing it to conduct business; a corporation can have many owners but is treated in the eyes of the law as one person
   EXAMPLE: That **corporation** decided to hire 50 new workers next month.

excise tax
   (EK syz TAKS) chart, page 173—a type of tax on the making of goods
   EXAMPLE: In order to manufacture fishing rods, the Gold Company had to pay an **excise tax.**

Senator Lloyd Bentsen of Texas conducts a budget meeting. What kinds of things might be discussed in a budget meeting?

1 ▶ Nearly $3 billion a day, $120 million an hour, $2 million dollars a minute! The amounts are so large that it is difficult for us to understand just how much money it is. Yet, this is the amount spent by the federal government according to the 1989 budget figures. The total expenses for that year reached $1.1 trillion. That is over $1,000 billion, the highest figure in history. It is eight times the amount spent by the federal government 20 years before. What are the expenses of the federal government? Where does the federal government get such an amount to spend? Does the amount of money collected meet the expenses? This chapter will help you find answers to these questions.

2 ▶ It is the president's duty to draw up the budget for the federal government. The budget is a statement of expected income and expenses for the federal government for the following year. Of course, the president has help in this huge job. Cabinet members and heads of hundreds of government agencies give their planned budget to the president. The Office of Management and Budget goes over all of these budgets to see if they are reasonable. The same office looks for ways to reduce expenses or see where more money is needed. The president may have asked Congress to pass laws that call for more money for certain departments during the year. He includes this in the budget. Congress has the job of approving or refusing to accept the budget the president offers. Usually, Congress will make changes in the budget before it is passed. The final budget is the one passed by Congress.

3 ▶ Where does the money come from? The chart on page 173 shows the money collected by the federal government in taxes in 1989. Study the chart carefully.

- What is the source of greatest income for the federal government?

- What is the next highest source?

- Notice the income from taxes on the income of corporations (businesses). How much money was collected from incomes of both individuals and corporations?

- For every $10 the government collects in taxes, how much is collected from individual and corporation incomes?

- What amount is collected from excise taxes?

- How much is collected from customs duties?

4 ▶ The chart shows that the federal government receives money from many

Enlargement of the Individual Income Tax Return. How important are individual taxes to the federal budget?

different sources. The gasoline tax amounts to over 14 cents on each gallon purchased. A pack of cigarettes will cost 20 cents more than a person might pay because of federal tax. Ten percent of the cost of an airplane ticket is added for that trip you might take within the United States. When people die and leave their savings to relatives, there is a tax (an estate tax) to be paid, too. Many kinds of goods brought into the country from foreign lands are also taxed (customs duties).

5▶ Where does the money go? How is the income of the federal government spent? All citizens have a right to ask these questions. The chart on page 174 shows the amount of money spent by large departments and agencies in 1990. Study the chart on page 174, then answer the questions on page 175.

FEDERAL GOVERNMENT

Income From Taxes, 1990

Sources of Government Income	Amount (billions of dollars)
Individual income taxes	$466.9
Corporation income taxes	93.5
Social insurance taxes (old age, disability, hospital, federal, and state unemployment)	380.0
Excise taxes	17.1
Highway fund (trucks, trailers, buses, fuel)	13.9
Estate and gift taxes	11.5
Airport and airways (fuels, air travel, plane registration)	16.7
Customs duties	16.7
Others (telephones, coin games, betting, earnings of Federal Reserve)	27.5
TOTAL INCOME FROM TAXES	$1,031.5

Source: Office of Management and Budget

FEDERAL GOVERNMENT

Expenses (Outlays of Money), 1990

Expense	Amount (billions of dollars)
Legislature	$2.3
Judiciary	1.7
President and Executive Office	.2
Departments:	
Agriculture	47.5
Commerce	3.9
Defense	315.0
Education	22.9
Energy	12.3
Health and Human Services, including Social Security	437.3
Housing and Urban Development (HUD)	21.4
Interior	6.1
Justice	6.9
Labor	25.5
State	3.8
Transportation	28.5
Treasury	252.4
Veterans Affairs	29.3
Environmental Protection Agency (EPA)	5.3
National Aeronautics and Space Administration (NASA)	12.1
Independent Agencies	83.6
Other	33.4
TOTAL	1,264.3

Source: Office of Management and Budget

- What was the greatest expense of the federal government? The next highest?
- How much interest was paid on the amount the government borrowed to meet its expenses? (See page 177.)
- Why do you think aid to veterans amounted to over $29 billion?
- What is meant by Health and Human Services?
- What is meant by Independent Agencies?
- Which item in the budget was the most costly: research on energy, science and space exploration, or pollution control?

6▶ Have you noticed the total of income and expenses shown on the chart? *Income:* $1,031.5 billion; *Expenses:* $1,264.3 billion. The federal government planned to spend $232 billion more than it received. This **deficit** (the amount by which expenses are greater than income) has become a yearly problem. Since 1960, the budget has been **balanced** in only one year. In a balanced

Sally Ride, the first U.S. woman in space.

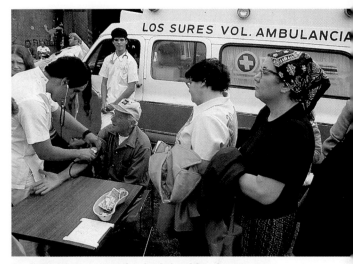

Senior citizens are checked for blood pressure. What federal expenses do the pictures on pages 175 and 176 represent?

budget, income is equal to or greater than expenses. When we personally spend more than we take in, we owe money. We are in debt. The government is in debt, too. After years of "unbalanced" budgets, the debt of the federal government is now more than one trillion dollars.

7▶ Why are government expenses so high? Experts in politics give us some explanations. Our people have come to expect many services and much help from the federal government. The more services, and the more aid from government, the greater the cost of government. In the expenses shown on the chart, there are payments to senior citizens in the form of Social Security and medical care. There are pensions for veterans and those retired from military careers. States and cities also receive aid. Because over 5 percent of our work force was unemployed, payments to those without work add to the expense.

Low-income housing project.

8 ► Our population has grown, too. And our population has changed. There are more elderly people than ever in history. Each year more people who will receive some kind of pension from the federal government are retiring from their jobs. Government help to those in need has increased. At present the Social Security system provides benefits to over 39 million retired and disabled persons, their children, and others. Workers for the federal government and members of the armed forces receive pay raises as workers in factories do. One can also look at the billions spent for national defense (the army, navy, air force, and new weapons). After the Soviet Union broke up in 1991, the threat of war was reduced. This resulted in proposals for less spending for armaments. But American armed forces became involved in the Persian Gulf War and other international crises. These expenses again added billions to the national defense budget.

9 ► How can government budgets be balanced? There are two ways: increase income or reduce expenses. Increasing government income usually means higher taxes. President Reagan tried another method called supply-side economics. In theory, a cut in taxes leaves people with more money to invest in new machines and new products. This means new jobs. With more people working and lower taxes, there would be more money to buy goods. As a result, the government would receive more money, even with lower taxes.

10 ► Under Reagan's plan, unemployment fell and people spent more buying goods. But income from taxes still did not meet expenses. In 1985, Congress passed the Gramm-Rudman bill intended to balance the budget by 1995. But these reductions were not enough. In 1990, President Bush signed a bill increasing taxes on wealthier citizens and luxury items. However, the growing federal debt was still a major issue in the 1992 presidential elections. President Clinton's plan for reducing the deficit decreased government spending. President Clinton also called for increasing certain taxes that would affect mainly the wealthier Americans.

11 ► If federal expenses are to be re-

duced, what items should be cut from the budget? Many of the expenses of the national budget are the result of laws passed by our representatives and senators in Congress. Only they can make changes in the national budget. What should be reduced: health care, pensions, pay for government workers, money for defense, aid for college students, aid to cities, help for needy families? As citizens and voters, you will have to answer these questions and let your representatives know what you think.

Understanding the National Debt

Expense items included $240 billion of interest on the debt of the federal government. To whom does the government owe money? Chiefly, to banks, insurance companies, other businesses, and even foreign nations that own government bonds. It may owe money to you, if you own one or more government bonds.

A bond is a promise to pay a set amount of money on a given date. This is how bonds are used. Suppose the government needs money to pay its bills. Bonds are printed by the government. The government says you may buy a bond for $900 and it will pay you back $1,000 in 10 years time. It wants your money now and is willing to pay you interest on this loan.

During the ten-year period of the bond, the government may pay you interest on your loan. If the interest is 8 percent, you will get 8 percent X $900 or $72 a year. Over 10 years, this amounts to $720. So for your loan of $900, you will receive $720 over 10 years, and your bond is still worth $1,000. Some of the interest paid to you on these bonds is not taxed. That's another reason why you might want to buy them. You must, however, pay federal income tax on savings bonds and treasury notes.

But the amount of interest to be paid on these bonds (and other government securities) increases each year. The government continues to borrow money as its income does not meet expenses. In 1990, interest payments on the national debt amounted to more than $8,000 for each person in the United States. As the budget continues to be unbalanced, it can be predicted that interest payments on the debt will rise also.

CHAPTER 23 REVIEW

★ UNDERSTANDING WHAT YOU HAVE READ

1. A good title for paragraph 8 might be
   a. Slowing Down the Arms Race
   b. Government Payroll Soars Higher
   c. Why the High Cost of Government

2. The budget of the federal government is
   a. prepared by a committee of the Senate
   b. prepared by the president, approved by Congress
   c. passed by Congress and approved by the Office of Management and Budget

3. President Reagan planned to reduce the budget deficit by:
   a. lowering taxes on businesses and individuals
   b. raising taxes on businesses only
   c. reducing spending for defense

4. The greatest source of tax money for the federal government comes from
   a. taxes on gasoline and tobacco
   b. taxes on estates and gifts
   c. taxes on incomes

5. In 1989, the expense budget of the federal government was about how much a year?
   a. Over $750 billion
   b. Over $900 billion
   c. Over $1 trillion dollars

6. One reason why government costs have risen is that
   a. citizens expect more and more services from government
   b. states have reduced taxes; the federal government must make up this loss
   c. budgets are difficult to balance

7. All of these are taxed by the federal government EXCEPT
   a. land on which homes are built
   b. telephone use
   c. some goods brought in from foreign countries

8. A budget is **balanced** when
   a. income equals expenses
   b. expenses are greater than income
   c. the government debt remains the same

★ DEVELOPING CRITICAL THINKING SKILLS

A. Finding Support for Statements

Below are several statements about the federal budget. For each statement, give one or two facts from chapter 23 that support it.

1. If spending for veterans' affairs were completely done away with, the federal government would still be in debt.

2. The president does not prepare the budget alone.

3. Congress has a great deal to say about the budget of the federal government.

4. The greatest share of government income comes from taxes on incomes.

5. Pensions for those employed by the federal government are a major item in the federal budget.

B. Interpreting Cartoons

1. What does the cartoonist mean by "Landing unknown?"

2. Name at least three federal expenses that some believe may be growing out of control.

3. Give two reasons why each of the expenses listed in number two is difficult to control.

C. Writing About Citizenship

Consider the statement, "If income is increased, it won't matter if expenses continue to grow." In one or two well-organized paragraphs, give reasons why you agree or disagree with the statement.

LANDING UNKNOWN.

D. Looking at Your Priorities

If you were a representative in the House of Representatives or a United States senator, you would have to face the problem of approving a budget for the government each year. Suppose you believe the budget should be balanced. From among the items listed below, choose those budget items that you would reduce. List them in order: the one you would reduce first, then second, and so forth. Give a reason why you would reduce each of the items you have chosen.

Department of Agriculture

Department of Health and Human Services

Department of Defense

Department of Housing and Urban Development

Energy Research

Environmental Protection Agency

Space Exploration

Department of Veterans' Affairs

These are examples of some of the large expenses of the federal government. You are free to choose to cut expenses elsewhere in the budget, if there are other items that concern you more.

Unit 5 ★

STATE AND LOCAL GOVERNMENTS

A public park. Funding parks is one of the many functions of state and local governments.

24

STATE GOVERNMENTS: THEIR POWERS

PURPOSES FOR READING

1. To learn the nature and powers of state governments
2. To understand how state governments are alike—and different
3. To learn the duties of the branches of state government

KNOWING NEW WORDS

vaccinations
(vak suh NAY shuns) paragraph 3—acts of giving medicine to prevent disease
EXAMPLE: They may need to have several **vaccinations** before they can enter the United States.

polluting
(puh LOOT ing) paragraph 6—making dirty
EXAMPLE: Smoke from factories and gases from cars are **polluting** the air.

violation
(vi uh LAY shun) paragraph 9—the act of breaking or failing to obey a law
EXAMPLE: Since the driver was going 60 miles an hour, he was found guilty of a **violation** of the town speed limit of 40 miles an hour.

State Capitol, Atlanta, Georgia.

"My best friend Tommy's very sick with the measles. His mother forgot to get his shots. Mommy said he might never get all better. I wish his mother didn't forget."

"Mi mejor amigo Tommy está muy enfermo con sarampión. Su mamá se olvidó de hacerlo vacunar. Mi mamá dice que quizás nunca se mejore. Ojalá que su mamá no se hubiese olvidado."

New York poster urging parents to get vaccinations for children. This poster appears in both Spanish and English. Why is this a good idea?

1 ▶ You are a citizen of the United States. If you live in one of the 50 states, you are also a citizen of that state. Both the federal and state governments are republics. That means the leaders of government are chosen by the people. Both governments are also democratic. The Constitution of the United States has granted powers to the federal government. It has also **reserved,** or saved, other powers for the states. Some powers are shared by the states and federal government. (See the chart on page 113.) Each state also has its own constitution that limits the powers and kinds of laws it may pass.

2 ▶ Both federal and state governments have become "big governments." There are five times as many people in California today as there were in the entire United States in 1789. The leaders who wrote the Constitution could not have known how the machine age would change the American way of life. They could not have pictured a nation with over 100 million cars. They could not have thought of coast-to-coast travel by air in five hours. They could not have known of our giant businesses.

Nor could they have predicted the need for labor unions and how they have grown in strength. In order to protect the rights of people in all walks of life, state laws cover thousands of activities. We have seen how the interests of the federal government have spread. So have those of the state.

3 ▶ The list of state powers is a long one. You attend school because state laws require it. Public school buildings and all the equipment in them have been paid for by state and local taxes. State laws require you to have vaccinations against certain diseases before you attend school. The roads that lead from one part of the state to another have been built chiefly with state money. You are protected by state police while traveling on those highways. Drivers are licensed by the state. Doctors, lawyers, teachers, and barbers must be licensed by the state before they are allowed to practice their professions. Cooks and waiters in restaurants must follow health rules set forth in state laws. The milk you drink and the meat you eat have been inspected by the state. Where you fish and hunt, and what you are allowed to catch, are regulated by

Nebraska's state legislature. How is Nebraska's state legislature different from other state legislatures?

state laws. And states have the power to pass tax laws to raise money for their activities.

4▶ The 50 states are alike in many ways. All have their constitutions. Each of these is somewhat like the Constitution of the national, the federal, government. All have a bill of rights. All separate the powers of government among the executive, legislative, and judicial branches. Forty-nine states have legislatures, lawmaking bodies, of two houses, as does the federal government. One, Nebraska, has a one-house legislature. In all states except North Carolina, the governor has the power to veto bills passed by the legislature. All states have a governor elected by the voters of the state.

5▶ The work of state lawmakers is important to you. Many laws that affect your daily life are state laws. State laws are passed by state legislatures. Much of the work of legislatures is done by committees, as in the Congress. The number of members in each state legislature differs from state to state. Nebraska's one-house legislature has 49 members—the smallest num-

ber. In New Hampshire there are 424 lawmakers, the largest number. The lower house is usually called the House of Representatives. Sometimes it is called the Assembly. In Virginia it is known as the House of Delegates. Members of the lower house are elected according to the population of the state. Many of the top officials in state and federal governments began their careers as lawmakers in their state.

6▶ Even though states have the same powers, laws may be very different from state to state. Most states allow drinks containing alcohol to be sold in restaurants. A few states do not. You can begin to drive a car in some states at age 15. In many others, you must wait until age 18. In Utah both girls and boys can be married with the consent of their parents at age 14. In many other states, an age of 18 is required. In California you can be fined if your car is polluting the air. Few of the other states

How does this picture show one of the powers of state government?

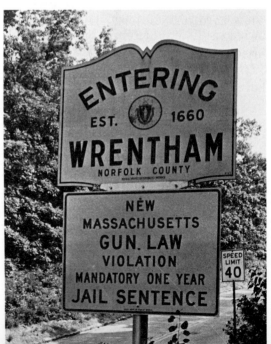

have laws regarding auto pollution. As you drive into Massachusetts, signs warn you that a year in prison awaits anyone carrying a gun without a license to do so. A license from another state does not help you. Some states tax individual incomes; others do not. Capital punishment, a death sentence, is legal in some states, but not in others.

7▶ The highest official in the state is the governor. The duties and interests of the 50 governors are similar in every state. But governors serve different terms of office. Most are elected for a four-year term. In three states, the term is only two years. In a few states, the governor cannot be elected for two terms in a row. The govenor's pay varies from state to state. The average yearly salary of all governors is about $66,000 a year. New York's governor receives $130,000. The governor of Arkansas is paid $35,000.

8▶ Many state governors have been candidates for the presidency. William McKinley, Theodore Roosevelt, Woodrow Wilson, Calvin Coolidge, Franklin Roosevelt, Jimmy Carter, Ronald Reagan, and Bill Clinton were governors before they were elected president. In 1925, Nellie Taylor Ross of Wyoming became the first elected woman governor. There were several women governors in the 1980s. In 1990, women were elected governors in Texas, Kansas, and Oregon.

9▶ The duties of the governor of a state are like those of the president of the United States. Governors are chief executives, in charge of enforcing the laws of the state. The governor commands the state guard and state police. The governor prepares the budget for the state and presents it to the

Ann Richards was elected governor of Texas in 1990. List the duties of the governor of a state.

legislature. He or she can send messages to the legislature asking that certain laws be passed. The governor may call the legislature into a special session. The governor appoints many state officials. He or she appoints the state judges of the supreme court in some states. However, the secretary of state is elected in most states. The governor also has the power to grant pardons for crimes committed in violation of state laws.

10▶ Every state has a system of courts. In most states, the state supreme court is the highest court. In some cases, the judges are elected by the people. In others, they are appointed by the governor. The state supreme court interprets state laws and hears appeals on the rulings of lower courts. Unlike the judges of the United States Supreme Court, state judges have a set term of office. There are also lower courts and district courts. Cities and towns may have their own courts. These deal with less important cases and the breaking of local laws.

185

CHAPTER 24 REVIEW

★ **UNDERSTANDING WHAT YOU HAVE READ**

1. The main idea of paragraph 4 is that
   a. all states have legislatures
   b. state governors are elected by people of the state
   c. state constitutions are somewhat like the federal Constitution

2. To grant a pardon for a crime (paragraph 9) is to
   a. set a penalty
   b. forgive
   c. find guilty

3. A republic (paragraph 1) is usually considered to be a
   a. dictatorship
   b. representative government
   c. federal government

4. State governments have been called "big governments" because
   a. state laws cover many different activities
   b. states have greater powers than the federal government
   c. states take care of all education within their borders

5. State governments are like the federal government in that
   a. the governor of each state serves a four-year term
   b. all states have a legislature of two separate houses
   c. all states have divided the powers of government among executive, legislative, and judicial branches

6. A reason why many state governors have been candidates for president might be that
   a. the duties of the governor are much like the duties of the president
   b. the president and the governor must have the same qualifications
   c. all governors serve the same number of terms as the president

7. Some state laws are the same in that all states provide for
   a. capital punishment for some serious crimes
   b. a system of free public education
   c. strict gun-control laws

8. Which of these is NOT a power of state governments?
   a. Inspecting food and those who handle food
   b. Passing laws that tax individual incomes
   c. Taxing goods that come into the state from another state

9. The governor of a state may
   a. prepare the budget for the state
   b. have a vote in the Congress of the United States
   c. grant a pardon for a federal crime

10. Judges of a state supreme court
    a. interpret the meaning of state laws
    b. are appointed by governors in each state
    c. hear cases in which city laws are broken

★ DEVELOPING CRITICAL THINKING SKILLS

A. Categorizing

Tell whether each of the following statements could be a law passed by the federal government (F), or by a state government (S), or a law that could be passed by both federal and state governments (B). Write the numbers from 1 to 6 in your notebook. Then, for each statement, write the letter of the best answer next to each number.

1. A person may vote in the election of a president of the United States at age 18.

2. All cars manufactured for sale in the United States must have a way of controlling pollution from auto gases.

3. People who make a living by installing plumbing in homes must pass a test before they can do such work.

4. Persons found guilty of kidnapping another person and taking the captured person from one state to another will be sent to prison for life.

5. For each package of cigarettes sold, there will be a tax of three cents.

6. The term of office of the governor of the state will be four years.

B. Making Comparisons

The following are some characteristics of state legislatures. Study each one. If they are the same as Congress, write **Same.** If they are different from Congress, explain in one or two sentences how there is a difference.

1. In a majority of states, members of the State Senate serve four-year terms.

2. In some states, lawmakers are paid only when the legislature is in session.

3. Most state legislatures meet for only a few months a year.

4. A bill must pass both Houses of a state legislature before it can become a law.

5. The Speaker for the House of Representatives is usually a member of the majority party.

6. The Senate in most states has fewer members than the House of Representatives.

C. Writing About Citizenship

Write a brief essay on the following topic: What sorts of problems do you think might arise because different states have different laws? In what ways do you think states might work together to relieve some of these problems?

25 STATE GOVERNMENTS: THEIR PROBLEMS

PURPOSES FOR READING

1. To understand why the costs of running state governments are high
2. To learn how states get the funds needed to provide services for their citizens
3. To learn what the federal government does to help states solve their problems

KNOWING NEW WORDS

revenue
(REV uh noo) paragraph 7—government income
EXAMPLE: All the tax money did not provide enough **revenue** to pay expenses.

levy
(LEV ee) paragraph 4—to order to be paid or collected
EXAMPLE: State lawmakers voted to **levy** a tax on theater tickets.

Toll booths on state highways are one source of money for state governments. What other means of collecting money does a state have?

188

Students on a state university campus. Education is just one of the services making demands on state funds. In what ways does the state raise the money to run its government?

1▶ Some called the year 1978 the year of the "Tax Revolt." In many parts of the country, taxpayers showed that they were not pleased about the number of taxes they had to pay and the increasing cost of those taxes. Leaders often stated they were "fed up" with the high taxes of state, city, and town governments. The "revolt" received its greatest boost when California voters approved a plan to limit taxes on property. This was known as Proposition 13. As a result of that vote, taxes on property in California were cut. It will be difficult for the state to raise property taxes in the future. This was the beginning. From states as far apart as Hawaii and Massachusetts, Michigan and Texas, people demanded a chance to approve such limits on taxes in their own states. What does this mean for state governments?

2▶ As the demand for lower tax rates increased, states have been called on to spend more and more money. Many states were able to meet this challenge in the 1980s. Some even had budget surpluses. But this success was short-lived. The amount of federal aid to states has been reduced. As states had to spend more money for prisons, hospitals, and improvements in transportation, the economy suffered a downturn. People bought less and the unemployment rate rose. Income from taxes dropped, but more unemployment benefits had to be paid. Fuel costs rose. Thirty states reported serious deficits in their budgets as the 1990s began. Sharp cuts had to be made in services and state payrolls. In some cases, state taxes were increased.

3▶ States receive federal aid. Likewise, states grant funds to cities and towns to help them solve their problems. Much of the cost of city welfare payments is paid for by the state. States give money to cities to operate their schools and transportation systems. Towns also have money problems, and call for more money from the state. If state budgets are balanced, cities and towns get more. When states show rising debts, cities and towns suffer.

4▶ States help smaller governments in other ways, too. Labor experts from the state help to settle labor disputes. State and local health departments assist each other. Buyers are protected from high costs of gas and electricity by state rules. All of these services cost money. Where does the money come from? The table on page 190 shows the amount of money collected by the 50 states in taxes in 1989. There are many kinds of taxes that states levy in order to get money for their needs.

STATE GOVERNMENT TAX COLLECTION, 1989

Sales taxes...$138.3 billion

General sales	93.4 billion
Motor fuels	18.0
Alcoholic beverages	3.1
Tobacco products	5.0
Insurance	7.3
Public utilities	6.1
Others	5.2

Licenses..$17.7 billion

Motor vehicles	9.4
Corporations	3.0
Driver	.8
Hunting/fishing	.8
Alcoholic beverages	.2
Others	3.5

Individual incomes	$88.7 billion
Corporation income taxes	23.9
Property taxes	5.4
Death, gift taxes	3.5
Other	6.6

TOTAL COLLECTED TAXES ....$284 billion

Source: Bureau of the Census

- What kind of taxes brought the greatest income for states?

- What total was collected in taxes?

- How much was collected from individual income taxes?

- Do states depend heavily on income from property taxes?

- How much was collected from licenses of all kinds?

- Which gave states the greater income— auto license fees or taxes on tobacco sales?

- Which taxes are the same kinds as those listed on the incomes from federal taxes (see table—page 173)?

5▶ Not all states have the same kinds of taxes. Seven states have no income tax at all. Almost all states have some kind of sales tax. The amount of that tax varies from state to state. The most common taxes are levied against alcohol, gasoline, and tobacco. Nearly half the states have lotteries. Money collected from the sale of lottery tickets is often used for a specific purpose, such as education. States also tax property and the buildings on it. This is not one of the big sources of income for states. However, property taxes are one of the main sources of income for city, town, and village governments.

6▶ The table on page 190 shows that states collected over $280 billion from many kinds of taxes and fees. Yet, this amount has not always provided states with enough money to carry out the jobs expected of them. More than $123 billion was granted to state and local governments by the federal government in the same year.

7▶ Money from Washington has come in the form of **grants-in-aid.** These funds have to be used in ways the federal government decides. In 1972, the federal government started **revenue sharing.** In this program, several billion dollars were given to the states each year. The states used these funds as they saw fit. Congress decided, however, to eliminate revenue sharing as one means of reducing the expenses of the federal government. In 1981, Congress passed a **block grant** program. Fifty-seven federal aid programs were brought together in nine blocks or groups. States were given funds for each block. (See chart on page 193.)

8▶ States must cooperate with each

Federal lunch program. What other grants-in-aid does the federal government provide?

other in solving some of their problems. There are good examples of this cooperation. The Port Authority of New York and New Jersey is a corporation that builds and operates bridges, tunnels, and docks in New York Harbor. The harbor contains waterways that lie between New York and New Jersey. Eight states along the Ohio River have an agreement to develop water uses and stop pollution in that river. States in the Southwest have agreements about oil production and costs. Four states along the Delaware River have joined with the federal government to regulate the flow of the water, build dams, and control pollution. Forty states have agreed to accept teachers who are licensed by one state, as licensed in all states. Marriages in one state are accepted in all, as are drivers' licenses. The governors of the states meet each year. At this conference, they discuss and reach an understanding on common problems faced by the 50 states.

CHAPTER 25 REVIEW

★ UNDERSTANDING WHAT YOU HAVE READ

1. An important idea of this chapter is that
   a. the federal government is giving less money to states
   b. people have demanded many services from state governments
   c. drivers' licenses are accepted in all states

2. The main idea of paragraph 1 is that
   a. taxes in California have been reduced
   b. citizens across the country have been demanding a limit on taxes
   c. states cannot raise property taxes

3. An important idea of this chapter is that
   a. states help city and village governments in several ways
   b. city and town governments grant money to states for the states' use
   c. most city and town governments need little help from their states

4. Throughout the country, states receive the greatest amount of revenue from
   a. property taxes
   b. licenses
   c. sales taxes

5. Each of these would be a part of the income of both the states and the federal government EXCEPT
   a. sales taxes
   b. auto license fees
   c. income taxes

6. Which of these statements about sales taxes is true?

   a. The amount of tax on sales is the same in all states
   b. Some states have no sales tax at all
   c. The federal government sets the amount of tax a state may levy

7. States have cooperated with each other in all these ways EXCEPT:
   a. Marriages in one state are legal in other states.
   b. States have made agreements to control pollution along rivers they share.
   c. States have agreed that all should have an income tax.

8. The amount of money states collect in taxes each year
   a. covers all of state expenses
   b. is used only for highways, schools, and school lunches
   c. is not enough to pay for the services people want

9. Governors of states probably like revenue sharing because
   a. they can use the money received for those things they think are needed by the state
   b. the money received must be used to build needed housing in the state
   c. states cannot afford to pay for the cost of school lunches

10. If you were a licensed teacher in your state, you would
    a. be able to teach in most other states
    b. not be able to teach in any other state
    c. have to be licensed by the federal government to teach in another state

★ **DEVELOPING SOCIAL STUDIES SKILLS**

A. Using Tables

Study the table below. Then answer the questions that follow it.

HOW THE FEDERAL GOVERNMENT HELPS STATE AND LOCAL GOVERNMENTS

Outlays of Money, 1989*

Purpose	Amount of money (in billions of dollars)
Medicaid	$34.2
Education	22.4
Highway construction	13.5
Other Public Assistance	11.3
Housing problems	9.1
Child nutrition	4.5
Mass transportation—cities	3.4
Employment and training	3.1
Community development—block grants	3.0
Social Services	2.7
Food stamps	1.4

*estimated
Source: Office of Management and Budget

1. The federal government helps state and local governments in many ways. List and briefly describe ten of those ways. You may have to infer the meaning of some of the purposes listed on the chart. The first two are done for you.
   1. Medicaid—health care for the elderly
   2. Child nutrition—nourishing food for youngsters
   3-10. List others in the same way.

2. In which area does the federal government give state and local governments the most money—subway and bus lines, employment help, or apartments for people of low income? In which of these areas does it provide the least money?

3. How much was granted under "block grants"? What are these funds used for?

4. What do you think is meant by the term public assistance? By the term agricultural price supports?

5. Many federal grants to states and local governments have come with what states call "government red tape." These grants are given to states only if they meet certain conditions. For example, highway funds may be granted only if the state enforces federal speed limit laws. In an organized paragraph, tell why states might object to such grants. Highways are only one of several examples.

B. Interpreting a Graph

Study the graph below. Then answer the questions that follow it.

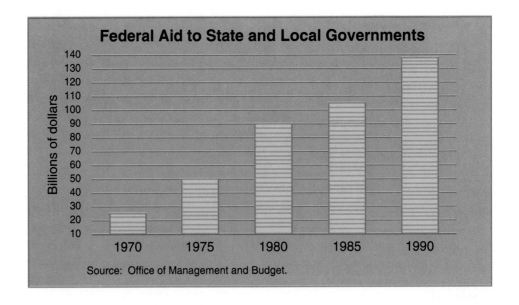

Federal Aid to State and Local Governments

Billions of dollars

1970 1975 1980 1985 1990

Source: Office of Management and Budget.

1. What was the amount of federal aid in 1980? in 1985? in 1990?

2. In which year did the amount of federal aid reach $49 billion? $105 billion?

3. In which period was there the fastest growth in federal aid—from 1975 to 1980, or from 1985 to 1990?

4. Which year showed the greatest amount in federal aid?

5. During which five-year period was there the least increase in the amount of aid?

6. Which of these statements best describes federal aid to states and local governments since 1970?
   a. Federal aid has doubled each year since 1970.
   b. Federal aid to states was greatest in 1985.
   c. There has been a steady increase in federal aid since 1970.

★ DEVELOPING CRITICAL THINKING SKILLS

A. Drawing Conclusions

Do you agree with these conclusions? Give reasons for your answers.

1. States are having problems with the increasing costs of state governments.

2. To provide needed services, cities and villages expect more help from the states.

3. The amount of federal government help to states will continue to increase for several years.

4. States have helped smaller governments in many ways.

5. States would be deeply in debt if it were not for money received from sales taxes.

6. States have been able to balance their budgets with incomes from taxes alone.

7. Some states feel they have no need for a tax on incomes.

8. A good feature of federal aid to states is that states can do whatever they wish with all the money received.

B. Writing About Citizenship

Write an essay answering the following questions: Do you agree with the way federal grants to states are spent? Why or why not? Would you spend the money differently? Tell what you would do, and give your reasons.

26

THE ROLE OF LOCAL GOVERNMENT

PURPOSES FOR READING

1. To understand the kinds of local governments and the powers they have
2. To understand the workings of county governments
3. To recognize some problems of local governments

KNOWING NEW WORDS

duplication
(doo pluh KAY shun) paragraph 10—the act of doing double work or the same thing as another

EXAMPLE: Louise collected money for the Red Cross. By asking for money from the same people, Sherry's work was a **duplication** of effort.

A small town. Why do you think small towns are important to American life?

INC.
VILLAGE OF OCEAN BEACH
NO
AUTO OR BICYCLE RIDING
NO DOGS ALLOWED ON BEACH
NO SOLICITING OR PEDDLING
NO TOPLESS BATHING SUITS ON WALKS
NO DISROBING ON BEACH
NO FOOD OR DRINKS ON BEACH
DOGS MUST BE MUZZLED OR
LEASHED ON WALKS
KEEP OFF DUNES
ORDINANCES STRICTLY ENFORCED
OCEAN BEACH P.D.

Incorporated villages' laws are posted. In what ways does this sign show that the village people influenced the local government?

1 ▶ If you live in a city, you have probably had fun in your city parks. If you take a drive outside the city for 30 miles or so, you might see signs like these along the highway: "Stoneham Village Park," "Bedford Town Park," "Chester County Park," "Forest State Park." You might even see directions to a national park. This wide variety of parks tells you about the different forms of government in our nation—from the village, the smallest, to the national or federal government, the largest. In this chapter, we will learn about local governments, the smallest forms of government . . . village, town, and county. We will look at city governments in the following chapter.

2 ▶ **Villages** make up the smallest unit of government. They are also the government that is closest to the people. It is the government of the local community in which they live. But all villages are not small. They can be of any size. Each state decides what makes up a village. The United States Census Bureau calls communities with more than 2,500 people cities. But there are villages with 50,000 people near large cities. In the same state there are other villages with as few as 200 people.

3 ▶ When enough people have settled in an area, 200 in some states, they can ask the state to be called a village. They are then given certain rights by the state. They are called **incorporated villages.** Incorporated villages can collect taxes and borrow money to pay for such services as education, garbage disposal, and street repairs. A mayor and village council or trustees usually run the village affairs. They are elected by the people. These are only part-time jobs, however. There is not enough village business to have full-time officials. People in the village probably know more about their local government than any other. Since people know what is going on, they can easily tell village officials what they like and don't like.

4 ▶ In many states, there is a **town** government. In most cases, the town is the next unit of government above a village. There may be several villages within a town. (See map page 198.) There are town laws and town taxes as there are village laws and village taxes. In other states, the **township** is the land around and outside of incorporated villages. It may include those villages that have not been granted their own governments by the state. Such villages are

Governments in Two Counties

Legend:
- County Line
- Town Lines
- Incorporated Villages
- Unincorporated Villages

called **unincorporated villages.** For people in unincorporated villages and in rural areas, the town government is the local government. The town has its own police department, collects taxes, builds and repairs roads, and has its own parks. Towns are most often run by a board of supervisors, elected by the people.

5▶ The New England town holds a special place in the history of local government in the United States. The New England town may cover a wide area and include several villages. At one time, when towns had few people, the people of the town met once a month in the local church to make their laws and elect officials. This was pure democracy at work. What the majority of people wanted became the rules of the town. Towns grew too large to continue this practice. But town meetings are still held once a year. Elected officials carry out town business in the period between meetings. Usually three officials called **selectmen** head the town govern-

ment. An important official is the **town clerk.** The clerk records births, marriages, deaths, election results, and issues licenses. There is also a town judge, called the justice of the peace, a road supervisor, and a school committee among others.

6▶ Several towns and villages, and sometimes cities, make up the next highest unit of government, the **county.** This is the largest of local governments. (States are divided into counties; counties into towns or towns and incorporated villages.) Only three states do not have a county system of government—Alaska, Connecticut, and Rhode Island. In Louisiana, a county is called a **parish.** The idea of a county goes back to the early American colonies. New England had its towns. In southern colonies, the county became the important unit of government.

7▶ County governments are not as important as they once were. Many county duties have been taken over by the states or large cities within a county. Yet, they still

New England town meeting. In what ways are the people in this picture showing good citizenship?

have important duties, especially where people are scattered over a wide area. As in other local governments, there is no set size for a county. Cook County, Illinois, includes the city of Chicago. Los Angeles County, California, has over 6 million people. Kings County, New York, is another name for Brooklyn. It has over $2\frac{1}{2}$ million people. Dade County, Florida, includes the city of Miami. There are counties in western states, however, that cover a thousand square miles where only a few hundred people live.

8▶ In most cases, county governments are headed by a group of officials. They are called **county supervisors** or **commissioners.** In recent years a county with a large population may have one person at the head—a **county executive.** This official serves the county much as the governor serves the state. A few counties now have an elected legislature that makes laws for the entire county. As with other local governments, county governments are granted powers by the state. They can borrow money and collect taxes, build roads, establish police forces, and the like.

9▶ County offices are not the same throughout the country. But there are many kinds of county officials that are common to all. There are **judges** who hear criminal cases. They also hear civil cases (those in which there are claims by one person against another). The county **sheriff** supervises the county jail and calls people to jury duty. The **district attorney** represents the

Joaquin Avino, County Manager for Dade County in Florida.

County Court House, Santa Barbara, California. How does the architecture of this building reflect the West Coast region of the country?

county in criminal cases. This official also presents charges against those who have been arrested for crimes. When the cause of death is unclear, a **coroner** investigates (studies closely) the death. The coroner is involved in investigating accidental deaths or where murder is suspected. The county **clerk** keeps records of court cases, the findings of juries, and the sentences given by the court. A **recorder** keeps a record of all land ownership in the county. Another important official is the **assessor**. This county officer determines the value of all property in the county for tax purposes. You will learn more about the assessor's duties in chapter 28.

10 ▶ Have you ever seen rugs lying on a floor with one rug partly on top of another? Two smaller rugs cover the floor when one larger rug would do the job. This is an example of **overlapping.** This means that two or more things do a job that one alone could do. Several governments may perform the same services, too. It may be that such services overlap and can be wasteful.

We call this a **duplication of services.** Some experts think this is one of the problems of local governments.

11 ▶ County, city, town, and state governments all have certain powers. They have the power to tax, to support schools, to build and maintain roads. A person could be paying village taxes, town taxes, county taxes, and state taxes. The roads a person uses within a few miles of home could be village roads, county roads, and state roads. One writer tells of the problem of plowing snow in the area of an eastern city. The state, county, city, and town governments all have highway departments. A state snowplow raises and lowers its plow over and over again as it passes through town, city, and county lines along the highway. There are city police forces, county police forces, and village police forces all within the same county. Some people believe there are too many governments. Others want to keep their local governments as close to the people as possible. What do you think?

CHAPTER 26 REVIEW

★ UNDERSTANDING WHAT YOU HAVE READ

1. An important idea of this chapter is that
   a. village governments are independent of other governments
   b. every village has its own government
   c. there are several kinds of governments in each state

2. The main idea of paragraph 11 is that
   a. local governments have the power to tax
   b. the powers of local governments sometimes overlap
   c. towns may build and repair roads

3. Which is the most accurate statement?
   a. A town may include several counties.
   b. A village is made up of several towns.
   c. A county may include villages and towns.

4. Powers of village governments are granted by the
   a. state
   b. federal government
   c. city

5. A coroner and recorder would be officials of which government?
   a. Village
   b. Town
   c. County

6. An incorporated village is one that
   a. has its own government
   b. has the same powers as cities
   c. is ruled by county laws only

7. Government offices that are full-time jobs would most likely be found at which level of government?
   a. Incorporated villages
   b. Unincorporated villages
   c. Counties

8. The New England town meeting is called an example of pure democracy because
   a. representatives are elected by the people to run the town government
   b. all citizens meet and make rules for the town
   c. selectmen head the town government

9. A county
   a. may be any size with any number of people
   b. is any area that has more than 2,500 people
   c. is the only local government allowed to collect taxes

10. For people in unincorporated villages, the government closest to them is the
    a. town
    b. county
    c. state

★ DEVELOPING SOCIAL STUDIES SKILLS

A. Using Map Keys and Scales

The map on page 202 shows the problems of overlapping governments within one county, Onondaga County, in New York State. Study the map and answer the questions that follow. Note that the county includes the city government of Syracuse.

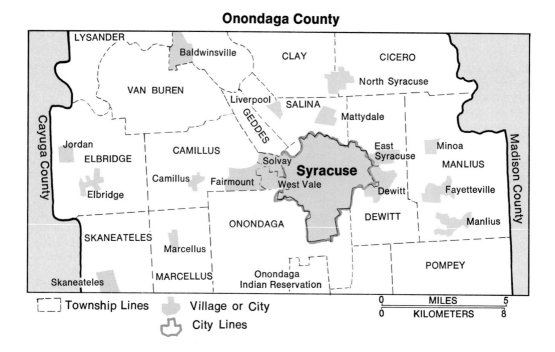

Onondaga County

1. How many types of government are shown on the map?

2. How many towns (townships) are shown on the map?

3. How many governments serve the village of Fayetteville?

4. Many people leave the village of Fayetteville, travel through the village of DeWitt, to work in Syracuse. Approximately how far do they travel?

5. Do the people of Syracuse have to obey the laws of Onondaga County? Give reasons to support your answer.

B. Overlapping Governments

1. Use the map above as a guide. Suppose the city of Syracuse (or any city like it) wanted a six-lane highway to bring workers and visitors into the city faster. What other governments might have a part in planning the highway? Who might want such a highway? Who might not want it?

2. Check on services that might be overlapping. In a phone book, look under the headings for county, town, and village governments. Is there a health department for each government? Are there any other cases in which there is a separate department under the listing for each government? Try highways, streets, sanitation, among others.

HELPING YOUR COMMUNITY

Good citizens should be interested in the quality of life of the people in their community. In Bowie, Maryland, students had many people sign petitions in a campaign to have the city council pass a "bottle" law. As a result, the council banned bottles that were "non-returnable." In Longwood, New York, junior high school students formed a group called Students Together Against Racism, (STAR). Later, as high school students, they conducted "anti-bias" workshops, trying to eliminate the ignorance that causes racism. These are examples of the kind of action civic-minded students can take.

You can also get involved and help your community. By using the following steps, it may be possible for the students in your class and possibly your school to help your community.

1. Each member of your class should write down two or three problems that, if solved, would improve the quality of life in your community.

2. In small groups, you and your fellow students should place these problems in order of importance.

3. The results from each group should be shared with your class and a class list of problems be made.

4. You, your classmates, and your teacher should then decide which problem would be best to try to help solve. If it is a problem that could be solved by providing people with information, do research on it and publish a pamphlet or fact sheet. For example, if you have chosen tenants' rights as a topic, the pamphlet might be entitled "What Tenants Need to Know." The information in it might be about their rights in regard to rent, eviction, heat, upkeep of the building, and so forth. The pamphlet could then be given out with the aid of parent and other civic groups.

Another way a problem might be solved is to bring it to public attention. You and fellow students might publicize the problem in school and around town. You might produce announcements, flyers, posters, and letters to leading citizens. You might want to get your whole school involved. If so, choose a representative to speak to the student government and the principal.

Another approach is to make up a petition and have as many people as possible sign it. The petition would then be presented to the proper official. You would need to know who is in your local government.

You might decide to support an existing organization already working on solving the problem. Then you could organize a fund raiser such as a bake sale, special ball game, or a danceathon.

Do not assume that you will be entirely successful with your project. After you have completed the project, discuss what went right and what went wrong, and why. If you were to do it again, what would you do differently?

THE CHALLENGES OF CITY GOVERNMENT

27

PURPOSES FOR READING

1. To learn the powers and duties of city governments
2. To understand the kinds of city governments
3. To appreciate some of the problems facing cities in the United States

KNOWING NEW WORDS

city council
(SIT ee KOUN sul) paragraph 5—a group of people who make city laws
EXAMPLE: Voters crowded into the meeting room when the **city council** talked over the idea of a city income tax.

career
(kuh REER) paragraph 6—an occupation or job that a person takes as his or her life's work
EXAMPLE: Tom helped Mr. Fox cut pipe as the first step in making plumbing his **career.**

1. Who is being hit with snowballs?

2. What do the snowballs represent?

3. Why doesn't the central figure escape?

4. Who might come to the help of the city?

5. What is a good title for this cartoon?

1 ▶ The cartoon on page 204 shows us some problems of our older cities. If you cannot answer some of the questions, you will be able to answer them after you have studied this chapter. But first, we will see how cities are governed.

2 ▶ Cities, like the governments you studied in chapter 26, are "children" of the state. The parent government, the state, grants powers to city governments in a **charter.** The charter states the rights of the city government—the laws it is allowed to pass. The charter is the constitution of the city. Not all city charters are the same. They may be different even from city to city within the same state.

3 ▶ How many people make a city? The number differs from state to state. The United States Bureau of the Census counts 5,000 people living in one place under one government as a city. One thousand people may be called a city in Nebraska. It takes 10,000 people to make a city in Pennsylvania. In other states, there are villages with more people than the cities next to them. A city exists when the state says it does— when it is granted a charter. The city can offer many services to its people. Cities have charge over streets, sewers, water supply, public schools, police and fire departments, health services, and zoning laws. States do not give cities power to make all kinds of laws, however. For example, cities can only levy and collect taxes the state allows.

4 ▶ The charter tells the type of government the city may have. The oldest form of city government is the **mayor-council** type. The largest cities in the United States have this form. The mayor is the chief executive

of the city. He or she is elected by the people. The job of mayor in the city is like that of governor in the state. As the head of the city government, the mayor is in charge of the city budget. Other duties include signing city laws and naming the heads of police, education, health, and other city departments.

5 ▶ In the mayor-council form of government, the members of the city council make the laws for the city. They are also elected by the people. The mayor may veto a law passed by the council, and the council may pass a law over the mayor's veto. In most city governments of this type, citizens may attend council meetings. Often citizens

Fifth Avenue, New York City. Why are big cities important to American life?

Citizen speaking at a city council meeting, Worcester, Massachusetts. What important American freedom does this scene represent?

are given a chance to speak out during council sessions.

6▶ Another type of city government is the **city-manager** form. There is a council here also, and it is the lawmaking body for the city. But there is no elected mayor. Instead, the council chooses a manager to run the city. Managers have studied about cities and make a career of running cities. This is their profession. The city manager of a large city probably spent some years as the manager of a smaller city first. San Antonio in Texas, Norfolk in Virginia, and Cincinnati in Ohio are three of the large cities that have this kind of government.

7▶ Other cities such as Portland, Oregon, and Tulsa, Oklahoma, have the **commission type** of government. They are governed by commissioners. The voters elect commissioners to run the city government. The commissioners not only make city laws, they also direct city departments. They are not people who specialize in city government as the city managers do. They can be business people, workers, professional people—whomever the voters elect.

The commissioners elect a mayor, but he or she has little power.

8▶ Many people believe cities should have more power to run their affairs than their states give them. This power is called **home rule.** People who want more home rule want the voters of the city to make their own charter. This would mean that

George Caravalho, city manager of Santa Clarita, California.

cities could raise money without asking the state government if they are allowed to do so. Cities have found that they must ask their state legislatures for money each year. It is argued that many members of state legislatures do not live in cities. Yet, they have a vote in deciding what taxes cities can collect.

9 ▶ Large cities throughout the country, but chiefly in the North and East, are having problems. The cost of city governments continues to rise. Large cities are running out of ways to raise money for the services they provide. More and more cities are depending on help from federal and state governments to see them through each year. Cities get their incomes chiefly from taxes on property, sales taxes, license fees, and some income taxes. (You will learn more about these taxes in Chapter 28.) Yet, these sources have not been enough to meet the cities' needs. The cities need more help to solve their problems.

10 ▶ One cause of the many problems of cities is that people have been leaving the older cities of the country. The **suburbs,** the smaller cities and towns around the large cities, have grown in size. People are now moving even farther away into rural areas. Or, they are moving to newer cities in the South and West. These have been called the **Sunbelt** cities. (The chart on page 208 shows some of the fastest-growing cities in the nation.)

11 ▶ Many metropolitan areas have also grown in recent years. A metropolitan area consists of a large central city and nearby smaller cities and towns. Among the fastest-growing metropolitan areas are Atlanta, Georgia; Dallas-Fort Worth, Texas; Houston-Galveston, Texas; Orlando, Florida; San Diego, California; and Phoenix, Arizona.

12 ▶ Those people who leave cities are usually ones with good incomes. When they leave, the city loses people who are

Skyline of Houston, Texas. Why do you think people move to Sunbelt cities?

LARGE CITIES OF THE UNITED STATES SHOWING GREAT GAINS IN POPULATION FROM 1980–1990

City	Population	Percent Gain
Irvine, California	110,360	77.6
Las Vegas, Nevada	258,295	56.3
Virginia Beach, Virginia	393,069	49.9
Scottsdale, Arizona	130,069	45.2
San Bernadino, California	164,164	36.4
Reno, Nevada	133,850	32.8
Austin, Texas	465,622	25.0
El Paso, Texas	515,342	21.2
Columbus, Ohio	632,910	12.0

Note: A 20 percent gain means that one person has been added to the population for each five people who lived there in 1970.

able to pay the taxes that provide the city with income for its services. Those that stay must pay higher taxes. Yet, those that remain are often the poorer families, unable to keep up the quality of city life. If the money does not come into the city treasury, roads are not repaired, streets are not cleaned, trains and buses are not kept in good condition, and workers cannot be paid. The city runs down.

13▶ There are other problems as a result of the movement of people out of the city. Businesses in the city need customers. If the customers, and those with good incomes, leave the city, some stores and businesses will have to close down. People lose jobs as a result. As these conditions continue and the city becomes poorer, problems multiply. Crime also increases. Problems cause more people to leave for the suburbs and beyond. Add heavy traffic and pollution to the problems of crime, poverty, and unemployment, and city governments find they need help. These governments look to other sources for help in solving their problems.

CHAPTER 27 REVIEW

1. The main idea of paragraph 9 is that
   a. large cities cannot raise enough money to pay for needed services
   b. cities have many ways of raising money
   c. towns and village governments are helping cities

2. A large city newspaper has said that "the cities are becoming the homes of the poor." This idea is contained in paragraph
   a. 8
   b. 10
   c. 12

3. **Home rule** refers to
   a. federal help for cities
   b. the mayor-council type of government
   c. the power of cities to run their own affairs

4. The type of city government that is most like the federal government is the
   a. mayor-council form
   b. city-manager form
   c. commission form

5. The taxing powers of city governments are limited because
   a. no property can be taxed
   b. the state decides what the tax powers of city governments are
   c. cities cannot tax the incomes of people

6. Some people favor more home rule for cities because
   a. the city would then raise money without having to ask permission of state lawmakers
   b. cities would then be independent of state governments
   c. the federal government would then give more aid to cities

7. It is said that city governments are "children" of parent state governments because
   a. people have left cities in search of a better life
   b. states give charters to cities listing their rights and duties
   c. a city's income is dependent chiefly on an "allowance" from the state

8. The most important job of the city council is that of
   a. naming the heads of city departments
   b. preparing the city budget
   c. passing city laws

9. The cities in the United States that are growing fastest in population are located
   a. in the Northeast
   b. along or near the Great Lakes
   c. in the South and West

★ **DEVELOPING SOCIAL STUDIES SKILLS**

Study the graph on the next page. It shows the populations of large cities in the United States. Answer the questions that follow the graph.

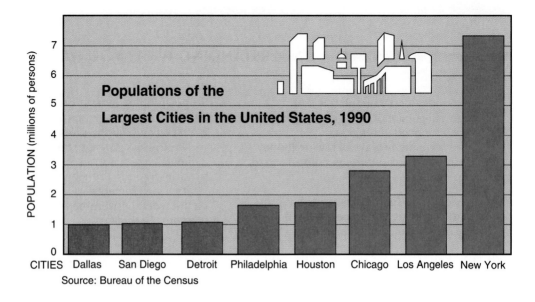

Populations of the Largest Cities in the United States, 1990

POPULATION (millions of persons)

CITIES: Dallas, San Diego, Detroit, Philadelphia, Houston, Chicago, Los Angeles, New York

Source: Bureau of the Census

1. Which city on the graph had the largest metropolitan area population in 1990?

2. Which city on the graph had the smallest metropolitan area populaton in 1990?

3. In which part of the United States are most of the cities located?

4 How many cities are located in the eastern part of the country?

5. How many are located in the western part?

6. Make a generalization that shows what the graph tells us.

★ DEVELOPING CRITICAL THINKING SKILLS

A. Making Generalizations

Tell whether these generalizations are correct or incorrect. Rewrite each incorrect generalization to make it correct.

1. In all forms of city government, city laws are made by elected officials.

2. Cities are depending more and more on money from the state and federal governments to provide services.

3. The city-manager form of government is used in some large cities of our country.

4. The right of a city to provide water supply, hospitals, and police is granted by its charter.

5. City charters are the same throughout the country.

6. In cities that have a commission type of government, the commissioners have made a career of managing city governments.

7. The largest number of state governors believe that cities should have more power to govern themselves.

8. Like other costs, the costs of running city governments are rising.

INCOME FOR LOCAL GOVERNMENTS

PURPOSES FOR READING

1. To learn the sources of moneys needed by local governments to provide services for their citizens
2. To understand how property taxes are assessed, and how local governments depend upon them

Elizabeth Watson, the police chief of Houston, Texas.

1▶ In previous chapters you learned where federal and state governments get tax funds. In this chapter we will learn about the tax funds for local governments—counties, cities, towns, and villages. The table on page 212 should help you to compare sources of tax incomes of these local kinds of government.

MAJOR SOURCES OF GOVERNMENT INCOME

FEDERAL GOVERNMENT (1990)

Income taxes (personal and corporation)	$560.4 billion
Social insurance taxes	380.0 billion
Excise taxes	17.5 billion

STATE GOVERNMENTS (1989)

Sales taxes	$138.3 billion
Income taxes (personal and corporation)	112.6 billion
Property taxes	5.4 billion
Motor vehicles	9.4 billion

LOCAL GOVERNMENTS (1989)

Property taxes	$116.6 billion
Sales taxes	24.4 billion
Income taxes	9.6 billion
Public utilities taxes	4.1 billion
Tobacco and alcohol taxes	.5 billion

Source: Statistical Abstract of the U.S.

a. There are two kinds of taxes among the top three sources of tax incomes for federal and state governments. What are they?

b. The top three sources of revenue for state and local governments are the same. What are they?

c. What is the top source of income for the federal government? for state governments? for local governments?

Three kinds of taxes are the chief sources of revenue (income) for local governments. Yet, among the three kinds, local governments depend heavily on property taxes. Still, many local governments have sales taxes and some even have taxes on personal incomes. Let us see why these taxes are used, and how they work in practice.

2▶ Some people believe that the **income tax** is the fairest kind of tax. People pay taxes according to their ability to pay. The higher the income, the higher the tax rate. Persons with a low salary might pay 5 percent of their income in taxes. A person with a higher salary might pay 10 percent; a person with a still higher salary might pay 20 percent or 25 percent. This is called a **graduated tax**—it increases in steps as the income increases. This kind of tax was not always allowed by law. It took the 16th Amendment to the Constitution, in 1913, to allow Congress to tax incomes at different rates. Since that time, nearly all income taxes have been graduated taxes.

3▶ Local governments depend upon **sales taxes** for a good part of their income. Sales taxes are an easy way of raising money. A tax is placed on special articles that people buy often. The pennies, nickels, and dollars flow into the treasury of local governments with every purchase ($24.4 billion in 1989). But to many people, sales taxes are not fair. Everyone pays the same sales tax, rich and poor alike. A person who pays $75 for a jacket may pay $4.00 in tax also. For the person making $250 a week, this $4.00 in tax is a greater share of his or her income than it is for a person making $1,000 a week. Not all kinds of goods have a sales tax, however. Necessities, such as food and medicines, usually are not taxed.

4▶ **Property taxes** provide the largest income for local governments. Even states have property taxes. Property is the land and the buildings on it. For tax purposes, a value is placed on a piece of property. This may or may not be the real selling price of the land and buildings. The value is determined by the village, town, city, or county **assessor.** (See chapter 26, page 200.) The value of the property for tax purposes is called the **assessed value.** This amount may be raised if the building on the land is made larger or more attractive. The amount may be lowered if a building becomes old or is torn down. By adding together the value of all the land in the village, for example, the government then knows what the tax rate must be to raise money for village services.

5▶ The local government then sets a tax rate. That rate determines the amount of tax on each piece of property. Let us look at an example:

Suppose the tax rate is set at $2 for each $100 of assessed value. You own a house and land that has been valued at $25,000.

Sign announcing meeting against a tax hike. What might be the reasons *for* the tax hike? What might be the reasons *against* the tax hike?

There are 250 hundreds in $25,000, or 250 units of $100 each. Your tax is $2 for each $100 unit. Multiplying $2 by 250 units of $100, we find that your property tax is $500 a year.

Is your property valued at $100,000? In $100,000 there are 1,000 units of $100 each. Your property tax would be $2 times 1,000 units, or $2,000.

6► What happens if the local government needs more or less money to provide services? It can then either (1) raise or reduce the assessed value of your property, or (2) raise or reduce the tax rate. Since changing the value of all property in the village would be a big job, usually governments will simply raise or lower the tax rate. If it were reduced to $1.50 for each $100 of assessed value, in the example mentioned in paragraph 5, you would pay less property tax. If the rate were raised to $2.50 per $100 value, you would pay more property tax.

7► The map on this page shows a block in the imaginary village of TAXA. The money figure for each property is the assessed value of the property. You should learn several things about property taxes from the map.

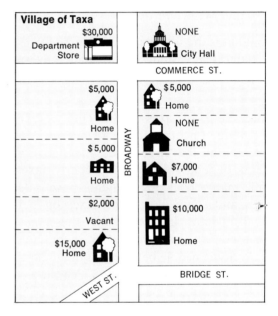

- Do all homes and property have the same assessed value?

- What would cause some property to have a higher value than others?

- Why does the vacant land have a lower value than the others?

- Why does the department store have a higher value than even the largest home and land?

- Why do you think city hall and the church have no assessed value listed? Would there be other properties with no property tax?

High school chemistry class. What methods are local governments using to get support for education?

8► You can tell from the study of property taxes that the governments of some communities have more money than others. Those with large homes will receive a larger amount in property taxes. Businesses, including factories, also add to the property tax paid. If houses and buildings are not kept up, however, they will lose value. Owners will then pay lower taxes. This means that the city or village will have to raise the taxes of others or reduce services. Either way, this may cause people to look elsewhere to live or set up businesses. This is what is happening in many communities today.

9► Supporting schools is another problem. Local governments have provided for schools from taxes on property. This means that communities with more valuable homes can pay more for their schools than poorer communities. Some believe this is unfair. Rich communities have a lot of money for schools. Poor communities do not. Many states are now trying to find ways to support education other than through property taxes alone. Some states are supporting education in poorer com-

munities with a greater share of state money than is given to wealthier communities.

10► There are other sources of money

Firefighters. New equipment has helped to put out fires more quickly. It is also more expensive. What are some ways cities can raise money for such equipment?

215

The pictures on this page represent different kinds of taxes: sales tax and income tax. Which do you think is the fairest tax for all the people? Why? What other kinds of taxes are there?

for local governments. One is by selling bonds. (See page 177.) Bonds are usually sold when the local government has an expense that can be paid off over several years. Such an expense might be a new building, a sewage treatment plant, or new fire-fighting equipment. The community has the use of the building or equipment while the holders of bonds are being repaid. State and federal governments are also sources of money. Both give a great amount of aid to local governments as you have read. (See chapter 25, page 189.) States, in turn, look for help from the federal government, too. For many cities, money from the state and federal governments is so important that cities cannot provide services without that help. State and federal aid make up one-third of the total income of some cities.

CHAPTER 28 REVIEW

★ UNDERSTANDING WHAT YOU HAVE READ

1. A good title for paragraph 3 might be
   a. "Sales Tax—A Tax on the Rich"
   b. "Sales Tax—Easy to Collect, But Unfair"
   c. "Sales Tax—Taking Food From the Family"

2. The main idea of paragraph 9 is that
   a. schools are usually supported from taxes on property
   b. towns have a problem in supporting schools
   c. property taxes favor poor communities

3. Which of these is matched correctly with its chief source of income?
   a. Federal government—income tax
   b. State government—property tax
   c. City and village governments—sales tax

4. If a community were to build a new plant for treating garbage, it would probably get the money from
   a. sales taxes
   b. property taxes
   c. the sale of bonds

5. Which of these is usually a graduated tax?
   a. Income tax
   b. Sales tax
   c. Property tax

6. If a building on a piece of property is torn down, the
   a. assessed value remains the same
   b. assessed value is lowered
   c. assessed value is raised

7. The property tax rate is $1 for each $100 of assessed value. Your property is assessed at $10,000. Your property tax would be
   a. $10
   b. $100
   c. $1,000

8. Which of these statements is true?
   a. All homes and property on the same block will have the same value.
   b. Vacant property will probably have a lower assessed value than the same size property with a house on it.
   c. Churches and government buildings pay property taxes.

9. People will probably begin to move away from some cities and villages when

   a. property has a growing value and taxes are low
   b. a tax is placed on some special items in stores
   c. the value of property drops and taxes are high

10. A growing source of income for local governments comes from
   a. state and federal governments
   b. a tax on tobacco
   c. auto license fees

★ DEVELOPING CRITICAL THINKING SKILLS

A. Interpreting a Cartoon

1. What would be a good title for this cartoon?

2. Why are the federal and state governments, as well as citizens, shown in this cartoon?

3. Which is the most important source of income for local government?

4. When consumers buy things, what tax might they have to pay to local government?

B. Interpreting a Table

What do local governments do with their income from taxes, bonds, and state and federal aid? Not every one spends its income the same way. One might spend much on education, while another might spend more on fire protection. The table on page 219 shows how Kansas City, Missouri, used its income in a recent year.

Spending for Each Dollar of Income in
Kansas City, Missouri

Police and fire protection	20 cents
Water utility	8 cents
Airports	7 cents
Housing	6 cents
Sewage	6 cents
Education	5 cents
Highways	5 cents
Payment of debts	5 cents
Hospitals	4 cents
Other	34 cents

Source: Bureau of the Census

1. The most money is spent by the city for what purpose?

2. Which takes more of the government's income—airports or education?

3. How much of the city income is spent paying back money owed by the city?

4. What might be some of the expenses listed under "Others"?

5. How much money is needed to take care of all health needs, including hospitals?

6. If the community wanted to build two new hospitals and equip them, where would the money come from?

C. Writing About Citizenship

Write a brief essay on the following topic: Do you think that the local governments' method of getting revenue is equally fair to everybody? Why or why not? If you do not think it is fair, what would you do to make it more fair?

★ KNOWING NEW TERMS

Match the terms in Column A with the description in Column B.

Column A

1. Council
2. Assessor
3. Charter
4. Revenue

Column B

a. The "constitution" of city government
b. Refers to income of government
c. The lawmaking body of city government
d. One who determines the value of property

Unit 6

OUR SYSTEM OF JUSTICE

The Supreme Court Building, Washington, D.C.

CRIME AND CRIMINALS

29

PURPOSES FOR READING

1. To understand the serious nature of the crime problem in the United States
2. To know the kinds of people who most often commit crimes
3. To learn something about the victims of crime

KNOWING NEW WORDS

assault
(uh SAWLT) paragraph 2—violent attack
EXAMPLE: During the **assault**, the men were beaten.

devices
(div VYS iz) paragraphv 8—machines or things made for particular purposes
EXAMPLE: We asked her to put locks or other **devices** on the doors to ensure our safety.

crime rate
(KRYM rayt) paragraph 3—the number of crimes for a certain part of the population
EXAMPLE: The **crime rate** in the United States is increasing.

traits
(TRAYTS) paragraph 6— features, qualities, characteristics of a person
EXAMPLE: You can tell from actions that kindness and honesty are his outstanding **traits.**

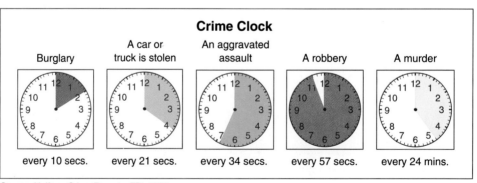

Crime Clock

Burglary	A car or truck is stolen	An aggravated assault	A robbery	A murder
every 10 secs.	every 21 secs.	every 34 secs.	every 57 secs.	every 24 mins.

Source: Uniform Crime Reports, FBI, 1989.

This robbery took place in a small auto-repair shop.

1► The information in the "Crime Clock" at the bottom of page 222 tells the story of crime in the United States. When people in large cities are asked what they consider to be their chief problem, "crime" is usually the answer. Crime is mentioned more often than the cost of living. It troubles people more than poor housing or pollution.

2► Unfortunately, crime has been on the rise since the 1960s. The largest percentage of crimes are crimes against property such as burglary and auto theft. About 10 percent of crimes are violent crimes against people, such as assault and murder. Drug-related crimes have shown a particularly alarming growth. In many people's minds, crime is especially related to large cities. While many crimes do occur in cities, and such cities have the highest crime rates, crime in suburbs and rural areas has been growing at a faster rate than in the large cities. Suburbs are no longer safe from serious crimes. It has been found that the number of criminals who repeatedly commit crimes has also been growing in the suburbs.

3► How accurate is our information on the number of crimes? The government gets information only about crimes that are reported to the police. The decrease in the number of crimes is good news. However, some experts in police work believe there are many crimes not reported to the police. Some insist that the **crime rate** in some large cities is twice as high as that reported. The figures on crime cannot be completely accurate. A large number of Americans simply do not feel that it is worthwhile to report that they have been victims of criminal acts. It is known that some victims are afraid to appear in court.

They do not want to face the person they accuse of attacking them. Others may not want to take time from work to appear in court. In some cases, they may have to appear five times or more before a case is decided.

4▶ How the nation is doing in the battle against crime is determined by the crime rate. (Paragraph 2 stated there is a rising crime rate in the suburbs.) This is different from the number of crimes committed. You would expect that there would be more criminal acts among 100 people than among 10. And you would expect more crime among 1,000 than among 100. In

determining the crime rate, we note the number of crimes for a certain part of the population. The FBI gets information about crimes in cities, towns, and rural areas. The FBI figures out each area's murder rate, that is, the number of murders for each 100,000 people. In the table on this page, for example, see St. Louis, Missouri. How could you find the approximate number of murders from this information? Multiply the rate (71.8) times the number of times 100,000 goes into the population figure (404,000÷100,000 = 4.04). In this case, 71.8 X 4.04 = 290. So St. Louis had approximately 290 murders.

Murder Rates Among Large Cities		
City	Murder Rate per 100,000	Population
St. Louis, MO	71.8	404,000
Richmond, VA	39.9	213,000
Miami, Fl	34.2	371,000
Dallas, TX	31.9	987,000
Atlanta, GA	27.1	420,000
Chicago, IL	22.2	2,977,000
New York, NY	19.5	7,300,000
Boston, MA	15.5	578,000
Denver, CO	15.0	492,000
Seattle, WA	12.4	502,000
Minneapolis, MN	7.8	345,000

Source: Uniform Crime Report, FBI, 1989.

What does the table on page 224 tell us about crime rates? See if you can tell whether these statements are true or false.

a. Atlanta had a higher murder rate than did Dallas.

b. All the large cities had the highest murder rates.

c. There was a greater number of murders in Seattle than in Miami.

d. There were over 70 murders in Richmond in the year reported.

5▶ Why has there been an increase in crime? The rapid increase in the sale and use of drugs has a great deal to do with the growth of crime. In the nation's three largest cities, more than seven out of ten men tested positive for drugs when they were arrested. In other large cities, almost half the women suspects tested positive for drugs. The drug menace has spread to the suburbs and rural areas as well. People who are addicted to drugs commit crimes to get the money to buy drugs. The behavior of a person under the influence of drugs cannot be predicted. Even though an increasing number of drug dealers have been jailed, this has made only a small dent in the drug trade. The drug culture has become a threat to the quality of life in the nation.

6▶ What kind of person commits a crime? Studies have been made to find answers to this question. Many different answers have been suggested. A prison doctor in the 1800s said that there is such a thing as a "criminal type." Those traits that make up a criminal are born in a person. Others claim that poverty is a chief cause of crime. Some who study how people

behave believe that persons turn to crime as a result of things that have happened to them in early life. Law officials have looked into cases of those who commit violent crimes. They offer some answers.

7▶ Most murders are not planned. They are the result of "a mad moment of anger." Most are caused by a family argument or a dispute with a friend. The victim is most often someone the murderer knows. Some murders happen during robberies. The robbery was planned but the killing was accidental. Over 90 percent of murders are committed by males against males. Two-thirds of accused murderers have had criminal records. Most violent crimes are committed by people between the ages of 16 and 25. These criminals usually come from families with low incomes. More often than not, they live in large cities. In many cases, the offender is living with one parent or none at all. Of course most people are not criminals—no matter what their background or living conditions.

8▶ Who are the victims of violent crimes? Most victims know their attackers. In addition, African Americans are usually victims of other African Americans. Whites are most often victims of whites. Nearly half the murder victims have drugs

When people are arrested, they are fingerprinted. Why do you think this is done?

or alcohol in their blood. Half of the victims have had some kind of criminal record. Males are normally the victims of crime. Elderly people who live in cities have been a growing target for criminals. Many of the elderly live in older neighborhoods where there is likely to be more crime. They are easy targets for the professional thief or gangs of teenagers. These older people often walk to stores and parks or use public transportation. They can't afford safety devices in their homes or apartments. Often, they don't report crimes. Sometimes they are afraid to. They are poor. The largest number of victims are poor and live in the poorest sections of cities.

9 ► What are the causes of crime? Many studies have been made. But no one can give one sure answer to the question. Poverty and poor living conditions seem to be important parts of the crime picture. Violent criminals and their victims are most often persons with low incomes from poor neighborhoods. Racial discrimination is linked with poverty. Poor African Americans and Hispanic Americans often

have special problems. Some jobs are closed to them because of prejudice against either their skin color or language. There are also many poor whites who cannot get jobs. Many from all these groups drop out of school and cannot find work. Some are so discouraged that they drop out of the job market, too. They join the hard-core unemployed. They may turn to crime to get what they want or need, or simply for excitement. They may begin to use or sell drugs, or both. It is difficult to   break this cycle.Throughout the nation's history, these conditions have been true for members of many groups who suffered from prejudice and poverty.

10 ► What are other causes of crime? The FBI points out that there is about one serious crime every two seconds. Of these crimes, only one in five ends in arrest. Witnesses are needed to make an arrest. Police say that many people who could help in making an arrest do not speak up. When witnesses do not speak up, they are helping the spread of crime. Some people say it is too easy to get handguns. Most murders kill their victims with handguns.

To help stop crimes against the elderly, many young people have volunteered to escort senior citizens as they travel around the city.

As already noted, there is a connection between drug use and crime. Some people believe there is too much violence on TV. They claim that people of weak character try to carry out the violent acts they have seen on the screen. There are those who say there is not enough police protection. Many blame the number of crimes on light sentences received by those who have been found guilty.

11▶ There are all types of crimes and criminals. Not all criminals commit violent acts. There are also white-collar criminals. These are most often adults. Many have above-average incomes. These are the people who steal secretly from businesses where they work. The use of computers has made business crimes easier. An embezzler can get $100,000 by simply changing information in a computer. Other white-collar criminals cheat on income tax returns or forge checks. These criminals like to think that no one else is hurt by the

Criminals are found in all income groups and among all professions.

crimes they commit. White-collar crimes cost billions of dollars more than the violent crimes that are committed throughout the nation.

CHAPTER 29 REVIEW

★ UNDERSTANDING WHAT YOU HAVE READ

1. A summary of the ideas in paragraphs 7 and 8 might be the following:
   a. It doesn't take much thought to commit a robbery.
   b. Victims of violent crimes are often poor.
   c. The elderly are prisoners of fear.

2. Most victims of violent crimes are
   a. poor
   b. wealthy
   c. middle class

3. Which of these is **not** offered as a cause of crime?
   a. There are criminal types.
   b. There are not enough police.
   c. Guilty persons receive long prison terms.

4. The best meaning for "hard-core unemployed" in paragraph 9 is
   a. very strong people
   b. people who are almost never able to get jobs
   c. people who fight for their rights

5. Social conditions **always** refer to
   a. people
   b. taxes
   c. housing

6. Most crimes in cities are committed in
   a. neighborhoods of well-to-do people
   b. neighborhoods of middle-class people
   c. neighborhoods of poor people

7. Which of these may be called white-collar crime?

a. Robbing a bank
b. Signing another person's name to a check
c. Threatening to damage a store unless the owner pays for protection

8. Which of these is often connected with the crime of murder?
   a. Forged checks
   b. Handguns
   c. Shoplifted property

★ DEVELOPING CRITICAL THINKING SKILLS

A. Looking at Both Sides

Some people believe that there would be less crime if gun-control laws were more strict. They have tried to get Congress to pass a national law to control the ownership of guns. The National Rifle Association has led the fight against such laws. It believes that such laws would limit the freedom of Americans. The following are arguments for and against gun-control laws. After reading each argument, answer the questions that follow it.

Further Firearms Laws Aren't Needed

The majority of privately owned firearms in American homes (handguns included) are in collections or are used for hunting . . . or recreational shooting, or self-defense.

. . . In areas with a high rate of ownership of firearms, burglary rates dip below those of their neighbors who don't own guns. . . .

Those who revert to murder to solve family disputes are people with long histories of violent and criminal behavior. They have, on the average, prior arrest records, . . . their victims had nearly as many, and they [the murderers] are, for the most part, mentally disturbed and drunk during the argument. They are already prohibited [forbidden] by federal law from owning guns. Violent people and alcohol spell potential for murder, regardless of the weapon available.

A nationwide poll of American opinion of firearms ownership and gun-control laws . . . found that a majority of those keeping firearms for self-protection were inner-city minority members. These people are not street criminals, but rather law-abiding owners of small businesses who struggle daily, without benefit of theft insurance . . . or effective police protection given their more affluent [wealthier] neighbors.

John Aquilino, Editor,
Reports from Washington.
National Rifle Association

In your notebook, write ONLY those arguments with which Mr. Aquilino would agree.

1. Most people have guns for self-defense.

2. People who commit the crime of murder have been arrested before.

3. People who have records of violence and use alcohol may commit murder whether or not they have a gun.

4. Guns don't cause murder, people do.

5. Many people who own small businesses need guns in cities for self-defense.

6. Police protection is at its best in poorer sections of cities.

7. In neighborhoods where a large number of people have guns, there are few robberies.

It's Time to End Our Romance with Guns

Before the West was won, the gun was a trusted companion, a loyal servant and the instrument of law and order. It [leveled] the differences between the powerful and the weak, the educated and the unschooled, rich and poor. . . . The romance with handguns took root.

Like so many romances, this one soured. A popular, youthful President was gunned down. The greatest black leader in our lifetime and other national leaders were assassinated. Riots and snipers in cities across the country brought havoc [destruction] to city life.

. . . The mass media [TV, movies, newspapers] have drowned viewers in violence. . . . As a result, violence has become commonplace. . . . Guns are no longer romantic or repulsive. They are simply accepted as another part of the landscape. . . .

. . . Are guns the first line of defense against criminals? Then explain why there are so many accidental gun deaths, and why the family handgun is six times more likely to be used against a member of one's family or an acquaintance than against a criminal intruder? . . .

Gun-related homicides have become the leading cause of death among black males between the ages of 15 and 44—exceeding cancer and heart disease. . . . Americans are no more violent than other peoples. It's just that they are more lethal [deadly] because of their devotion to technology of all kinds and far easier access to murderous weapons.

John Conyers, member of Congress
from Michigan

In your notebook, write ONLY those statements with which Representative Conyers would agree.

1. Americans have always been in love with guns.

2. Americans are the most violent people on earth.

3. People use guns to kill members of their family and friends more often than to kill robbers.

4. The movies and TV have taught Americans to be shocked by violence.

5. Guns, in early American history, gave power to the weak against the strong.

6. There are a greater number of deaths from guns than from some diseases.

7. Getting a gun for personal use is too easy today.

After reading both Aquilino's and Conyers's opinions, answer these questions.

1. What single point, made by either person, impresses you the most?

2. In your opinion, which side has presented the stronger arguments?

3. What conclusion do you draw from the arguments? Give your reasons.

B. Finding Supporting Information

In your notebook, list the number of the paragraph where there is enough information to support the following headlines.

1. STUDIES SAY DRUG-RELATED CRIMES HAVE SKYROCKETED
   a. paragraph 2
   b. paragraph 4
   c. paragraph 10

2. HALF OF CRIMES GO UNREPORTED
   a. paragraph 2
   b. paragraph 3
   c. paragraph 9

3. BUSINESS CRIMES, AN UNTOLD STORY
   a. paragraph 5
   b. paragraph 9
   c. paragraph 11

4. THE ELDERLY, PRISONERS OF FEAR
   a. paragraph 2
   b. paragraph 6
   c. paragraph 8

C. Interpreting Generalizations

Tell whether each of these generalizations is accurate or inaccurate.

1. There appears to be no single explanation for the rise in the crime rate in the United States.

2. The rate of serious crimes is rising in the suburbs and rural areas.

3. There appears to be a connection between poverty and discrimination and a high crime rate.

4. All concerned with the crime problem agree that sentences for the guilty are too light.

5. People in poor neighborhoods are rarely the victims of violent crime.

6. It is generally agreed that not all crimes are reported to the police.

7. All studies show that most crimes are committed by people between the ages of 28 and 35.

D. Writing About Citizenship

What happens to people who are arrested for serious crimes, which are known as felonies? Here is how such arrests were dealt with in 1989.

For every 100 felony arrests, 43 of those arrested had the charges dismissed or were not prosecuted. Of the 57 remaining, 54 pleaded guilty. Only three went to trial. Of these, one was acquitted and two were found guilty.

Of the 56 who were convicted, 22 were placed on probation. Twenty-one were sentenced to a year or less in jail. Thirteen were sentenced to terms of longer than a year.

As a citizen interested in the prevention of crime, write a paragraph that expresses your reaction to this information. Write another paragraph that tells how a police officer might react to this information.

30

FIGHTERS AGAINST CRIME

PURPOSES FOR READING

1. To understand the nature of the police officer's job
2. To learn how police departments are changing and improving
3. To understand how you may help in the fight against crime

KNOWING NEW WORDS

indistinguishable
(in dih STING gwih shuh bul)
paragraph 9—appearing to be the
same; not having clear differences
EXAMPLE: In the darkness, enemies
and friends were **indistinguishable.**

snipers
(SNYP urs) paragraph 3—people
who shoot at others from a hiding
place
EXAMPLE: Two **snipers** on a rooftop
fired at the street patrol.

---

1 ▶ Perhaps there is no person who is more in the public eye than the police officer. What he or she does is judged by all kinds of people. Police officers are loved and hated, respected and feared. They have a difficult job. Many different demands are made on them. They must try to help their fellow citizens. They must enforce the law. Citizens can help police by cooperating with them, or they can stand in the way of an officer's duties, making the job more difficult.

2 ▶ What is the police officer's job? There are three main tasks. One task is to enforce the law. Another is to prevent crime. A third is to arrest persons believed to have committed crimes. Police will be quick to tell you that people expect more from them than these three jobs. During a tour of duty, officers sometimes have to break up family fights. They may have to give first aid to a person hurt in an accident, or they may have to chase a reckless driver. Other officers might be handing out tickets for traffic violations of protecting government leaders. Some may patrol at school crossings. Others direct traffic at busy street corners. Officers are also in

court as witnesses in trials and hearings. They write reports of accidents and crimes. Citizens will ask police to be present at celebrations in parks or at public meetings. At times, it may seem that stopping crime is only a small part of the police officer's job.

3▶ The police officer's job is a dangerous one. Officers never know when they will face an enraged person who will use a deadly weapon against them. There are people who show their lack of respect for law by attacking the police. Police have been attacked by name calling. They have been attacked with bullets and bombs. In 1989, 146 police officers in our country were killed while carrying out their duties. Others have been killed when off duty. They had gone to the aid of their fellow citizens. Some have been killed by snipers. Others have been killed while carrying out such routine jobs as writing out traffic tickets. Attacks on police harm all society. If officers fear traps, they may think twice before making an arrest or answering a call. If this happens, neighborhoods that most need police protection may not get it.

The police officer's job includes issuing traffic tickets to people who violate the law. Why is this an important task?

4▶ Police are an arm of government that enforces the law. However, some feel that the law best protects those who have money and property. Many in minority groups think that the laws have been made by well-to-do whites for well-to-do whites. They point out that until recent years many

Police bomb squad at work. How does this picture relate to the three main tasks of a police officer's job?

Police in action at the scene of a bank robbery.

laws kept thousands of minority group members from being successful. Few African Americans, Hispanic Americans, or Asian Americans were members of police forces. Some said that police did not understand the people in poor city neighborhoods. It appeared to some leaders that minorities were arrested for small offenses while whites were not. When people feel that government is not working for them, they can lose respect for the law.

5▶ In order to improve their ability to fight crime, police departments have become motorized. The modern police officer may spend five hours of his or her tour of duty riding in a patrol car. Police are therefore able to reach the scene of a crime more quickly. But this improvement can cause another problem. It makes it difficult for the police to meet the people they serve.

6▶ When the police and the community lose contact with each other, law enforcement is hurt. People feel safer when they know the police in their neighborhood. The motorized patrol may begin to see the community only through a car window. They may hear about it only over the car radio. They could easily begin to believe that their patrol area is filled with law-breakers only. Members of the community, on the other hand, may look upon police only as enforcers. They don't get the chance to meet their officers on the street. Several cities have tried teams of officers in a single neighborhood. In these cities, reports show that citizens have increased their cooperation with police. They feel that the officers they have come to know are a part of their community.

7▶ Police departments are putting into action many ideas to improve their crime prevention work. One police officer with many years of service put it this way. "In my day, we received four days training, were given a gun, and told to get out in the street." Now, police in most states do not

Police officers visit schools in their area to discuss many things, such as self-protection, crime prevention, community programs, and good citizenship.

begin their jobs until they have received weeks of schooling. They are taught when and how to make arrests. They study people—to understand them and their needs. They learn how to cooperate with the people they will meet on their beats. In several large cities, new police must study Spanish. They also learn to use computers in studying where crimes are committed. They study many other subjects.

8▶ Courts have complained that many criminals must go free. This is because police have not gathered enough evidence to convict the accused criminal in a court of law. Sometimes the evidence is not gathered in the proper way. The federal government has provided money for large cities to teach police how to solve crimes. Some now have police officers doing their own investigations instead of turning cases over to detectives. Police are also taught how to question witnesses and gather facts for trials.

9▶ Not long ago, nearly all police officers were white males. That is no longer true. Now 14 percent of all police officers are African Americans. In many places, candidates for police jobs had to be of a certain height and weight. This ruled out most women, Hispanic Americans, and Asian Americans. These rules are no longer in force. Today across the nation nearly 10 percent of all law enforcement officers are women. In major cities, 8 percent are Hispanic Americans. In New York City, a study of the work of women on the job reported that "the women's style of patrolling was almost indistinguishable from the men's."

10▶ The growth of crime has resulted in larger and better trained police departments all over the country. Good protection costs money. The cost of keeping federal, state, and local police across the nation has increased to over $28 billion. This was double the cost of ten years before. It amounts to $115 for each American. In some areas, police protection may cost as much as $200 a person. Preventing and solving crimes is expensive.

11▶ The job of the police is to see that laws are obeyed. This means that crimes are prevented. Police cannot do this job alone. If the law is broken, the officer's duty is clear. If laws are not broken, we would need few police. Good citizens know that laws are made by their representatives. Laws are made for the benefit of most people. If the laws are unjust, there are legal and orderly ways of changing them. By obeying laws, everyone can reduce crime. Citizens also know that there may be many causes of crime. They work to get rid of these causes. They help others who are working for this same goal. A police chief of a large city explained the drop in crime in his city this way: "We have pushed citizens to get involved in the fight against

A police officer on the job. More women are on the police force since the height and weight restrictions for police officers have changed.

crime, and it pays off." In what ways can you help in this fight?

CHAPTER 30 REVIEW

★ UNDERSTANDING WHAT YOU HAVE READ

1. We may expect our police to do many things for us. This may be a summary of
   a. paragraph 2
   b. paragraph 5
   c. paragraph 8

2. Police may use computers to
   a. write reports
   b. learn places where large numbers of crimes take place
   c. help them avoid snipers and traps

3. Several police forces require new police to study Spanish because
   a. two years of college is needed to become a police officer
   b. many people they serve speak Spanish
   c. their work will take them into neighboring countries

4. Motorized police are not a complete success because they
   a. are often delayed in traffic
   b. have many clerical jobs to perform
   c. lose contact with the people they serve

5. Women and members of minority groups have been added to police forces partly as a result of
   a. lowering of age requirements
   b. changing of rules about height and weight
   c. the fact that a police officer does not have to be a citizen

6. Which best describes how some police forces were trained in the past?
   a. "Here's a gun; get out on the beat."
   b. "We're sorry, get a college education first."
   c. "You must spend weeks studying evidence and the need to understand people."

7. Which of these statements is most accurate?
   a. The costs of solving crimes have remained the same for many years.
   b. Keeping all the police forces across the country costs each citizen about $10 per year.
   c. The cost of fighting crime has doubled in ten years.

8. Police officials believe that the greatest help they can get in fighting crime is
   a. more teams in patrol cars
   b. police who have attended college
   c. greater cooperation from citizens

9. Studies of women police officers show that women
   a. let their male partners make all the arrests
   b. officers and male officers perform in the same manner
   c. do not serve in high-crime areas

★ DEVELOPING CRITICAL THINKING SKILLS

A. Drawing Conclusions

Police complain that persons arrested and taken to court are soon "back on the street." Judges complain that police often do not get enough evidence to find some arrested persons guilty. Whoever is correct, it is certain that many crimes are committed by persons who did the same crime before. These people are called "repeaters."

This table shows what percentage of persons released from prison were arrested for the same crime or another crime and what punishment they received.

Record of Released State Prisoners		
Time After Release	Percent Arrested Again	Jailed Again
6 months	25.0%	8.4%
1 year	39.3%	18.6%
2 years	54.5%	32.8%
3 years	62.5%	41.4%

Source: Department of Justice

1. What conclusions might you reach from these facts? What do these conclusions mean for the ordinary citizen?

2. What does this kind of information mean to police departments in carrying out their duties?

B. Finding Supporting Information

Below are headlines from the nation's newspapers about police work. What is the number of the paragraph where support for the idea in the headline can be found?

1. ATTACKS ON POLICE CONTINUE
   a. paragraph 1
   b. paragraph 3
   c. paragraph 5

2. FOREIGN LANGUAGE PART OF POLICE TRAINING
   a. paragraph 6
   b. paragraph 7
   c. paragraph 8

3. COSTS OF POLICE PROTECTION RISING
   a. paragraph 4
   b. paragraph 10
   c. paragraph 11

4. POLICE SCHOOL WIDENS ITS STUDIES
   a. paragraph 7
   b. paragraph 9
   c. paragraph 11

5. POLICE TEAMS GETTING A TRYOUT
   a. paragraph 2
   b. paragraph 4
   c. paragraph 6

C. Making Decisions

1. You see a car speeding down the street near your home. Several people trying to cross the street jump back onto the sidewalk to avoid being hit. The car continues in a dangerous manner down the street and speeds around a corner. What would you do? What choices do you have? What are the possible results of each choice?

2. You hear glass breaking in the middle of the night. Then you hear another sound of shattered glass. It sounds as if it is in the house next door. You look out the window and see a figure running down the street from the house. What would you do? What choices do you have? What are the possible results of each choice?

D. Looking at Police Work

Study the photographs on page 239. Then answer the questions.

1. Describe what the officers are doing in each picture.

2. How do these jobs relate to the tasks described in paragraph 6?

3. Make a list of the different skills required to do each of the tasks pictured here.

4. Select one of the pictures. Write a short paragraph telling the story behind the picture.

E. Writing About Citizenship

Do you think that ordinary citizens should do more to prevent crimes? Or do you think crime prevention should be left entirely to the police? What facts do you have to support your opinion? If you think that ordinary citizens should do more to prevent crimes, what actions do you think they should take?

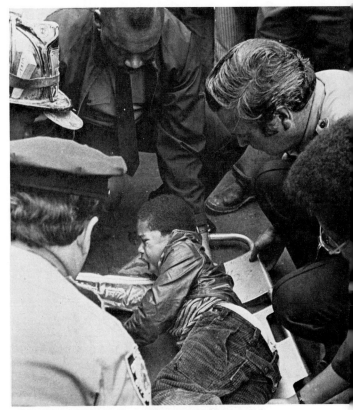

EQUAL JUSTICE UNDER THE LAW

31

PURPOSES FOR READING

1. To learn how the Constitution provides for a court system in the United States
2. To understand the duties of federal and state courts
3. To understand the roles of special courts, federal and state

Engraving from 1778 entitled "Justice." Why did the artist picture Justice blindfolded? In the photo is the United States Supreme Court in Washington, D.C.

1 ▶ The words in the title of this chapter tell us the purpose of the court system of the United States. **Justice** means being treated in a fair manner. Justice should be equal—the same for every person. Our courts are given the duty of seeing that justice is done. Note the second part of the chapter title—UNDER LAW. Justice is not what one person or a group of persons in power say it is. In our government, a ruler cannot say, ''I don't like you; I'm going to put you in prison.'' We are governed by a system of laws.

2 ▶ Article III of the Constitution provides for our court system—the judicial branch of government. It says very little about our courts. It sets up a Supreme Court and such lower courts as Congress feels are needed to judge cases fairly. The number of courts, the number of judges— these matters are left to Congress. The conditions that are a part of being treated fairly are stated in the Bill of Rights. These include not being arrested without a cause, the right to a speedy trial, and trial by jury, among others.

3 ▶ Our court system has two parts: the **federal courts** and **state courts**. Federal courts are those of the national govern- ment. They are headed by the Supreme Court of the United States, the only court mentioned in the Constitution. (See page 412.) Under the Supreme Court are **district courts.** There are 94 district courts. There is at least one district court in each state. States with larger numbers of people will have several district courts. It is in these courts that cases in which there are crimes against federal laws are first tried. Federal courts also hear cases when a foreign country or more than one state is involved. For example, a person robs a store near your home. The case would be tried in a local court. But if that person had robbed the house of the ambassador from Egypt, the case would be tried in a federal court. Here is another example. Two states have a dispute over how to stop pollution in a river that flows between the states. The federal courts would hear the case.

4 ▶ Another kind of federal court is the **court of appeals**. When people feel that they have not received fair treatment in a trial in a district court, they can appeal. This means they can ask a higher court to review the case. This is the work of the court of appeals. There are 12 such courts. Each state or territory is part of one of

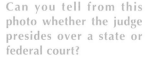

Can you tell from this photo whether the judge presides over a state or federal court?

these courts. (They are called **circuit** [SUR kit] **courts**—1st circuit court, 2nd circuit court, and so forth.) The judges in the circuit court study the claims of unfair treatment. The judges of the court can then do one of several things. The judges can rule that the decision of the district court was fair. They can reverse (change) the findings of the lower court. They can even return the case to the lower court for another trial.

5▶ Suppose that a person loses a case in a district court. The court of appeals also rules against him or her. That person may then ask the Supreme Court to hear the case. This is the highest court in the land. The Supreme Court only hears those cases that have been tried in lower courts. The Supreme Court may agree to listen to arguments in the case. Or the Court may refuse to hear the case if it finds that there was nothing to show that the lower courts were unfair. There is no appeal of a finding of the United States Supreme Court.

6▶ District courts hear a very large number of cases. From time to time, Congress has established other courts to hear special cases. This reduces the work load of the district courts. Among the special courts are these:

United States Claims Court—the oldest special court—handles cases of claims of citizens against the United States government.

United States Court of International Trade—hears cases about goods brought into the country from other countries.

United States Court of Military Appeals—hears claims of unfair treatment in courts of the armed forces.

United States Tax Court—handles cases on income tax matters.

7▶ Each state has a court system much like that of the federal government. State courts hear cases in which there is a violation of a state law. Most crimes committed are against state laws. In each state, there are lower courts, courts of appeals, and a higher court. The names of courts may differ from state to state. But they serve the same purpose as federal courts. All the rights guaranteed by the Constitution apply to all courts in the states as well.

8▶ The lowest of state courts are **justice of the peace** courts in farming areas and

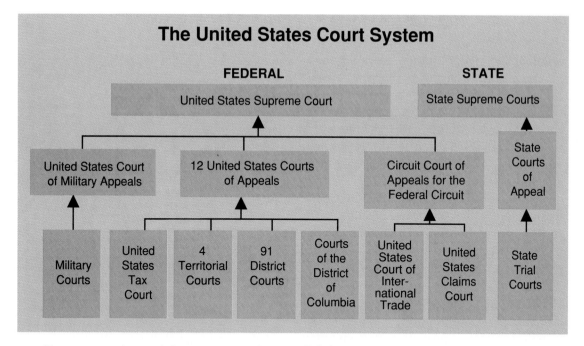

The United States Court System

FEDERAL

United States Supreme Court

- **United States Court of Military Appeals**
  - Military Courts
- **12 United States Courts of Appeals**
  - United States Tax Court
  - 4 Territorial Courts
  - 91 District Courts
  - Courts of the District of Columbia
- **Circuit Court of Appeals for the Federal Circuit**
  - United States Court of International Trade
  - United States Claims Court

STATE

State Supreme Courts

- **State Courts of Appeal**
  - State Trial Courts

small towns, and **municipal** (myoo NISS uh puhl) **courts** in cities. These courts handle small matters. They hear disputes among neighbors, claims on failure to pay bills, charges against drivers for improper parking, and the like. Justices of the peace do not necessarily have any training. Anyone elected to office may serve. In the municipal courts of cities, however, most judges are lawyers. They are elected to office. City courts look like the courts on TV. A justice of the peace may hear a case in the kitchen of his or her home.

9 ▶ Most serious criminal cases are handled by other state courts. Murder, assault, robbery, forgery, and the like, are state matters. These cases are usually brought before **trial courts.** These courts carry a great work load of cases. Trial courts are those that are most familiar to the public. Trials are held before a jury. Judges in trial courts are usually elected, but in some states they are appointed by the governor.

Trial courts have a variety of names: criminal courts, district courts, superior courts.

10 ▶ All states have courts that hear appeals from rulings and findings of lower courts. Some states, with large populations, have special courts of appeals as in the federal system. In all states, too, there is one highest court. It is usually called the state supreme court, but several states have other names for this court. In New York and Maryland, this court is called the state court of appeals. In Texas, there is a special highest court for appeals in criminal cases. Because of the importance of the states' highest courts, judges have longer terms of office than in lower courts. Rulings of the state supreme courts are usually final. However, an appeal can be made to the United States Supreme Court. This can happen if there is a claim that the ruling of the state court is not allowed by the Constitution of the United States.

11 ▶ Courts hear two kinds of cases:

criminal and **civil.** Criminal cases are those in which a crime has taken place. A serious crime is a **felony** (FEL uh nee). Stealing large amounts of money, mugging, forging checks, murder, lying when a witness at a trial—all are felonies. If a person is found guilty of a felony, a prison sentence usually follows. A less serious crime is a **misdemeanor** (mis dih MEE nur). Driving on the wrong side of the street and stealing small sums of money are kinds of misdemeanors.

12 ▶ **Civil** cases are those in which one person may have a claim against another. No criminal act is involved in a civil case. For example, a homeowner may claim that a repairman was paid to fix something, but it was not done properly. Persons may claim that a magazine printed a story about them that was untrue. Often, there is no jury in a civil trial, although one is allowed. There is no jail sentence in a civil case.

Speed limit sign. Which court would handle violations of speed limits?

Lawyer bringing the jury to the scene of the crime as part of his case for the prosecution. Why might this be helpful to justice? Why might it not be helpful to justice?

CHAPTER 31 REVIEW

★ UNDERSTANDING WHAT YOU HAVE READ

1. Another title for chapter 31 might be
   a. Courts of Appeals
   b. The Court System of the United States
   c. Crimes and Criminal Courts

2. The main idea of paragraph 4 is that
   a. appeals courts hear claims of unfair rulings of lower courts
   b. there are ten circuit courts in the United States
   c. courts of appeals may rule for a new trial in some cases

3. Article III of the Constitution names which court?
   a. The Supreme Court of the United States
   b. United States Court of Appeals
   c. United States Court of Claims

4. Crimes against the federal government are first heard in
   a. state criminal courts
   b. United States district courts
   c. United States courts of appeals

5. The Supreme Court of the United States hears cases
   a. of serious crimes against the United States
   b. in which there is a serious crime such as murder or arson
   c. which have already been tried in lower courts

6. In a small town, a person accused of driving 30 miles an hour in a 15-mile-an-hour zone, would first appear before

   a. the justice of the peace
   b. the trial judge
   c. a municipal judge

7. In which of these cases could a trial be held without a jury?
   a. A person is accused of stealing suits from a clothing store.
   b. A person is accused of signing another person's name to several checks.
   c. Mr. X accuses Ms. Y of planting rose bushes on the property of Mr. X.

8. Which of these cases would probably be tried in a federal court?
   a. A driver, while drunk, drove a car through the window of a grocery store.
   b. Several people are arrested when their boat is found in San Francisco harbor loaded with drugs brought from Mexico.
   c. A person is accused of not paying state income tax for the last five years.

9. Congress has set up a special court to hear cases concerning
   a. claims that a military court denied people their rights
   b. claims that bank officers stole funds from their bank
   c. claims that the Supreme Court of the United States made an improper ruling

10. Which of these statements is true?
    a. Judges of state supreme courts serve a term of ten years.
    b. All judges of state supreme courts are elected by the people of their state.
    c. There is no set number of years that all state supreme court judges serve.

★ DEVELOPING CRITICAL THINKING SKILLS

A. Fact or Opinion

Tell whether these statements are facts or someone's opinion. Write the word "Fact" or "Opinion" next to the number of each statement in your notebook.

1. Because of their importance, all judges on the highest courts should serve for life.

2. In the future, each state will have the same number of United States district courts.

3. Every person has the right to a fair and speedy trial.

4. Because there are so many cases awaiting trial in criminal courts, more judges are needed now.

5. The courts of our country are doing a better job in seeing that justice is done than courts of 100 years ago.

6. A large number of courts have been set up as a result of acts of Congress.

7. There is no way to appeal a ruling of the United States Supreme Court.

8. In civil cases, no crime has been committed.

9. A large number of appeals to higher courts places our court system in danger.

10. The Supreme Court of the United States has too much power.

B. Looking at Both Sides

A law professor in a large university law school has said, "Good judges can make even bad laws achieve justice. Poor judges can defeat even the best system of laws."

Study the following two lists. (One has arguments in favor of appointing judges. The other favors electing judges.) Then answer the questions that follow.

Judges Should Be Appointed	Judges Should Be Elected
1. Judges don't have to please large groups of people or any political party. They have no pressure on them to favor anyone in their decisions.	1. Judges should be close to the people. They should know what the people want from their judges.
2. The best lawyers do not want to go through an election campaign. Campaigns cost money and they are tiring. Yet they want to be judges.	2. A poor or dishonest judge must run for re-election. He of she can be removed from office by the voters.

3. Judges could be elected through the work of a small group of people who pay for the election campaign.

3. A person who is a friend of the governor can be appointed a judge for a long term, even though that person may not be qualified to be a judge.

4. Criminal groups or dishonest people may want to see a judge elected. They may hope to get favors from that person in the future.

4. In a democratic country, the people should decide who their judges are.

5. The voters don't know enough about persons running for judge to make a wise choice.

5. The people can make as good a choice as a governor. In an election campaign, they can get to know their candidates very well. Good judges have been elected in the past.

1. What is your conclusion? Should judges be appointed or elected? Support your opinion.

2. Which arguments seem to you to be the strongest? Why?

3. Suppose your choice were limited to having judges appointed either by a governor or a mayor. Which do you think would be the best way? Why?

4. Research how Canada selects judges.

C. Categorizing

1. Which is the more serious crime—a felony or a misdemeanor?

2. Ms. Jackson is accused of lying during a trial. The case would be heard in which kind of court—a criminal or a civil court?

3. Which is the higher court—a United States district court or a United States circuit court?

4. Which would hear a case about an ambassador to the United States from a foreign country—a state court or a federal court?

5. Mr. Lent claims that a judge would not hear some evidence at his criminal trial. Which court would hear his claim—a trial court or a Court of Appeals?

D. Writing About Citizenship

Write a brief essay on the following topic: Do you believe that this country really practices "equal justice under law," as the title of this chapter says? Why do you think so? Do you think that we could make any changes in the justice system to make it more fair? What would those changes be? Give reasons for your opinions.

FROM ARREST TO VERDICT

PURPOSES FOR READING

1. To learn what happens when a person is arrested for a crime
2. To learn the duties of the grand jury and the jury at a trial
3. To understand the difference between criminal and civil trials

KNOWING NEW WORDS

preliminary
(prih LIM uh ner ee) paragraph 4—coming before the main action
EXAMPLE: Taking a test is a **preliminary** step before entering college.

excessive
(ik SES iv) paragraph 4—extreme; higher than might be expected
EXAMPLE: Hector felt that staying in for the whole weekend was **excessive** punishment.

burglary
(BUR gluh ree) paragraph 1—the act of breaking into and entering a building to commit a crime
EXAMPLE: Witnesses said the suspect did break into the company office to commit a **burglary.**

probation
(proh BAY shun) paragraph 9—a sentence from a court is held off, on the promise of good behavior
EXAMPLE: The judge said that Martin should be placed on probation rather than given a prison sentence.

advise
(ad VYZ) paragraph 3—to give information to; to tell what to do
EXAMPLE: Kim asked her father to **advise** her in making out her tax return.

parole
(puh ROHL) paragraph 9—to free a prisoner before the sentence is finished; the paroled person is under supervision until the end of the time he or she was sentenced to serve
EXAMPLE: The prison board felt that Jane's behavior in prison was good and voted to **parole** her at the end of one year.

reject
(rih JEKT) paragraph 7—to refuse; deny; turn down
EXAMPLE: Voters will get a chance to approve or **reject** the tax plan at the next election.

On left, police officers stop violence and then make several arrests. Below, a verdict has been reached. The judge passes sentence. What happens between arrest and verdict?

1 ▶ The sirens of police cars are heard in the night. An alarm has sounded in a store, telling the police of a possible burglary. The police arrive in time to see a young man running from the store. He is caught by one of the officers. The officers search the suspect and find $200 in his pocket. He is arrested. The police take the suspect to the police station. What happens between the time of arrest and the end of a trial?

2 ▶ Several features about the arrest should be noted first. The officers had no trouble in making the arrest. The suspect did not try to resist the police officers. These officers were carrying out the duties the people expect of them. Officers may use whatever reasonable force they need to use in making an arrest. When a suspect resists arrest, problems result that could be avoided. The suspect was searched. Officers

249

Police frisking a suspect. Under what circumstances can the police search a suspect?

may carry out a search if they have reason to believe the suspect has a weapon, is a danger to the officers, or is hiding evidence. This is a reasonable search allowed by the Bill of Rights.

3► At the police station, a charge of **burglary** is entered against the suspect. (Let's call hin by his last name, Robbins.) Burglary means that a house or building was entered by force—breaking into the building. Before the suspected lawbreaker can be questions, however, he must be informed of his rights. This was not always so. In 1967 the United States Supreme Court ruled that the Constitution provides certain rights for persons who are arrested. The police will advise Robbins of his rights. These are rights that people held for questioning have: (1) **They have the right to remain silent.** (2) **Anything they say can be used against them at a trial.** (3) **They have the right to have a lawyer present when they are questioned.** If Robbins does not have a lawyer of his own, he will be provided with a lawyer.

4► The next step is a **preliminary** hearing. The hearing is usually held one or two days after the arrest. It takes place before a judge. The judge hears the charges against the suspect and asks him how he pleads. If Robbins says he is not guilty, the judge can take one of several actions. If Robbins has no police record, the judge may release him, believing that he will appear at a trial when he is called. The judge may set **bail.** This means Robbins must place a sum of money on deposit. This is to make sure that he will appear for the trial. If Robbins does not, he will lose the money he has deposited as bail. The judge has a third choice. He may keep the suspect in jail until the trial. If Robbins has a record of previous crimes, the judge may set a high bail. Or the judge may keep Robbins in jail without any bail. The Constitution forbids **excessive bail.** This means that bail cannot be too heavy for the crime committed.

What steps must the police follow in order to arrest a suspect?

Police look for finger- prints. Fingerprints are one form of evidence. What other forms of evidence can you name?

Whether or not the bail is excessive is a cause for arguments in many arrests.

5► Robbins's case must go before a **grand jury.** In most cases, a grand jury is made up of 23 citizens. The jury listens to the charges against the suspect and the evidence against him. The district attorney presents the case against Robbins to the grand jury. The jury then decides whether or not a trial should be held. If they believe there is strong evidence against Robbins, they will present an **indictment** (in DIGHT munt). This is a formal charge. An indictment is not a finding of guilt. It means that a trial should be held in this case. The grand jury meets in secret. This protects innocent persons from having charges against them made public.

6► Robbins, as well as other accused persons, has the right to a speedy trial. This should mean that the case should be finished in a month or a few weeks. But today, courts all over the country are jammed with cases awaiting trial. Robbins's case may not come before a judge for several months. Meanwhile, his lawyer goes over his case. He will try to prove Robbins is innocent. He may want to prove that there are conditions about the burglary that would lead to

a light sentence. The district attorney will present evidence against Robbins. She must prove that Robbins is guilty "beyond a reasonable doubt." Both sides will call witnesses to support their arguments.

7► Robbins can plead guilty before the trial is held. If he does, the judge will pass sentence. If he does not plead guilty, the trial is held. A jury of 12 citizens will be chosen to hear the case. The process of choosing a jury takes time. Robbins's attorney, the district attorney, and the judge all take part in choosing the jury. All of them can question those who have been called for jury duty. Any one of them can reject a person for the jury by giving a reason. A certain number of possible members of the jury can be rejected without giving a reason. Once the jury is chosen, the judge swears them in. The members of the jury promise they will give a fair decision in the case.

8► At the end of the trial, after all the witnesses have been heard, both Robbins's lawyer and the district attorney give summaries of the case to the jury. Both will try to show the jury how the evidence supports their side of the trial. The judge will then give instructions to the jury. The jury goes

251

Trial by jury. What is the role of the jurors in a trial by jury?

into a room where they can talk over the case in secret. In this case, all 12 jurors must agree on a decision. The decision is called a **verdict** (VUR dikt). The verdict is reported to the judge in person. If the verdict is guilty, the judge will set a date to inform Robbins of his sentence. If the verdict is not guilty, Robbins goes free. If the jury cannot agree on a verdict after many hours of trying, a new trial may be held.

9 ▶ What kind of sentence will Robbins receive if he is found guilty? He could be **fined,** but this is not likely in a case in which a store was robbed. He could be placed on **probation** for a period of time. This might happen if it is the first offense for Robbins, or if he is found guilty of taking only a small amount of money. This means that his behavior will be watched for a year or more. If he breaks no laws during this time, there will be no prison sentence. Robbins might be sentenced to jail—either a county jail or a state prison. It is possible that he may receive a **parole** before the sentence is finished. This would depend upon his behavior while in prison.

10 ▶ In a civil case, the steps in the trial process are much the same. However, no one is arrested in a civil case. One person has a complaint against another. The person making the complaint is called the **plaintiff** (PLAYN tif). The one who is accused is the **defendant.** In a civil case, there may or may not be a jury. Sometimes, law-

Scene in the isolation cellblock at a federal penitentiary.

yers for each side may agree that they want only the judge to decide the case. If so, the judge gives the verdict in the trial. If the verdict is in favor of the plaintiff, **damages** (a sum of money) are awarded. The costs of holding the trial, paying for witnesses and jury, are usually paid by the side that loses the case.

CHAPTER 32 REVIEW

★ UNDERSTANDING WHAT YOU HAVE READ

1. The main idea of paragraph 3 is that
   a. a suspect is arrested
   b. Robbins did not use force to enter the building
   c. arrested persons must be told their rights

2. Police officers may search a person thought to have committed a crime if
   a. they believe the suspect has a weapon
   b. the suspect has been informed of his or her rights
   c. a lawyer is present

3. At a preliminary hearing, a judge may decide
   a. whether a person is guilty or not guilty
   b. to send a person to jail until charges are prepared
   c. to hold a suspect in jail without bail

4. The purpose of a grand jury is to
   a. decide whether an accused person is guilty or not guilty
   b. listen to lawyers for a suspect and the district attorney
   c. decide whether there is enough evidence against a suspect to hold a trial

5. Which step in the road from arrest to trial is held in secret?
   a. The preliminary hearing
   b. The grand jury hearing
   c. The jury announcing its verdict

6. Which of these has a say in choosing a jury?
   a. The district attorney only
   b. The district attorney and the lawyer for the accused person
   c. The district attorney, the lawyer for the accused, and the judge

7. A civil case is different from a criminal case because in a civil case
   a. no jury ever hears a case
   b. no one is arrested
   c. there is no judge

8. Suppose an arrested person has no lawyer she can speak with at the police station. In this case
   a. a lawyer will be provided for her if she asks for one
   b. no lawyer is allowed before a hearing
   c. a person cannot be arrested without a lawyer present

9. A judge may NOT
   a. set bail for a person accused of a crime
   b. send an accused person to jail unless the accused has been told the charges against him or her
   c. allow a jury to meet in secret

10. Accused persons may not have the speedy trial they expect, partly because
    a. many witnesses have to be heard
    b. courts all over the country have a heavy load of cases waiting for trial
    c. judges often set a high bail for serious crimes

★ **DEVELOPING CRITICAL THINKING SKILLS**

Looking at Both Sides—Plea Bargaining

When people buy an item in some stores or a market, they often bargain with the seller over price. The buyer may offer $5 for a clock, while the seller asks for $8. They bargain, that is, each makes several offers back and forth before a price is agreed upon. The price will likely be somewhere in the middle.

There is a practice in the arrest-trial process where a suspect may "bargain." In the case of Robbins in this chapter, Robbins might have claimed that he was guilty of a crime, but a lesser crime than the one with which he was charged. His lawyer might tell the judge that Robbins will plead guilty, but to a lesser crime. For example, instead of Robbins being charged with breaking into the store and stealing from it, he might plead guilty to the stealing only. If the district attorney agrees, the "bargain" might be accepted by the judge. Robbins would receive a lighter sentence for the lesser charge. In this way he avoids standing trial on the more serious charge. He avoids the chance of being found guilty on the more serious charge.

Plea bargaining is common. Nine of ten serious crimes in the country are now settled by plea bargaining. There are arguments for and against this practice. Read the arguments for and against plea bargaining. Then answer the questions that follow the chart.

For Plea Bargaining	Against Plea Bargaining
1. It reduces the need for a trial. The costs of operating courts are reduced.	1. People who are guilty of a serious crime should receive the punishment they deserve for that crime.
2. It cuts the work load of judges. The number of cases awaiting trial has jammed our courts.	2. It encourages crimes. Criminals know they will receive punishment for a lesser crime.
3. It speeds up a decision in cases. An accused person does not have to wait so long for a decision.	3. It tends to make innocent people plead guilty to a crime they did not commit—to get the matter settled quickly.
4. It is fair because an accused person does not have to spend a long time in jail awaiting trial.	4. People who are in jail awaiting trial may want to plead guilty to a lesser charge, just to get out of jail.
5. In less serious crimes, it cuts the time spent by attorneys in preparing less important cases.	

1. Have you studied the arguments for and against plea bargaining? What arguments seem to you to be the most reasonable?

2. Does plea bargaining improve the chances for "equal justice under the law"?

3. What conclusion did you reach after studying the arguments?

4. Why do you think some states have forbidden the practice of plea bargaining?

5. Research to find out whether or not your state allows plea bargaining.

★ SUMMARIZING THE CHAPTER

A. Building Vocabulary Skills

Match the following terms in Column A with the definitions in Column B. There is an extra item in Column B.

Column A

1. civil case

2. plaintiff

3. indictment

4. verdict

5. parole

6. probation

7. grand jury

Column B

a. A prisoner is freed before the jail sentence is finished.

b. The jury reports how it has decided a case.

c. The first step toward an arrest.

d. A finding that there is enough evidence to hold a trial.

e. When one person has a complaint against another.

f. Is made up of 23 persons.

g. The person making a complaint against another person.

h. A convicted person is not sentenced. But the person's behavior is watched by a special officer for a period of time.

B. Writing About Citizenship

Reread the list of rights that people held for questioning have (page 250). Then write a brief essay which answers these questions: Why do you think that all people have these rights? Do you think that they are important rights? Why or why not? How do you think they help or hurt the justice system? Give reasons for your answers.

JUVENILE DELINQUENCY AND JUVENILE COURTS

33

PURPOSES FOR READING

1. To learn about the kinds of offenses for which young people may appear in court
2. To learn how juvenile courts are different from criminal courts
3. To learn the rights of juveniles before a court
4. To understand some suggestions made for improving the treatment of youthful offenders

KNOWING NEW WORDS

juveniles
(JOO vun nuls) paragraph 1—
young people, not yet adults
EXAMPLE: At the party, the adults enjoyed the old-time songs, but the **juveniles** seemed bored.

delinquents
(dih LING kwunts) paragraph 3—
those not doing what is required by law
EXAMPLE: Since Bob and Sue had not paid their income tax in full, the government notified them that they must make the tax payments. They were **delinquents.**

supervision
(soo pur VIZH un) paragraph 4—
the act of directing or watching over someone's behavior
EXAMPLE: Since more than 200 children came to the schoolyard each day, Mrs. Tower's **supervision** was needed.

publicity
(puh BLIS ih tee) paragraph 6—
information given to the public; public attention
EXAMPLE: The war veterans wanted **publicity** for the parade on November 11 so there would be a good number of marchers.

A police officer conducts a school program. Programs such as these can help young students learn about the law.

Newspapers often carry headlines like these:

YOUNG VANDALS DESTROY SWINGS IN PARK

- New Orleans, Louisiana

TEENAGER HELD FOR ASSAULT ON ELDERLY

- New York, New York

13-YEAR-OLDS ACCUSED OF SETTING FIRE; 1 DEAD, 2 INJURED

- Miami, Florida

THREE TEENAGERS HELD IN $6,000 BANK ROBBERY

- El Paso, Texas

1 ▶ The news stories on page 257 tell us some of the crimes that have been committed by young people. Almost half of those arrested for auto thefts and a third of those arrested for burglaries are teenagers. In a recent year over 30,000 youngsters ten years of age or younger were arrested for serious crimes. One federal law enforcement official says, "This is not 'kid stuff' we're talking about. This is serious crime committed by juveniles." How do our courts handle the cases of youngsters who get into serious trouble? We will learn about that in this chapter.

2 ▶ A juvenile is defined as a person who is not yet considered to be an adult. Juveniles are not thought to be able to judge the results of their acts as adults might. As a result, they are treated differently by our courts. In most states, 18 years of age is the beginning of adult life. In

IT'S ONLY MONEY— OURS

What is the meaning of this cartoon?

Young people roaming the streets. Why do many people think this could lead to trouble?

some states, the difference in court treatment ends at age 16.

3▶ The headlines at the beginning of this chapter describe some offenses committed by juveniles. These would be considered serious crimes if they were committed by adults. But they are considered lesser offenses or delinquent acts when committed by teenagers. Young people who commit such acts are called **juvenile delinquents.** (They have failed to live up to the law or their obligations as young people.) When appearing before a court, these young people are not treated as adult criminals.

4▶ Young people used to be called juvenile delinquents for other reasons. They might behave in such a manner as to show that their parents have no control over them. For example, young people might run away from home over and over again. Or they might roam the streets of the community day or night. Perhaps they refused to go to school. Such young people might cause trouble at home, too. These actions are different from those described in the headlines at the beginning of the chapter. These activities would not be defined as crimes even if they were committed by adults. But such young people often have to appear before a court. They are in need of court-ordered supervision. They are now commonly called PINS (Persons In Need of Supervision) instead of juvenile delinquents.

5▶ Early in the country's history, the laws provided the same treatment for young people and adults. The punishment for a crime was the same, no matter who committed it. In 1847 the state of Massachusetts began separate prisons for adults and juveniles. **Reform** schools were established for juveniles. The name of this kind of school is a clue to its purpose. It is to reform, to change, juveniles who have not acted the way society expected them to. This plan spread in the years that followed. Separate courts for juveniles first appeared in Illinois 50 years later. Today, all states have juvenile courts and reform schools. The purpose of our juvenile court system is not to punish but to guide young people to

Probation officer conducts an interview with a young man on probation.

change their ways from crime to good citizenship.

6▶ In a juvenile court, there is no trial. A **hearing** is held before a judge. The judge hears the evidence in the case. He or she may listen to the police, parents, school officials, and the accused youth. The Supreme Court has ruled that a jury is not an absolute right in juvenile courts. The hearing is not given publicity. Young people are protected from getting a bad reputation as a result of a delinquent act.

7▶ The judge decides what should be done. The case could be dismissed or the juvenile given a warning. The offender could be placed on **probation.** This means that the juvenile lives at home. An officer of the court, a probation officer, is named to help the youth for a few months, perhaps a year. The officer tries to help the juvenile overcome the problems that caused troubles in the first place. The judge could decide that reform school would provide the best treatment. The purpose of the judge's action, however, remains the same—to try to change the behavior of the offender.

8▶ In 1967 the United States Supreme Court set down rules for the treatment of juveniles in trouble with the law. It is known as the **Gault decision.** Gerald Gault was a 15-year-old from Arizona whose case was heard in juvenile court. His case was taken to the Supreme Court because he felt that he had been denied certain rights. The Court ruled that:

1. Juveniles must be told they do not have to make a confession of wrongdoing.

2. Juveniles must have a lawyer when accused of a crime for which an adult would have a lawyer.

3. Juveniles must be told the charges against them before a hearing.

4. Juveniles can cross-examine witnesses at a hearing. The witnesses at such a hearing must swear that the statements they give are true.

A few years later, the court held that juveniles must be guilty "beyond a reasonable doubt" if the judge's verdict sends a youth to reform school.

9▶ What can be done to improve the juvenile court system? How can juvenile justice stop teenage violence? Many studies have been made about this problem. State lawmakers across the nation have made changes in the juvenile court system from time to time. Police, lawyers, teachers, and counselors are just as interested in solving the problem. Some of these people believe the following:

1. Judges should have to write out the reasons for their decisions. Others can then study them and learn from them.

2. Laws about juvenile delinquency should be the same in all states.

3. Juvenile offenses that are not crimes by adults should not be handled by courts. They should be treated by government departments that deal with family problems.

4. Reform schools are not doing the job of turning young people from paths

of crime. In reform schools, they say, teenagers may learn how to become real criminals.

5. There should be special homes for special problems. Runaways should be separated from those who have committed violent acts.

6. There should be more probation officers. Most of these officers now have more than 100 people each to help. The officers cannot see them very often.

7. People who were once drug users should teach teenagers the dangerous effects of using drugs.

10 ▶ There are others concerned with juvenile crimes who believe that our courts are not working to prevent crime because they are "too soft" on juvenile crime. They point to the growing number of crimes committed by youngsters between the ages of 10 and 17. Every state in the country now allows 13- to 15-year-olds to be given a trial in criminal court. Trials are allowed only for the most serious crimes. A full study is made in each case. A judge or district attorney may then recommend that the case be turned over to a juvenile court. If not, it becomes a criminal case. The sentence may be the same as an adult might receive for the same crime. Is this the answer to the problem? What is the best solution for juvenile delinquency? As a good citizen, someday you may be called upon to help supply the answers to these questions.

CHAPTER 33 REVIEW

★ UNDERSTANDING WHAT YOU HAVE READ

1. The main idea of paragraph 4 is that
   a. juveniles often appear in court
   b. juveniles may appear in court for reasons other than committing a crime
   c. juveniles may have a court hearing because of troubles at home

2. An important idea of this chapter is that
   a. some acts that are crimes for adults are not crimes for juveniles
   b. juvenile courts are not doing their job
   c. laws about juveniles are the same in all states

3. Separate courts for adults and juveniles

   a. have always been a part of our court system
   b. were started less than 100 years ago
   c. are found in less than half the states

4. In a hearing in a juvenile court, you probably will NOT find a
   a. witness
   b. jury
   c. parent

5. The purpose of a judge's decision in a juvenile court is to
   a. punish the offender
   b. dismiss the case
   c. change the offender's behavior

6. The Supreme Court has ruled that juveniles must have all of these rights EXCEPT
   a. trial by a jury
   b. the right to be told the charges against them
   c. the right to have a lawyer in certain cases

7. A person who believes that juvenile courts are "soft on crime" might say that

   a. there needs to be more probation officers
   b. government departments should deal with family problems
   c. teenagers should receive the same sentence as adults for some crimes

8. Which of these statements is true?

a. In a juvenile court, there is no trial.
b. Judges have to write out the reasons for their decisions in juvenile courts.
c. A youth running away from home commits a crime.

9. The offenses listed in the headlines at the beginning of the chapter would properly be called
   a. delinquent acts
   b. crimes
   c. "white-collar" crimes

10. Which of these would be a PINS referral to a court?
    a. Stealing candy from a store
    b. Refusing to come home at night
    c. Destroying benches in a public park

★ DEVELOPING CRITICAL THINKING SKILLS

A. Looking at Both Sides

Here are two news stories that tell about some of the ideas found in this chapter. Read each one and answer the questions that follow.

1. New York State passed a law in July 1978 that allowed criminal courts instead of juvenile courts (Family Court) to hear cases of teenagers who are accused of serious crimes. After several years of experience with the law, the following news article presents a summary of the law's results.

GET-TOUGH JUVENILE LAW PERSISTS AS CONTROVERSY

"The law is not cutting down on crime," said New York City's commissioner of juvenile justice. He and some other criminal justice officials say that all it has done is increase overcrowding in prisons.

Others say it is at least an improvement over the old system because it puts the most violent offenders behind bars.

"The law has allowed us to prosecute juveniles in accordance with the crimes they commit," says the chief of the juvenile crime unit in the Manhattan district attorney's office. "Before the law was passed, a juvenile who committed a violent crime received no more than a slap on the wrist."

The law has stiffened jail sentence for teenagers. It permits prosecution of 13-, 14-, and 15-year-olds in adult criminal courts for violent crimes such as murder, rape, and armed robbery.

Two State Division of Youth leaders say that . . . "Juveniles should be tried in a court designed to understand and correct their problems, which this law does not even attempt to do." Another [leader said], "The criminal courts are too harsh and not designed to deal with this kind of criminal. But the family courts are too lenient."

United Press International

Tell whether these statements are true or false—based on the article you have just read. If the statement is false, rewrite it to make it true.

a. Law enforcement officials believe that the law should be continued.

b. More teenagers are receiving stiffer sentences today for serious crimes than before the law was passed.

c There are those who believe that teenagers do not receive just sentences in either adult or juvenile courts.

d. Nearly everyone connected with the handling of juvenile offenders believes that the law is a good one.

2. A newspaper editor, in disagreement with the handling of a serious juvenile offender, in the state of Massachusetts, presents this point of view.

America is a nation, fortunately, that cares about its young. That concern has been demonstrated in thousands of ways. One of them is special legislation that separates juveniles from adults in the court process.

. . . As it now stands in Massachusetts, a juvenile cannot be convicted on a charge of murder if he [or she] is tried in a juvenile court session. The only finding permissible [allowed] in juvenile court is delinquency, not conviction. A juvenile court judge is restricted to committing a delinquent to the custody of the state Department of Youth Services. That agency, in turn, has no other choice but to release [the offender on his or her] . . . birthday.

. . . The theory that juveniles are not yet hardened criminals and thus prime candidates for special handling and possible rehabilitation is a good one. But at some point society must use common sense and draw a line. Giving murder the same value as larceny, assault, or breaking and entering is absurd.

In this instance a single individual, a judge, invoked a rule that will return a confessed killer of three to society in a very short time. The sentence amounts to not much more than wagging a finger.

The victims, on the other hand, were themselves sentenced by a single individual—but to eternity.

Kenneth J. Botty,
Editor,
Worcester Telegram,
September 1, 1985

Tell whether these statements about this editorial and the previous news articles are true or false. If the statement is false, rewrite it to make it true.

a. The writer of the editorial is not sure whether juveniles accused of serious offenses should be tried in adult courts.

b. Other states have passed laws similar to New York's regarding the treatment of juvenile offenders.

c. A juvenile who has a trial in juvenile court in Massachusetts can only be found delinquent.

d. The editorial writer believes in separate courts for juvenile and adult cases.

e. The last newspaper article represents the writer's opinion.

f. The last article gives specific facts about the results of the juvenile law in New York state.

B. Writing About Citizenship

How do you think the criminal justice system should treat juvenile offenders? Do you think the system should be more lenient with juvenile offenders because they are not adults? Or should people be responsible for their own actions, no matter how old they are? Write your own editorial about juvenile justice.

★SUMMARIZING THE CHAPTER

Tell where the action described in each statement would take place. The choices are these: in a juvenile court or family court only (J), in a criminal court (C), or in both kinds of courts (B). Use the knowledge you have gained from chapters 32 and 33. Write the letter of your answer next to the numbers in your notebooks.

1. A grand jury listens to charges against an accused person.

2. A hearing is held before a judge. The public is not told of the hearing or its results.

3. The accused are told their rights before making a statement.

4. Offenders can be placed on probation.

5. Accused persons can be sent to a state prison.

6. A jury is not needed to decide the case.

7. A complaint can be made even though no crime was committed.

8. The accused could be sent to a reform school.

9. An accused person can be treated as an adult.

10. An accused person must be found guilty "beyond a reasonable doubt."

PARTICIPATION IN GOVERNMENT

PROVIDING COMMUNITY SERVICE

Sometimes people who break the law are forced to perform "community service" as their punishment. The offenders are required to give a period of their time to help their community. They are forced to be "good citizens." But good citizens should not have to be *forced* to help their neighbors. They should help because they are both interested in and respect other people.

In 1984, students throughout the country showed how much they cared for others. They collected money and food to aid the starving people of East Africa. It was a tremendous effort involving thousands of young people—and it continued with aid to earthquake victims in Mexico and to people whose homes were destroyed in the mud slides of Puerto Rico. In an eastern high school, students volunteered to handle the phones of the city's ambulance service when personnel were not available.

But service to others need not be as dramatic as these. There are "little things" everyone can do. Some can form a team or club and visit the handicapped or shut-ins. Others can perform errands for them, do their shopping, read to those who cannot, or merely chat. The last contribution may be more important than all others. Writing letters may be a big help. During the summer months, mowing lawns can be an important service. Students can even help other students with problems they may have in their schoolwork. The choice of service to be performed is yours, but the opportunities to demonstrate your civic awareness are all around you.

Unit 7 ★

OUR ECONOMIC SYSTEM

The New York Stock Exchange on Wall Street is an important part of our free enterprise system.

34 FREE ENTERPRISE IN AMERICA

PURPOSES FOR READING
1. To understand the freedoms that are part of our economic system
2. To appreciate the benefits of our economic system
3. To understand some differences between our economic system and that of Communist nations

KNOWING NEW WORDS

resources
(ree SOHRS ez) paragraph 3—a supply of something that can be used when needed, as coal, lumber, water
EXAMPLE: We have often wasted our **resources** of oil.

enterprise
(EN tur pryz) paragraph 4—an important, difficult, or dangerous undertaking

EXAMPLE: Opening a store on that block was an **enterprise** that took a lot of luck to succeed.

competition
(kom pih TISH un) paragraph 6—the act of trying against others for a prize or profit
EXAMPLE: The **competition** between the Ace Soap Company and the Brace Soap Company is strong in the Chicago area.

1► In how many of the world's nations could we say that people live in freedom? Freedom House is a group that studies governments throughout the world. In a recent year, it listed only about a third of the world's nations as "free." This means that the people in these nations enjoy rights such as the freedoms of speech, press, assembly, and religion. Nearly two-thirds of the world's nations do not allow these freedoms. These nations are ruled by various kinds of dictatorships or monarchies. They include Communist nations such as China, North Korea, Vietnam, and Cuba. There are also such countries as Iran and Libya, where one person rules the country or where only one political party is allowed. In some other countries where people do not live in freedom, elections are held, but they are not honest.

Consumers shopping in a store. The U.S. economic system provides consumers with an almost unlimited variety of goods and choices.

2► The United States is among the nations whose citizens have many important freedoms. But the United States is not only a leader in the rights its people enjoy. Few other peoples anywhere in the world have such a choice of goods and services. Few other people are fed so well. No other nation has as many cars, telephones, radios, and TV sets. No other country can boast of such a system of free public schools. American workers are among the highest paid workers in the world. The lowest pay American workers can receive is higher than normal pay in most other nations. Yet, there are 35 million Americans who are poor. (1) How has our country come to be so rich in so many ways? (2) How is it that all Americans do not enjoy its riches? As you study this unit, you will learn some of the answers to these questions.

3► There can be many answers to the first question. The United States is rich in natural resources. Americans have been hard workers. Schools in the United States have educated millions of citizens. The na-

tion has grown with the idea that all people can improve their positions in life. The United States has combined the talents of people of many races and nationalities. Americans have felt that they have been free to work and to create. They can profit from their talents. The freedom of Americans has extended to economic life as well.

4► A country's economic system determines how the people produce, manage, and divide their riches. The American economic system is called **capitalism.** One of the basic features of capitalism is **free enterprise.** This means that people are free to think and to act. They may enter a business or career of their own choosing. They are free to try something that others may not have tried before. When people are able to act as they wish, they seem to work hard at it. It is this freedom to think and act that has encouraged Americans to invent the steamboat and design many improvements for the motor car and television.

5► The American economic system also includes the right to own **private property.**

People may own land and a house. They may own a business. They may call their car and their clothes their own. This right to own things, property, extends to everyone. Each person enjoys this freedom. Of course, if one person does not respect the property of another, then the government may step in to make sure the rights of all are protected.

6▶ **Competition** is an important activity in the American economic system. You take part in competition when your team plays against another team. Or it may be that you are trying to beat others in a race. You want to win, to do better than the others who are competing with you. This is what businesses also try to do. They try to sell as many of the products they make as they can. They try to get you to buy what they have to offer. Their advertising is for the same purpose—to make you feel you need their goods. A business will try to give you good service, too, so you will buy from them a second and third time. Competition makes a business look for new and

cheaper ways to make the goods that people want. However, if businesses cheat or are dishonest, it is the government's job to protect you, the buyer.

7▶ A person starts a business to make a **profit.** The American economic system is a profit system. Just as you will take a job to make money, so business owners want to make money also. If a business does not make money, it cannot continue. When people start a business or farmers plant a crop, they take a risk. They are using their money to get started. Through the use of their money, they hope to produce a product and be able to sell it. They hope that their sales will bring them more money than they used to make the product—a profit. It is this desire to make a profit that makes the free enterprise system work. If people could not make a profit, there might be little reason to start a business, to plant a crop, or to do any kind of work.

8▶ Members of the clergy, plumbers, social workers, teachers, doctors, and nurses don't make goods. They provide a

What right in the American economic system allows the owner to put up the sign shown in the picture?

This shopping mall has many different stores that sell the same kinds of goods. How do you think competition plays an important role in the American economy?

service. So do people who are lawyers, gardeners, sales people, and waiters. Many businesses provide services instead of goods. Airline companies and insurance companies are examples. They are also an important part of the economic system.

9 ► Communist countries have an economic system very different from the American one. In a Communist country, the government, rather than individuals, makes the important economic decisions. Communist governments do not allow their citizens the rights that many Americans take for granted. For example, there is very little freedom of speech, press, and assembly. This means that Communist government officials are not elected in free elections. So the leaders who control the Communist economic system may not truly represent the people's wishes. In Communist countries, people have little freedom to choose a business or job. Businesses do not compete with one another to provide a wide choice of goods. There is little or no private property. The government decides what kinds of goods, services, factories, and workers are needed. It decides who will continue in school to learn a skill. It decides what crops to grow, and who will work on the farms. The government also decides how the goods that are produced are to be divided among the people.

10 ► Communist countries are finding that the lack of freedom hurts their production of food and other goods. People just will not work as hard when they are told when and where to work. People want to be able to enjoy the things they make or grow themselves. In recent years, some Communist countries have allowed people to sell their goods in small shops and stands. Some workers in factories have been allowed to make decisions about what products they shall make. Communist leaders have found that rewards for good

Private enterprise stand in China. Compare this picture to the one above. How are they alike? How are they different?

Wichita Falls oil refinery in Texas. In what ways does the American free enterprise system encourage the growth of industry?

work result in greater production. Despite changes, many Communist governments still did not meet their peoples' needs.

11▶ By the 1980s, Communist governments in the Soviet Union and Eastern Europe were facing major problems. Greater freedom of speech and loosened controls on business in the Soviet Union sparked unrest. In 1989, the Berlin Wall came down. Without Soviet support, Communist governments in Eastern Europe fell. Then, in 1991, the Soviet Union crumbled. In its place, 15 nations formed. Many are trying to rebuild economies based on free enterprise.

CHAPTER 34 REVIEW

★ UNDERSTANDING WHAT YOU HAVE READ

1. The main idea of paragraph 4 is that
   a. Americans are free to enter any business or field of work
   b. Americans have made many important inventions
   c. the American people have proven to be hard workers

2. When several companies make the same kinds of goods for sale, and each tries to sell more of the goods than the other, they are taking part in
   a. competition
   b. profit sharing
   c. Communist economics

3. When one person's property rights are not respected by others,
   a. the result is free enterprise
   b. competition will settle the problem
   c. the government steps in to protect the rights of each person

4. The chief reason why most people take risks in starting a business is to
   a. make a profit
   b. increase the number of workers
   c. let the government decide what should be produced

5. Which of these kinds of work can be called a service?
   a. Making paper
   b. Growing wheat
   c. Providing medical care

6. Which of these statements about a Communist economic system is true?
   a. All people have the right to own private businesses.
   b. Government officials are not elected in free elections.

   c. Farmers are able to make large profits from the sales of their crops.

7. The chapter tells us that
   a. people in Communist countries have many political and economic freedoms
   b. many of the people in the world live in countries that do not allow much freedom
   c. most people in the world enjoy the same rights that Americans do.

★ DEVELOPING CRITICAL THINKING SKILLS

A. Making Comparisons

This table compares a free enterprise economy, such as the U.S. economy, to a centralized economy, which is the kind of economy that can be found in Communist countries. After studying the table, answer the questions on page 274.

	Free Enterprise Economy	Centralized Economy
Ownership	Land, resources, and industry are privately owned.	Land, resources, and industry are owned by the government.
Decision-Making	Individuals and private businesses make their own economic decisions based on supply and demand.	Government planners make decisions based on what is important to the government.
Competition	Businesses compete with one another to sell their products to consumers. Competition leads to the production of a great variety of goods and services. Companies try to outsell competitors either by making higher quality goods or by lowering prices. They also often invent new products.	There is no competition because the government controls the production of goods and services. There is a small selection of products. Producers have little reason to lower prices or produce high quality products because consumers have no choice but to buy their products.
Profit	Goal of businesses is to earn profit.	Goal of businesses is to produce goods and services.

1. a.) What is the goal of businesses in a free enterprise economy? b.) What is the goal of businesses in a centralized economy?

2. Who makes economic decisions in a centralized economy?

3. How is the ownership of land, resources, and industry different in a free enterprise economy than in a centralized economy?

4. According to this table, why do many goods and services produced in a free enterprise economy tend to be lower in price and higher in quality than the goods and services that are produced in a centralized economy?

5. Do you think the free enterprise system leads to more inventions of goods and services than the centralized economy? Why or why not?

6. As you read in this chapter, the U.S. economic system is a free enterprise system. Based on this table, how do businesses in the United States make economic decisions?

B. Finding Support for Decisions

Decide whether you agree or disagree with the following statements. What paragraph or table in this chapter will help you support your decisions?

1. People in many nations, such as China, North Korea, and Cuba, do not have the same freedoms as people in the United States.

2. In some nations that are run by dictators, there are as many or more cars than there are in the United States.

3. The laws of the United States allow persons complete freedom to do what they want with their property.

4. A business advertises its goods so people will buy them and it can make a profit.

5. The American economic system is partly based upon the desire of people to make a profit from their business.

C. Writing About Citizenship

Write a brief essay on the following topic: What are the advantages and disadvantages of living in a country with a free enterprise system economy? Do you think that there are more advantages or disadvantages? Give reasons for your answer.

35

HOW CAPITALISM WORKS FOR US

PURPOSES FOR READING

1. To understand the meaning of and uses for capital
2. To learn the ways businesses are organized
3. To learn how governments place controls on what businesses can do

KNOWING NEW WORDS

corporation
(kor puh RAY shun) paragraph 4—a group of people who carry out business as one person
EXAMPLE: Rather than start a business by himself, Stewart asked others to join with him to form a **corporation.**

cycle
(SY kul) paragraph 8—an event that is repeated at particular times
EXAMPLE: The **cycle** of the seasons includes spring, summer, fall, and winter.

inflation
(in FLAY shun) paragraph 11—a period when there is a lot of money, few goods, and high prices
EXAMPLE: The family found that it was hard to pay all its bills during the period of **inflation.**

depression
(dih PRESH un) paragraph 8—a period of falling prices, low wages, and people out of work
EXAMPLE: People stood in lines to get bread and a cup of soup during the **depression** of the 1930s.

Who owns the automobile companies in the United States?

Who owns the airlines in the United States?

Who owns the oil wells in the United States?

Who owns the electronic companies in the United States?

Who owns the tobacco fields in the United States?

Who owns the telephone systems in the United States?

1 ▶ Have you thought about these questions? If you answered "people" or "private companies" to all these questions, you are right. People own and control the wealth and the riches of this country. This system, as you learned in the last chapter, is called the free enterprise system. It is also called **capitalism** (KAP ah TUL ism). In "pure" capitalism, people can own and control all kinds of wealth without limits. In capitalism in the United States there are limits. Those limits are set by the government. The government has placed some controls on how wealth is used. In this chapter we will see how American capitalism works in business.

2 ▶ It takes more than a person's wish to make a business. It takes money. Land for a building is needed. The building must be bought or rented. There is also a need for tools and equipment. The machines, building, and equipment are called **capital.** They will be used to produce goods and make a profit for the business. But capital is still not enough. Workers must be hired to run and repair machines, to keep records, to sell what the business makes. Capitalism cannot operate without good, skilled workers. Our business life, then, is made up of capital and **labor** (the workers). Neither can do without the other. They use natural resources to make goods and provide services. These resources are called **land.** Minerals, water power, wild life, soil, timber, and other natural resources are included in this definition of land.

3 ▶ A business can be owned by a single person. That person takes all the risks, but also makes all the profit. It is hard for a single owner to get the money needed to make a business grow. A business with only one owner is usually a small one. But there are more single-owner businesses than any other kind. Some businesses are owned by partners. Two or more owners means there is more capital to make a business a success. The risks are also shared. But partners do not always agree about the way the business should be run. One partner may pile up debts that the other must also pay. A partnership ends when one of the partners dies. Suppose one partner wishes to sell his or her portion of the business. The other partner may not accept the new part-

Worker in a modern factory. How does this picture illustrate both capital and labor?

ner. Even if the old partner does accept the new one, a new partnership agreement must be formed. Partnerships are most often found among doctors, lawyers, or where large amounts of money are not needed to get a business started.

4 ▶ The largest businesses in the United States are **corporations.** They are fewer in number than single-owner firms, but their sales are much greater. Some corporations will have sales in the hundreds of millions of dollars in a year. Of course there are thousands of small corporations too. A corporation can be started by a group of people who get a **charter** from the state government. This is written permission to form a corporation. The charter states the name of the corporation and why it was formed. It also states the powers that the corporation has. The owners of the corporation are those who have put money into it.

5 ▶ How does a corporation work? Let us suppose that ten people decide to start a business. They need money. Each of the ten people decides to put $10,000 into the business. They now have $100,000, but they need more. They try to interest others in their idea. These people would also be expected to put $10,000 into the new business. They find 40 more people who agree they will risk $10,000 of their money to get started. The group is able to get a charter from the state, and the John Doe Corporation is formed. It has a capital of $500,000, that is, $10,000 from each of 50 people. Each person, therefore, has an equal **share** in the corporation. If others want to own part of the corporation, they can buy a share for $10,000. It is these **shareholders** who own the corporation.

6 ▶ The corporation now is a real person under the law. Business is carried on by the John Doe Corporation, not by any single person. The shareholders will elect a board

Stock certificate. Who can purchase stock in a corporation? According to paragraph 5, what is the name for stock owners?

A shareholder's meeting. What do shareholders expect of the corporation? What is the responsibility of the board of directors?

of directors to decide how the business will be run. The board will have to decide what materials to buy, when to buy them, and the kinds of products to be made. The business may borrow money as any single person might. People who own shares of the corporation hope to make a profit. If the business makes money, each share may be worth more money. If the business loses money, each share may be worth less money. Shareholders may sell their shares if they wish. They may get more or less than the $10,000 they put in the business.

7 ▶ The John Doe Corporation will make a product that is being made by several other companies. It will be in competition with them. It will try to make a better product or come up with a new idea for something already in use. It may try to sell its goods at lower prices than those of other companies. It has to sell its goods in order to make a profit. This competition for sales is an important part of the free enterprise system. Soap companies bring out "new and improved" products every few years. The ball-point pen was a new idea only forty years ago. It became popular. People wanted ball-point pens instead of fountain pens. The camera that gives a finished picture in a minute forced other companies to make the same kind of product. Competition brings new products to the American people.

8 ▶ Economic systems have "ups" and "downs." Prices rise and fall. Wages and profits go up and down. When prices, profits, wages, and production of goods are rising and there are many jobs, it is a period of boom. When there is growing unemployment and falling profits, wages, and production, it is a **recession.** If conditions

Bread line during the depression of the 1930s. What is a depression? What causes recessions and depressions?

become even worse, it is called a **depression**—the low point. This is one result of the free enterprise system. We call this change from boom to depression a **business cycle.**

9 ▶ In our system, the government does not set the price of most goods. It does not set the wages of most workers. A company will charge the price that will bring it the most profit. Workers will work for the best wage they are able to receive from their employers. When prices keep rising and wages do not rise with them, people cannot buy goods. When people buy less, businesses will make fewer goods, since they cannot sell as much as before. If a company makes fewer goods, it needs fewer workers. The number of people out of work grows. Fewer people are able to buy goods. Then business may lower prices. When business is able to sell goods again, the whole cycle begins anew.

10 ▶ Our government has tried to solve some of the problems that arise in our capitalistic system. The government places controls on what a business may or may not do. Laws have been passed to make sure that competition among businesses is fair. The first such laws were passed in the late 19th century. (See page 154.) Before that time, most Americans felt that government should let business run itself. However, in 1887, the government set up an agency to stop unfair practices of railroad companies. About the same time, some businesses making the same kinds of goods agreed to charge the same prices for their products. Their prices were lower than those of other companies. This plan would cause the other companies to go out of business.

Dealer caught watering milk, New York City, late 19th century. Practices such as this caused the government to pass laws to regulate business.

Then the businesses that made the first agreement would again set their prices high. They would have no competition. Congress forbade this practice as early as 1890. Another unfair business practice occurs when businesses agree to hold back their goods from sale. This causes the goods' prices to rise. The Federal Trade Commission was set up by Congress in 1914. It tries to stop attempts at unfair competition. It also tries to prevent advertising that misleads the public.

11 ▶ From time to time, the government has tried to stop the "ups" and "downs" of the business cycle. A big problem is **inflation.** This is the sharp rise in prices, wages, and profits. There have been times when the government has "frozen" prices and wages. They have been kept at a certain level. However, these controls have never lasted for a long time. This kind of control has been used only when there were serious economic problems. Congress set up the

Federal Reserve System in 1913. This is our national banking system. Federal Reserve Banks can control the amount of money in use. Through their controls, our people are sometimes saved from the "ups" and "downs" of the business cycle. (See page 304.)

12▶ Most Americans believe in some controls on our capitalistic system. If there were no controls, businesses, labor unions, and banks could do whatever they pleased. There have been harmful practices in the past. Each bit of control, however, takes away some freedom from our economic system. How much freedom should be allowed? The American people have to answer this question. It would be wonderful if our system worked for everyone's benefit without controls. So far, this has not been possible.

CHAPTER 35 REVIEW

★UNDERSTANDING WHAT YOU HAVE READ

1. A good title for paragraph 9 might be
   a. Prices and Wages in the Business Cycle
   b. Let Business Alone
   c. Government Keeps Business Honest

2. The main idea of paragraph 10 is that
   a. prices and wages are always at the same level
   b. our economic system does have some government control of business
   c. government has tried to reduce the "ups and downs" of business life

3. Money, buildings, and tools used to produce goods and make a profit are called
   a. a cycle
   b. capital
   c. corporations

4. When wages are low and many are out of work, it is called
   a. a depression
   b. inflation
   c. competition

5. The capitalism of the United States can be described as
   a. government control of all business life

   b. complete freedom of choice and action
   c. freedom of choice and action, with some limits

6. The owners of a corporation are the
   a. partners
   b. banks
   c. shareholders

7. A feature of a partnership is that
   a. only one person takes risks
   b. one partner may have debts the other must also pay
   c. debts cannot be applied to either partner

8. One of the jobs of the Federal Trade Commission is to
   a. stop false advertising
   b. reduce railroad rates
   c. control the amount of money banks can lend

9. Several companies agree to sell the same product at the same price. This is called
   a. free enterprise
   b. an unfair business practice
   c. capitalism within limits

10. Which is likely to be a large business?
    a. A trucking firm that moves furniture across the country
    b. A locksmith
    c. The law firm of Lopez and Son

11. The three most important parts of our capitalistic system are
    a. capital, business, and banks
    b. capital, land, and mines
    c. capital, labor, and land

★ DEVELOPING SOCIAL STUDIES SKILLS

A. Interpreting a Cartoon

Study the cartoon below. Then answer the questions.

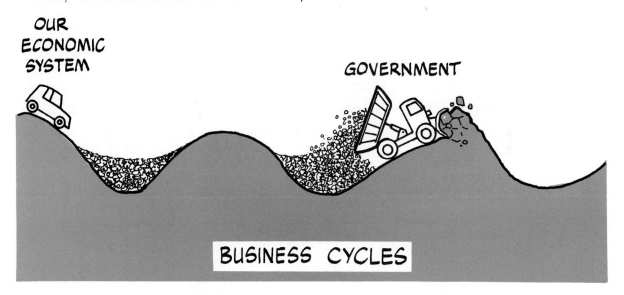

1. How are business cycles shown on the cartoon?

2. What problems does the economic system face in the cartoon?

3. How is the government trying to overcome the problems shown?

4. How does the government try to create a "smoother road" for the economic system as described in Chapter 35?

5. What would be a good title for the cartoon?

B. Interpreting Graphs

Study the graph, then answer the questions that follow.

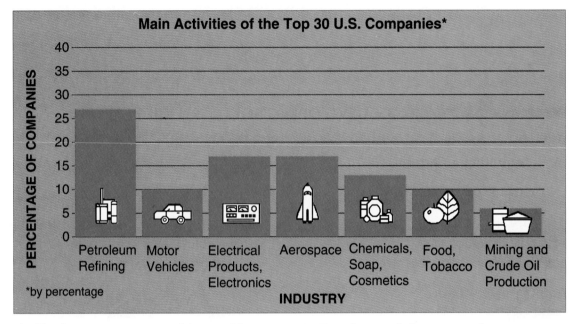

Main Activities of the Top 30 U.S. Companies*

PERCENTAGE OF COMPANIES

40 35 30 25 20 15 10 5 0

Petroleum Refining — Motor Vehicles — Electrical Products, Electronics — Aerospace — Chemicals, Soap, Cosmetics — Food, Tobacco — Mining and Crude Oil Production

*by percentage

INDUSTRY

1. The largest percentage of the top 30 companies
   a. refine petroleum
   b. produce motor vehicles
   c. produce crude oil.

2. Of the top 30 companies
   a. aerospace companies equal those that produce electronics
   b. food and tobacco companies are the highest in number
   c. chemical, soap, and cosmetic companies equal motor vehicle companies.

3. Which of these companies have the same percentage in the top 30?
   a. petroleum refining and aerospace
   b. mining and crude oil and aerospace
   c. electronics, electrical, and aerospace.

4. Petroleum refining companies
   a. outnumber aerospace companies by more than 3 to 1
   b. outnumber food and tobacco companies
   c. have the same percentage as electronics and electrical companies.

5. Electronics companies
   a. have a smaller percentage of top 30 companies than mining and crude oil companies
   b. are tied for the second highest percentage of top 30 companies
   c. have no companies in the top 30.

C. Studying How a Business Works

Study the following description. Then answer the questions.

Dick and Dell are a married couple in their mid-twenties. They have saved some money and want to open a quick-food stand. Each one has saved $5,000. They find they need more than that to get started. They are able to borrow money from a bank. They plan to open the small business near their home. The stand will sell hamburgers, frankfurters, and beef sandwiches. There are other stands that serve the same foods near them. They hope to make their business successful with good food and good service.

They get the necessary permit from the city and build their stand. Their business is a success. They have more customers than they ever dreamed of having. People come to Dell's as the place is called, because of the fast and courteous service they receive. Health inspectors from the city give Dell's the highest ratings.

Because of their success, they plan to open a second Dell's about a mile away. They choose a place for their stand, but the city says they cannot build there. The spot they chose is in a section where only private homes can be built. They find another good place for their stand and build there. They cannot complete the stand fast enough to take care of the people who want to eat at Dell's.

Their success is repeated at the new place. Since their first stand opened, three older food stands have gone out of business in that neighborhood. Dick and Dell realize that they are offering something people want. They decide to build another Dell's in a nearby town.

Soon, they are trying to gather more money to widen their business. Within ten years there are 30 Dell's across the state. Along the way to this success, they received a charter from the state that allowed others to put money into their business. Dell's is now a business owned by more than 50 shareholders.

1. What kind of business organization did Dick and Dell have when they opened their first food stand?

2. How does this story show "freedom of enterprise"?

3. What does the story tell us about competition among businesses?

4. What capital did Dick and Dell have to start their business?

5. What kinds of capital did Dick and Dell add to their business?

6. When the owners needed additional capital, how did they get it?

7. At what point did the Dell's stands become a corporation?

8. What are three ways that governments controlled what Dick and Dell did with their business?

36 WORKERS AND THEIR GOVERNMENT

PURPOSES FOR READING

1. To understand how the government and public looked upon the problems of workers early in our history
2. To understand how and why labor unions were formed
3. To learn the attitude of the government and public toward disputes between employers and workers

---

KNOWING NEW WORDS

federation
(fed uh RAY shuN) paragraph 7—a group of several organizations; a union by agreement
EXAMPLE: Our federal government is a **federation** of 50 states.

industry
(IN duh stree) paragraph 7—manufacturing products for business
EXAMPLE: Many workers are employed in the steel **industry.**

collective
(kuh LEK tiv) paragraph 8—of a group rather than of separate individuals
EXAMPLE: In the Soviet Union, there are **collective** farms where farm families work together on the same land.

security
(sih KYOOR ih tee) paragraph 9—freedom from danger or risk; safety
EXAMPLE: People want **security** from fear and need in their old age.

---

1 ▶ Some workers were hired to build homes at 65 cents a day. A week's work would give workers $3.90 to take care of their families as best they could. Workers built miserable huts on the grounds where they were working. Then they decided to join together and ask for higher pay. When they asked their employer for 87 cents a day, they were refused. The workers went on strike. The employer then hired others to take their places. The workers on strike fought with the newly hired workers

for their jobs. The government sent in a large force to stop the violence. The newcomers were protected in their work. The workers who asked for more pay and went on strike lost their jobs. A strange story? It couldn't happen? It did, in the United States, many times, only a little over a hundred years ago.

2 ▶ Paragraph 1 helps us to understand the position of workers in our economic system during the 1800s. People who looked for jobs would have to work for the pay offered to them. If the pay was small, they could refuse the job. But a plant manager could easily find the workers needed. There were many others who were happy to have a job, even at low pay. The plant could hire women and children instead of men and pay them lower wages. As long as there were plenty of people who wanted jobs, workers were forced to take whatever an employer offered them. Business owners wanted to hold down costs and make a greater profit. Workers, on the other hand, wanted to get better pay and working conditions. Government usually kept out of arguments between employers and workers, except to keep peace.

3 ▶ Farms, factories, and mills cannot do without workers. Capital is of little value unless it is put to use. People, on the other hand, need capital. It is capital that creates jobs, and people need jobs. Capital and labor would seem to be a team of equals. But, they were not. As the factory system grew in the 1800s, workers had almost no power to get better wages and shorter hours of work. Businesses held the jobs and therefore had the power.

4 ▶ Workers began to feel that the only

The Homestead Strike, 1892. Strikes such as this one of steel workers helped to demonstrate the need for unions.

way to get better pay and shorter hours of work was to join together. One worker who asked for more pay had little power. But workers thought that if all of them demanded better pay, all would not be fired. The first modern unions were formed in the 1820s. They were small unions. The members were those with a trade. These were skilled workers. They called strikes and won many of them. Since they had skills, employers could not replace them so quickly. But, courts often ruled that strikes were against the law. Also, during hard times, many workers lost their jobs. They could not pay union dues. Most of the early unions slowly passed away.

5 ▶ Late in the 1800s, the problems of workers were much the same, or worse. Millions of people were coming to America from Europe. They looked for work in the factories of our cities. The number of people looking for jobs was greater than ever. Only unions of skilled workers could strike for higher pay with any success. As businesses

Women march in a labor parade in 1912. Explain the meaning of the signs the women are carrying.

became bigger and bigger, it was even harder to form unions. If workers went on strike in one plant, the owners would shut down the plant. This is called a **lockout.** Most workers had no savings. As a result, they had to return to work on the owner's terms in a few weeks.

6 ▶ Besides the lockout, there were other ways business could keep unions from forming. Workers could get a job only if they agreed not to join a union. Employers also kept lists of workers who were active in forming unions. If such persons wanted a job, no employer would hire them. This is called a **blacklist.** Then, too, the government and the public were not friendly to unions. Unions caused trouble, they felt. Government officials were quick to send troops to keep the peace. The result was help for businesses in labor troubles. Courts hurt unions, too. Courts issued orders that forbade workers to strike. Strikes, they said, hurt an employer's business. To call a strike was unfair to the employer.

7 ▶ In spite of these problems, workers did organize into unions. The American Federation of Labor was established in 1886. These were unions of skilled workers.

Since they received higher wages, they could pay higher union dues. Many strikes called by the A.F. of L. led to success. But the large numbers of unskilled workers were still without power. It was not until 1935 that these workers were organized. The Congress of Industrial Organizations

Factory closing, late 1800s. Business problems affected both management and labor. If the business could not make profits, it closed, and workers lost their jobs. The families of the workers were often the hardest hit.

(CIO) brought workers in a single industry into one union. Skilled and unskilled workers in steel plants were in one union. Auto workers made up another. Workers in transportation formed another, and so on. The result was that several million workers were now in unions. A change in the attitudes of the public and government made this growth possible.

8 ▶ For most of American history, government had helped business. It had not placed many controls on what business could do. During the terms of office of President Franklin D. Roosevelt, that picture changed. In the 1930s the country was suffering from the worst depression in its history. Congress passed several laws that helped workers and unions. The National Labor Relations Act of 1935 guaranteed workers the right of **collective bargaining.** This meant that employers had to meet with workers to talk over wages, hours, and conditions of work. Employers cannot say, "We're not going to speak to you." They must meet with their workers. Workers may choose whomever they wish to speak for them. They may vote and pick a union of their choice.

9 ▶ The Social Security Act was also passed in 1935. This law helps protect workers against the problems of old age. Workers and their employers put aside a certain amount of money. When workers retire, they receive a monthly check. The law also provides help for workers when they cannot find jobs. States also passed laws that helped workers if they were hurt on the job or were sick for a long time. Three years later, the Wages and Hours Act was passed. This law forbade a business

President Roosevelt signs the Social Security Act in 1935. What was the purpose of this law?

that operates in more than one state to pay workers less than 40 cents an hour. This is called a minimum wage—the lowest legal wage that can be paid. That figure has been raised many times since then. Also, workers were not to work more than 40 hours a week for regular wages. If workers agreed to work longer than that, they would have a higher rate of pay. Other laws set the minimum age for holding a job. Laws also limited the number of hours children could work.

10 ▶ Unions, protected by new laws, began to grow quickly after 1935. By 1940, 10 million workers belonged to unions. That number grew to a peak of 23 million by 1975. By 1990, however, union membership had dropped to 17 million workers. Most workers today do not belong to unions. To some people, unions had too much power. In 1947, Congress passed another labor law, the Taft-Hartley Act. This new law cut into some union powers. The president was to delay a strike in important industries for 80 days. The time

287

Present-day strikers. Compare this picture with the one on page 285. How are they alike? Why are they different?

was to be used to settle the dispute. The law also allows states to pass "right to work laws." These laws allow a business to hire non-union workers, even though the business has a contract with a union.

11 ▶ Labor as well as business is controlled by the government in some ways. The government often steps in to settle a strike. Strikes by sanitation workers or police can tie up an entire city. Strikes by workers in coal mines or steel plants affect the entire country. In chapter 35 unfair practices by business were discussed. The public can suffer when either business or labor has too much power. The government, therefore, no longer keeps "hands off" business and labor. Rather, it tries to find ways to control the powers of both.

CHAPTER 36 REVIEW

★ UNDERSTANDING WHAT YOU HAVE READ

1. The main idea of paragraph 4 is that
   a. the first unions of workers were started in the 1820s
   b. early unions of skilled workers had little power
   c. skilled workers were the first to form unions

2. The main idea of paragraph 6 is that
   a. many workers could not get a job if they joined a union
   b. both the government and business hurt early attempts to form labor unions
   c. courts often forbade strikes

3. Wages of workers are likely to be low when
   a. there are few jobs and many people want work
   b. the number of workers in unions is growing
   c. there are many jobs and few people are looking for work

4. When workers went on strike, an employer would shut down the business. This is called
   a. a lockout
   b. a blacklist
   c. collective bargaining

5. In the 1800s, when workers called a strike the courts would usually

a. make employers meet with the leaders of the workers
b. make both sides pay a fine if they did not settle the dispute
c. rule that the strike was against the law

6. One of the reasons for the early success of the American Federation of Labor (A.F. of L.) was that it
a. was a union of skilled workers
b. formed unions from all workers in one plant
c. had the support of the laws of the United States

7. Congress passed several laws that helped workers and their unions during which period?
a. 1820–1835
b. 1886–1910
c. 1935–1940

8. Which of these laws made sure that workers had the right to form unions and meet with their employers to talk over their conditions of work?
a. National Labor Relations Act
b. Social Security Act
c. Taft-Hartley Act

★ DEVELOPING CRITICAL THINKING SKILLS

A. Looking at Both Sides: Strikes by Public Workers

Some states have laws that forbid strikes by persons who work for local and state governments. But public workers have walked off their jobs in many cities and towns across the country. Public workers include teachers, police officers, fire fighters, and sanitation and transportation workers. In some cases, cities had run out of money. So workers had not been paid for some weeks. In others, workers have felt that they were not paid as well as other workers in private industry.

Here are some arguments used for and against strikes by public workers. Study both sides. Then answer the questions that follow.

Public Workers Should Be Allowed to Strike	Public Workers Should Not Be Allowed to Strike
1. Workers are people no matter where they work. Public workers deserve good pay as much as workers anywhere else.	1. Workers usually ask for more money than they deserve for the work they do.
2. The public takes the work of police officers, fire fighters, teachers, and others for granted. The strike makes people realize how valuable their work is.	2. Taxpayers pay the wages of public workers. Governments do not make a profit. Public workers cannot be paid as much as people who work for a business that makes a profit.

3. The public should provide for the welfare of the people who work for them.	3. Most governments are in debt. The public pays heavy taxes now. They cannot pay more.
4. A strike is the only way workers have of telling the public when they are being treated unfairly.	4. Public safety is more important than the pay of individuals. When public workers strike, the welfare of all people is in danger.
5. Other workers can strike. Public workers should not be denied the rights others have. They are citizens, too.	5. People know when they become public workers that they cannot strike because of the job they have. No one forced them to take the jobs they have.

1. Which argument in favor of strikes by public workers seems to you to be the strongest? Why?

2. In your opinion, what is the strongest argument against such strikes? Support your opinion.

3. Do you think public workers should or should not have the same rights as other workers? Why?

4. Do you think the safety of the public is more important than the rights of individuals? Why?

5. How would you settle the dispute between the two points of view?

B. Workers Under Free Enterprise and Centralized Economic Systems

Study the comparisons below between workers in a free enterprise system and those under a centralized government. Then answer the questions.

	Free Enterprise System	Centralized Economy
Unions	Workers have a free choice of forming unions or joining them.	Unions represent what the government wants them to do. Chief purpose is to urge workers to produce more goods.
Choice of Job	Workers are free to choose their jobs and change jobs if they wish.	People work where the government says they are needed. Skilled workers are changing jobs more now than in previous years.

Wages	Unions can bargain with employers to determine pay, hours, and conditions of work. Workers may strike if disputes cannot be settled any other way.	Wages are often set by plant managers. If workers produce more, they may get rewards of some kind. Strikes are forbidden.
Security (Pensions)	Unions work out pension plans with employers. Social Security helps provide for workers when retired or ill.	Almost all workers receive pensions when they retire. Those who are disabled or blind may receive pensions before that. Pensions are at half pay or more.
Women	Women are employed in almost all fields of work. However, women often do not receive the same pay as men for equal work.	Women work on the same terms as men. Women have done heavy work, driving trucks and tractors, and working in factories.
Government	Allows as much freedom as possible. Laws guarantee workers' rights.	Plans for business and farms are made by the government. The government has the final word. Some governments have begun to allow managers and farmers greater freedom in planning.

1. In which economic system do workers seem to have the most power to decide their way of life?

2. In which system does the government act as a peacemaker rather than as a dictator of business and labor?

3. In which economic system have women been accepted as an important part of the labor force?

4. In China's system, does it seem that workers have security in their old age?

5. In which system are workers likely to improve their pay more easily?

6. What generalization or summary statement can you make from the facts in the chart?

C. Fact or Opinion

Tell whether the statements on page 292 are facts or someone's opinion. If the statement is an opinion, tell whether you agree or disagree with it. Give your reasons.

1. Collective bargaining is the best way for workers and employers to decide on the conditions of workers.

2. The problems of workers did not change much from the 1820s to 1900.

3. Capital and labor should be equal in power if each is to have a fair settlement of disputes.

4. Workers should not have to be members of a union in order to get a job.

5. The Congress of Industrial Organiza-tions (CIO) allowed both skilled and unskilled workers to become union members.

6. After 1935, workers could not be fired from their jobs because they were union members.

7. In our past history, it seemed that the government ruled with business against workers.

8. The profits of business are more impor-tant to our economic system than the wages of workers.

PARTICIPATION IN GOVERNMENT

USING SMALL CLAIMS COURTS

Small claims courts are especially designed to help people who have a claim of only a few hundred dollars and who cannot afford to hire a lawyer. Nearly 4,000,000 people use these courts every year. Cases most often involve such issues as complaints against stores, problems with neighbors, broken contracts, and poorly performed services.

In order to file your claim, call the small claims court in your area and ask for advice. Forms to file your complaint will be provided for you at the courthouse. You will have to pay a small fee to file, probably no more than $20, and often much less.

Be sure that you've collected all of the information that you will need to present your case in court. Judges require actual proof, not just opinions. Gather your receipts, contracts, names and addresses of concerned parties, and any other records you might need. Get as much in writing as possible. If you have any reliable witnesses, make arrangements for them to appear with you. Plan in advance what you wish to say.

Most small claims courts are open in the evenings and weekends for your convenience. When you are scheduled to appear, get to court early. You may have to wait until your case is heard. But if you are late for the hearing, the case will be dismissed. Arriving early will also give you the opportunity to watch court proceedings. Don't hesitate to ask for advice and help if there is something that is unclear to you.

The person making the complaint is known as the *plaintiff*. The person defending him- or herself against the claim is the *defendant*. Both parties will be under oath, that is, sworn to tell the truth.

After all of the evidence has been presented to the court, the jude will make a decision. The judge may not grant the exact settlement you wish. But whether of not your claim is accepted, you will have the satisfaction of knowing that our system of justice has allowed your complaint to be hear, at little cost to you.

37

THE AMERICAN FARMER AND SURPLUS CROPS

PURPOSES FOR READING

1. To understand how American farming has changed in the last 50 years
2. To understand the problems of American farmers
3. To learn how the federal government has tried to solve farm problems

KNOWING NEW WORDS

specialize
(SPESH uh lyz) paragraph 4—to follow a special line of work
EXAMPLE: Some stores **specialize** in selling flowers.

parity
(PAR ih tee) paragraph 8—equality in value or amount
EXAMPLE: The star baseball players enjoyed **parity** in salary.

Farmers today. What changes in farming over the last 50 years are evident in this picture?

1. What does Uncle Sam represent in the drawing?

2. What does the truck represent?

3. What are we told in the picture by the overflowing basket?

4. What is the artist's purpose in making this drawing?

5. What would be a good title for the drawing?

1▶ When settlers first arrived from Europe in the 1600s, families had to grow their own food. Each member of the family had a job to do. If the job wasn't done, people simply did not eat. Over 200 years later, most people in the United States still lived on farms. Many farm families raised just enough food to feed themselves. A little of the crop might have been left over to buy seed and pay their bills. But the machine age came to the farms as well as to industry. By 1900, about one-third of the American people lived on farms. The number has dropped sharply since then. Now only one American in 50 makes a living from farm work. The reason is a simple one. Fewer farmers are needed to grow all the food Americans need.

2▶ The cartoon on this page and the graphs on page 295 tell us the story of American farmers today. They do much more than feed their own families. One farmer in the United States can raise enough food to feed 78 people. But there is even more to the farm story. American farmers grow so much food that they can feed much of the rest of the world, too. The United States exports more wheat, corn, barley, and oats than all the rest of the world combined. Because of the output of

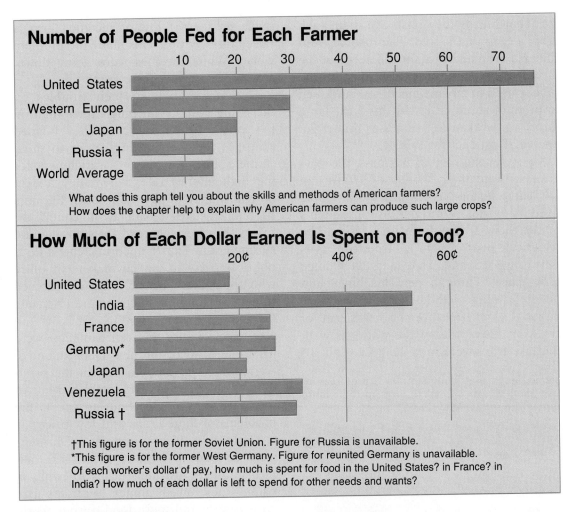

Number of People Fed for Each Farmer

| | 10 | 20 | 30 | 40 | 50 | 60 | 70 |

United States
Western Europe
Japan
Russia †
World Average

What does this graph tell you about the skills and methods of American farmers?
How does the chapter help to explain why American farmers can produce such large crops?

How Much of Each Dollar Earned Is Spent on Food?

| | 20¢ | 40¢ | 60¢ |

United States
India
France
Germany*
Japan
Venezuela
Russia †

†This figure is for the former Soviet Union. Figure for Russia is unavailable.
*This figure is for the former West Germany. Figure for reunited Germany is unavailable.
Of each worker's dollar of pay, how much is spent for food in the United States? in France? in India? How much of each dollar is left to spend for other needs and wants?

Source: Department of Agriculture

our farms, Americans are well fed, and the cost of food is low. (See graph above.) Americans also have a wide variety of food at their meals.

3 ▶ Today's farmers use all kinds of new machinery. Machinery costs money. (A grain combine can cost $85,000 and be used only a few weeks of the year.) This machinery is just too expensive to use on a small farm. As a result, American farmers have become "big" farmers, running their fields much like a factory. It is true that more than half the country's farmers live on smaller farms. But their incomes are small, too. Most have other jobs that provide much of their income.

4 ▶ Only 15 percent of the farms in this country take in $65 of every $100 that farmers make from the sale of crops and animals. These are big farms. Most **special-**

ize. That means they raise one main cash crop, a crop that is sold. The income from the cash crop provides for the needs of the farm family and more. It also provides the money used to buy the machinery and seed to produce more grain. In this way, large farms are worked as businesses that make one chief product for sale.

5 ▶ As in the case of business, the government kept their "hands off" farms in our early history. After all, most people lived on farms. Our first five presidents made their living from the land. The American people were a farming people. Between 1865 and 1900, a great change took place. Through new machines and better farming methods, farm crops were larger than ever before. This was true of crops in other parts of the world as well. Because crops were so large, prices fell. To

Signing away the family farm. List three reasons why people were forced to give up their farms during the period 1865-1900.

make up for the loss of income, farmers raised larger crops. This made the problem worse. While incomes were going down, costs to the farmer were rising.

6 ▶ Farmers blamed their troubles on the rising costs of farming rather than on low prices for their crops. They blamed railroads for charging high rates to small farmers. Farmers blamed warehouses for the high interest rates when they had to borrow money to pay their debts. Farmers tried to get states to pass laws to control the prices they were charged for shipping and storing grain. They helped to create a third political party to get lawmakers in office who understood farmers. They did succeed in getting Congress to create the Interstate Commerce Commission in 1887. Its job was to make sure that railroad rates were just. The head of the new Department of Agriculture was made a part of the president's cabinet two years later. Neither of these actions brought about an end to the problems of large crops and low prices.

7 ▶ In the 1920s, problems of farmers were so bad that many more left their farms. Others lost their farms to banks to whom they owed money. Farmers had grown more and more food during World War I. Many borrowed money to buy more land and machinery. After the war, however, farm prices returned to normal. Farmers could not pay back the money they borrowed. In the 1930s the price of corn had fallen so low that farmers burned it instead of coal. Dairy farmers refused to sell milk unless the price was raised. Farmers continued to lose their land and homes because of debts. It was time for the government to act.

A bumper corn harvest in Illinois. How does the government help regulate surplus crops?

8 ▶ Have you heard the expression, "That's par for the course"? You may have played or watched golf on TV. If a golfer scores what is expected, he or she shoots par. It is a good score, a fair score. In the 1930s several laws were passed by Congress to give farmers a **par** price for their crops. It is called **parity.** The idea is that the prices for farm crops should allow farmers to live as well as people in other kinds of work. These prices would be par, or parity prices. Parity prices were to be those that farmers received in 1910–1914. They are like minimum wages that workers receive. Prices cannot go below the par figure. Other laws set up ways that the government would keep farm prices at parity.

9 ▶ The Department of Agriculture has the job of keeping up the prices of some crops. It buys **surplus** crops. (A surplus is more of something than is needed.) The government pays farmers for these crops at a price near parity. The surplus is then stored by the government. In other cases, the government must pay farmers the difference between the price for grain and parity. For example, the farmer can sell a bushel of corn for $2.00. Parity is $2.20. The government pays the farmer 20 cents a bushel for each bushel the farmer sells. Loans are also given to farmers to pay their bills at harvest time. Farmers don't have to sell their crops right away. They can wait until prices are higher. When crops are sold, they can pay back the loan.

10 ▶ The big problem for farmers has been that they grow too much. When there is too much of a crop, its value drops. Farmers are encouraged to plant less of their land. The government tells farmers how many acres to plant. If farmers want parity prices and loans, they have to follow government orders. This has not always worked out the way it was planned. American farmers have even grown a surplus when less land has been planted. The government also pays farmers for not planting some of their land in grain. Grasses are planted for a few years to keep the soil fertile. Then the land can be planted with crops again. This is called a **soil bank.**

11 ▶ Farm problems will continue. In the

1980s, farmers complained of high interest rates on their loans. In addition, crop sales to foreign countries declined. More countries were now able to grow enough grain to feed themselves and also to sell. This increased the world's supply of grain. Farm prices dropped and the income of American farmers fell. Because of these conditions, farm debts increased to dangerous levels. All of these problems continued despite aid from the federal government, which had multiplied five times in three years. Thousands had to give up their farms. How can the problems of farmers whose work is so vital to everyone be solved? You as a citizen will be called on to suggest and approve solutions.

CHAPTER 37 REVIEW

★ UNDERSTANDING WHAT YOU HAVE READ

1. The main idea of paragraph 6 is that
   a. farmers tried to solve their problems by seeking the help of the government
   b. the government began to control railroad rates
   c. farm prices dropped lower than ever

2. This chapter tells us that
   a. the number of people living on farms has dropped sharply
   b. about half our people live on farms today
   c. the number of farms in the United States is growing

3. An important idea of this chapter is that
   a. only one other country grows as much food as the United States farmers
   b. United States farmers produce more food than Americans eat
   c. most of our food is grown on small farms

4. When farmers specialize, they
   a. obtain loans to pay their bills
   b. grow one main crop for sale
   c. use costly labor to harvest crops

5. During the early history of the United States
   a. most people lived on farms
   b. the government helped farmers get good prices for their crops
   c. farms were much like the factories of today

6. Perhaps the chief problem of farmers in our history has been
   a. the high cost of farm machinery
   b. too much government control of farm life
   c. low prices and high costs

7. The government helps farmers in all these ways EXCEPT:
   a. It buys surplus crops.
   b. It makes loans to farmers.
   c. It gives farmers surplus land to grow surplus crops.

8. A parity price is a kind of
   a. soil bank
   b. minimum price for crops
   c. business cycle

9. Keeping up the prices of some crops is the job of the
   a. Federal Trade Commission
   b. Interstate Commerce Commission
   c. Department of Agriculture

A. Making Comparisons

Read the chart below and then answer the questions on page 300.

	Farming in 1890	Farming Today
Farm Residents	Over 40% of the total U.S. population lived on farms.	Less than 2% of the total U.S. population lives on farms. More than half of all working people who live on farms have jobs in nonfarm occupations.
Size of Farms	Farms were generally small. The average farm size was 137 acres.	The average size of farms has increased as small farms are replaced by large corporate farms. In 1991, the average farm size was 467 acres. Most of the crops sold are produced by large farms owned by corporations.
Number of Farms	The total number of farms in the United States was 4,565,000.	The number of farms is steadily decreasing because small farms have trouble competing with large corporate farms. By 1991, the total number of farms had fallen to 2,105,000.
Equipment	Farming equipment was simple and relatively inexpensive.	Equipment has become much more expensive. Small farmers often can not afford machinery which would increase production.
Crop Production	Before 1850, farms often produced what people needed to live on and only a small surplus. By 1890, new farming technology allowed farmers to raise more crops. Crop prices fell. Many people lost their farms.	Farming technology continues to improve and the amount that can be grown per acre has increased. U.S. farmers usually produce a large surplus of crops. The government tries to control this surplus.
Government in Farming	Government did not have many programs to deal with the problems of large crops and low prices.	Government has many programs to help farmers, including setting up parity prices, buying surplus crops, and creating a soil bank.

1. a.) What was the percentage of the total U.S. population that lived on farms in 1890? b.) What is the percentage of farm residents today?

2. a.) How has the average size of farms changed from 1890 to today? b.) Why has farm size changed?

3. How do you predict that the total number of farms in the United States will change in the future?

4. How did farming technology change crop production after the 1850s?

5. How do you think the rising cost of farming equipment will affect the ability of small farms to compete with large corporate farms?

6. Based on this table and the information you read in this chapter, why does the U.S. government try to regulate surplus crop production?

B. True or False

Tell whether these statements are true or false. The underlined words may be true or false. If the word makes the statement false, replace it with a word that would make the statement true.

1. Each United States farmer grows enough food to feed <u>five</u> people.

2. Each family in the United States spends <u>about 23 cents</u> of each dollar earned for food. (See graph on page 295.)

3. The United States exports more <u>wheat</u> than any other country in the world.

4. The income of farmers is <u>smaller</u> on large farms.

5. <u>Trucks</u> were first blamed by farmers for the high cost of shipping grain to market.

6. <u>Parity</u> is a price set for farm products that gives farmers a fair income for their work.

7. The <u>Department of Agriculture</u> keeps prices at a fair level.

8. In 1800, most people in the United States lived on farms. Today, <u>fewer</u> people live on farms.

9. Some farmers raise one crop for sale. This is called a <u>loan</u> crop.

C. Writing About Citizenship

Write one or two well-organized paragraphs that answer the following question: How do you think the government should try to help farmers with their economic problems? Suggest one or two things the government might do.

38

MONEY
AND BANKING

PURPOSES FOR READING

1. To understand how money works as a means of exchange
2. To learn the meaning of several forms of money
3. To learn the purposes of the Federal Reserve System
4. To understand how the Federal Reserve System tries to regulate our economic system

KNOWING NEW WORDS

circulation
(sur kyuh LAY shun) paragraph 3— the movement of something through a system; money passing from one person to others as in trade
EXAMPLE: If people kept all they earned, there would be no money in **circulation.**

reserve
(rih ZURV) paragraph 11— something kept back or saved for the future
EXAMPLE: I didn't spend all of the $100; I kept $20 in **reserve.**

discount
(DIS kount) paragraph 9— a reduction; payment of interest in advance of receiving a loan
EXAMPLE: She borrowed $1,000 from the bank. But she received $920. The bank had subtracted an $80 **discount** from her $1,000.

How many different kinds of money can you identify in this picture?

The average new home costs over $100,000. Most home buyers have not saved up that much money. They borrow most of the money from banks. How do banks benefit from loaning money to home buyers?

1▶ "I'll swap you for it!" You've heard someone say that many times. It simply means, "I'll give you something you want. You give me something I want." Through much of history, one person might give another something in exchange for something else. A bag of grain might be given in exchange for some logs. This is called **barter,** or trading of goods. Each person involved in barter had something another person needed. There are problems with barter. How could people save up wealth when some of the products used for barter might spoil? Or what if one person wanted a chicken, but all that person had to offer in trade was a horse? In some places certain kinds of things were accepted as payment. Some Indian groups used beads made from shells to trade or buy what they wanted. In World War II, American soldiers in Europe used cigarettes or chocolate to buy what they wanted. Whatever has value, is worth something, can be used to buy or trade. In our economic system, we place a value on things in terms of money.

2▶ To be of use, people must accept money in exchange for goods. Everyone must know what the value of the money is. When our country first declared its independence in 1776, each state made its own kind of money. This caused endless arguments. In the United States today, there is one money system. The federal government has the power to set up a money system. It has the power to coin money. The money we use is **legal tender.** That means it must be accepted by all as a means of payment for goods and debts. It is valuable because everyone uses it. It is accepted in everyday business.

3▶ Gold was once the most widely accepted form of money. Everyone wanted gold. Today, most of our money is in the form of paper. Until 1933, paper money was backed by gold and, at times, silver. A person could take a paper dollar to a bank and get a dollar's worth of gold for it. Then, there were only as many dollars in circulation as there was gold in the treasury of the United States. This is not so today. The government does not hold a dollar's worth of gold for each paper dollar. The government can print more paper money when more money would help the economy. The government can also take money out of circulation. It might do this to try to stop inflation. But, at any time, the value of money is what it can buy.

4► Much of our business is carried on by other forms of paper. They, too, are parts of our money system. A large part of payments for goods is by **check.** When people write checks, they are saying that they have money on deposit in a bank. The person who receives the check will get money from the bank. **Credit** is another form of money. People buy clothes and pay for them at a later time. Much of our business life is based on credit. Many Americans have become "credit card" people. Most people buy their homes on credit. They will pay for them over a long period of time. They will also pay **interest** to the bank for the use of the money that was borrowed. Governments, too, get money from borrowing, to be paid back at a later time.

5► Banks in our country are an important part of our money system. They are not owned by the government. They are private corporations, owned by shareholders. Banks, like corporations, have charters to operate. (See chapter 35.) If the bank has a charter from a federal government, it is a national bank. If it has a charter from a state, it is a state bank. Banks help to make our system of free enterprise work. The government watches over banks to make sure their activities are honest. The federal government also set up a special insurance agency. It insures people's bank deposits against loss should the bank fail.

6► Our government has tried several kinds of banking systems. In 1913 Congress set up the present system. It is called the **Federal Reserve System.** This system guides all the large banks in the United States. This is how it works: The country is divided into 12 districts. Each district has a Federal Reserve Bank. All banks with charters from the federal government are members of the system. Some state banks are also members. The Federal Reserve Bank in each district is owned by its member banks. Member banks own shares in the district bank, as in a corporation. The district bank is then a "bank for bankers."

7► Banks use the Federal Reserve Bank as you might use your own bank. You deposit money in your bank. Your bank deposits money in the Federal Reserve Bank. You borrow money from your bank. Your bank borrows money from the Federal Reserve Bank. You go to your bank for money. Your bank goes to the Federal Reserve Bank for money.

Many people use credit cards, rather than cash, for both large and small purchases.

Banks offer many services to their customers. This woman is able to do her banking without seeing a bank teller. What other services does a bank offer?

8▶ Federal Reserve Banks get money from their member banks. The member banks are required to keep a certain percentage of their money on deposit with their district bank. Each of the 12 district banks can issue **Federal Reserve notes,** based upon the money it has. Your paper money has Federal Reserve note written across the face of the bill. The district bank can lend money to member banks. It also inspects the workings of member banks.

9▶ All banks expect to make a profit from lending money. When money is loaned, often a **discount** is made at the time of the loan. For example, you may borrow $100 from a bank at 10 percent interest. You will pay back to the bank $110. The bank makes a profit of $10 on the loan. Sometimes the bank will take off the amount of the interest before making the loan. The bank will give you $90. You will then pay back $100. This is called **discounting** a loan. It is clear that if the interest rates are low, you and others are more likely to want to borrow money. If interest rates are high, you may not want to ask for a loan.

10▶ When member banks borrow money from the Federal Reserve Bank, their loans are discounted in the same way. Since this is a bank loan to another bank, it is called a **rediscount.** If member banks must pay a high rate of discount to the Federal Reserve Bank, they will ask for a higher rate from you when you want a loan. If the Federal Reserve Bank has a lower discount rate, you will borrow at a lower rate of interest. Federal Reserve Banks can, therefore, control how much money is being borrowed by the public. If there is a need for people to spend money, the rediscount rate will be low. When there is inflation—too much money being spent—the rediscount rate will be raised.

11▶ All the money that people put in a bank is not kept at the bank. The bank tries to make more money through loans and buying stocks and bonds. In this way, it is able to pay interest to people who have deposited there. But banks must keep a set amount of money on hand. The Federal Reserve Board sets this amount. It is called a **reserve.** If the bank's reserve is a small amount of money, they can make more loans. If the reserve is high, they can make fewer loans. The amount of the reserve and the rediscount rate are important in the American economic system. Through these means, the Federal Reserve system tries to control the "ups" and "downs" of the economic system.

Chairman of the Federal Reserve Board Alan Greenspan and Wendy Gramm, chairperson of the Commodity Futures Trading Commission. What is the role of the Federal Reserve Board?

12► The Federal Reserve System is headed by a Board of Governors. The president of the United States names the seven members of the board. They serve a term of 14 years. None of the governors may be named a second time. By law, the members of the board must come from different parts of our economic life. Business people, bankers, and farmers must be represented. It is this board that sets interest rates for the 12 district banks. It decides how much cash the district banks and member banks must have on hand.

13► The Federal Reserve System has nothing to do with the printing or coining of money, however. Our money system is managed by the Treasury Department. It is headed by the secretary of the treasury, a member of the president's cabinet. Congress has given this department the power to coin money. Coins are made at the United States Mint in two places, Philadelphia and Denver. All paper money, including Federal Reserve notes, is printed by the federal government. The Treasury Department is in charge of the printing. It also collects taxes and advises the president on economic policy.

CHAPTER 38 REVIEW

★ UNDERSTANDING WHAT YOU HAVE READ

1. The main idea of paragraph 4 is that
   a. people pay interest on loans from banks
   b. checks can be written only when there is money on deposit in a bank
   c. business is carried on with several kinds of money besides legal tender

2. An important idea of this chapter is that
   a. the federal government has placed controls on the business of banking
   b. the United States national banking system was created by the Constitution
   c. credit is only a small part of the United States money system

3. Banks in this country are
   a. owned by the federal government
   b. owned by shareholders
   c. called national banks

4. The Treasury Department has the power to
   a. print paper money
   b. set interest rates for banks
   c. decide how much money banks can have

5. The amount of money in circulation in the United States
   a. is always the same amount
   b. depends on the rulings of the Federal Reserve Board
   c. is set by the Treasury Department

6. Which statement about the United States money system is TRUE?
   a. A person can turn in a dollar bill at a bank and get $1 worth of gold.
   b. United States money is accepted by everyone as a payment for goods.

   c. Several states have their own money systems.

7. How many Federal Reserve Banks are there?
   a. One, in Washington
   b. Twelve district banks
   c. One in each state

8. If a bank must have a high **reserve,** it
   a. cannot make as many loans as it might with a low reserve
   b. keeps less money back for future use
   c. will advertise that loans are easy to get

9. The Federal Reserve System tries to control the "ups" and "downs" of our economic system through
   a. barter and exchange
   b. credit and charters
   c. reserves and the rediscount rate

10. The paper money we use today is called
    a. gold certificates
    b. silver notes
    c. Federal Reserve notes

★ DEVELOPING SOCIAL STUDIES SKILLS

Interpreting a Diagram

Study the diagram. Then answer the questions that follow it.

How Our Economic System Has Highs and Lows

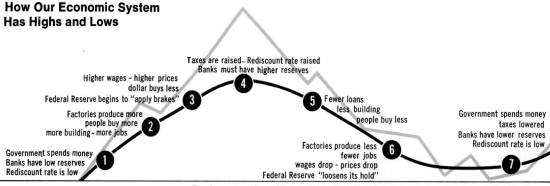

Taxes are raised – Rediscount rate raised
Banks must have higher reserves

Higher wages – higher prices
dollar buys less

Federal Reserve begins to "apply brakes"

Factories produce more
people buy more
more building – more jobs

Government spends money
Banks have low reserves
Rediscount rate is low

Fewer loans
less building
people buy less

Government spends money
taxes lowered
Banks have lower reserves
Rediscount rate is low

Factories produce less
fewer jobs
wages drop – prices drop
Federal Reserve "loosens its hold"

— Business cycle, with controls by government (Federal Reserve System)

　 Business cycle without government controls

1. What conditions cause businesses to grow, and good times for workers? Which conditions are controlled by the Federal Reserve System?

2. What is meant by the statement, "The Federal Reserve begins to put on the brakes"? How can the Federal Reserve System "slow up" the rise in business conditions?

3. What may cause business activity to slow

and perhaps start on a downward path?

4. What is meant by the statement, "the Federal Reserve loosens its hold"?

5. What part of the curve might include inflation?

6. What might the curve look like if there were no government controls in the economic system?

★ DEVELOPING CRITICAL THINKING SKILLS

A. Proving Statements

Some statements can be proved either correct or incorrect. Others cannot be proved or are difficult to prove. In each of the following pairs of statements, select the statement that is *more difficult* to prove correct or incorrect.

1. a. Some Native American groups used beads to trade for the materials they wanted.
   b. A farmer's use of bushels of potatoes to pay his or her lawyer's fees is a good trade.

2. a. State banks have made loans that borrowers will have difficulty in repaying.
   b. State banks have loaned money beyond the amount they have held in reserve.

3. a. The amount people owe on their credit card purchases throughout the country has reached a dangerous level.
   b. The amount of purchases through credit cards has reached the level of the previous year.

B. Writing About Citizenship

Write one or two well-organized paragraphs that answer these questions: What are some of the advantages and disadvantages of buying things on credit? Do you think that there are more advantages, or more disadvantages? Give reasons for your opinions.

PROTECTION FOR THE CONSUMER

PURPOSES FOR READING

1. To understand how the actions of businesses and consumers combine to set prices for goods
2. To recognize how some advertising presents problems for buyers
3. To learn how governments and private groups try to protect consumers
4. To learn ways by which consumers can protect themselves against unwise buying

KNOWING NEW WORDS

snob
(SNOB) paragraph 4—one who acts as though others were inferior
EXAMPLE: Neighbors called him a **snob** because he would not go to their parties, only to those at expensive hotels.

register
(REJ ih stur) paragraph 10, number 4—in a store, a machine that shows the amount of a sale
EXAMPLE: The **register** showed that eggs were 85 cents a dozen.

sensational
(sen SAY shuh nul) paragraph 10, number 9—concerning something that makes a person strongly interested; outstanding, exciting
EXAMPLE: The tearing down of the Berlin Wall was really **sensational** news.

"All Suits 20% Off"

"You'll Find Brand X in Only the Finest Stores."

"Now, New and Improved. Contains XXX-6."

"Now with 20% Greater Cleaning Power"

"Try Brand X. You can lose weight while you sleep."

1▶ How often have you read statements like those on page 308? Or heard them on radio or TV? They are meant to interest you. You are a **consumer,** a user of goods and services. In fact, everyone is a consumer. Everyone eats and wears clothes. Everyone uses some kind of medical service and enjoys some form of entertainment. Even those who make the goods are consumers. Businesses make goods in order to make a profit when people buy the goods. The ads at the beginning of this chapter are meant to make you want what is advertised. What to buy and when to buy are questions every consumer has to answer.

2▶ How are prices of goods set? The business that makes goods wants to make a profit. That profit is only part of the price. Many people must be paid along the way from raw material to finished product. The raw materials cost money. Workers must be paid for their labor. There is the expense of heat, light, rent, and repairs in the factory where goods are made. The goods must be sent by truck or train to stores. Drivers receive wages and fuel costs money. The store where the goods are sold also must

make a profit. All of these costs are included in the price you pay for the goods you buy.

3▶ Prices also depend on demand and supply. Consumers buy what they **need** and what they **want.** Businesses make what they think people will buy. There is no reason for a product to be made if people do not want it. But the producer will try to make people want a product. Goods will be advertised and presented to buyers in a way that attracts them to buy. Producers try to increase the demand for their goods and services. If enough people buy a product or service at the price offered, someone will continue to make it. If more people want to buy a product (high demand), and there are few such products for sale (low supply), the price of the goods will rise. If enough consumers do not buy (low demand, high supply), the price will be lowered, or the product will be taken off the market. In a free enterprise system, the ones who really decide what goods and services are offered for sale are the consumers.

4▶ Consumers face some real problems in using their money wisely. Let's look at

Consumer looking at used car. What kind of protection does a consumer have when buying a used car? Are there any agencies that protect consumers?

the ads at the beginning of the chapter.

- Suits are 20 percent off. Off what price? Yesterday's price, or last week's, or any price set by the store or business?

- The second ad suggests that you will be doing something special if you buy their product. You will be known as one who shops at the finest stores. You will be part of the "smart set." This is known as snob appeal. Is this a good reason for buying a product?

- In the next ad, one might wonder what XXX-6 really is. It could be something new and good. It could be anything given a fancy name that suggests science has discovered something of value. Shouldn't buyers know what XXX-6 is before they buy?

- ". . . 20% more cleaning power." More power than what? The old cleaner? Another cleaner? How can 20% more cleaning power be measured?

- "You can lose weight while you sleep." How much time must be spent in sleep to lose weight? Is it good for your health? Why haven't others tried this easy way of losing weight? (A company that did advertise in this way was fined $50,000 for false advertising.)

5▶ Help for the consumer has come from government. The Federal Trade Commission tries to protect people against false advertising. Through the work of the FTC, cigarette packs must carry the message that smoking is dangerous to your health. The Food and Drug Administration tries to protect the public against the sale of harmful drugs. The Consumer Product Safety Commission has the power to stop the making of goods that are unsafe. It can force companies to correct errors in radios, toasters, and the like that are dangerous to the people who use them.

6▶ There are other aids from the government, too. The U.S. Postal Service has the power to stop those who use the mail to cheat consumers or use false advertising. The Truth-in-Lending Act of 1968 protects against "hidden" interest rates. Businesses must tell the truth about the interest people will pay when buying on credit. Federal, state, and some local governments inspect food. The Department of Agriculture grades all the meat sold in this country. Many

USDA (United States Department of Agriculture) inspector. Why is it important for a government agency, rather than private business, to inspect food?

THE BETTER BUSINESS BUREAU

What is the role of the Better Business Bureau?

governments have a department of consumer affairs. It looks into complaints from consumers and takes action on them through the courts.

7► Consumers can get advice and help from private sources, too. Most businesses want to be fair with their customers. They want people to buy from them again and again. Business people have set up a way in which honest business people can be protected from dishonest ones. It is called the Better Business Bureau. There are over 174 in the United States. No business wants a bad name. If a person feels he or she has been treated unfairly, the bureau can be called. If there are several complaints about the same business, the bureau will take action. It will investigate and try to get the business to correct unfair practices.

8► Many radio and TV stations make consumer affairs a part of their news reporting. Some have "action" programs. A person may write or call in a complaint. The station will select some complaints,

check them out, and tell listeners about their findings. A business does not like to have thousands of people hear about a possible dishonest deal or sale. Most businessess are quick to make things right. *Consumer Reports* is a magazine published each month by Consumers Union. This is a private organization. It tests hundreds of items for sale, from cars to children's toys. Its findings are printed in *Consumer Reports*.

9► One of the best-known spokespersons for consumers in this country is Ralph Nader. He wrote a book about how cars are made in this country. In it, he accused car makers of being more interested in sales than in safety. Laws to provide greater safety in cars today are the result of Nader's work. He and a large number of people who work with him continue to study consumer products and various industries. From time to time Nader's groups supply Congress with information about consumer interests.

Ralph Nader. Do you think people such as Ralph Nader help or hurt business? Why? Why not?

10► The best advice for consumers is "Protect Yourself First." Know what you want to buy and how much money you can pay. Then buy wisely. Some good advice for shoppers comes from the New York City Department of Consumer Affairs. As you read each item, think how it might help you save money.

1. See that the store has a scale that can be easily read. Find out if in your area scales are required to bear an official seal of approval of the Department of Consumer Affairs.

2. Get the price per pound before you buy food.

3. Figure the total price yourself. Question any higher amount.

4. Check what you have bought against the register tapes and read the total on the tape.

5. You are entitled to the net (or actual) weight of your purchases. This should not include the weight of boxes, cartons, bags, or wrapping paper.

6. Buy fresh fruits and vegetables in season. They taste better and are much lower in price.

7. Don't be fooled by the size of the container or box; look for the weight or content statement.

8. Wherever possible, buy in person. If you must order by phone, ask for an itemized bill sent with your order.

Wise consumers inspect merchandise. Why is this the best method of consumer protection?

9. Be very careful of sensational claims or cuts in prices that are ridiculous.

10. If a store (with a good reputation) has a special sale, stock up. Do this if the sale is of everyday foods and canned goods.

11. Make sure that sale items are charged as advertised.

12. Ask the sales person to put on the bill any claims made, such as "all silk" and "handmade"

13. All goods on display in the store must have their prices clearly marked on a tag, sign, or poster.

Good Rules for Buying:

1. Never be pushed into spending cash or signing a contract.

2. Be patient. Look at several stores and compare their goods and prices.

3. Buy only at places you can trust.

4. Beware of strangers with offers.

Be Careful of These Words. They May Spell Danger:

· "I can get it for you wholesale."

· A price tag worded: "Value $15, price $9.95." "Reduced from" or "Factory priced" can also be used to fool you.

· "Don't you want to help your child?" You may be shamed into buying costly books.

· "Trial Offer." Don't sign a receipt for trial goods. It may turn out to be a sales contract.

· "Quick Profits." Some companies offer materials for you to make at home and they will buy them from you. There are many examples where this never came true.

· "We're sold out of the model advertised in the paper." This is a way to talk you into buying a higher priced model.

CHAPTER 39 REVIEW

★ UNDERSTANDING WHAT YOU HAVE READ

1. A title for paragraph 4 might be
   a. Checking Out Sales Slogans
   b. The Real Problem With Most Products
   c. Something Fancy, Something Cheap

2. If you wanted to find what tests tell about new upright refrigerators, you might
   a. call the Better Business Bureau
   b. read *Consumer Reports*
   c. write the U.S. Postal Service

3. The best buy in shopping for any product:
   a. The best product at the lowest price
   b. The product with the most weight at the lowest price
   c. A good product at a high price

4. The best meaning of the word **consumers**:
   a. People who work for a living
   b. Everyone who uses goods and services
   c. Shoppers for food

5. Making sure that electric ovens for sale are not dangerous to the people who use them is the job of the
   a. Federal Trade Commission
   b. Consumer Product Safety Commission
   c. Department of Agriculture

6. The government protects consumers in all these ways EXCEPT
   a. taking action against those who cheat customers through the mail
   b. making sure buyers know how much interest they pay in buying on credit
   c. inspecting prices in stores to see if they are fair

7. Ralph Nader became famous as a fighter for consumers as the result of a book about

a. dirty conditions in meat-packing plants
b. the way TV repairs are handled
c. the ways cars are made

8. Which of the following is good advice for any buyer?
   a. Be patient. Wait for the right sale.
   b. Order most goods by phone. There can be no mistake.
   c. Buy when you see something you like. Fast buys are often the best buys.

9. Which statement about the ideas in this chapter is true?
   a. There are many places consumers can go to make a complaint.
   b. Congress has failed to pass laws that help consumers.
   c. A person should always buy from a place that does a lot of advertising.

★ DEVELOPING CRITICAL THINKING SKILLS

A. Interpreting a Cartoon

Tell whether the shoppers in these cartoons are foolish or wise. What advice are they taking, or ignoring?

What advice should you remember in each of these situations?

GOOD CONSUMER/BAD CONSUMER

"I'll buy this cereal because it's cheaper."

"I've been waiting three weeks for these shirts to go on sale!"

B. Becoming a Careful Consumer

What advice should you remember in each of these situations?

1. A salesperson says to you, "Be sure to sign here to receive your trial offer."

2. A salesperson says to you, "I'm sorry you're just a little bit late. We sold out the TV sets we advertised. This one here is really much better. Of course, it costs more."

3. You see a sign in a store that says, "Best Buy in Town."

4. You complain to a friend, "I think the salesclerk cheated me, but I'm not sure."

5. An ad in the paper says, "All famous brand-name dresses, Slashed—Everything at half price."

C. Consumer Goods in Other Countries

Read the following descriptions and answer the questions on page 316.

Russia

Economic problems helped lead to the collapse of the Soviet Union in 1991. Soon after, Russian leader Boris Yeltsin began to take steps to change from a centralized to a free enterprise economy. He ended price controls on most products, except for essentials like milk, bread, and medicine. Yeltsin also tried to change some government-owned industries to private businesses based on supply and demand.

These changes led to confusion and misery. Prices skyrocketed. The prices of basic items like meat and sugar rose so fast that they could double overnight. Problems with shortages of goods under the old economic system had meant that consumers usually had to wait in long lines. They could not find some products at all. Under the new system, these shortages continued. However, prices were much higher. Many people could not afford to buy even basic items.

Although new businesses started, many could not get the supplies they needed. Others had problems with transporting their goods to consumers. Russia's economy is still very weak. It remains to be seen if Russia can successfully change to a free enterprise economy.

China

China began reforms of its centralized economic system in the early 1980s. Some plant management ideas were borrowed from capitalism. Prices of goods were allowed to follow supply and demand instead of being set by the government. Then, in 1989, the economy slumped after the government crushed a massive demonstration. However, by the early 1990s, it was clear that China would continue its economic reforms.

The average income per year of a city dweller is $261. In rural areas, it is half that figure. The average living space in a city is a room 10 feet by 7 feet. Costs are high in relation to wages. More than half a family's income was spent for food in 1990, compared with the world average of a quarter. The Chinese must save for years to buy even a bicycle, which costs about $100. But a Chinese family cannot do without one.

Western-style clothing is popular in China. A man's suit may cost more than a month's pay. A woman's blouse would take a half-month's wages. There is no buying on the installment plan—everything is paid for in cash. Since most homes do not have a refrigerator, fresh food is bought daily. Some member of the family has to go to the store each morning and stand in line for meat, eggs, and other foodstuffs. There are lines for bicycle parts and haircuts. Shoppers can't be sure they'll find what they want at the store either. Billboards often advertise goods that are not available.

1. What might be the reasons for shortages of consumer goods in these countries?

2. Is there competition among businesses to make goods that people want at the prices they are willing to pay?

3. What are some of the things that make these economic systems different from the economic system of the United States?

4. Do shortages of goods sometimes take place in the United States? What might cause shortages? Have you ever seen lines for goods because people wanted the small amount offered for sale?

D. Writing About Citizenship

Write one or two well-organized paragraphs making a generalization or summary statement about consumer goods under a totalitarian form of government.

★ THINGS TO DO

CONSUMER ACTION

1. Makers of products sometimes create consumer demand for a product you may never have thought of. For example: There are times products sold that were not part of our life in large numbers 10 or 15 years ago. Men's cosmetics is a hundred-million-dollar business. TV electronic games are another relative newcomer on the market. Can you think of other recent products that have become big sellers?

2. In a supermarket, go down the aisle where mouthwashes are on the shelf. List the names of different brands you see. List the sizes of bottles on the shelves and their prices. What problems are presented to the person who wishes to get a good value for the money?

3. Over the course of a week, check newpaper or TV ads for cars, jewelry, perfumes, and so forth. What kinds of appeals do advertisers make to atrract customers?

4. Spend half an hour at a supermarket. Watch the people at the register. Count those who add up the amount on the sales slip. What do your findings tell you about how most people shop?

40

POVERTY AND WEALTH

PURPOSES FOR READING

1. To learn who are the poor in the United States
2. To understand some of the reasons for poverty in our country
3. To learn what governments have done to help the poor and to reduce the number of poor

KNOWING NEW WORDS

efficient

(ih FISH unt) paragraph 2—very able; doing things without waste
EXAMPLE: The more **efficient** they became, the more goods they were able to produce.

This picture from 1874 shows a man selling stale meat to children. What has the government done to prevent this kind of thing from happening today?

1▶ Despite the wealth produced by the American economic system, the picture is not a pleasant one for every person. There are over 31 million people in the United States who live in poverty. They live each day hoping to make ends meet. They do not look for a great change in their lives in the future. The federal government describes the level of poverty in these terms: a family of four making less than $12,092 a year is living in poverty.

2▶ Some poverty can be blamed on loss of jobs due to improvements in machinery. A business making goods for sale wants to make a profit. Therefore, new, more efficient machines are bought to take the place of the old ones. Machines, rather than people, are used to regulate and control other machines. This is called **automation.** Many of these machines can do the jobs that once were done by many workers. For example, coal-cutters are machines that reduce the need for a number of miners. Giant farm machines do the work of many farm hands. Fruit-picking machines mean fewer people are needed to pick fruit by hand. People who work for newspapers are put out of work by new methods of printing. These people must look for other kinds of work. They are victims of the desire to make everything more efficient and faster.

3▶ Miners, farmers, and others put out of work by machines may move to cities to find work. There, they may face hard times, too. They may not have the skills that industry needs. They will find that there are few good jobs open to people without skills. They may take jobs in small stores, gas stations, and hospitals. In these jobs, the pay is usually low and the hours of work are long. Also, they will find thousands of others who can fill the same jobs. Among these are high school dropouts. Without education, those without skills fill the ranks of the unemployed in and around large cities.

The cost of a college education continues to increase. From the information in paragraph 3, what problems might many people face in the future?

WHO ARE THE POOR?

(Based on the Department of Labor standard of poverty income)

1 of every 8 Americans
1 of every 10 whites
1 of every 3 African Americans
1 of every 4 Hispanic Americans
1 of every 8 people age 65 or older
1 of every 5 children under 18 years

(Figures have been rounded off from percentages)

Source: Bureau of the Census

EDUCATION AND EARNINGS IN THE UNITED STATES

Heads of Families Median Earnings*	Women	Men
8 years elementary school	$11,712	$17,204
4 years high school	16,865	25,859
4 years college	25,908	36,845

*Median means middle. There are the same number of people with earnings above and below this figure.

Source: Bureau of the Census

1. What does the table show about the link between education and income?

2. How might a high-school dropout's income compare with the income of a person who at least finishes high school?

4▶ Large numbers of people live in poverty. For example, in 1988, one in five teenagers lived in households with incomes below the poverty level. This is a higher percentage of poor than in any other age group. Many were those who did not finish school. They did not have the skills that employers wanted. Others may have finished high school, but employers wanted workers with some experience on the job.

5▶ Older people are having a hard time meeting the costs of living. The number of older people in our country is growing steadily. This is caused, in part, by improved medical care. Most older people receive some kind of pension. Most often, they get Social Security payments from the government. But these payments were never meant to give older people enough money to meet all the costs of living. As costs go up, people on fixed pensions are not able to buy as much with their money. Many have had to move out of homes they held for many years. Workers also lose jobs when a factory closes or moves elsewhere. People of middle age who lose jobs find it hard to get new ones. It is not easy to learn a new trade or skill in later life.

MEDIAN FAMILY INCOME	
Whites	$33,915
Hispanic Americans	21,769
African Americans	19,323

Source: Bureau of the Census, 1989

What paragraph in the chapter gives information that helps to support the information in the table?

6▶ Poverty affects people of all racial and ethnic groups. Most of the poor families in our country are white. About one of every ten whites is poor. Ten million African Americans live in poverty. This is over one third of the African American population. One in four Hispanic Americans lives below the poverty level. Some of them are workers who travel from farm to farm picking crops of fruits and vegetables. They are called migrant workers (see page 65). Most American Indians have incomes that are well below the poverty level. The average income of American Indians is one fifth that of all

Mexican-American migrant farm workers. This kind of farm work is among the lowest-paying kind of work in the country.

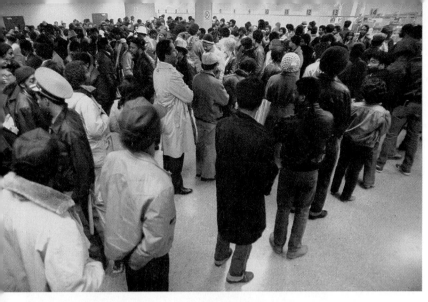

Long unemployment lines. From information in this chapter, list what seps the government has taken to help solve the problem of unemployment.

Americans. The poor in America have found little escape from their poverty. The poor are younger than ever and most of them live in cities.

7▶ Since the 1950s, our country has made much progress in removing discrimination in jobs. More people of minority groups have gotten good jobs than ever before. But when jobs are lost, people in minority groups have suffered the most. People who have held jobs for a long time are able to keep their jobs. Those who were hired last are the first to lose their jobs. The expression, "Last hired, first fired," has been true for thousands of African Americans and Hispanic Americans.

8▶ Most of the poor, no matter where they live or the color of their skin, are people who are not able to work. These are the very young and the very old. They depend upon others to care for them. They also include women who are heads of families. Many cannot take jobs because they must care for their children. Those who can work may have to take jobs at low pay. Sick people, too, fill the ranks of the poor. Employers want workers who can be present every day. They do not like to hire persons with a history of illness.

9▶ Our country always has had poor people. Before the 1930s the job of caring for the poor was left to state and local governments. Poor people were placed in county homes. There, they worked at jobs for low pay. The "hard times" of the 1930s caused a great increase in the number of poor. Local governments could not handle the problem. Congress then began programs to help the needy. Most people thought that such help would be needed for only a short time. It would end when business got back on its feet and there were jobs once more. But this help, **welfare** payments, has grown beyond anything our leaders dreamed. (See graph, page 324.)

10▶ Social Security payments also began during the 1930s. The amount of payments has risen several times since then. In 1964, President Lyndon Johnson declared a "War on Poverty." A Job Corps was begun. Young men and women who were out of work could go to a camp for two years to get special job training. A program called VISTA was begun. Volunteers with special skills worked in cities, renewing houses and parks, and teaching job skills. Project Head Start set up learning programs for preschool chil-

People waiting in the Social Security Office. How does the Social Security program help Americans? Are there ways you think this program is harmful to society?

dren. Neighborhoods established Community Action Programs. These gave needed services, including child care for working mothers.

11► The "War on Poverty" had many sides. Congress passed a law raising the minimum wage. Money was given to cities to rebuild housing. Poor families received rent payments when they moved into better housing. Families below and near the poverty level were also given help toward better meals. The food stamp plan was begun. People obtained food stamps from the government at little or no cost. They are able to buy food with the stamps. Over 19 million people now benefit from the use of food stamps. They are able to buy a wide variety of food. Congress also passed a plan of medical care for older people. It is called **Medicare.** For low-income people, money from the states and federal government helps provide better health care. This plan is called **Medicaid.**

12► All the programs of the War on Poverty cost money. Costs increased greatly as the years passed. President Reagan believed spending for many social programs should be reduced. He felt that the American people could not afford to continue to spend billions of dollars to maintain them. He wanted to cut the huge debt owed by the federal government. However, the "truly needy" would not be harmed by the budget cuts he proposed. Congress approved a reduction in the number of people who would receive Medicaid and food stamps. Fewer children received free school lunches. Some job training programs were reduced or done away with. The president believed that states and cities should take over responsibility for some social programs. He did not believe that spending by the federal government was the answer to the problem of poverty. To him, getting the able-bodied poor into a job was a better solution.

13▶ Since 1980, it has been the policy of the federal government that business people and private citizens should assume a greater role in caring for the poor. Most Americans believe that every person should have a decent life. People should not have to struggle for the things they need. Plans to reduce poverty have cost taxpayers billions of dollars. Yet there are still millions of poor people. No solution yet proposed has been successful. Helping to end poverty is a concern of every citizen.

CHAPTER 40 REVIEW

★ UNDERSTANDING WHAT YOU HAVE READ

1. The main idea of paragraphs 10 and 11 is that
   a. under President Lyndon Johnson, several programs to help the poor were begun
   b. most government programs helped to improve housing
   c. poor families moved into better homes

2. Welfare is best described as
   a. government payments to those in need
   b. a plan to teach skills to young people
   c. monthly payments to retired people

3. The number of people living in poverty in the United States today is about
   a. 10 million
   b. 32 million
   c. 50 million

4. Which of these is an example of discrimination?
   a. School dropouts find it hard to get a high-paying job.
   b. Goods are produced by workers with low pay.
   c. A person is denied a job because she has a Spanish name.

5. From this chapter you learn that
   a. black and Hispanic families have lower average incomes than white families
   b. education has little to do with the income a person can receive
   c. the pay of whites and all others who finished high school is the same

6. Which is an example of automation?
   a. Ten workers, each doing a different job in making kitchen chairs
   b. A machine that fills milk cartons faster than ten people can do the job
   c. A clerk in a store adding up the amount of a bill

7. "Last hired, first fired" sometimes applies to
   a. factory managers
   b. workers who are minority group members
   c. migrant workers.

8. The federal government began programs to help the poor because
   a. many people did not ask for food stamps
   b. there were food strikes in the 1960s
   c. the problem became too great for local governments to handle

9. Which of these would not help people with low incomes?
   a. Increasing all the taxes on goods and services
   b. Providing rent payments for better housing
   c. Providing Medicaid and increased Social Security payments

10. Many older people now live below the poverty level because
    a. the number of older people is becoming smaller
    b. they live on fixed incomes that buy less as costs rise
    c. wages have gone down almost as fast as prices of goods

★ DEVELOPING SOCIAL STUDIES SKILLS

A. Interpreting a Graph

Study the graph below. Then tell whether the statements on page 325 are true or false.

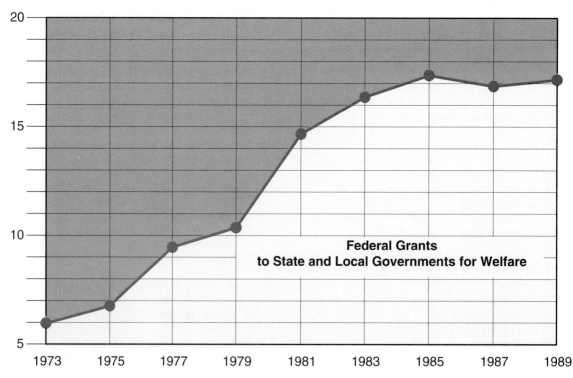

(In billions of dollars)

Federal Grants to State and Local Governments for Welfare

Source: Department of Commerce

Federal aid on the graph includes many programs: public assistance payments, child nutrition, food stamp, and food donation programs, and low-income energy assistance programs.

Are these statements *true* or *false?*

1. The graph shows welfare grants in millions of dollars.
2. More federal money was provided for welfare in 1979 than in 1989.
3. The graph gives us information about both federal and state welfare costs.
4. The graph indicates that more grants will be provided for welfare in the years to come.
5. The most federal money provided for welfare was in 1985.
6. The graphs tells us that there are millions of people on welfare.

B. Interpreting Tables

UNEMPLOYMENT RATES, 1985 AND 1990

	1985	1990
All workers	7.2%	5.5%
White adults	5.5	4.2
African American adults	13.1	10.0
White teenagers	15.7	13.4
African American teenagers	40.2	31.1
Hispanic Americans	10.5	8.0
Agricultural wage and salary workers	13.2	9.7

Source: Bureau of Labor Statistics

Choose the best answer based on the information in the table.

1. Over the five-year period, unemployment among wage and salary workers
   a. increased.
   b. decreased.
   c. remained the same.

2. Over the five-year period, unemployment was the most serious problem for
   a. white teenagers.
   b. Hispanic Americans.
   c. African American teenagers.

3. An important idea of the table is that
   a. African Americans have had the most serious unemployment problem.
   b. there were more people employed in 1985 than in 1990.
   c. employment among Hispanic Americans has always been high.

4. An important idea of the table is that
   a. the percentage of all workers unemployed was lower in 1990 than in 1985.
   b. a larger number of women in the work force may have caused increased employment.

   c. unemployment has dropped every year from 1985 to 1990.

5. One idea of the table is that
   a. unemployment among African Americans and Hispanic Americans has remained at the same level
   b. African American adult and teenage unemployment has been higher than Hispanic American unemployment
   c. only agricultural wage and salary workers have a lower unemployment rate than Hispanic Americans.

6. The table shows that in 1985
   a. there was a greater percentage of white teenagers working than African American teenagers
   b. the percentage of white teenagers working in 1985 was less than in 1990
   c. white teenagers make up only a small part of the labor force.

7. The table reveals that
   a. Hispanic Americans had the greatest drop in unemployment from 1985 to 1990
   b. African American adults and teenager had higher rates of unemployment in 1985 than in 1990
   c. among all workers, rates of unemployment were lower in 1985 than 1990.

8. The table tells us that
   a. the jobless rate was higher in 1985 than in 1990
   b. white adult unemployment did not improve in the five-year period
   c. 1990 African American unemployment was more than double that of white adult unemployment.

★ DEVELOPING CRITICAL THINKING SKILLS

Tell why you agree or disagree with each of the following conclusions. Which paragraph or chart helped in making your decision? What conclusions may have influenced your decision?

1. The more education people have, the higher income they might expect to receive.

2. Our system of competition among businesses makes sure that all people can fill their needs.

3. There are few good jobs open to people without skills.

4. People whose incomes are below poverty level live in cities and on farms.

5. Most people who live in cities are poor.

6. People with fixed incomes suffer when prices of goods rise.

7. The average income of American Indian families is below that of the average income of all American families.

8. Most of the 35 million poor are people who could get good jobs if they wanted to work.

9. The federal government began programs to help the poor as far back as the time of George Washington's presidency.

10. The cost of programs to reduce poverty has risen sharply in the 1980s.

PARTICIPATION IN GOVERNMENT

USING COMMUNITY SERVICES

Your community offers many services to its residents. You and your family should know what they are. In addition to schools and hospitals, you may find the following:

- Health Clinics
- Parks
- Swimming Pools
- Gymnasiums
- Political Clubs
- Churches
- Synagogues
- Civic Associations

- Welfare Departments
- Police Stations
- Fire Stations
- Libraries
- Narcotics Programs
- Block Associations
- Youth Organizations
- Y.M.C.A.

You can get information about these and other services by writing to the appropriate organization and asking speakers to come to your class, or you can visit the organization. Your class can place each service organization on a community map. With the help of your school's parents' association, such a map can be distributed to homes. The map will show the location of services. It will not tell what each one does. In visiting any of these organizations, you may wish to use a survey form like the following:

- Your name and date
- Name of service organization
- Address and phone number
- Name of person in charge
- Business hours per day, per week
- Number of employees
- Number of people who use the service

- Who should use the service
- What the service does
- What the service would like to accomplish
- How you or your parents can support the service
- What problems the organization faces

SAVING OUR RESOURCES

PURPOSES FOR READING

1. To understand the dangers of air and water pollution
2. To learn government measures to reduce pollution
3. To learn how resources have been wasted
4. To learn what is being done to increase sources of energy

KNOWING NEW WORDS

pollution
(puh LOO shun) paragraph 1—dirt; something impure
EXAMPLE: We are breathing dirt into our lungs from **pollution** in the air.

reservoirs
(REZ ur vwars) paragraph 2—places where water is stored; reserves of water
EXAMPLE: Water for the people of Los Angeles comes from **reservoirs** a hundred miles away.

exhausts
(ig ZOSTS) paragraph 5—fumes; used steam, gasoline, and so forth, that escape from engines
EXAMPLE: Many of the people in traffic were coughing from the **exhausts**.

erosion
(ih ROH zhun) paragraph 7—the process of wearing away
EXAMPLE: Maria's farm lost much of its valuable topsoil because of wind and water **erosion.**

- What is the artist's point of view as shown in the cartoon?
- Do you think the artist is giving a warning or telling a joke?
- What in the cartoon shows there is pollution of the air?
- What would be a good title for the cartoon?

1▶ The cartoon deals with air and water pollution. These are two ways that **natural resources** are wasted. Air, water, forests, soil, metals, and minerals are natural resources. They are part of the reason for the wealth of the United States. **Human resources** are another. People are human resources. The American people have used natural resources to make the country rich. They also have wasted them and abused them. The American people have already used as much coal, oil, and iron ore as all the people before them in history. Even now, the United States is using as much as the rest of the world combined. At the same time, many Americans have allowed the way they use resources to pollute the **environment.** How long can they continue to abuse their natural wealth?

2▶ People cannot live without water. The people of the United States use 150 gallons per person each day. Factories use great amounts of water. It takes 100,000 gallons of water, for example, to make one automobile. Farms might use half the water supply if there were no limits on water use. In the western states, water is carried over long distances to make the desert bloom with plants. People in some cities get water from reservoirs that are miles away. A large supply of clean, fresh water is needed more than ever today. Yet, people have allowed the water systems to be damaged by pollution.

3▶ Not long ago the national government found that nearly all rivers in the United States were polluted in some way. Sewage and wastes from factories and mills are the greatest causes of this pollution. Congress has passed laws that will reduce pollution. Our government spends billions of dollars to build plants to treat (clean up) sewage. Plants that dump wastes into lakes and streams now face a heavy fine. The government has taken over the

Cartoon from 1880. Compare this cartoon with the one on page 328. How are they alike? How are they different?

job of making sure that our drinking water is safe. Saving water is another matter. That water can be saved has been shown by people in all parts of the United States. Conservation methods on Long Island in New York State, for example, have brought about a 15 percent drop in water usage within five years.

4▶ Air is like water in this way: we cannot live without it. The pollution of air is a serious health problem. People who live in cities are in the greatest danger from polluted air. Over half our air pollution is caused by automobiles. (See pictograph, page 335.) Factories and power plants are also big offenders. A mass of warm air over a city can trap dirty air beneath it. The result is smog—a foglike smoke. Pollutants from factories form an acid in the air. This acid falls to earth with rain or snow. Known as "acid rain," this pollutant kills fish, changes soils, and destroys forests.

5▶ Congress has passed Clean Air laws to try to control pollution of several kinds. The job of fighting pollution is headed by the Environmental Protection Agency (EPA). The EPA is in charge of government plans to safeguard resources from abuse. In 1990, President Bush signed the latest Clean Air Act. The new law requires tougher controls on auto manufacturers to reduce gases from car exhausts. It also requires coal-burning plants to greatly reduce pollutants that cause acid rain. In addition, businesses must now install new equipment to capture toxic chemicals given off in the manufacturing process.

6▶ When people from Europe first came to America, it was a land of forests and fertile soil. By 1900, fires and careless cut-

What kind of pollution is shown in this photograph? Why is it a serious problem?

ting of trees had destroyed half the forest land. Today, the picture is brighter. Trees are a resource that can be restored. Trees are now cut after careful planning. More are planted than are cut down. There is more forest land in the United States today than 100 years ago.

7▶ The waste of soils became serious in the 1930s. Tons of topsoil were being washed away each year by floods. Winds blew good soils from some of the richest farmland. It was feared that large parts of the country would become desert. Something had to be done. The government began several programs to save the soils. Trees were planted on acres of land to protect them from erosion. Grasses were planted on unused land to enrich the soil. Farmers were taught to plow their fields in a way that kept soils from washing away. Fertilizers (FUR tuh ly zurs) have brought good crops to poor lands. Erosion has not been stopped completely. Valuable topsoil is still being lost on much of our crop land. But fortunately, the rate of loss has been slowed.

8 ▶ The Tennessee Valley Authority (TVA) was created in the 1930s. It is part of the program to save water and soil. Floods had washed away good farmland. Dams were built on the Tennessee River. The dams stopped the flooding. The dams also supplied water power for electricity. The TVA plan has been a success. Farmlands are again growing good crops. Homes in the river valley have electricity at cheaper rates than they might get from a private company. Parks have been made from land once thought to be useless.

9 ▶ At one time people believed that there was no end to the supply of metals. The United States had rich deposits of iron ore. Today most of the rich ores have been used. One-third of the iron ore used in the United States steel mills is imported. (Unlike trees, ores cannot be replaced.) This nation is still the world's largest producer of copper. But other important metals are imported. These include tin, tungsten, and chrome.

10 ▶ A serious concern to Americans today is the use of resources that provide **energy.** The United States has a giant supply of coal. Coal has been used as a fuel for hundreds of years. It still provides one-fifth of the nation's energy. There is little danger of a coal shortage now. However, much of the coal is expensive to remove from the earth. In the future, other fuels may become even more expensive. Natural gas has become more widely used as a fuel. Because of this, the United States' supply of natural gas has been greatly reduced. Now, much of this fuel must come from other countries. Water can provide a continuing source of power. Many places use water power to make electricity. But places where water can be used to make power cannot be found all over the nation. Water

Dust bowl, 1936. Why were scenes such as this called a "dust bowl"?

A hydroelectric power plant, Grand Coulee Dam, Washington. What source of energy is pictured here?

technology fills only a small part of our energy needs.

11▶ Oil is the chief source of energy for the nation's factories, homes, and transportation. The United States is easily the world leader in the use of oil. In the early 1970s, nearly half the oil used in the nation was imported. Much of it came from the Arab nations of the Middle East. For a time in 1973 and 1974, there was an oil crisis. Arab nations refused to ship oil to the United States. The **scarcity** of oil that resulted drove up the price. Many businesses had to cut down their use of oil. People had to wait in long lines to buy gasoline for their cars.

12▶ The nation's dependence on foreign oil cannot be completely eliminated. The United States uses far more oil than it produces. More than half the oil consumed by Americans is used for transportation. Because of the scare caused by the oil crisis, steps were taken to reduce the need for as much oil from other countries as was imported before 1973. Oil companies stepped up their drilling in the waters off the coasts of the United States. The pipeline bringing oil from northern Alaska to southern Alaska was opened in 1977. In 1977, Congress created the Department of Energy. The head of this department is a member of the president's cabinet. Federal laws also required automobile makers to produce cars that use less gasoline. Congress also passed laws allowing homeowners tax credits if they used energy-saving devices in their homes. Tax credits were also given to those who used solar energy—the energy from the sun. A "Strategic Petroleum Reserve" was started.

This reserve, which now has over 400 million barrels of oil, is stored in caverns in Texas and Louisiana.

13▶ For a time, these measures and those taken by individuals sharply reduced the country's use of oil. But, as time passed, the oil shortage of the 1970s dimmed in the public mind, and imports of foreign oil grew once more. By 1990, 45 of every 100 barrels used in the United States were imported. Then in August, 1990, armed forces from Iraq invaded and overran neighboring Kuwait. Iraq's forces also threatened Saudi Arabia. If successful in establishing control of the Middle East, Saddam Hussein, the Iraqi dictator, could have controlled over 40 percent of the world's oil supply. President Bush sent American troops and naval and air forces to the Middle East to prevent further aggression by Iraq and restore the independence of Kuwait. The United States was supported by the Security Council of the United Nations. Joining the United States forces were those from Egypt, Great Britain, France, Italy, Kuwait, and others.

14▶ Many places in the country are testing the use of solar energy now. Water is heated by the rays of the sun. The heated water can be stored for later use. Sunlight costs nothing. But the equipment need to collect and store solar energy is still expensive. Whether solar energy can be widely and cheaply used is yet to be seen.

15▶ Some experts think that atomic power (nuclear power) is the power of the future. The United States and other countries already have atomic plants now. About 4 percent of the total energy used in the United States comes from these plants. Many people feel that nuclear energy is very dangerous. Accidents in nuclear power plants, such as the accident in the Soviet Union in 1986, are a major threat. Radioactive materials are a threat even to people who are far away from the accident site. Nuclear reactors give off wastes that remain radioactive for a long time. In some parts of the country, people have demonstrated against nuclear power plants planned near their homes. Many others, however, think they are safe. They argue that nuclear power plants could provide energy for another thousand years.

In 1986 a major accident took place at this nuclear power plant in Chernobyl in the Soviet Union. A number of people were killed and radioactive material was detected in many parts of Europe. The accident occurred seven years after a smaller incident at Three Mile Island in Pennsylvania.

CHAPTER 41 REVIEW

★ **UNDERSTANDING WHAT YOU HAVE READ**

1. The main idea of paragraph 12 is that
   a. an oil shortage led to measures to reduce dependence on foreign oil
   b. tax credits for those who save oil are a good idea
   c. the Alaskan pipeline solved an oil shortage

2. An argument against the use of nuclear power is that
   a. it can be used in only a few places in the country
   b. plants take up too much space
   c. radioactive wastes can be dangerous to health

3. The United States has enough of which of these?
   a. Natural gas
   b. Coal
   c. Iron ore

4. The American people could not live without
   a. oil
   b. steel
   c. water

5. The "Strategic Petroleum Reserve" refers to
   a. stepping up off-shore drilling for oil
   b. storing oil in underground caves for use in an emergency
   c. increasing imports of oil from nations outside the Middle East

6. In dealing with soil erosion, the United States has

   a. failed to do much about it
   b. completely solved the problem
   c. had much success in the last 50 years

7. An important idea of this chapter is that
   a. farmland in the United States has not recovered from the waste of years ago
   b. the government has done several things to save the country's natural resources
   c. the United States leads the world in producing all important metals

8. This chapter makes which of the following points?
   a. Pollution wastes human and natural resources.
   b. The American people have always tried to save their natural resources.
   c. The government takes little interest in saving human and natural resources.

9. The government is fighting water pollution by
   a. providing money to build plants to treat sewage
   b. placing taxes on heavy users of water
   c. cutting down on the amount of water auto plants use

10. Human resources can be wasted. An example of this would happen when
    a. a person is able to work but has no job
    b. a worker throws away materials that could be used on the job
    c. a worker plants trees on unused farmland

★ **DEVELOPING SOCIAL STUDIES SKILLS**

A. Reading a Pictograph

Study the pictograph on page 335. Then answer the questions that follow it.

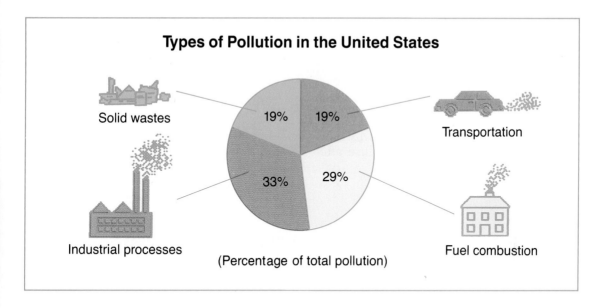

Types of Pollution in the United States

Solid wastes — 19%

19% — Transportation

Industrial processes — 33%

29% — Fuel combustion

(Percentage of total pollution)

1. What causes the greatest amount of pollution?

2. What is the second-worst pollutant?

3. Which causes air pollution?

4. Which pollutants hurt the eyes?

5. How could pollution from heating be reduced?

6. Which paragraphs in the chapter tell what the government is doing to reduce the kinds of pollution shown in the pictograph?

B. Interpreting Graphs

Study the graphs. Then answer the questions at the top of page 336.

Kinds of Energy Used in the United States

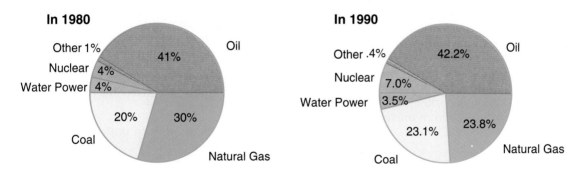

In 1980

Other 1%
Nuclear 4%
Water Power 4%
Oil 41%
Coal 20%
Natural Gas 30%

In 1990

Other .4%
Nuclear 7.0%
Water Power 3.5%
Oil 42.2%
Coal 23.1%
Natural Gas 23.8%

Source: Monthly Energy Review

1. What was the largest source of energy for the United States in 1980? In 1990?

2. Which sources of energy increased in use from 1980 to 1990?

3. Which sources of energy declined from 1980 to 1990?

4. Which energy source appears to have remained at the same level of use after the 10-year period?

5. How do the graphs and chapter tell us what problems in energy the United States will face in the future?

6. What paragraphs in the chapter tell what is being done to solve the problems?

7. From what the graphs and the chapter tell us, what suggestions might you make for solving the energy problems in the United States?

★USING SOURCE MATERIALS

Read the following newspaper article and answer the questions that follow.

"Cars Lead Pollution Parade"

If it were possible to vacuum all the pollution out of the El Paso and Juárez skies and freeze it in little blocks, 31 giant dump trucks would be needed to haul it away—every day.

Each year, state estimates show, the cars, trucks, factories, and homes of El Paso and Juárez spew 340,800 tons of pollution. That's 9.37 tons on an average day, enough to fill 31 dump trucks, each with a capacity to haul 30 tons.

Without a doubt, experts say, automobiles are the biggest source of contamination in the El Paso-Juárez basin. "Together with other pollutants, vehicles from both cities are estimated to contribute 583.2 tons of pollution—enough to fill almost 20 of our dump trucks."

Open burning—of leaves and trash in El Paso; of wood, cardboard, and tires in Juárez—is another source. Together with clouds of dust raised from unpaved roads and alleys, it is the second largest source of air pollution.

Industry, of course, is the third major cause of pollution. It accounts for perhaps 10 to 15 percent of air problems.

Smaller sources of pollution in Juárez include 367 bakeries and 200 tortilla makers (using wood and natural gas for cooking), 500 small brick factories (using sawdust, wood, or natural gas), and about five small iron foundries.

Source: the El Paso Times, March 25, 1984

1. How does the first paragraph tell us that pollutants are often "hidden pollutants"?

2. Which type of pollutant described in the article is most easily seen? What are some of the "hidden pollutants"?

3. How much of the pollution in the El Paso-Juárez region is caused by automobiles? By industries?

4. What other sources of pollution are mentioned in the article?

★ EXAMINING AMERICAN ECONOMICS

A. Categorizing

In this unit, you have learned about the American economic system. There are three main kinds of economic systems:

1. Government has no control over business, farms, banks, and workers. This is a completely free system.

2. Businesses, farms, banks, and workers have a great deal of freedom, but government uses some controls to bring the most benefits to the most people.

3. Government controls all sections of the economic system. It runs banks, businesses, farms, railroads, and sets prices and wages of workers.

How would you describe the economic system of the United States? Which of the above is the best description?

B. Examining Government Action

In this unit you learned how the government is involved in the American economic system. For each topic, name at least one way in which the government has taken action or can become involved. Write the answers in your notebook.

1. Several people want to form a corporation.

2. Employers blacklist workers who want to join a union.

3. Employers will not talk over conditions of work with their workers.

4. The public thinks there are too many strikes in important industries.

5. A company sells drugs that are harmful to people's health.

6. Many people want to borrow money, or too few people want to borrow money.

7. A company sells a radio that can give you a shock when you turn a dial.

8. Older people are often forced to live at poverty level.

9. Poor families are not able to buy proper foods.

10. Mothers who are heads of families cannot leave their children to get a job.

C. Writing About Citizenship

Write a brief essay that answers the following: Do you think that the government does enough to help individuals with their economic problems? Why do you think so, or why do you not think so? What more could the government do? Give reasons for your opinions.

Unit
8 ★

OUR FOREIGN POLICY

The American Embassy in London. The United States maintains embassies in many countries.

MAKING A FOREIGN POLICY

PURPOSES FOR READING

1. To learn how the foreign policy of the United States first developed
2. To learn how the United States tried to stay neutral in foreign disputes
3. To learn how the foreign policy of the United States changed as its power grew

KNOWING NEW WORDS

entanglements
(en TANG gul munts) paragraph 3—acts or things that cause problems
EXAMPLE: George Washington said that the United States should avoid any foreign **entanglements.**

foreign
(FOR in) paragraph 2—having to do with other countries; coming from outside one's own country
EXAMPLE: Louise enjoyed her trip to Europe. She can speak **foreign** languages well.

policy
(POL ih see) paragraph 2—a plan; a way of acting toward others
EXAMPLE: We should know what our **policy** will be if the landlord raises our rent.

neutral
(NOO trul) paragraph 3—not taking sides in a dispute

EXAMPLE: You can't get me to tell Juan he's wrong about Tom. I'm **neutral.**

isolation
(eye suh LAY shun) paragraph 3—complete separation; being alone
EXAMPLE: The prisoner was taken away from the others and placed in **isolation**

treaties
(TREE tees) paragraph 3—contracts, or agreements between two or more countries
EXAMPLE: The **treaties** signed at Paris ended the war for independence from England.

alliances
(uh LY uns is) paragraph 2—agreements between nations to cooperate in special ways
EXAMPLE: The country entered into military **alliances** to protect itself against enemies.

Why did George Washington think that the best foreign policy for the United States was, in effect, not to "get involved?"

1► Can you picture what it might be like to move into a new neighborhood? For some time you may know only a few people. You are not sure of the customs of the other people on your block or in your building. You try not to be "overly friendly" at first. You want to be sure that you are accepted in your new home. You would like others to show friendship toward you. You want to be the kind of person others will like and want to know better. In a short time, you will learn that there are others around you who do not have the same likes and dislikes as you do. But you want to get along with them also. In 1783 our new nation, the United States, was much like you in a new neighborhood.

2► The new nation had to find its place in the world neighborhood. George Washington, the first president, stated the way in which we would like to live among the countries of the world. He said, in effect, "Let's do business with others. Let's be friendly with everyone. But, let us not get involved in their troubles, in their politics." Washington thought that the distance of 3,000 miles between the United States and Europe would help the country stay out of Europe's wars and troubles. Washington was right. The United States was able to stay out of most disputes between European countries for over a hundred years. His policy and advice was to "steer clear of permanent alliances with any portion of the Foreign World." This was the first **foreign policy.**

3► The new nation tried to carry out the policy of no **entanglements.** But treaties were made with England and Spain. Louisiana was bought from France. These moves removed some dangers to the United States from three European powers. However, even though the United States tried to remain neutral in Europe's troubles, war came. The War of 1812 was fought with England over the right of the United States to trade with whomever it wished. The desire to be free of foreign entanglements remained after the war. President Monroe, in effect, told European

What was the message President Monroe gave the world in 1823? Why is it called the Monroe Doctrine?

nations to stay out of North and South America. In turn, we would not interfere in Europe's affairs. The policy of **isolation**—"leave us alone"—continued.

4 ▶ The United States managed to stay at peace with foreign countries through most of the 1800s. Treaties ended disputes with England. Both countries agreed to set the boundary line between the United States and Canada. But a boundary dispute brought war with Mexico. Victory in that war added a large piece of land to our territory in the Southwest. In 1867, Alaska was purchased from Russia. This ended Russia's claim to any land in the Americas.

5 ▶ The turn away from the policy of isolation began in the Far East. The United States had built up a large trade with China. It had opened Japan to trade with Western nations. Later, it took over Hawaii and islands in the Pacific. These gave it stepping stones across the Pacific Ocean.

European nations had forced China's local rulers to give them special rights in trade. The United States wanted to stop this practice. It wanted American businesses to have an equal chance to compete. The United States declared that all nations could trade with China on an equal footing. This was called the **Open Door policy.** China welcomed this policy of the United States.

6 ▶ The United States remained neutral in the affairs of Europe and the Far East. It did not stay neutral in Latin America. In 1898, the United States went to war with Spain. Through this short war, Cuba gained freedom from Spain. But the United States stayed its protector for over 30 years. The United States also took the Philippines, Guam, and Puerto Rico from Spain. Our country was once a colony of England. Now, it had colonies itself. There followed a greater interest in Latin America. Under President Monroe, our nation

President Woodrow Wilson speaking in support of the League of Nations. Why did Wilson think the United States should join the League?

had warned the countries of Europe to keep out of Latin America. Now our nation went further. President Theodore Roosevelt built the Panama Canal and bases to protect it. We took control of several countries to keep European powers out. It was said that the Caribbean Sea had become an "American lake."

7▶ War broke out in Europe in 1914. The United States tried to remain neutral. But it could not. American ships were sunk without warning by German submarines. In 1917, the United States entered the war on the side of France, Britain, and Italy. President Wilson said that the American goal in the war was "to make the world safe for democracy." He hoped that peace after the war would bring about more **interdependence.** Wilson wanted the United States to join the League of Nations. This was a world organization to keep peace in

the world. Afraid of entanglements in the troubles of other nations, the Senate voted down his plan. In the 1920s, the United States once more had a policy of isolation in world affairs.

8▶ The United States did begin to change its policy in Latin America. In 1933, a meeting of all American nations was held. The United States agreed to the right of Latin American countries to control their own affairs. A few years later, United States troops were brought home from Cuba and other neighbors to the south. A Good Neighbor policy was begun.

9▶ War broke out in Europe again in 1939 (World War II). And again, the United States tried to remain neutral. Hopes of staying out of the war were dashed when Japan attacked Pearl Harbor in 1941. The United States joined other nations in fighting against Japan, Italy, and

President Truman signs the United Nations Security Charter in 1945. Why did the United States decide to support the United Nations after World War II?

Germany. Shortly before the war ended, four years later, 50 nations met to draw up plans for peace. They formed the United Nations organization. This time, the United States was a leader in the world organization.

10▶ After World War II the United States was the most powerful country in the world. It was the leader of nations that believed in democracy. It had just led a fight against dictators who threatened the democratic way of life. The American people were tired of war. But another threat to

freedom grew out of the war. This was the spread of communism. The United States and the Soviet Union were allies during the war. But that cooperation came to an end as soon as the war was over. Communists took over nearly all the countries of Eastern Europe. The United States decided to stop this new threat before it took over the world. American relations with other countries changed to meet this threat. The United States was ready to enter into permanent economic and military alliances with other countries.

CHAPTER 42 REVIEW

★ UNDERSTANDING WHAT YOU HAVE READ

1. A good title for paragraph 2 might be
   a. Let's Do Business with Europe
   b. Our First Foreign Policy
   c. The First President
2. The first foreign policy of the United States may be described as
   a. "Don't interfere with us; we won't interfere with you"
   b. "Speak tough and back it up"
   c. "Victory at any cost"
3. The main idea of paragraph 5 is that
   a. the United States took an active interest in the affairs of the Far East
   b. Japan began to trade with the United States
   c. the United States took over islands in the Pacific
4. Which event took place first?
   a. President Monroe warned nations of Europe to stay out of America.
   b. The United States went to war with Spain.
   c. The Panama Canal was built.
5. "It is hard not to take sides when our ships

are being sunk." This is an idea found in
   a. paragraph 3
   b. paragraph 6
   c. paragraph 7
6. As the United States spread its interest outside North America, it took over all of these EXCEPT
   a. Guam
   b. Puerto Rico
   c. China
7. Which president and his policy are INCORRECTLY matched?
   a. Wilson—make the world safe for democracy
   b. Monroe—Good Neighbor policy
   c. Washington—no permanent alliances
8. When World War II broke out in Europe, the United States
   a. declared war on Germany at once
   b. tried to remain neutral
   c. met with other nations to work out a plan for peace
9. Which of these became a threat to freedom after World War II?

a. The growing power of Japan
b. The setting up of European colonies in Latin America
c. The spread of communism to many countries

10. In the 1800s, the United States stayed neutral in foreign troubles EXCEPT in
a. Latin America
b. China
c. Europe

★DEVELOPING CRITICAL THINKING SKILLS

Interpreting Cartoons

These are some illustrations of events and policies you read about in this chapter. Study the illustrations. Then answer the questions that follow them.

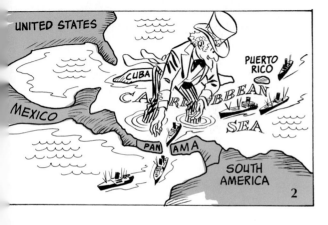

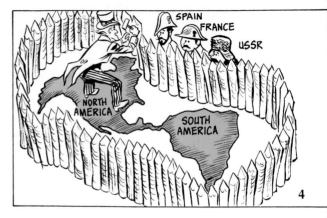

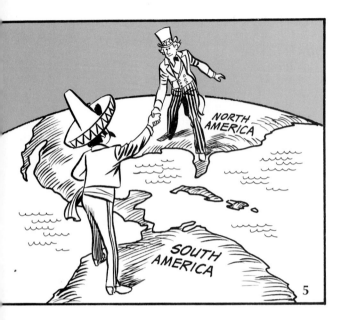

1. Which policy is shown by number 1? Which paragraph will help to support your answer?

2. Which event is described by number 2? Which paragraph refers to this event?

3. Which event is described by number 3? Which paragraph refers to this event?

4. Which policy is shown by number 4? Which paragraph will help to support your answer?

5. Which policy is shown by number 5? Which paragraph will help to support your answer?

6. Which event is described by number 6? Which paragraph refers to this event? What was United States foreign policy at the time of this event?

7. Which number shows the desire of the United States to be neutral in world troubles?

8. Which number shows the desire of the United States to keep peace?

9. Which number would be in agreement with George Washington's idea of "isolation" from entanglements in the affairs of other countries?

B. Writing About Citizenship

Do you think that the United States should be heavily involved in foreign policy, or should the government be more concerned with policy "at home"? Why do you think so? What are the reasons for your opinion?

THE CHALLENGES OF FOREIGN POLICY

PURPOSES FOR READING

1. To learn how the United States met the growing power of communism after World War II
2. To learn how the United States's policy of containment has worked in Europe, Latin America, and Asia
3. To learn steps taken by the United States to reduce the chance of a nuclear war
4. To understand the policy of the United States toward the human rights of all people

KNOWING NEW WORDS

recognition
(rek ug NISH un) paragraph 4—an official act by which one country admits that another country exists
EXAMPLE: France granted **recognition** to the new United States of America.

Planes and helicopters stand ready on the United States aircraft carrier in Saudi Arabia, 1990. What event started the Middle East crisis in 1990? Why were United States aircraft stationed there?

The United States sent aid to Europe after World War II under a program called the Marshall Plan. George Marshall was secretary of state in 1947 and presented a plan to send aid to Europe to help rebuild from the damage done by World War II. Congress approved the plan in 1948.

1 ▶ Have you ever faced the problem of a leak in a roof? Suddenly, there is water dripping from the ceiling onto the floor. You can't fix the roof at once. The important thing is to keep the water from spreading all over the room. Most likely, you will place a pan under the drip to catch the water. You try to "contain" it, to keep it in one place. The United States and other Western democracies had the same policy toward communism after World War II. Communists, with help from the Soviet Union, had taken over much of Eastern Europe after World War II. The United States wanted to contain the spread of communism.

2 ▶ The United States met the Communist threat in several ways. Millions of dollars were sent to Greece to crush a revolt there led by Communists. Millions more were sent to Turkey to strengthen its armed forces against threats from the Soviet Union. More United States aid went to help

nations of Europe "get on their feet" after the war. The United States joined with other nations of the Americas in forming the OAS (Organization of American States). The United States also helped to form a powerful military alliance. It is called NATO (North Atlantic Treaty Organization). NATO is made up of over a dozen nations. The United States, Canada, most of the countries of Western Europe, and Greece and Turkey are members. Both the OAS and NATO were formed to stop the spread of communism. The United States also put a stop to the Soviet move to build missile bases in Cuba. The policy of "containing" communism had some success in Europe and Latin America.

3 ▶ The policy did not work out so well in Asia. The Communists won a great victory in China. With that victory, one-fourth of the world's people came under Communist dictatorship. When armies from Communist North Korea invaded South Korea,

Vietnam War. Why did some Americans support United States involvement in the war and others did not?

United Nations forces were sent to stop the attack. The armed forces of the United States led the fighting against North Korean and Chinese troops. South Korea was kept free from Communist control.

4▶ American troops were sent also to Vietnam. In that bloody war, hundreds of thousands of Vietnamese and over 58,000 Americans died. But Communist rule came to South Vietnam anyway. This war divided the American people. Many did not believe that the effort in Vietnam was worth the cost of so many lives. Many felt that the policy of containment should be changed. It was during the Vietnam War that President Nixon visited China. The trip was the beginning of a change in foreign policy. The visit was the beginning of meetings between our leaders and those of China. In 1979, the United States opened official relations with China. President Carter granted recognition to China. This meant that the United States and China

began to have the same relations that most countries have with other countries. Trade increased between the two countries.

5▶ The United States has a deep interest in the Middle East. That area has the world's largest oil reserves. The state of Israel is also in the Middle East. Arab leaders want to destroy Israel. Four wars have been fought over Israel's freedom. The United States has always supported Israel with money and supplies. At the same time, aid has been sent to Arab nations to keep their friendship and lessen Communist influence. In 1978, President Carter met with the leaders of Israel and Egypt. From that meeting came a plan for peace between the two nations. American forces were sent to the Middle East in 1990 in response to Iraq's invasion of tiny but oil-rich Kuwait. President Bush announced his aims were to protect Saudi Arabia from invasion, convince the Iraqis to leave Kuwait, and restore its government.

President Carter, Israeli Prime Minister Menachem Begin, and Egyptian President Anwar al-Sadat meet to discuss Middle East peace. Why was this an important conference?

6► After World War II, several African countries came under Communist control. Ethiopia was one of these. Yet the United States donated food and supplies to relieve hunger in Ethiopia, Somalia, Sudan, and eastern Africa. In South Africa, U.S. foreign policy helped force the government to change. For years, a white minority controlled a much larger black majority. Blacks were treated as inferior in a system known as *apartheid* (uh PART hyt). The United States and other nations protested this system. In the early 1990s, South Africa began to change its policies. The government freed the imprisoned leader of the African National Congress, Nelson Mandela. Apartheid was outlawed. The government agreed to hold elections that both blacks and whites could vote in. The United States will push for changes until whites and blacks are equal in South Africa.

7► Leaders of countries in Central and South America have felt that the United States had not given their peoples enough help. President Kennedy offered to spend millions of dollars to help the economy of Latin American countries. He also started the Peace Corps. Americans with special skills lived among the poor, teaching them how to improve their lives. Under President Carter, the United States agreed to give up control of the Panama Canal to Panama. In the 1980s, the United States government followed a policy of stopping the spread of Cuban and Soviet influence in Latin America. Under President Reagan, secret aid was given to rebels in Nicaragua. In El Salvador, the United States aided the government against rebels. The rebels, it was claimed, were receiving help from Cuba and the Soviet Union. In 1989, President Bush ordered American forces into Panama. President Manuel Noriega was captured and brought back to the

Panama Canal. President Carter signed a peace treaty with Panama. What does the treaty tell us about U.S. foreign policy?

United States to stand trial for trafficking in drugs and using government funds for his personal gain. The United Nations General Assembly "strongly deplored" the United States invasion.

8▶ Since the destruction of Hiroshima by an atomic bomb in 1945, the world has faced the threat of nuclear weapons in warfare. There have been many attempts to deal with this threat. In 1963, the United States and the Soviet Union signed a treaty ending tests of nuclear weapons in the air, on the ground, and under water. In 1972, the two powers signed the SALT (Strategic Arms Limitation Treaty) agreement. Strategic weapons are those capable of destroying an enemy's population and its ability to produce war materials. A new agreement was signed in 1979, but the United States Senate did not give its consent to the treaty.

9▶ In 1987, the two powers agreed to eliminate all medium- and shorter-range nuclear missiles. In mid-1991, Bush and Gorbachev agreed to reduce strategic arms. When the Soviet Union broke up in late 1991, the new countries wanted to keep their nuclear weapons under central control. However, by 1992, these countries stated that the United States would have to deal with each of them separately to make arms reduction agreements. The uncertainty of control over former Soviet nuclear weapons would remain a concern during the early 1990s.

10▶ The human rights of all people concern Americans. This concern has lead the United States to cut off or reduce economic ties to several countries. For example, after the Chinese government

Minuteman missile being launched. What is the main purpose of a missile program?

brutally crushed a peaceful student demonstration in 1989, the United States imposed trade restrictions on China for over a year. Since then, the United States has warned China about its human rights abuses. Some political prisoners who have been freed from oppressive governments in Latin America have given the human rights policy of the United States credit for their freedom. Yet, there are nations friendly to the United States that deny their people basic human rights. Can the United States force or persuade other nations to grant civil and political rights to their people? Should it break off relations with nations that do not treat their people humanely?

11 ▶ In chapter 42 and this chapter, you have learned something of the history of our foreign policy. What is foreign policy then? It is the way a country carries on its dealings with other nations. United States foreign policy tries to protect the nation from outside enemies. It tries to help the American people in their dealings with people and governments of other countries. It tries to keep the United States at peace. It tries to promote peace throughout the world.

12 ▶ Leaders in the government have to take specific actions in order to achieve their foreign policy objectives. It is not easy to shape foreign policy because there are always many decisions to make. Each new foreign policy decision depends on all the decisions that leaders made before. Each decision may change the lives of many people in many different countries, as well as in the United States.

13 ▶ What is the foreign policy of the United States today?

1. The United States attempts to provide security for its people. This means that the nation should be free of threats from other nations and be able to defend itself against possible enemies.

2. The United States offers economic and military aid to friendly nations. It enters into alliances with other nations to assist them in defending themselves.

3. The United States is committed to help those in need, regardless of their political beliefs.

4. The United States promotes peace throughout the world in cooperation with the United Nations. It attempts to halt a race in armaments and the spread of nuclear weapons.

1990
ECONOMIC SUMMIT
OF
INDUSTRIALIZED
NATIONS

HOUSTON TEXAS

President Bush addressing an economic summit in Houston, Texas, 1990. What do you think are the major issues discussed at an economic summit?

5. The United States encourages the growth of democracy throughout the world. It supports the efforts of people to choose their own governments.

6. The United States seeks open trade arrangements. It wants to be able to buy goods from others and enable American producers to sell their goods.

CHAPTER 43 REVIEW

★ UNDERSTANDING WHAT YOU HAVE READ

1. The main idea of paragraph 5 is that
   a. the United States wants peace in the Middle East
   b. Israel controls great oil reserves
   c. the United States has sent aid to both Israel and Arab nations

2. A victory for the policy of containing communism took place in
   a. Vietnam
   b. China
   c. Korea

3. The United States has joined with other nations in the OAS and NATO to
   a. rebuild places damaged by war
   b. put down revolts in countries of Europe
   c. stop the spread of communism

4. A result of the war in Vietnam was that
   a. communism lost its power in Asia
   b. China agreed to stop making atomic bombs
   c. the United States made changes in its policy of containment

5. A goal of the United States in Latin America has been to
   a. oppose Cuban and Soviet influence in the region
   b. halt the spread of nuclear weapons
   c. stop Latin American trade with Europe

6. Under Presidents Reagan and Bush

   a. the size of the Peace Corps was increased
   b. the United States sent armed forces into Latin America
   c. the United States ended its protests against apartheid.

7. The main purpose of the foreign policy of the United States is to
   a. spread the American kind of government throughout the world
   b. keep our country safe and at peace
   c. force foreign nations to give us the goods we need

8. "Because we are free, we cannot turn our backs on those who are not free." This thought is the main idea of the
   a. policy of containment
   b. Human Rights policy
   c. Peace Corps

9. After World War II, the United States
   a. did not give up its policy of isolation
   b. decided not to have any say in world affairs
   c. planned to contain the spread of communism everywhere in the world.

10. Which nation did the United States invade in 1989?
    a. Korea
    b. Grenada
    c. Panama

★ DEVELOPING CRITICAL THINKING SKILLS

A. Interpreting Maps and Charts

FOREIGN TRADE OF THE UNITED STATES, 1988

Exports and Imports (In millions)

Country	Exports	Imports	Balance
Canada	$69,223	$80,921	-$11,688
West Germany	14,331	26,503	-12,172
Mexico	10,331	26,503	-12,172
Great Britain	18,404	18,042	+362
Soviet Union	202	681	-479
Israel	3,248	2,978	+270
Saudi Arabia	3,799	5,504	-1,795
South Korea	11,290	20,189	-8,899
Japan	37,732	89,802	-52,070
Egypt	2,340	221	+2,119

Source: Statistical Abstract of the U.S., 1990

Write the answers to the following questions in your notebook.

1. Which nation is the leading trading partner of the United States in combined imports and exports?

2. From which nation did the United States import the greatest amount of goods?

3. To which nation did the United States export the greatest amount of goods?

4. With which countries did the United States have more exports than imports?

5 From what you have studied, what may be the reasons for the small amount of trade with the Soviet Union?

6. Why do you think there is a great imbalance in trade with Egypt?

7. What does the table tell us about the interdependence of nations?

UNITED STATES MILITARY AND ECONOMIC ASSISTANCE

Foreign Aid, 1988 (in millions)

Country	Military Aid	Economic Aid
Egypt	$1,302	$718
Israel	1,800	1,200
Turkey	494	32
Pakistan	261	385
Philippines	128	78
El Salvador	82	266
Honduras	91	130

Source: United States Agency for International Development

Write the answers to the following questions in your notebook.

1. Which country received the largest amount of combined aid in 1988?

2. Which country received the most military aid in 1988?

3. Which countries received more economic that military aid?

4. From what you have read in chapter 43, why do you think Israel received such a large amount of military aid?

5. Which region of the world received the most military aid? The least amount?

6. Using a world map, determine why military aid to Turkey is of great importance to the United States.

7. What conclusions can you draw from this table?

B. Writing About Citizenship

"Presidents are responsible for the foreign policy of the United States. There are times when presidents must make tough decisions that affect the lives of Americans."

1. In your notebook, list some of the decisions that presidents have made that were mentioned in this chapter.

2. In one or two well-organized paragraphs, support the quotation about presidents and foreign policy.

HOW FOREIGN POLICY IS MADE

PURPOSES FOR READING

1. To learn the powers of the president and Congress in making foreign policy
2. To learn the workings of the State Department in making and carrying out foreign policy
3. To learn how the president receives advice from many sources in making foreign policy

KNOWING NEW WORDS

embarrass
(em BAR us) paragraph 3—to make a person feel uncomfortable, uneasy
EXAMPLE: Harry has no money with him so let's not **embarrass** him by asking him to pay the bill.

league
(LEEG) paragraph 3—an organization of states that acts together
EXAMPLE: The **League** of Nations was supposed to work together to keep peace in the world.

adviser
(ad VY zur) paragraph 5—one who offers advice, who suggests what can be done
EXAMPLE: The student asked the college **adviser** about help for his science class.

personnel
(pur suh NEL) paragraph 10—the people who work together in one place or for one group
EXAMPLE: The office **personnel** included clerks, typists, and secretaries.

President Bush meets with the foreign minister of Kuwait during the Middle East crisis. What do you think the purpose of this meeting might have been?

President Dwight D. Ei-
senhower meets with
Senator Jacob K. Javits.
What role does the Senate
play in approving treaties
and ambassadors?

1► When you awake in the morning you most likely will think about the day ahead of you. You will think of school and the people you will meet. You may wonder about how prepared you are to meet the classes on your schedule. Your thoughts may turn to music or the game to be played. You may look forward to your plans for the evening. It would seem strange if you were greeted by a member of your family with the latest world news. Probably no one will tell you what happened in China, or England, or South Africa. These places seem far removed from what you expect of a brand-new day. But there are people for whom the latest news is one of the first items each day. It is that way for the president of the United States. The president has to be prepared to speak for us before the entire world.

2► The Constitution lists the powers of the president. One of these powers is the power to make treaties with foreign coun-

tries. Congress can advise the president about a treaty that may be made. The Senate must approve any treaty by a two-thirds vote. But only the president makes a treaty. And only the president speaks for the United States in dealing with other countries. The president also names representatives of the United States to foreign lands. These are ambassadors. They represent the president. When they speak, they speak with the voice of the United States government. Ambassadors must also be approved by the Senate.

3► The powers of Congress are important ones. Presidents like to have the support of Congress when they are dealing with a foreign country. Presidents do not want the Senate to say no to a treaty they have made. This can embarrass the president. This part of the American democratic system is hard for leaders of other nations to understand. They will say: "We made an agreement with the president. But we don't know if there is an agreement. The Senate has to vote. That may take months. We may not have any agreement after all." There have been times when the Senate has voted down a treaty made by the president. It did not agree to our joining the League of Nations after World War I. In 1977 President Carter signed treaties with Panama. These agreements provided for the takeover of the canal by Panama by the year 2000. In 1978 the Senate approved the treaties by only one vote.

4▶ Congress has another control over the president's power. It controls government spending. Suppose that a president promises to send aid to a foreign country. Congress will have to give the money to support the president's plan. If Congress does not like the plan, it may refuse to do so. Presidents, therefore, try to get the support of Congress. They will meet with leaders of Congress. In most cases, they will "let Congress in" on a planned agreement. When President Reagan did not do this with his Iran policy, he had problems with Congress.

5▶ The secretary of state is the president's chief adviser in foreign affairs. Some presidents have been bold leaders in these matters. They left little for their secretary of state to do. But for others, the secretary of state does a great deal. Henry Kissinger, secretary of state under Presidents Nixon and Ford, was among the most active. He flew hundreds of thousands of miles trying to bring about peace in many parts of the world. In the Middle East, he flew back and forth between the leaders of Israel and Arab nations. These flights were made almost every day for weeks at a time. His travel record may be surpassed by that of James Baker, Secretary of State for President George Bush. The following is a record of his travels during November, 1990. In all of these visits, Secretary Baker is carrying out the policies of his president.

Nov. 4-5	Visits King Fahd in Saudi Arabia
Nov. 6	Visits President Mubarak of Egypt
Nov. 7	Talks in Ankara with the president of Turkey
Nov. 8	Meets with President Gorbachev of the Soviet Union in Moscow
Nov. 9	Meets with Prime Minster Thatcher of Britain in London
Nov. 10	Has talks with President Mitterand in Paris

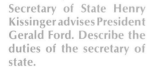

Secretary of State Henry Kissinger advises President Gerald Ford. Describe the duties of the secretary of state.

President Bush and Secretary of State James Baker. Secretary Baker was President Bush's chief adviser on foreign policy.

Nov. 15-16 In Brussels, Belgium, for European Community Commission

Nov. 17 To Geneva, Switzerland, with foreign ministers of Côte d'Ivoire, Ethiopia, Zaire, and members of the UN Security Council

Nov. 18 Meets with other UN Security Council members in Paris

Nov. 21-22 Back to Saudi Arabia, Egypt, and Yemen

Nov. 24 Travels to Colombia to confer with President Gaviria

Nov. 24 Same day, in Los Angeles with Malaysian Foreign Minister

Nov. 29 In New York, chairman of meeting of UN Security Council

1. What world problem caused the secretary's hurried visits during November, 1990?

2. How many continents did Secretary Baker visit in one month?

3. In chapter 43, you read of the North Atlantic Treaty Organization (NATO). Which visits included leaders of countries in NATO?

4. What may explain Secretary Baker's visits to Saudi Arabia and Egypt?

6 ▶ The secretary of states has a large staff. There are five chief assistants. These assistant secretaries have special interests: Europe and Canada, Africa, East Asia and the Pacific, the Near East and Southern Asia, and the rest of the Western Hemisphere. Each of these has smaller offices that deal with a single country. The men and women who work in these offices are specialist. They have to keep their assistant secretary up to date on all matters of importance.

7 ▶ Over twenty-five thousand people work for the State Department. Sixteen

American troops in Saudi Arabia in 1990. Why did President Bush think it was necessary to send troops to Saudi Arabia? What did most Americans think?

thousand of them work outside the United States. These are members of the **Foreign Service.** These people have spent long periods of training for the jobs they hold. They are the "eyes and ears" of our foreign policy. They report to the State Department about conditions in the country where they work, and they offer help to Americans who may be traveling there. Americans will find an office of the State Department —a consulate or embassy—in almost all the world's important cities.

8 ▶ The president makes American foreign policy. The State Department is an arm of the president. But there are other voices that are heard in making policy. Presidents have their own special advisers. These are people who have had great experience in studying foreign policy. Some may be friends of the president. Because they are chosen by the president, their advice can carry great weight.

9 ▶ The president receives advice from the **National Security Council.** This body was formed by Congress in 1947. The president is a member of the National

Security Council. So is the vice-president. Others are the secretaries of state and defense and the director of the Office of Emergency Planning. The council's job is to give advice to the president about the safety of the nation. Because it is concerned with the nation's strength, all meetings are held in secret.

10 ▶ The president receives reports about safety from the Department of Defense. The president is the commander of the armed forces. The armed forces of the United States must, at times, carry out foreign policy. The United States is a member of NATO. (See page 348.) The United States supplies arms and personnel to carry out its duties as a member of NATO. The American policy of trying to stop the spread of communism brought the United States into wars in Korea and Vietnam. Marines were sent to the Dominican Republic in 1965. President Johnson thought there was a Communist threat in that small nation.

11 ▶ Sometimes, domestic policy interferes with foreign policy. For example,

United States farmers have unintentionally grown a surplus of certain crops. The United States then sold some of these crops to other countries at a very low price. The sale created friction between the United States and its allies because the allies needed to sell the same crops. However, they could not sell their crops because the United States was selling the same ones at a lower price. The president must try to balance foreign and domestic policy.

12► The people of the nation are also advisers to the president. Citizens know more about foreign affairs than ever before. TV, radio, and newspapers tell people about foreign events almost as soon as they take place. Speedy means of travel place all parts of the world at our doorsteps. The United States needs a wise and knowing public with **empathy** for people in other countries. The public has an important effect on foreign policy.

CHAPTER 44 REVIEW

★ UNDERSTANDING WHAT YOU HAVE READ

1. The main idea of paragraph 2 is that
   a. ambassadors represent the United States government in foreign countries
   b. the Senate must approve a treaty made by the president
   c. the Constitution gives the president powers in foreign affairs

2. Congress may have some voice in what the president does in foreign affairs by
   a. not giving money to support the president
   b. making treaties themselves
   c. training people for jobs in the Foreign Service

3. Presidents want the support of Congress in foreign affairs because
   a. members of Congress visit foreign countries too
   b. the Senate must approve any treaty that is made
   c. Congress names the secretary of state

4. Presidents have given much of the work in foreign affairs to the
   a. secretary of state
   b. secretary of defense
   c. National Security Council

5. Which of these statements is most accurate?
   a. There are few employees of the United States in foreign lands.
   b. The president makes American foreign policy.
   c. Few people can give advice to the president about foreign policy.

6. "The State Department is the arm of the president." This means that
   a. the State Department carries out the wishes of the president
   b. presidents have their own close advisers
   c. the Foreign Service helps Americans in foreign lands

7. Who is NOT a member of the National Security Council?
   a. The secretary of defense
   b. The vice-president
   c. The chief justice of the Supreme Court

8. Which of these is usually the first step in making foreign policy?
   a. The Senate votes on a treaty.
   b. The president makes an agreement with a foreign country.
   c. The president receives advice from Congress, cabinet members, and the public.

9. Which of these statements is TRUE?
   a. There are times when the armed forces carry out the foreign policy of the United States.
   b. All members of the cabinet are members of the National Security Council.
   c. The Senate has never turned down a treaty made by a president.

10. The "eyes and ears" of our foreign policy are the members of the
    a. Foreign Service
    b. president's cabinet
    c. Congress

★DEVELOPING CRITICAL THINKING SKILLS

A. Studying Foreign Policy Statements and Decisions

Read each foreign policy statement or decision. Then answer the questions.

George Washington's Farewell Address

> George Washington, in his Farewell Address in 1796, made this statement:
>
> The great rule of conduct for us, in regard to foreign Nations, is, in extending our commercial relations [trade], to have with them as little political connection as possible. . . . Europe has a set of primary interests which to us have none, or a very remote [far-off] relation. . . . Our detached and distant situation invites and enables us to pursue a different course. . . . Why forego the advantages of so peculiar a situation [3,000 miles of ocean between the United States and Europe]? Why quit our own to stand on foreign ground?—Why, by interweaving our destiny with that of any part of Europe, entangle our peace and prosperity in the toils of European ambition?

1. What did President Washington think the policy of the United States should be concerning the countries of Europe?

2. What kind of relations do you think the United States should today have with Europe? Why?

3. What is the name given to Washington's policy?

Franklin D. Roosevelt's Four Freedoms

In January 1941, Europe was at war. President Roosevelt, in his message to Congress, explained his hopes for the world.

. . . In the future . . . we look forward to a world founded upon four essential freedoms.

The first is freedom of speech and expression everywhere in the world

The second is freedom of every person to worship God in his [or her] own way everywhere in the world.

The third is freedom from want, which . . . means economic understanding which will secure to every nation a healthy peacetime life for its inhabitants everywhere in the world.

The fourth is freedom from fear which . . . means a world-wide reduction of armaments to such a point and in such a thorough fashion that no nation will be in a position to commit an act of physical aggression [war] against any neighbor—anywhere in the world.

(Within a year after he announced this policy, President Roosevelt was leading our nation in a war to defend this policy.)

1. The statement is sometimes called "The Four Freedoms." Has this policy been accepted in the world today? Explain your answer.

2. In your study of foreign policy, you have learned what the United States has done to bring these freedoms into being throughout the world.

   a. Has the United States had a policy about freedom of speech and expression elsewhere in the world? Support your answer.

   b. Has the United States tried to make sure all people have freedom to practice their own religion? Support your answer.

   c. Has the United States had a policy that would help people elsewhere in the world to be free from want? Support your answer.

   d. Has the United States had a policy that would lead to disarming of nations to end the chance of war? Support your answer.

Harry S Truman's Decision for Military Action

In June 1950, North Korea, a Communist state, invaded South Korea. President Harry S Truman made the decision to send United States troops to defend South Korea. In his own words, he tells how he came to this decision.

. . . I had time to think aboard the plane [from Kansas City to Washington]. In my generation, this was not the first occasion when the strong had attacked the weak. I recalled some earlier instances: Manchuria (1931), Ethiopia (1935), Austria (1938). I remembered how each time that the democracies failed to act it had encouraged the aggressors [invaders] to keep going ahead. Communism was acting in Korea just as Hitler, Mussolini, and the Japanese had acted ten, fifteen, twenty years earlier. I felt certain that if South Korea were allowed to fold, Communist leaders would be emboldened [encouraged] to override nations close to our own shores. . . . It was also clear to me that the foundations and principles of the United Nations were at stake unless this unprovoked [without a reason] attack on Korea would be stopped."

Source: Truman, Harry S, *Memoirs,*
Vol. II, pp 332–33. 1956, Time, Inc.

1. How did President Truman describe the attack on South Korea?

2. What did the president think would happen if the United States failed to act in South Korea?

3. The president compared Communist leaders with what other leaders who were aggressors in the past?

4. Why did the president make the decision to send troops to South Korea?

B. Writing About Citizenship

Write a short essay on the following topic: If you were the secretary of state, what do you think your greatest concern would be? Would it be a communist threat to another nation? Would it be the Middle East? Or would it be something else altogether? Be sure to support your opinions.

PARTICIPATION IN GOVERNMENT

WRITING LETTERS TO GOVERNMENT LEADERS

Many students are concerned about pollution in our global environment. The United States has many environment problems it must work on. However, some of the worst polluters of the environment are other countries. Many countries in Eastern Europe and those that used to be a part of the Soviet Union did not have strict laws to control pollution. These countries often built their factories, mining operations, and other industries without considering how this would affect the environment. When the Soviet Union collapsed, these countries tried to build their industries even more rapidly to catch up to the rest of Europe. This has led to a serious environmental crisis.

Some concerned citizens in the United States want these countries to clean up their industries. They want U.S. government leaders to put pressure on these countries. They want foreign policy decisions that support cleaning up the environment. If you wanted to influence U.S. foreign policy about the environment, what could you do? How would you let the president and other government representatives know what concerns you? Write to them!

Write a formal letter discussing your concerns. Give reasons why these issues are important and try to give ways the problems might be solved. If you can, give specific foreign policy suggestions. Be sure to include your full name and address so that you can receive a reply to your letter. When you are finished writing, have a friend proofread your letter. Then send it to your senator, representative, or the president.

45

THE UNITED NATIONS ORGANIZATION

PURPOSES FOR READING

1. To learn why the United Nations was formed
2. To learn how the United Nations carries out its work of keeping peace in the world
3. To learn how the United Nations has succeeded and where it has failed

KNOWING NEW WORDS

disputes
(dih SPYOOTS) paragraph 1—arguments; differences of opinion
EXAMPLE: Jennifer and Carlos agreed with each other about most things, but they had serious **disputes** over politics.

permanent
(PUR muh nunt) paragraph 5—fixed; cannot be changed

EXAMPLE: Fred didn't want an office that would be changed every day. He wanted a **permanent** one.

trustee
(truh STEE) paragraph 9—one who holds property for another and does business for that person or group
EXAMPLE: A parent is sometimes a **trustee** of the bank accounts of his or her children.

Meeting of the UN General Assembly. What are the main aims of the United Nations?

1 ► How can people settle disputes without fighting? Most arguments can be settled by talking it over. Often arguments take place when one person or group does not understand the other. When each side can sit down with the other, an agreement often follows. The sides may even ask a third person or group to help them settle their disputes. Nations disagree with one another too. Can they settle their disputes in the same way individuals do? After World War I, the League of Nations was formed. It hoped to bring nations together to bring peace to the world. But the United States did not even join it. The League of Nations failed to stop the dictators in their rush to war in 1939.

2 ► During World War II, the United States, the Soviet Union, and Britain ("The Big Three") agreed to help form a new world organization to keep peace. They wrote a charter—a set of rules—for it. It was called the United Nations organization (UN). Fifty-one nations agreed to the charter before the war ended. The Senate gave its approval and the United States was among the first to join the UN. The United States had given up its policy of isolation. That policy had not kept it out of World War II. The United States became the host for the nations of the world. The headquarters of the UN is in New York City.

3 ► The aims of the UN are stated in the charter. (1) It hopes to save the people of the world from the evils of war. (2) It hopes to improve the living standard of all people. (3) It hopes that all people will be treated with the dignity they deserve as humans. Men and women are to have equal rights. Large and small nations are

UN buildings in New York City. Why was New York City a good choice for UN headquarters?

to have equal rights. To reach these goals, the UN was set up with six chief parts or bodies.

4 ► The **General Assembly** is made up of delegates from all the member nations. Each member has one vote in the General Assembly. This body discusses problems that are a threat to world peace. It can suggest that the UN take certain actions. A two-thirds vote of members is needed on important matters.

5 ► The **Security Council** is the action body of the UN. It has five permanent members. These are the United States, the Russian Federation, the United Kingdom, France, and the People's Republic of China. These five are always members of the council. Ten other members are elected for two-year terms. This body decides what the UN should do when trouble arises. The council can do two things. It can ask member nations with disputes to work out an agreement. Or, if this cannot be done, it can work out an agreement by itself. The council can act against a nation if the council finds that the nation is standing in the way of peace. It can ask UN members

367

UN forces in Lebanon. What has been the usual role of UN troops?

not to trade with that nation. It can even take military action against that nation.

6 ▶ The Security Council needs at least 9 of the 15 members to approve of an action. However, any of the 5 permanent members can stop an action by a **veto,** or a negative vote. Although the UN has no armed forces of its own, members supply arms and troops when necessary. Several times the UN has been given troops to patrol borders between nations with disputes. In 1950, members of the UN sent armed forces to South Korea to stop an invasion by North Korea. In 1990, the Security Council gave Saddam Hussein of Iraq a deadline to withdraw has troops from Kuwait, which he had invaded. When he did not withdraw in January 1991, UN members, including the United States, went to war to force Hussein out of Kuwait.

7 ▶ The **International Court of Justice** decides questions of law between nations. It is sometimes called the World Court. UN members do not have to take their disputes to the World Court. But, if they do, they agree to obey the court's rulings. This part of the UN is located in the Netherlands.

8 ▶ A fourth body of the UN is the **Economic and Social Council.** Of all the bodies of the UN, this one has had the most success. This council has 54 members elected by the General Assembly for three-year terms. It collects facts and figures on social and economic conditions around the world.

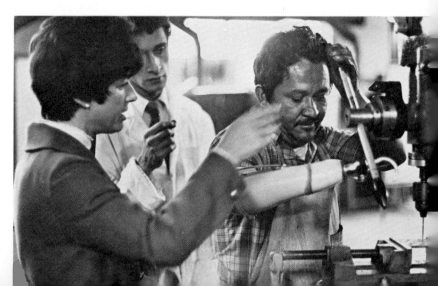

UN expert in job training for disabled people helps a worker in Latin America as part of the UN Development Program.

It gives advice to the General Assembly. It works with many important branches of the UN. Each branch does a different kind of work. Some of the following branches are very important. The World Health Organization (WHO) fights the spread of disease in countries around the world. The Food and Agricultural Organization (FAO) tries to improve the food and farming methods in many lands. Workers are helped through the International Labor Organization (ILO). One of the most useful branches is UNESCO (uh NES koh). The letters stand for United Nations Educational, Scientific, and Cultural Organization. It tries to get scientists and artists of different countries to work together. It works for justice and human rights.

9▶ The **Trusteeship Council** watched over the way some nations ruled certain areas that had once been colonies of other nations. The council would choose a nation to be a trustee of a colony. As a trustee, the ruling nation helped the people of the colony toward self-government. All but one trust area have become independent countries. This council, therefore, has very little work to do.

10▶ The sixth main body of the UN is the **Secretariat** (sek rih TAIR ee ut). Here is where the office work is done. This body has several thousand clerks, secretaries, and translators (those who speak several languages). It keeps records, makes reports, and plans meetings. It makes sure that the work of the UN runs smoothly. The head of this body is the secretary-general. This is the highest office of the UN. The holder of this office is elected by the General Assembly. The secretary-

One of the missions of the UN is to fight malnutrition. This UN-sponsored program taught nutrition, gardening, and health care to mothers in India.

general may inform the Security Council of any matter that is a danger to world peace. Boutros Boutros-Ghali, of Egypt, was elected secretary-general in 1992.

11▶ The UN has not been able to work as its founders hoped it would. It depends upon its members to make decisions. Members must also carry them out. Sometimes, differences between member nations have made this difficult. Often, the Security Council cannot act. This is because one or more of the five great powers often vetoes suggested actions. The Security Council can only ask its members to take some actions.

12▶ Another problem is the great growth in the number of UN members. There were 51 members in 1945. Now, almost all nations are members. It is harder to get things done in the assembly. Many new nations are small. Yet each has the same vote as a great power. Many were once colonies of Western European nations. They often disagree strongly with the United States and Western European nations on important policy matters.

369

Dr. Ralph Bunche and UN team leave for the Middle East in 1948.

13► The UN has also suffered from lack of money. Some nations do not have the money to pay their dues. Others refuse to pay. Some have refused to pay when they have not agreed with UN actions. The United States pays one-fourth of the entire regular UN budget. But our country refused to pay its share of education programs at one time. This was to protest UNESCO actions against Israel.

14► The UN has had successes, too. Dr. Ralph Bunche headed a UN team that brought an end to fighting between Israel and Arab nations in 1948. In the next 20 years, it was able to stop more than a dozen disputes among nations. In Korea, a UN army stopped the invading North Koreans.

In the Congo and Cyprus, UN forces helped to restore peace. It issued the Declaration of Human Rights in 1948. This statement is based on the United States Bill of Rights. The UN has held meetings to try to get nations to reduce the size of armies and navies. Its agencies have stamped out disease in some parts of the world. It has helped poor nations to start factories to support themselves. It has taught farmers how to grow a greater amount of crops. It has taught about healthful foods.

15► In other cases, the UN has voted to condemn the actions of certain member nations. At times, the UN has not been able to enforce its decisions. The Security Council asked members not to trade with Rhodesia. Trade continued. It also ordered members not to supply arms to South Africa. Some nations continued to do so. In 1974, it went so far as to forbid South Africa to take part in the meetings of the General Assembly. In Rhodesia and South Africa, a small white minority held power despite a large black majority. Rhodesia, renamed Zimbabwe, now has a black prime minister. But UN actions have made little change in South African policies.

16► Some people believe that the UN

This picture is an example of racial segregation in South Africa. What steps did the UN take to condemn this kind of discrimination?

could do more if there were some changes in its charter. But it would be almost impossible to make such changes. Every large nation in the Security Council would have to agree to charter changes. It is not likely that large nations would vote to reduce the power they already have. The UN has not fulfilled all hopes for it. But cooperation among the major powers in condemning the 1990 invasion of Kuwait revived hope for future successes. The lessening of tensions after the fall of the Soviet Union also contributed to this brighter outlook. So long as nations talk at the UN, as the world listens, nations may think twice before going to war.

CHAPTER 45 REVIEW

★ UNDERSTANDING WHAT YOU HAVE READ

1. The Security Council would have a hard time taking action against the United States or France because they
   a. could veto the action
   b. have stronger armed forces than those used by the UN
   c. do not belong to the Security Council

2. An important idea of this chapter is that
   a. the UN has little power unless the United States and the Russian Federation support its votes
   b. armed forces of the UN are ready to stop trouble in any part of the world
   c. the General Assembly is the "action body" of the UN

3. When the UN was formed, the United States
   a. was against the idea of a world organization
   b. was among the first to join the new organization
   c. helped to get it started but did not join until 1960

4. The United States could not join the UN without
   a. a vote by citizens
   b. the consent of two-thirds of the Senate
   c. approval of both houses of Congress

5. The UN body that would vote to stop trade with a member nation is the
   a. General Assembly
   b. Security Council
   c. Trusteeship Council

6. All of these are permanent members of the Security Council EXCEPT
   a. the People's Republic of China
   b. France
   c. Germany

7. To some, the increase in the number of nations who are members of the UN has caused a problem. The problem is that
   a. most new nations are small with the same voting power as large nations
   b. none of the new nations pays to support the UN
   c. some new nations have veto power in the Security Council

8. Which statement is TRUE?
   a. The UN has never condemned the action of a member nation.
   b. The UN has not asked members to stop fighting each other.
   c. The UN has been able to stop some serious disputes among nations.

★ **DEVELOPING CRITICAL THINKING**

A. Interpreting A Graph

Study this graph. Then answer the questions that follow it.

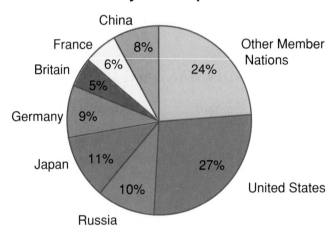

Who Pays UN Expenses

Source: UN Secretariat

1. Which nation pays the largest amount of the expenses of the UN?

2. Which nation pays the second highest amount?

3. Does the United States pay twice as much as Russia?

4. How many nations pay 10 percent or more of the total expenses?

5. About what percentage of the UN budget is paid by the "other member nations"?

B. Using Word Clues

The following words or terms are used in this chapter. In your notebook write the meanings of these words. Also list the clue in the paragraph that helped you to know the meaning of the word.

charter—paragraph 2

bodies of the UN—paragraph 3

translators—paragraph 10

C. Finding Proof for Statements

Tell whether the following statements are true or false. Which paragraph provided information that helped you to reach your decision? Write the answers in your notebook.

1. The United States was in favor of a world organization for peace after World War II.

2. The United States vote can stop any action by the Security Council.

3. Large and small nations have the same voting power in the General Assembly.

4. The UN is not concerned with living standards of people all over the world.

5. In the world today, there are few areas that are held in trust by larger nations.

6. An increase in the number of members has ended problems in getting things done quickly in the General Assembly.

7. The Security Council has worked just as the founders of the UN hoped it would.

8. All member nations pay an equal amount in support of the UN.

9. The UN has not always been successful in actions it has taken against member nations.

D. Categorizing

In your notebook, write the letter of the UN body that fits each description.

　　a. General Assembly
　　b. Security Council
　　c. Economic and Social Council
　　d. Trusteeship Council
　　e. World Court
　　f. Secretariat

1. Has five permanent members.

2. Decides questions of law among nations.

3. Is made up of delegates from every member nation.

4. Does the office work of the UN.

5. Helped guide several former colonies to self-government and full independence.

6. One of its branches helps to stamp out disease.

E. Writing About Citizenship

Write a brief essay on the following topic: Do you think that the UN has done a good job of achieving its aims? Why or why not? Give evidence to support your opinions.

46

FOREIGN POLICY AND GLOBAL RELATIONSHIPS

PURPOSES FOR READING

1. To learn the place of the United States in today's "shrinking world"
2. To learn why the problems of hunger and growing world population affect the foreign policy of the United States
3. To understand that all people depend upon one another
4. To understand the problems that stand in the way of peace in the world

Live Aid, a huge concert in Philadelphia to help feed the victims of famine in Ethiopia and Sudan. Millions of dollars were raised by the event. Why do Americans help the needy in other parts of the world?

"...for the first time in American experience, we can neither escape from the world nor dominate it."
Henry Kissinger,
Former secretary of state,
December 1976

1 ▶ The first foreign policy of the United States was one of isolation from the troubles of Europe. People in the United States thought that 3,000 miles of ocean could keep them at peace. In a sense, Americans wanted to escape from the world and its troubles. As late as the 1930s the United States tried to be neutral in foreign affairs. Americans wanted to be left alone. Without foreign problems, Americans felt free to work out their own destiny. In the quotation on page 374, Kissinger says there is no escape from the world. Americans are in it and part of it. What world conditions will influence the relations of the United States with other peoples?

2 ▶ First, let us see the place the people of the United States hold in the world. There are over 5 billion people in the world today. That is a large number. To think of 5 billion of anything is not easy. Let us imagine that the world is a town of 1,000 people. Then, of that 1,000 people, only 60 would be people from the United States. About 300 of the 1,000 would be white. The other 700 would be other races. About 700

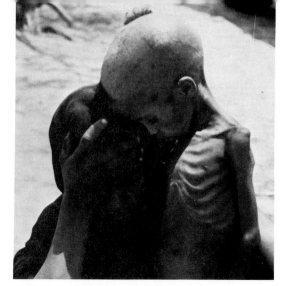

Famine and drought cause starvation conditions in West Africa.

of the people would have religious beliefs that are not Protestant, Catholic, or Jewish. The 60 from the United States would have almost half the world's wealth. The other 940 would share the other half.

3 ▶ A good part of the Western world is living on the best land and making use of its resources. Most of these people have a high standard of living. They can look forward to an average life span of 70 years. But these are only a small part of the world's people. Only seven countries in the world now grow more food than their

Squatters' shacks in Mexico. In many places in the world, over-population has made it necessary for people to live in makeshift huts. Sometimes they are side by side with rich people's homes, as in this photo.

people can eat. One-third of the world's people live in 50 hungry nations. All of these are in Asia, Africa, and Latin America. Ten thousand people a day die of starvation in these parts of the world. A good part of the world's unrest is due to widespread hunger. Even in the United States, there are over 30 million people who live in poverty. Can Americans allow this condition to continue? How can Americans help poor people everywhere to improve their ways of living?

4▶ Why are Americans interested in helping others? First, because all people are humans. People have a dignity because they are human. Then, Americans believe the earth has too many riches for millions to go hungry. Third, by helping others, Americans help themselves. As other people raise their standard of living, they will be able to trade with the United States. And, people who are well fed and housed will be able to have other interests. They will want to be better informed about their own government and the world. They will be better able to resist wars and ambitious persons who might try to rule them.

5▶ Another world problem is that of a growing population. The increase is greatest in the poor parts of the world. Is there a limit to the number of people who can live on earth? Scientists have found that when they put two mice in a cage, they get along well. When 20 mice are put in the same cage, they fight. The space is too small for so many. Is the earth reaching its limit? If world population grows at the same rate as in the last 100 years, there will be 6 billion people on earth in another 15 years. Can the world's riches care for so many people? Experts give different answers to this question.

6▶ Most of the world's people have religious beliefs and cultures that are different from those of the majority of the American people. Their values are not always the same as those held by Americans. Americans feel that their form of government and economic system is the best in the world. They want other peoples to share their beliefs, freedoms, and wealth. But the good intentions of Americans are not accepted everywhere in the world. **Terrorist** acts against Americans have increased. Bombings and hijackings are some of the latest examples of terrorism. The nations of the

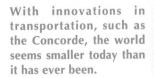

With innovations in transportation, such as the Concorde, the world seems smaller today than it has ever been.

Hiroshima, Japan, after the United States dropped the atomic bomb in 1945. How does this picture support the statements in paragraph 9?

world have not yet agreed on how to deal with terrorist groups.

7► The earth remains the same size. It just seems to be getting smaller. Some have called it our shrinking world. It seems smaller in one way because there are more people. It also seems smaller because of the changes in transportation and communication. Today news travels around the world almost as fast as it happens. Ideas spread just as fast from one part of the world to another. We watch the president of the United States travel to Russia or China. An airplane crosses the ocean in a little more than three hours. These improvements mean that more Americans travel to other lands. At the same time, about 20 million people visit the United States each year. Under such conditions, can the United States isolate itself from today's world?

8► Nations of the world depend upon each other. Americans do not produce all they need for their high standard of living. Coffee, bananas, peppers, and coconuts are not grown in the United States. Americans import oil, tin, iron ore, uranium, and other materials. The United States sells billions of dollars worth of goods to other countries each year. As the United States depends on others, so others depend upon the United States. This interdependence means that people need each other. That need should lead to friendship.

9► The horrors of war are worse today than they have ever been. One reason for this increased fear of war is the threat of nuclear weapons. Six nations have tested nuclear arms. The United States and the former Soviet Union agreed to limit the testing of nuclear weapons. But some nations have refused to do so. The threat of chemical and germ warfare also haunts the world. Iraq and Libya have reportedly used such weapons in recent wars. New and more deadly weapons continue to be made. People ask why science cannot be used for the benefit of people of the world rather than for their destruction.

10► More than 40 wars have broken out since the end of World War II. A few have been large, as in Korea and Vietnam. Most have been small wars. Many of these small wars begin with a group that is against the government in power. Small bands hold out in mountains or jungles. From time to time, they attack villages, cities, or government buildings. Then they return to hide

Guerrilla troops in El Salvador. How old do you think these soldiers are?

again. This is called **guerrilla** (guh RIL uh) warfare. As the bands succeed, they grow larger and stronger. Sometimes they may have the support of a foreign government. Some Communists have taught that guerrilla warfare is the only way poor people can gain a share of the world's riches. American foreign policy must be concerned with this type of warfare. When are such groups right in their actions? When should they be supported? What governments should the United States support against such bands?

11 ▶ There are many issues that foreign policy makers face. These issues include poverty, hunger, race discrimination, the hopes of people for freedom and human rights, the interdependence of people, a growing population, the nearness of people to each other, nuclear weapons, and guerilla warfare. There is hope. After the fall of Communism in Eastern Europe and the collapse of the Soviet Union, the Cold War ended. Many leaders of nations believe that nuclear war might bring only losers. There might be no winner. More people are growing enough food to feed themselves. Diseases that once killed millions have been stamped out. Science is working to conquer cancer, AIDS, and other terrible diseases. Soon, perhaps all nations can live in peace.

CHAPTER 46 REVIEW

★ UNDERSTANDING WHAT YOU HAVE READ

1. The main idea of paragraph 7 is that
   a. modern means of travel and communication have brought people of the world closer together
   b. more and more visitors are coming to the United States each year
   c. television and radio affect the foreign policy of the United States

2. An important idea of paragraph 2 is that
   a. over half the people of the world live in poverty

   b. the world has over a billion people
   c. the United States has more riches than any other country in the world

3. Which of these continents holds a good part of the world's hungry people?
   a. Africa
   b. Europe
   c. Australia

4. Which of these statements is an example of a policy of isolation?

a. The poor treatment of any people in the world is our business.

b. We cannot allow events in Asia and Africa to affect the way we act.

c. We will not allow friendly nations to be invaded by Communist powers.

5. Which statement is TRUE?
   a. There are more whites than nonwhites in the world.
   b. There are more nonwhites than whites in the world.
   c. The number of whites and nonwhites in the world is about the same.

6. Which best describes guerrilla warfare?
   a. Thousands of people parade in front of a government building.
   b. A group of 50 men and women blows up a warehouse during the night.
   c. A group of tanks crosses the border into a foreign country.

7. A likely result of improved transportation and communication is that people
   a. will tend to keep to themselves
   b. in different areas will become more dependent on each other
   c. will not move as often

8. Which statement is correct?
   a. The United States has all the mineral resources it needs.
   b. No nation in the world grows enough to feed its people.
   c. Other nations supply the United States with important minerals and valuable foods.

9. In the quotation at the beginning of the chapter, Kissinger is saying that
   a. we can neither separate ourselves from the world nor tell the rest of the world what to do
   b. since we are a part of the world, we should make sure that all people follow our way of life
   c. we should step into disputes among nations and tell them how to solve their disputes

10. In which of these areas did the United States and the former Soviet Union reach an agreement?
    a. Stopping guerrilla warfare
    b. Giving all people a voice in their own government
    c. Stopping many kinds of nuclear weapons tests

★DEVELOPING CRITICAL THINKING SKILLS

Separating Facts from Opinions

Read each of the following statements. Decide whether they are facts or opinions.

1. Only seven countries in the world now grow more food than their people eat.

2. Millions of people should visit the United States to learn about modern farms and factories.

3. The six nations that have nuclear weapons ought to agree not to test them in the air.

4. The United States should decide not to establish relations with any Communist nations.

5. The United States does not produce all the goods and services it needs for its citizens' high standard of living.

Unit 9

CAREERS IN GOVERNMENT

The U.S. Postal Service office. Over 3 million workers are employed by the federal government.

JOBS IN GOVERNMENT SERVICE

PURPOSES FOR READING

1. To understand why there has been a great increase in the number of government jobs
2. To learn why government jobs are desirable
3. To understand how the civil service system works
4. To understand the kinds of jobs that are available in government service

KNOWING NEW WORDS

employees
(em PLOI eez) paragraph 1—persons who work for another
EXAMPLE: **Employees** of the store asked the manager for a meeting about their pay.

employers
(em PLOI urs) paragraph 1—people or businesses that hire people to work for them

EXAMPLE: **Employers** want to hire the best people for the jobs they have to fill.

politicians
(pol ih TISH uns) paragraph 3—people who hold a public office; those who take part in the work of a political party
EXAMPLE: **Politicians** want to win elections and keep their party in power.

People Working for Government

	State and Local Governments	Federal Government	
1970	10,147,000	2,881,000	**TOTAL** **13,028,000**

	State and Local Governments	Federal Government	
1989	14,406,000	3,112,000	**TOTAL** **17,518,000**

Source: Bureau of Labor Statistics

- What does the graph on page 382 show about the number of workers for governments in the years from 1970 to 1989?
- In which governments have the number of workers increased the most from 1970 to 1989?

1▶ When the United States began, there were only three departments in the federal government. The State Department had nine employees. Today, one of every six American workers is working for their local, state, or national government. Governments are the biggest employers in the United States. The number of federal workers has not changed much in the last 15 years. A greater growth had taken place in state and local jobs. There, the number of workers has actually increased over the last two decades. Many people, however, have urged the government to try to cut payroll expenses. Yet, in preparing for a life's work, more and more people are looking toward jobs with government.

2▶ Why has there been such a growth in government jobs? As the United States grew, the needs of the people grew also. Farmers needed help. Businesses needed help. Workers needed help. Then, as you learned in Unit 4, the actions of many groups had to be regulated. The government had to be sure that all groups were treated fairly. The government began to provide care for the large number of poor. The rights of minorities had to be protected. The United States began to explore space. It started programs to protect the environment. The numer of departments and bureaus grew and grew. State and local governments had to carry out laws passed by the federal government. People were needed to staff the growing number of departments created by governments.

3▶ Most federal government jobs are in the **civil service**. The Office of Personnel and Management, which used to be called the Civil Service Commission, prepares tests for government jobs. About eight of every ten government jobs come under

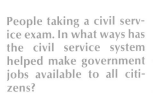

People taking a civil service exam. In what ways has the civil service system helped make government jobs available to all citizens?

civil service. Before 1883, when the Civil Service Commission was established, politicians chose people for government jobs. This system helped politicians gain support for their re-election and their programs. People owed their jobs to a person in government. They would never be sure how long the job would last. They were expected to turn over a part of their pay to the party in power. Suppose the politician who got the worker a job lost an election. Then the government worker also lost his or her job. Government workers had to be loyal first to the person who got them their job.

4 ▶ The civil service system changed all that in the federal government. Now, only the holders of top jobs in each department are appointed. To get a civil service job, people must pass a test. There may be thousands who take the same test. But, there may be only a few openings for the position the test takers want. People with the highest scores on the test are hired first. Once civil service workers get a job, they cannot be fired without a good reason. They have the job so long as they do their work in a satisfactory manner. Thousands of people have made the civil service their career.

5 ▶ Getting a government job is not easy. There are good reasons why thousands of people think government jobs are better than those with private businesses. Years ago, government workers were paid less than workers in private businesses. This is not true any longer. The changes in yearly earnings are shown in the following chart.

AVERAGE YEARLY EARNINGS			
Government Workers	**1980**	**1984**	**1988**
Federal	$18,340	$23,867	$27,470
State and Local	$14,933	$19,915	$18,110
Civilian Workers	$14,946	$18,897	$21,580

Government workers at the National Aeronautics and Space Administration in Houston, Texas.

Traffic controller in civil service job. This job and those pictured on page 384 require technical training. Give examples of jobs that do not require technical training.

1. What does the chart (page 384) show about the earnings of workers in government and private businesses?

2. What does it show about the earnings of workers for the federal government and those in state and local governments?

Besides pay, there are other benefits in government work. Pay raises are given for years of service. No test has to be taken to earn such a raise. Government workers are less likely to lose jobs when business is bad. However, in the past few years, many cities have had money problems. In order to reduce money spent, workers have been let go. Federal workers have good pension plans. They may retire at age 55 after 30 years of service.

6▶ The Office of Personnel Management has offices in most large cities. It has over 100 information centers. These tell where and when civil service tests are being given. A person takes the test first. Then the name goes on a list of those who passed the test. When there is a job opening anywhere in the country, the office will ask the commission for the names of people who can fill the job.

7▶ What kind of job can a person get with the federal government? The number runs into the thousands. Look at this chart. It lists the number of employees in some of the most important agencies of the federal government.

NUMBER OF EMPLOYEES IN SOME IMPORTANT FEDERAL DEPARTMENTS AND AGENCIES	
Congress	19,200
Executive Office of the President	1,554
United States Courts	21,161
Cabinet Departments:	
State	25,635
Defense	1,049,619
Interior	78,216
Agriculture	120,869
Commerce	52,819
Labor	18,178
Health and Human Services	123,270
Treasury	160,516
Housing and Urban Development	13,342
Transportation	63,506
Justice	76,515
Energy	17,473
Education	4,831
Veterans Affairs	248,174
Environmental Protection Agency (EPA)	15,309
Office of Personnel Management	6,673
National Aeronautics and Space Administration (NASA)	23,130
Postal Service	831,956

Source: Office of Personnel Management

8▶ All these departments need people to handle the office work. They need workers to keep records and make and file reports. They need typists and clerks. They also need people to explain their work and programs to the public. But there are other jobs that people might not think of when they think about or look for government work. Here are some civil service jobs.

Aerospace Engineer
Air-conditioning
    Mechanic
Air Traffic Controller
Architect
Counselor
Forester
Geologist
Lawyer
Meteorologist
Mining Engineer
Office Machine
    Operator
Public Relations
Security Guard
Surveyor
Technical Writer
Urban Planner

Accountant
Bank Examiner
Building Inspector
Carpenter
Civil Engineer
Clerk
Computer
    Programmer
Corrections Officer
Court Stenographer
Electrician
Elevator Mechanic
Firefighter
Hospital Worker
Housing Manager
Librarian
Nurse
Painter
Parks
    Personnel Officer
Motor Vehicle
    Operator
Plumber
Police Officer
Pollution Control
Road Maintenance
Roofer
Sanitation Worker
Steam Fitter
Stenographer
Social Worker
Teacher
Traffic Control
Transportation
Typist
Water Inspector

These are only a few of the specialized jobs needed by federal departments. There are others that are much like the positions in state and local governments.

9▶ What jobs are available in state and local governments? Most state and local governments now have a civil service system. People can find out a great deal about civil service positions from their newspapers. Large cities may have a newspaper that specializes in civil service news only. One such paper in New York City is *The Chief.* This paper gives information about tests to be given, the results of the tests, information about preparing for tests, and explanations of all kinds of information about government workers. In one issue of *The Chief,* information about these jobs was given.

Sanitation workers are employed by the city or local government. These services help protect the health and welfare of citizens.

10 ▶ Many people want jobs with governments. For some positions there are as many as 12 people who apply for each job opening. People wanting these jobs must be prepared if they are to succeed. In the next chapter, you will learn about preparing for a career. You will also learn about preparing for a career in politics.

CHAPTER 47 REVIEW

★ UNDERSTANDING WHAT YOU HAVE READ

1. The main idea of paragraph 1 is that
   a. the number of people working for state governments has increased
   b. the United States had few employees when it began
   c. governments are the biggest employers in the United States

2. A reason for the growth in government jobs is that
   a. a test is necessary to get a government job
   b. a great increase in the number of departments and bureaus answers the needs of a growing population
   c. the space program has more workers than any other government department

3. Many government jobs are civil service jobs. This means that
   a. members of Congress name most people to jobs
   b. people get jobs because they belong to a political party
   c. people get jobs because they have shown they have ability on a test

4. People seem to want government jobs because
   a. they can improve the power of their political party while they work on the job
   b. pay and pension plans are as good or better than in private business
   c. they are easy to get

5. Which statement is true about the pay of government workers?
   a. The average pay of workers for state government is higher than the pay of workers for the federal government.
   b. The average pay of federal workers is higher than the pay of those in private businesses.
   c. The average pay of workers in private businesses is higher than the pay of workers for the federal goernment.

6. Which statement is TRUE?
   a. When business is bad, government workers have less fear of losing their jobs than those in private business.
   b. There are few clerks or typists among government workers.
   c. The number of federal government workers has increased faster than state or local government workers.

7. Which of these federal departments has the most employees?
   a. Health, Education, and Welfare
   b. Agriculture
   c. Labor

8. The department of the federal government with the most employees is the
   a. Department of Agriculture
   b. Department of Health and Human Services
   c. Defense Department

9. Which of these would most likely be a civil service job of a state or local government?

   a. Police officer
   b. Aerospace engineer
   c. Geologist

10. Which of these positions in the federal government is not a civil service job?
    a. Highway inspector in the Department of Transportation
    b. Ambassador to France
    c. Forest ranger

★DEVELOPING CRITICAL THINKING SKILLS

Interpreting a Cartoon

1. What would be a good title for the cartoon?

2. What do the "selections" represent?

3. What selection would you make?

4. Who is making a selection?

B. Writing About Citizenship

Write one or two well-organized paragraphs on the following topics: Do you think that you would ever want to work in a government job? Why or why not? What might be some of the rewards of a government career? What might be some of the drawbacks? If you know someone who works in a government career, you may want to talk with that person so that you can get a better idea about the different advantages and drawbacks of government careers.

PARTICIPATION IN GOVERNMENT

CONTACTING PUBLIC SPEAKERS

Speakers from a variety of community offices can help you to understand your role as a citizen in a larger community. In addition to forming personal relationships, you will be given the opportunity to ask these contacts questions and get immediate answers.

Speakers who would be of special interest to you in studying government are:

- Representatives of your local newspaper—to learn how news is gathered
- Representatives of the federal government—to help you understand how federal, state, and local governments, though separate, cooperate with each other
- A member of your state legislature or city council—to explain special procedures in passing laws
- A judge or attorney—to explain how court schedules are made; why there are delays in hearing cases; how a jury is selected
- Representatives of police and fire departments—to help you understand how both departments must be organized in order for things to run smoothly
- Representatives of local, state, or federal governments (or private agencies)—to tell how they deal with the problem of narcotics and narcotics users
- A naturalized citizen—to tell you how he or she became a citizen

48 CAREERS IN GOVERNMENT AND POLITICS

PURPOSES FOR READING

1. To learn some things you can do before choosing a career
2. To examine reasons that people choose some careers
3. To learn how some high government positions are filled
4. To learn how careers in politics are made

KNOWING NEW WORDS

aerospace
(AIR uh spays) paragraph 4—concerned with the designing and making of missiles and other means of traveling within and beyond the earth's atmosphere
EXAMPLE: People preparing to guide a spaceship to the moon are first of all **aerospace** engineers.

prestige
(preh STEEJ) paragraph 5—standing, reputation, or influence based on what is known of one's abilities, deeds, friends, and so forth
EXAMPLE: Being chairman of the Fourth of July parade did not pay any money, but it gave Tom great **prestige.**

Many high schools and colleges have classes in technical training as part of their educational programs.

1 ▶ How many kinds of jobs are there? Your public library may have a book entitled *Dictionary of Occupational Titles*. It lists more than 40,000 different kinds of jobs. More are always being added to the list. There are lists of jobs at your local employment office. Your guidance counselor can tell you of jobs in career fields. There are hundreds of jobs in health, law, transportation, and the like. You aren't expected to know all the jobs you might hold. But these lists will give you a "taste" of the choices you have.

2 ▶ It is likely that it is too early for you to make a final choice of a career. If you know now what you want to do in life, you could start to prepare for your career right now. However, most young people will not be sure what they want to be. This is normal. A person's interests may change as he or she grows older. In a few years, there could be a new career field that doesn't even exist now.

3 ▶ You should begin to learn about careers, however. And you should take a look at yourself. What are your interests? What are your talents? In what school subjects have you had the greatest success? Do you speak up in class, giving your opinion often? Are you shy, not wanting to stand out in a group? Are you a leader, having many friends? Are you a happy person, eager to be with other people? Do you have good health? How do other people rate you? These are some of the questions you should ask yourself. Not all persons are suited for the same kind of career.

4 ▶ In chapter 47, you read some lists of job titles. Many of these are jobs in both private business and government service. Both need office managers, typists, computer programmers, and electricians. Even in the aerospace field, there are private and public careers. There are other careers that only the government can use. You could plan a political career and seek to be elected to public office. You could be hired for work in the Foreign Service. You might want to be an expert who can settle labor disputes. You could be interested in working for the United States Postal Service.

5 ▶ What reasons do people have for choosing the job they hold? One reason is money. Money means people can buy the things they **need.** But a good-paying job means workers can also buy the extra things they **want.** To some people it is more important to do something that is **satisfying.** Money is less important. These people enjoy doing something that they think is worthwhile. Others like the high **prestige** of certain jobs. They may think a job title

The job of a government administrator may sound glamorous, but it can be very difficult and require long hours of work.

sounds important. They like the idea that others look upon them as having a powerful position. There are those who put **security** first. They want their job to give them the things they need. At the same time, they want to know their job will last. Then, they will be able to take care of themselves in their old age. These different needs can be filled by jobs in government service.

6▶ Civil service jobs are available for people with many educational backgrounds. However, nearly all civil service jobs require at least a high school education. A great many require additional education or training, such as a college degree or graduation from a business or technical school. Yearly salaries for jobs in the federal government averaged over $25,000 in 1990. People with advanced skills in statistics, economics, chemistry, engineering, and computer science earn more. Administrative positions also pay well. And advancement to higher levels, which pay more, is always possible.

7▶ You have learned that those holding high positions in government are chosen by the chief executive. This chief executive could be the president, a governor, or a mayor. Some of the people chosen have had long careers in government. They

began civil service jobs early in their lives. They worked their way up "through the ranks." They became known for the high quality of their work. Others have come from outside the government. A person who runs a large business well is likely to manage a government bureau well too. An expert farmer could be of value on the staff of the Department of Agriculture. A person with business contacts in a foreign country

Cathy Villapando, the United States Treasurer, being sworn in.

may be a valuable employee of the State Department.

8 ▶ Many people welcome the chance to work in government. In many cases, they will accept a position for less money. They believe that government work is the highest kind of service. There are those, too, who want to be elected to high office in government. Voters may come to know them through government work. But there are good people who don't like government service for the same reasons. They don't want to be "in the public eye." They don't want the public to judge everything they do. Also, many successful people can make much more money in their private jobs than they can receive for government positions.

9 ▶ A career in politics is open to everyone. You may want to hold public office. Perhaps your desire is to be a United States senator, even president. This is a lofty goal and few ever reach it. But there are important offices in your state and community. How does a person get elected to public office?

10 ▶ Most people start early in their own community. First, you show you have an interest in politics. You want good government. You are interested in the good of your neighbors. You can become a worker and leader in your block association, taxpayers' group, or parents' club. You can volunteer to work for your political party at elections. You do things for other citizens. You can help with their tax returns. You can give advice on voting or tell them where to make complaints. You may learn to speak well and people will listen to you. Your local party leaders may see in you a person whom people like and respect. In time they may ask you to run for a local office. Or you could be appointed as an assistant to a member of the city or town council or the state legislature. This could be a beginning.

11 ▶ You learn a lot in this first political job. You decide that you want to run for the state legislature. Your party leaders think you would make a good lawmaker. (You don't need the support of the party. You can run on your own. But having a party behind you can be a big help.) You are elected. Now, you have a chance to become known state-wide. If your work gains the respect of the public, you can aim higher. You can run for state senator, Congress, or governor. Of the eight presidents

Young man campaigning for his candidate. Why are campaigners important in the election process?

since 1933, five had been members of Congress. Three had been governors. The important thing is that you like politics. You enjoy being in the public eye. You can take criticism. You want to serve your community. And you have the ability to serve the public well.

12 ▶ Some careers in politics begin in our judicial system. Lawyers know the law and the courts. They can help people with problems in ways others cannot. Some lawyers become well known through the cases they handle. They are seen and heard by the public. Their names appear in newspapers. Their faces become familiar through programs on TV. A district attorney has a good chance to become known. A popular district attorney is often chosen by the party to run for higher office. There are more lawyers in Congress than those from any other profession. And more lawyers have become president than have people from any other profession.

13 ▶ There is no way you can learn about all careers open to you. As you begin a job, you may learn of other jobs you have not heard of. But, whatever you do, you should find out all you can about your job. You should enter your career with the idea that you are going to be the best in whatever you do. In trying to improve yourself, you will keep interest in your work. Moreover, you will be of greater value to the people you serve.

President Clinton at a conference on the environment. If you were president, what would you do?

CHAPTER 48 REVIEW

★ UNDERSTANDING WHAT YOU HAVE READ

1. Which of these might be a summary statement of paragraph 8?
   a. Some people like high positions in government; others do not.
   b. Most people want to be elected to high office in government.
   c. Few people want to have their actions judged by voters.

2. Which of these skills would probably be the greatest help to a successful politician?
   a. Ability to speak clearly and smoothly in public
   b. Fast and accurate typing
   c. Knowledge of accounting and bookkeeping

3. A job as a manager of a government program to find ways to treat garbage would be
   a. an administrative position
   b. a clerical position
   c. an instructional position

4. Which of these careers is to be found ONLY in government service?
   a. Office manager
   b. Judge or justice
   c. Construction engineer

5. A college teacher, an expert in Asian history, is offered a high post in the State Department. The teacher turns down the offer. One reason may be
   a. the post would probably have only the beginning pay of a civil service worker
   b. the person may not want to have a job where the public will watch everything she does
   c. the public does not think highly of such a position

6. Another way of saying "worked their way up 'through the ranks'" as in paragraph 7 might be
   a. "took the first chance that came along"
   b. "started at the bottom and rose to the top"
   c. "one good turn deserved another"

7. If you want a job for the security it gives you, you want a job
   a. with high pay
   b. with an important-sounding title
   c. that you can only lose for a good reason

8. One thing you should be sure to do before choosing a career to follow is to
   a. take a good look at yourself, at your interests and talents
   b. go to college
   c. visit your local employment office

★ DEVELOPING CRITICAL THINKING SKILLS

A. Interpreting a Table

Study the table on page 396. Then answer the questions that follow it.

PROFILE OF THE 101ST CONGRESS

Professions of Members	House	Senate
Lawyers	170	52
Business People	111	19
Educators	51	7
Farmers	14	2
Journalists	18	5
Others	71	22

(Some lawmakers could not be reached for this information. Others list themselves in more than one profession.)

Sex of Members		
Men	408	98
Women	25	2
Race and Ethnic Background		
Whites	398	97
African Americans	24	0
Asian Americans	3	2
Hispanic Americans	10	0

Source: *Almanac of American Politics*

Tell whether the following statements are TRUE, as shown in the table. Or, tell whether there is no information in the table about the statement.

1. Most members of both the House of Representatives and Senate were lawyers.

2. The number of African Americans has dropped since the previous Congress.

3. Few women ran for election to the U.S. Senate.

4. A background as a teacher is likely to be better training for a political career than that of a farmer.

5. The members of Congress who have Asian backgrounds were from Alaska and Hawaii.

6. Over 100 members of the House of Representatives were business people or bankers.

7. African Americans, Asian Americans, and Hispanic Americans are members of both houses of Congress.

8. Farmers who were members of Congress were elected from states in the Midwest.

9. African Americans make up about one-tenth of the United States' population. They made up less than one-tenth of the members of Congress.

B. Looking at Both Sides

Do your talents and personality fit you for government work?

1. Make a list of your own talents and character traits under the headings of "Strengths" and "Weaknesses."

2. Which items might help you in a government career as a civil service worker? as a holder of political office?

3. Which weaknesses might make a career in government service difficult?

4. Do your strengths seem to fit you for a career in the civil service or in politics?

5. What conclusions can you make after your self-study?

C. Writing About Citizenship

In one or two well-organized paragraphs, answer the following questions: Do you think that you would like to have a career in politics? What might be some of the advantages of a career as a politician? What might be some of the drawbacks?

★ SUMMARIZING THE CHAPTER

1. Paragraph 5 lists some of the reasons why people choose the job they hold. How can each of these reasons be satisfied by a job in government service? Write the answer in your notebook.

   Good pay

   Doing something that is worthwhile

   Presitige of the job

   Security

2. "Public employees live in glass houses. People judge all government workers by what they know about a few of them." What is your opinion of this statement? Which paragraph contains this thought?

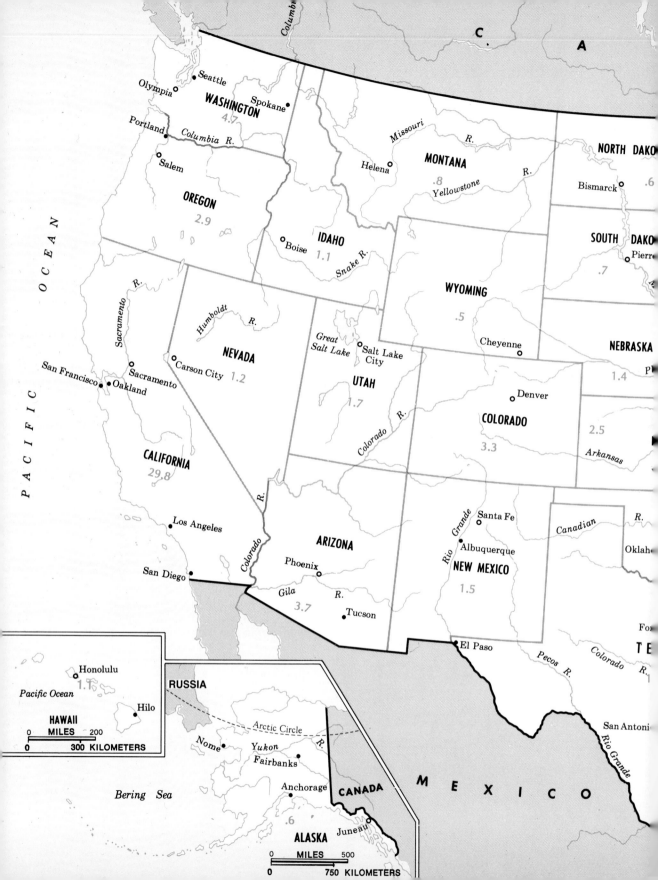

C   A

WASHINGTON
4.7

Olympia
Seattle
Spokane
Portland
Columbia R.
Salem

OREGON
2.9

MONTANA
.8
Helena
Missouri   R.
R.
Yellowstone

NORTH DAKO
Bismarck   .6

IDAHO
1.1
Boise
Snake R.

WYOMING
.5
Cheyenne

SOUTH DAKO
Pierre
.7

NEBRASKA
1.4   P

NEVADA
1.2
Carson City
Humboldt   R.
Sacramento   R.

UTAH
1.7
Great
Salt Lake
Salt Lake
City
Colorado   R.

COLORADO
3.3
Denver
2.5
Arkansas

San Francisco
Oakland
Sacramento

CALIFORNIA
29.8

Los Angeles

Colorado   R.

San Diego

ARIZONA
3.7
Phoenix
Gila   R.
Tucson

Santa Fe
Albuquerque
Rio Grande

NEW MEXICO
1.5

Canadian   R.
Oklaho

El Paso
Pecos   R.
Colorado   R.
Fo
TE

P A C I F I C   O C E A N

Honolulu
1.1
Pacific Ocean
Hilo

HAWAII
MILES   200
0
0   300 KILOMETERS

RUSSIA
Arctic Circle
Nome
Yukon   R.
Fairbanks
Anchorage
CANADA

Bering   Sea

.6
Juneau
ALASKA

MILES   500
0
0   750 KILOMETERS

M E X I C O

San Antoni
Rio Grande

THE UNITED STATES

Population in millions
★ National capital   ○ State capital

MILES 0 — 500
KILOMETERS — 750

THE DECLARATION OF INDEPENDENCE

The Unanimous Declaration of the Thirteen United States of America, July 4, 1776

When in the Course of human events, it becomes necessary for one people to dissolve the political bands which have connected them with another, and to assume among the powers of the earth, the separate and equal station to which the Laws of Nature and of Nature's God entitle them, a decent respect to the opinions of mankind requires that they should declare the causes which impel them to the separation. —We hold these truths to be self-evident, that all men are created equal, that they are endowed by their Creator with certain unalienable Rights, that among these are Life, Liberty and the pursuit of Happiness.—That to secure these rights, Governments are instituted among Men, deriving their just powers from the consent of the governed,—That whenever any Form of Government becomes destructive of these ends, it is the Right of the People to alter or to abolish it, and to institute a new Government, laying its foundation on such principles and organizing its powers in such form, as to them shall seem most likely to effect their Safety and Happiness. Prudence, indeed, will dictate that Governments long established should not be changed for light and transient causes; and accordingly all experience hath shown, that mankind are more disposed to suffer, while evils are sufferable, than to right themselves by abolishing the forms to which they are accustomed. But when a long train of abuses and usurpations, pursuing invariably the same Object evinces a design to reduce them under absolute Despotism, it is their right, it is their duty, to throw off such Government, and to provide new Guards for their future security.— Such has been the patient sufferance of these Colonies; and such is now the necessity which constrains them to alter their former Systems of Government. The history of the present King of Great Britain is a history of repeated injuries and usurpations, all having in direct object the establishment of an absolute Tyranny over these States. To prove this, let Facts be submitted to a candid world.—He has refused his Assent to Laws, the most wholesome and necessary for the public good.—He has forbidden his Governors to pass Laws of immediate and pressing importance, unless suspended in their operation till his Assent should be obtained; and when so suspended, he has utterly neglected to attend to them.—He has refused to pass other Laws for the accommodation of large districts of people, unless those people would relinquish the right of Representation in the Legislature, a right inestimable to them and formidable to tyrants only.—He has called together legislative bodies at places unusual, uncomfortable, and distant from the depository of their public Records, for the sole purpose of fatiguing them into compliance with his measures.—He has dissolved Representative Houses repeatedly, for opposing with manly firmness his invasion on the rights of the people.—He has refused for a long time, after such dissolutions, to cause others to be elected; whereby the Legislative powers, incapable of Annihilation, have returned to the People at large for their exercise; the State remaining in the mean time exposed to all the dangers of invasion from without, and convulsions within.—He has endeavoured to prevent the population of these States; for that purpose obstructing the Laws of Naturalization of Foreigners; refusing to pass others to encourage their migration hither, and raising the conditions of new Appropriations of Lands.— He has obstructed the Administration of Justice, by refusing his Assent to Laws for establishing Judiciary powers.—He has made Judges dependent on his Will alone, for the tenure of their offices, and the amount and payment of their salaries.—He has erected a multitude of New Offices, and sent hither swarms of Officers to harass our people, and eat out their substance.—He has kept among us, in times of peace, Standing Armies without the Consent of our legislatures.—He has affected to render the Military independent of and superior to the Civil power.—He has combined with others to subject us to a jurisdiction foreign to our constitution, and unacknowledged by our laws; giving his Assent to their Acts of pretended Legislation:—For quartering large bodies of armed troops among us:—For protecting them, by a mock Trial, from punishment for any Murders which they should commit on the Inhabitants of these States:—For cutting off our Trade with all parts of the world:—For imposing Taxes on us without our Consent:—For depriving us, in many cases, of the benefits of Trial by jury:—For transporting us beyond Seas to be tried for pretended offences:—For abolishing the free System of English Laws in a neighbouring Province, establishing therein an Arbitrary government, and enlarging its Boundaries so as to render it at once an example and fit instrument for introducing the same absolute rule into these Colonies:—For taking away our Charters, abolishing our most valuable Laws, and altering fundamentally the Forms of our Governments:—For suspending our own Legislatures, and declaring themselves invested with power to legislate for us in all cases whatsoever.—He has abdicated Government here, by declaring us out of his Protection and waging War against us.—He has plundered our seas, ravaged our Coasts, burnt our towns, and destroyed the lives of our people.—He is at this time transporting large Armies of foreign Mercenaries to complete the works of death, desolation and tyranny, already begun with circumstances of Cruelty & perfidy scarcely paralleled in the most barbarous ages, and totally unworthy the Head of a civilized nation.—He has constrained our fellow citizens taken Captive on the high Seas to bear Arms against their Country, to become the executioners of their friends and Brethren, or to fall themselves by their Hands.—He has excited domestic insurrections amongst us, and has endeavoured to bring on the inhabitants of our frontiers, the merciless Indian Savages, whose known rule of warfare, is an undistinguished destruction of all ages, sexes and conditions. In every stage of these Oppressions We have Petitioned for Redress in the most humble terms: Our repeated Petitions have been answered only by repeated injury. A Prince, whose character is thus marked by every act which may define a Tyrant, is unfit to be the ruler of a free people. Nor have We been wanting in attentions to our British brethren. We have warned them from time to time of attempts by their legislature to extend an unwarrantable jurisdiction over us. We have reminded them of the circumstances of our emigration and settlement here. We have appealed to their native justice and magnanimity, and we have conjured them by the ties of our common kindred to disavow these usurpations, which would inevitably interrupt our connections and correspondence. They too have been deaf to the voice of justice and of consanguinity. We must, therefore, acquiesce in the necessity, which denounces our Separation, and hold them, as we hold the rest of mankind, Enemies in War, in Peace Friends.—

WE, THEREFORE, THE REPRESENTATIVES OF THE UNITED STATES OF AMERICA, in General Congress, Assembled, appealing to the Supreme Judge of the world for the rectitude of our intentions, do, in the Name, and by authority of the good People of these Colonies, solemnly publish and declare, That these United Colonies are, and of Right ought to be FREE and INDEPENDENT STATES; that they are Absolved from all Allegiance to the British Crown, and that all political connection between them and the State of Great Britain, is and ought to be totally dissolved; and that as Free and Independent States, they have full Power to levy War, conclude Peace, contract Alliances, establish Commerce, and to do all other Acts and Things which Independent States may of right do.—And for the support of this Declaration, with a firm reliance on the protection of divine Providence, we mutually pledge to each other our Lives, our Fortunes and our sacred Honor.

THE CONSTITUTION

The exact text of the Constitution is given in the

Blue lines are used to cross

that have been changed by

PREAMBLE

The preamble, or introduction, to the Constitution lists the goals which the Founding Fathers hoped it would achieve.

ARTICLE I. THE LEGISLATIVE BRANCH

Section 1. *The Two Houses of Congress.* Congress is the legislature, or lawmaking body, of our federal government. It consists of two houses, the House of Representatives and the Senate.

Section 2. *The House of Representatives.* Representatives are elected by the people for a two-year term. In each state, people eligible to vote for the lower house of the state legislature are also eligible to vote for representatives. (In effect, each state decides the qualifications for voting in federal elections within its borders.)

To be a representative, a person must be at least 25 years old, a citizen of the United States for at least 7 years, and an inhabitant of the state that elects him or her.

The number of representatives from a state depends on its population. This includes all free persons and three-fifths of "all other persons"—that is, slaves. A census (count

WE, the people of the United States, in order to form a more perfect Union, establish justice, insure domestic tranquillity, provide for the common defence, promote the general welfare, and secure the blessings of liberty to ourselves and our posterity, do ordain and establish this Constitution for the United States of America.

ARTICLE I.

Section 1. All legislative powers herein granted, shall be vested in a Congress of the United States, which shall consist of a Senate and House of Representatives.

Section 2. The House of Representatives shall be composed of members chosen every second year by the people of the several States; and the electors in each State shall have the qualifications requisite for electors of the most numerous branch of the State Legislature.

No person shall be a representative who shall not have attained the age of twenty-five years, and been seven years a citizen of the United States, and who shall not, when elected, be an inhabitant of that State in which he shall be chosen.

Representatives and direct taxes shall be apportioned among the several States which may be included within this Union, according to their respective numbers, which shall be determined by adding to the whole number of free persons, including those bound to service for a term of years,

inner, colored area and explained in the outer.

out parts of the Constitution

amendments or other laws.

and excluding Indians not taxed, three fifths of all other persons. The actual enumeration shall be made within three years after the first meeting of the Congress of the United States, and within every subsequent term of ten years, in such manner as they shall by law direct. The number of representatives shall not exceed one for every thirty thousand, but each State shall have at least one representative, and until such enumeration shall be made, the state of New Hampshire shall be entitled to choose three, Massachusetts eight, Rhode Island and Providence Plantations one, Connecticut five, New York six, New Jersey four, Pennsylvania eight, Delaware one, Maryland six, Virginia ten, North Carolina five, South Carolina five, and Georgia three.

When vacancies happen in the representation from any State, the Executive authority thereof shall issue writs of election to fill such vacancies.

The House of Representatives shall choose their Speaker and other officers; and shall have the sole power of impeachment.

Section 3. The Senate of the United States shall be composed of two Senators from each State, chosen by the Legislature thereof, for six years; and each Senator shall have one vote.

Immediately after they shall be assembled, in consequence of the first election, they shall be divided equally as may be into three classes. The seats of the Senators of the first class shall be vacated at the expiration of the second year, of

of the population) is to be taken every ten years. But each state, no matter how small its population, must have at least one representative.

If a seat in the House becomes vacant (usually through the death of a representative), the governor of the state may appoint a substitute.

The House of Representatives chooses its Speaker and other officers. It has the special power to impeach federal officials.

Section 3. *The Senate.* The Senate consists of two senators from each state. Senators are chosen by the state legislature. (This was changed by the Seventeenth Amendment, on page 73.) A senator's term of office is six years.

One-third of the Senate is elected every two years. (This makes the Senate a continuous body.)

A senator must be at least thirty years old, a citizen for at least nine years, and an inhabitant of the state that elects him or her.

The vice-president of the Unites States serves as the presiding officer of the Senate. He or she may vote only in case of a tie.

The Senate chooses its other officers, including the president *pro tempore,* who serves as the presiding officer when the vice-president is absent.

The Senate tries impeachments. When the president is impeached, the chief justice of the Supreme Court serves as presiding officer. A two-thirds vote is needed for conviction.

Convicted persons are removed from office and may not hold any other federal office. They may also be tried for their offenses in the usual way.

Section 4. *Election and Meeting of Congress.* Each state regulates its own elections, but Congress may make rules for electing representatives. (Thus Election Day, set by Congress, is the same throughout the United States.)

Congress must meet at least once a year. (The date was changed by the Twentieth Amendment.)

the second class at the expiration of the fourth year, and of the third class at the expiration of the sixth year, so that one third may be chosen every second year; and if vacancies happen by resignation, or otherwise, during the recess of the Legislature of any State, the Executive thereof may make temporary appointments until the next meeting of the Legislature, which shall then fill such vacancies.

No person shall be a Senator who shall not have attained the age of thirty years, and been nine years a citizen of the United States, and who shall not, when elected, be an inhabitant of that State for which he shall be chosen.

The Vice President of the United States shall be president of the Senate, but shall have no vote, unless they be equally divided.

The Senate shall choose their other officers, and also a president *pro tempore,* in the absence of the Vice President, or when he shall exercise the office of President of the United States.

The Senate shall have the sole power to try all impeachments. When sitting for that purpose, they shall be on oath or affirmation. When the President of the United States is tried, the Chief Justice shall preside; and no person shall be convicted without the concurrence of two thirds of the members present.

Judgment in cases of impeachment shall not extend further than to removal from office, and disqualification to hold and enjoy any office of honour, trust or profit, under the United States; but the party convicted shall nevertheless be liable and subject to indictment, trial, judgment, and punishment according to law.

Section 4. The times, places and manner of holding elections for Senators and Representatives, shall be prescribed in each State by the Legislature thereof; but the Congress may at any time by law make or alter such regulations, except as to the places of choosing Senators.

The Congress shall assemble at least once in every year, and such meeting shall be on the first Monday in December, unless they shall by law appoint a different day.

Section 5. Each House shall be the judge of the elections, returns, and qualifications of its own members, and a majority of each shall constitute a quorum to do business; but a smaller number may adjourn from day to day, and may be authorized to compel the attendance of absent members, in such manner, and under such penalties, as each House may provide.

Each House may determine the rules of its proceedings, punish its members for disorderly behaviour, and, with the concurrence of two thirds, expel a member.

Each House shall keep a journal of its proceedings, and from time to time publish the same, excepting such parts as may, in their judgment, require secrecy; and the yeas and nays of the members of either House on any question, shall, at the desire of one fifth of those present, be entered on the journal.

Neither House, during the session of Congress, shall, without the consent of the other, adjourn for more than three days, nor to any other place than that in which the two Houses shall be sitting.

Section 6. The Senators and Representatives shall receive a compensation for their services, to be ascertained by law, and paid out of the Treasury of the United States. They shall, in all cases, except treason, felony, and breach of the peace, be privileged from arrest during their attendance at the session of their respective Houses, and in going to, and returning from, the same; and for any speech or debate in either House, they shall not be questioned in any other place.

No Senator or Representative shall, during the time for which he was elected, be appointed to any civil office under the authority of the United States, which shall have been created, or the emoluments whereof shall have been increased during such time; and no person holding any office under the United States, shall be a member of either House during his continuance in office.

Section 7. All bills for raising revenue shall originate in the House of Representatives; but the

Section 5. *Rules of Congress.* Each house of Congress decides whether its members have the necessary qualifications and have been fairly elected. A majority of the members must be present to do business. Absent members may be forced to attend.

Each house makes its own rules. It may punish a member for bad conduct. It may expel a member by a two-thirds vote.

Each house keeps a journal (the *Congressional Record*). How the members have voted on a certain bill is put into the record whenever one-fifth of the members ask that this be done.

Neither house may adjourn for more than three days or move to a different place without the consent of the other house.

Section 6. *Rights of Members of Congress.* Senators and representatives are paid by the federal government. Their salaries are fixed by law. They may not be arrested while Congress is in session, except for three offenses — "treason, felony, and breach of the peace." They may not be questioned (by the executive, the courts, or state officials) about anything they have said in Congress.

No senators or representatives may be appointed during their term of office to any position that was created or given a higher salary while they were in Congress. No federal officials may hold their position and serve in Congress at the same time.

Section 7. *The President's Veto.* Tax bills must start in the House of Representatives, but the Senate may change them.

After a bill has passed both houses, it is sent to the president. The president may either sign the bill or veto it ("return it with objections"). Congress may pass the bill over a veto by a two-thirds vote of each house. The vote must be recorded in its journal. If the president holds a bill for ten days (not counting Sundays), it becomes a law without the president's signature unless Congress has adjourned meanwhile. If Congress has adjourned, the bill dies after ten days (the "pocket veto").

The same procedure applies to any other action that requires the approval of both Congress and the president.

Section 8. *Powers of Congress.* To collect taxes, pay the government's debts, and provide for the defense and welfare of the nation;

To borrow money;

To regulate trade with foreign nations,

Senate may propose or concur with amendments as on other bills.

Every bill which shall have passed the House of Representatives and the Senate, shall, before it become a law, be presented to the President of the United States; if he approve he shall sign it, but if not he shall return it, with his objections, to that House in which it shall have originated, who shall enter the objections at large on their journal, and proceed to reconsider it. If after such reconsideration two thirds of that House agree to pass the bill, it shall be sent, together with the objections, to the other House, by which it shall likewise be reconsidered, and if approved by two thirds of that House, it shall become a law. But in all cases the votes of both Houses shall be determined by yeas and nays, and the names of the persons voting for and against the bill shall be entered on the journal of each House respectively. If any bill shall not be returned by the President within ten days, (Sundays excepted), after it shall have been presented to him, the same shall be a law, in like manner as if he had signed it, unless the Congress by their adjournment prevent its return, in which case it shall not be a law.

Every order, resolution, or vote, to which the concurrence of the Senate and House of Representatives may be necessary, (except on a question of adjournment), shall be presented to the President of the United States; and before the same shall take effect, shall be approved by him, or being disapproved by him, shall be re-passed by two thirds of the Senate and House of Representatives, according to the rules and limitations prescribed in the case of a bill.

Section 8. The Congress shall have power

To lay and collect taxes, duties, imposts and excises, to pay the debts, and provide for the common defence and general welfare of the United States; but all duties, imposts, and excises shall be uniform throughout the United States:

To borrow money on the credit of the United States:

To regulate commerce with foreign nations, and

among the several States, and with the Indian tribes:

To establish an uniform rule of naturalization, and uniform laws on the subject of bankruptcies throughout the United States:

To coin money, regulate the value thereof, and of foreign coin, and fix the standard of weights and measures:

To provide for the punishment of counterfeiting the securities and current coin of the United States:

To establish post offices and post roads:

To promote the progress of science and useful arts, by securing, for limited times, to authors and inventors, the exclusive right to their respective writings and discoveries:

To constitute tribunals inferior to the Supreme Court:

To define and punish piracies and felonies committed on the high seas, and offences against the law of nations:

To declare war, grant letters of marque and reprisal, and make rules concerning captures on land and water:

To raise and support armies: but no appropriation of money to that use shall be for a longer term than two years:

To provide and maintain a navy:

To make rules for the government and regulation of the land and naval forces:

To provide for calling forth the militia to execute the laws of the Union, suppress insurrections and repel invasions:

To provide for organizing, arming, and disciplining the militia, and for governing such part of them as may be employed in the service of the United States, reserving to the States respectively, the appointment of the officers, and the authority of training the militia according to the discipline prescribed by Congress:

To exercise exclusive legislation, in all cases whatsoever, over such district (not exceeding ten miles square) as may by cession of particular States, and the acceptance of Congress, become the seat of the government of the United States,

among the states (interstate commerce), and with the Indian tribes;

To make rules for naturalization (citizenship for foreigners) and for bankruptcy (business failure);

To coin money and regulate its value; to set standards for the weights and measures used in the United States;

To punish counterfeiters;

To establish post offices and build post roads;

To protect authors and inventors (by issuing copyrights and patents);

To set up a system of federal courts;

To punish piracy, other crimes committed on the high seas, and offenses against the law of nations (international law);

To declare war and give permission to privately owned ships to seize enemy vessels; (Such private ships were known as privateers, and the permission was called a "letter of marque and reprisal.")

To raise and support armies; (The two-year limit on funds for the army was intended to keep the president or a general from becoming a dictator.)

To support a navy;

To make rules for the armed forces;

To call up the militia (state troops) to carry out federal laws, put down uprisings, and stop foreign invasions;

To make rules for the militia, when called into federal service;

To rule the District of Columbia and other federal holdings;

To make all laws needed to carry out these powers. (This is the very important "elastic clause.")

Section 9. *Limits to Congress' Powers.* Congress may not end the slave trade until the year 1808.

The right of *habeas corpus* may be suspended only in case of rebellion or invasion. This is an order, signed by a judge, either to arrange a prisoner's early hearing or to set the prisoner free at once.

Bills of attainder and *ex post facto* laws are forbidden. (A bill of attainder is a law punishing a person without a regular trial in court. An *ex post facto* law makes certain actions illegal even if they were performed before the law was passed. Both kinds of laws had been passed by the British Parliament.)

Any direct tax must be based on the census. (This provision prevented Congress from taxing people more heavily in one state than in another. The income tax became an exception as a result of the Sixteenth Amendment.)

No tax may be put on exports, no port may be given an advantage over another, and ships going from one state to another may not be taxed.

The treasury can spend money only with Congress's permission. A statement of federal receipts and spending must be issued regularly. (This is our federal budget.)

No titles of nobility may be granted by the federal government. No federal official may accept a gift or title from a foreign nation without the consent of Congress.

Section 10. *Powers Forbidden to the*

and to exercise like authority over all places purchased by the consent of the legislature of the State in which the same shall be, for the erection of forts, magazines, arsenals, dock-yards, and other needful buildings. And,

To make all laws which shall be necessary and proper for carrying into execution the foregoing powers, and all other powers vested by this Constitution in the government of the United States, or in any department or officer thereof.

Section 9. The migration or importation of such persons as any of the States now existing shall think proper to admit, shall not be prohibited by the Congress prior to the year one thousand eight hundred and eight; but a tax or duty may be imposed on such importation, not exceeding ten dollars for each person.

The privilege of the writ of *habeas corpus* shall not be suspended, unless when in cases of rebellion or invasion the public safety may require it.

No bill of attainder or *ex post facto* law shall be passed.

No capitation, or other direct tax, shall be laid, unless in proportion to the *census* or enumeration herein before directed to be taken.

No tax or duty shall be laid on articles exported from any State. No preference shall be given by any regulation of commerce or revenue to the ports of one State over those of another; nor shall vessels bound to, or from, one State be obliged to enter, clear, or pay duties in another.

No money shall be drawn from the treasury, but in consequence of appropriations made by law; and a regular statement and account of the receipts and expenditures of all public money shall be published from time to time.

No title of nobility shall be granted by the United States; and no person holding any office of profit or trust under them, shall, without the consent of the Congress, accept of any present, emolument, office, or title of any kind whatever, from any king, prince, or foreign state.

Section 10. No State shall enter into any treaty, alliance, or confederation; grant letters of marque and reprisal; coin money; emit bills of credit;

make any thing but gold and silver coin a tender in payment of debts; pass any bill of attainder, *ex post facto* law, or law impairing the obligation of contracts, or grant any title of nobility.

No State shall, without the consent of the Congress, lay any imposts or duties on imports or exports, except what may be absolutely necessary for executing its inspection laws; and the net produce of all duties and imposts, laid by any State on imports or exports, shall be for the use of the treasury of the United States; and all such laws shall be subject to the revision and control of the Congress. No State shall, without the consent of Congress, lay any duty of tonnage, keep troops, or ships of war, in time of peace, enter into any agreement or compact with another State, or with a foreign power, or engage in war, unless actually invaded, or in such imminent danger as will not admit of delay.

ARTICLE II.

Section 1. The executive power shall be vested in a President of the United States of America. He shall hold his office during the term of four years, and together with the Vice President, chosen for the same term, be elected as follows:

Each State shall appoint, in such manner as the legislature thereof may direct, a number of electors equal to the whole number of Senators and Representatives to which the State may be entitled in the Congress; but no Senator or Representative, or person holding an office of trust or profit under the United States, shall be appointed an elector.

The electors shall meet in their respective States, and vote by ballot for two persons, of whom one at least shall not be an inhabitant of the same State with themselves. And they shall make a list of all the persons voted for, and of the number of votes for each; which list they shall sign and certify, and transmit sealed to the seat of the government of the United States, directed to the President of the Senate. The President of the Senate shall, in the presence of the Senate and House of Representatives, open all the certificates, and

States. The states may not make treaties, give permission to privateers, coin money, issue bills of credit (a kind of paper money), pass a bill of attainder or *ex post facto* law, impair a contract, or grant a title of nobility.

A state may tax imports or exports only with the consent of Congress and for purposes of inspection (to keep out infected plants and animals, for example).

A state may not keep troops or warships in peacetime, make agreements with other states or foreign nations, or wage war without the consent of Congress. It may, however, defend itself from a foreign invasion or other danger.

ARTICLE II. The Executive Branch

Section 1. *The Presidency.* Both the president, our chief executive, and the vice-president are elected for four-year terms.

Each state decides how its electors for president and vice-president are to be chosen. The number of electors from each state is equal to the number of its senators and representatives combined. Members of Congress and other federal officials may not serve as electors.

The electors meet in their own states (usually in the state capital) and vote for two persons. The votes are counted and the results are sent to the presiding officer of the Senate in a sealed envelope. These envelopes are opened and the electoral votes are counted before both houses of Congress. The person with the highest number of votes becomes president. The person with the second highest number of votes becomes vice-president. (This was changed by the Twelfth Amendment, under which

409

electors cast separate ballots for president and vice-president.) In case of a tie or the lack of a majority for any candidate, the House of Representatives chooses the president; the Senate chooses the vice-president. In such elections, each state casts only one vote.

Congress may set the dates on which electors are chosen and cast their ballots. (They are chosen on Election Day, but cast their ballots several weeks later.)

A candidate for president must be at least thirty-five years old and a citizen of the United States by birth. The president must have lived in the United States for at least fourteen years.

If the president dies, is unable to work, or is removed from office, the vice-president becomes president. Congress shall take care of cases in which no vice-president is available. (This has been changed by the Twenty-fifth Amendment.)

The president's salary may not be

the votes shall then be counted. The person having the greatest number of votes shall be the President, if such number be a majority of the whole number of electors appointed; and if there be more than one who have such majority, and have an equal number of votes, then the House of Representatives shall immediately choose by ballot one of them for President; and if no person have a majority, then from the five highest on the list the said House shall in like manner choose the President. But in choosing the President, the votes shall be taken by States, the representation from each State having one vote; a quorum for this purpose shall consist of a member or members from two thirds of the States, and a majority of all the States shall be necessary to a choice. In every case, after the choice of the President, the person having the greatest number of votes of the electors shall be the Vice President. But if there should remain two or more who have equal votes, the Senate shall choose from them by ballot the Vice President.

The Congress may determine the time of choosing the electors, and the day on which they shall give their votes; which day shall be the same throughout the United States.

No person except a natural born citizen, or a citizen of the United States, at the time of the adoption of this Constitution, shall be eligible to the office of President; neither shall any person be eligible to that office who shall not have attained the age of thirty-five years, and been fourteen years a resident within the United States.

In case of the removal of the President from office, or of his death, resignation, or inability to discharge the powers and duties of the said office, the same shall devolve on the Vice President, and the Congress may by law provide for the case of removal, death, resignation, or inability, both of the President and Vice President, declaring what officer shall then act as President, and such officer shall act accordingly until the disability be removed, or a President shall be elected.

The President shall at stated times, receive

for his services, a compensation, which shall neither be increased nor diminished during the period for which he shall have been elected, and he shall not receive within that period any other emolument from the United States or any of them.

Before he enter on the execution of his office, he shall take the following oath or affirmation:

"I do solemnly swear, (or affirm,) that I will faithfully execute the office of President of the United States, and will, to the best of my ability, preserve, protect, and defend the Constitution of the United States."

Section 2. The President shall be commander-in-chief of the army and navy of the United States, and of the militia of the several States, when called into the actual service of the United States; he may require the opinion, in writing, of the principal officer in each of the executive departments, upon any subject relating to the duties of their respective offices, and he shall have power to grant reprieves and pardons for offences against the United States, except in cases of impeachment.

He shall have power, by and with the advice and consent of the Senate, to make treaties, provided two thirds of the Senators present concur; and he shall nominate, and by and with the advice and consent of the Senate, shall appoint ambassadors, other public ministers and consuls, judges of the Supreme Court, and all other officers of the United States, whose appointments are not herein otherwise provided for, and which shall be established by law. But the Congress may by law vest the appointment of such inferior officers, as they think proper, in the President alone, in the courts of law, or in the heads of departments.

The President shall have power to fill up all vacancies that may happen during the recess of the Senate, by granting commissions which shall expire at the end of their session.

Section 3. He shall, from time to time, give to the Congress information of the state of the Union, and recommend to their consideration such meas-

changed during his or her term in office. The president may not receive any other payment from the federal government or any state during the term of office.

At the inauguration, the president takes an oath to perform the duties of the president and to defend the Constitution.

Section 2. *Powers of the President.* The president is commander in chief of the armed forces and of the state militia when called into federal service. The heads of the executive departments have to report to the president on the work of their departments. The president has the power to grant reprieves (delays of punishment) and pardons for offenses against the federal government.

The president makes treaties, with the consent of two-thirds of the Senate. The president appoints ambassadors, judges, and other high federal officials, with the consent of a majority of the Senate.

When the Senate is not in session, the president may make temporary appointments to these positions.

Section 3. *Powers of the President* (continued). The president gives Congress "information on the state of the Union" (see photo, page 122) and asks it to pass laws thought necessary. The president may call Congress together for special sessions. If the two houses cannot agree on when to adjourn, the president may set the date. The president receives ministers from foreign nations, takes care that the laws are "faithfully executed," and grants commissions to all officers in the armed forces.

Section 4. *Removal.* The president, vice-president, and other federal officials can be removed through impeachment and conviction on three charges — "treason, bribery, or other high crimes and misdemeanors."

ARTICLE III. The Judicial Branch

Section 1. *Protection of Judges.* The judicial department is made up of the Supreme Court and lower courts established by Congress. The judges hold office "during good behavior." Their pay may not be reduced while they are in office.

Section 2. *Jurisdiction of the Federal Courts.* Federal courts hear all cases 1. arising under the Constitution, laws, and treaties of the United States; 2. affecting foreign ministers; 3. occurring at sea; 4. in which the United States is a party; 5. between two or more states; 6. between a state and the citizen of another state; 7. between citizens of different states; 8. between citizens of the same state about land given them by different states; and 9. between a state and foreign states or people. (However, the Eleventh Amendment protects the states from being sued in a federal court by citizens of another state or by foreigners.)

Cases involving foreign ministers and state governments go directly to the Supreme Court. In other cases the Supreme Court may hear appeals if it wishes. Congress may,

ures as he shall judge necessary and expedient. He may on extraordinary occasions, convene both Houses, or either of them; and in case of disagreement between them, with respect to the time of adjournment, he may adjourn them to such time as he shall think proper. He shall receive ambassadors and other public ministers. He shall take care that the laws be faithfully executed; and shall commission all the officers of the United States.

Section 4. The President, Vice President, and all civil officers of the United States, shall be removed from office on impeachment for, and conviction of, treason, bribery, or other high crimes and misdemeanors.

ARTICLE III.

Section 1. The judicial power of the United States shall be vested in one Supreme Court, and in such inferior courts as the Congress may, from time to time, ordain and establish. The judges, both of the Supreme and inferior courts, shall hold their offices during good behaviour; and shall, at stated times, receive for their services, a compensation, which shall not be diminished during their continuance in office.

Section 2. The judicial power shall extend to all cases, in law and equity, arising under this Constitution, the laws of the United States, and treaties made, or which shall be made under their authority; to all cases affecting ambassadors, other public ministers, and consuls; to all cases of admiralty and maritime jurisdiction; to controversies to which the United States shall be a party; to controversies between two or more States, between a State and citizens of another State, between citizens of different States, between citizens of the same State claiming lands under grants of different States, and between a State, or the citizens thereof, and foreign States, citizens or subjects.

In all cases affecting ambassadors, other public ministers and consuls, and those in which a State shall be party, the Supreme Court shall have original jurisdiction. In all the other cases before mentioned, the Supreme Court shall have appellate jurisdiction, both as to law and fact, with such exceptions, and under such regulations, as the Congress shall make.

The trial of all crimes, except in cases of impeachment, shall be by jury; and such trial shall be held in the State where the said crimes shall have been committed; but when not committed within any State, the trial shall be at such place or places as the Congress may by law have directed.

Section 3. Treason against the United States, shall consist only in levying war against them, or in adhering to their enemies, giving them aid and comfort. No person shall be convicted of treason unless on the testimony of two witnesses to the same overt act, or on confession in open court.

The Congress shall have power to declare the punishment of treason, but no attainder of treason shall work corruption of blood, for forfeiture, except during the life of the person attainted.

ARTICLE IV.

Section 1. Full faith and credit shall be given in each State to the public acts, records, and judicial proceedings of every other State. And the Congress may by general laws prescribe the manner in which such acts, records, and proceedings shall be proved, and the effect thereof.

Section 2. The citizens of each State shall be entitled to all privileges and immunities of citizens in the several States.

A person charged in any State with treason, felony, or other crime, who shall flee from justice, and be found in another State, shall, on demand of the executive authority of the State from which he fled, be delivered up, to be removed to the State having jurisdiction of the crime.

No person held to service or labour in one State, under the laws thereof, escaping into another, shall, in consequence of any laws or regulation therein, be discharged from such service or labour, but shall be delivered up on claim of the

however, make regulations for such appeals.

All federal crimes are tried by a jury in the state in which they have been committed. Congress decides where a crime should be tried if it was not committed inside any state.

Section 3. *Treason.* Treason consists only of making war against the United States or giving "aid and comfort" to its enemies. A person can be convicted of treason only on the testimony of two witnesses or on his or her own confession in open court.

Congress can set the penalties for treason, but only the accused person may be punished. (In England, a traitor's entire family was often punished.)

ARTICLE IV. Cooperation Among the States

Section 1. *Acceptance of All State Actions.* Every state must accept the legal actions and records of the other states. (Marriages and divorces are the most common examples.)

Section 2. *Return of Fugitives.* A citizen of one state is entitled to equal treatment in the other states.

When a person charged with a serious crime has fled from one state to another, he or she must be returned at the governor's request.

A runaway slave or indentured servant must likewise be returned on demand.

Section 3. *Admission of New States.* Congress admits new states. It may not, however, form a new state from the territory of another state without that state's consent.

Congress governs the federal territories.

Section 4. *Protection of the States.* The United States guarantees every state a republican form of government. (That is, it must act to keep a monarchy or dictatorship from being set up.) It must protect a state from invasion and from "domestic violence" (an uprising) at the request of the state's legislature or governor.

ARTICLE V. Amending the Constitution. Congress may propose amendments by a two-thirds vote of both houses. If two-thirds of the states so request, Congress must call a special convention to propose amendments. Proposed amendments go into effect when they have been ratified by the legislatures or by special conventions in three-fourths of the states.

ARTICLE VI. Supremacy of the Fed-

party to whom such service or labour may be due.

Section 3. New States may be admitted by the Congress into this Union; but no new State shall be formed or erected within the jurisdiction of any other State; nor any State be formed by the junction of two or more States, or parts of States, without the consent of the legislatures of the States concerned, as well as of the Congress.

The Congress shall have power to dispose of and make all needful rules and regulations respecting the territory or other property belonging to the United States; and nothing in this Constitution shall be so construed as to prejudice any claims of the United States, or of any particular State.

Section 4. The United States shall guarantee to every State in this Union a republican form of government, and shall protect each of them against invasion; and on application of the legislature, or of the executive, (when the legislature cannot be convened) against domestic violence.

ARTICLE V.

The Congress, whenever two thirds of both Houses shall deem it necessary, shall propose amendments to this Constitution, or, on the application of the legislatures of two thirds of the several States, shall call a convention for proposing amendments, which, in either case, shall be valid to all intents and purposes, as part of this Constitution, when ratified by the legislatures of three fourths of the several States, or by conventions in three fourths thereof, as the one or the other mode of ratification may be proposed by the Congress; provided, that no amendment, which may be made prior to the year one thousand eight hundred and eight, shall in any manner affect the first and fourth clauses in the ninth section of the first article; and that no State, without its consent, shall be deprived of its equal suffrage in the Senate.

ARTICLE VI.

All debts contracted, and engagements entered

into, before the adoption of this Constitution, shall be as valid against the United States, under this Constitution, as under the confederation.

This Constitution, and the laws of the United States which shall be made in pursuance thereof, and all treaties made, or which shall be made, under the authority of the United States, shall be the supreme law of the land: and the judges, in every State, shall be bound thereby, any thing in the Constitution or laws of any State to the contrary notwithstanding.

The Senators and Representatives before mentioned, and the members of the several State legislatures, and all executive and judicial officers, both of the United States and of the several States, shall be bound, by oath or affirmation, to support this Constitution; but no religious test shall ever be required as a qualification to any office or public trust under the United States.

ARTICLE VII.

The ratification of the conventions of nine States, shall be sufficient for the establishment of this Constitution between the States so ratifying the same.

Done in Convention, by the unanimous consent of the States present, the seventeenth day of September, in the year of our Lord one thousand seven hundred and eighty-seven, and of the independence of the United States of America the twelfth. In witness whereof we have hereunto subscribed our names.

GEORGE WASHINGTON, PRESIDENT
and Deputy from Virginia.

(Following Washington's signature are those of the delegates from the states represented at the Convention.)

(On September 13, 1788, Congress certified that a sufficient number of states had ratified and that the Constitution should be put into operation.)

ERAL GOVERNMENT. The federal government accepts all debts and other obligations of the Confederation.

The Constitution and law or treaties made under it are the supreme law of the land. Judges in every state must recognize this fact.

Senators and representatives, members of the state legislatures, and other federal and state officials must take an oath to support the Constitution. But no religious test shall ever be required for any federal office.

ARTICLE VII. ADOPTING THE CONSTITUTION

The Constitution shall go into effect as soon as nine states have ratified it.

AMENDMENTS

ARTICLE I. *Freedom of Religion, Speech, Press, Assembly, and Petition.* Congress is forbidden to make laws about an "establishment of religion," or to prevent freedom of religion, freedom of speech and the press, the right of peaceful assembly, or the right of petition.

ARTICLE II. *The Right to Bear Arms.* A free country needs a "well regulated militia." So the government may not interfere with the people's right to bear arms.

ARTICLE III. *Security of the Home.* A soldier may not be stationed in a private home in peacetime without the owner's consent. This may be done in wartime, but only if Congress passes a law saying so.

ARTICLE IV. *Security of the Home* (continued). The people, their homes, and their possessions shall be safe from unreasonable searches and seizures. A search warrant may be issued only if witnesses give good reasons under oath. The warrant must describe the place to be searched and the persons or things to be seized.

ARTICLE V. *Rights of an Accused Person.* In serious crimes, a person must be indicted by a grand jury before being tried. The accused person may not be tried twice for the same offense. The accused person may not be forced to be a witness against himself or herself. The accused person may not have his or her life, liberty, or property taken away without due process of law. Private property may not be taken for public use without fair payment.

Amendments One through Ten, known as the Bill of Rights, took effect in 1791.

ARTICLE I. Congress shall make no law respecting an establishment of religion, or prohibiting the free exercise thereof; or abridging the freedom of speech, or of the press; or the right of the people peaceably to assemble, and to petition the government for a redress of grievances.

ARTICLE II. A well regulated militia being necessary to the security of a free State, the right of the people to keep and bear arms shall not be infringed.

ARTICLE III. No soldier shall, in time of peace, be quartered in any house without the consent of the owner; nor in time of war, but in a manner to be prescribed by law.

ARTICLE IV. The right of the people to be secure in their persons, houses, papers, and effects, against unreasonable searches and seizures, shall not be violated; and no warrants shall issue, but upon probable cause, supported by oath or affirmation, and particularly describing the place to be searched, and the persons or things to be seized.

ARTICLE V. No person shall be held to answer for a capital or otherwise infamous crime, unless on a presentment or indictment of a grand jury, except in cases arising in the land or naval forces, or in the militia, when in actual service, in time of war or public danger; nor shall any person be subject for the same offence to be twice put in jeopardy of life or limb; nor shall be compelled, in any criminal case, to be witness against himself; nor be deprived of life, liberty, or property, without due process of law; nor shall private property be taken for public use without just compensation.

ARTICLE VI. In all criminal prosecutions the accused shall enjoy the right to a speedy and public trial, by an impartial jury of the State and district wherein the crime shall have been committed, which district shall have been previously ascertained by law, and to be informed of the nature and cause of the accusation; to be confronted with the witnesses against him; to have compulsory process for obtaining witnesses in his favour; and to have the assistance of counsel for his defence.

ARTICLE VII. In suits at common law, where the value in controversy shall exceed twenty dollars, the right of trial by jury shall be preserved; and no fact tried by a jury shall be otherwise re-examined in any court of the United States than according to the rules of the common law.

ARTICLE VIII. Excessive bail shall not be required, nor excessive fines imposed, nor cruel and unusual punishments inflicted.

ARTICLE IX. The enumeration in the Constitution of certain rights, shall not be construed to deny or disparage others retained by the people.

ARTICLE X. The powers not delegated to the United States by the Constitution, nor prohibited by it to the States, are reserved to the States respectively or to the people.

ARTICLE XI. The Judicial power of the United States shall not be construed to extend to any suit in law or equity, commenced or prosecuted against one of the United States by Citizens of another State, or by Citizens or Subjects of any Foreign State.

ARTICLE VI. *Rights of an Accused Person* (continued). A person accused of a crime has the right to a speedy and public trial by a fair (impartial) jury in the district where the crime was committed. The accused person must be informed of the charges against him or her. The accused person has the right to know the witnesses against him or her, to summon witnesses in his or her favor, and to have a lawyer.

ARTICLE VII. *Rights of an Accused Person* (continued). A jury must be used in any lawsuit involving more than twenty dollars.

ARTICLE VIII. *Rights of an Accused Person* (concluded). Excessive bail, excessive fines, and cruel and unusual punishments are forbidden.

ARTICLE IX. *Reserved Rights.* The people have other rights besides those listed here.

ARTICLE X. *Reserved Rights* (continued). Powers not delegated to the federal government or forbidden to the states are reserved to the states and the people.

ARTICLE XI. *Jurisdiction of the Federal Courts* (1798). A case may not be brought against a state in a federal court by citizens of another state or a foreign nation.

ARTICLE XII. *Election of the President and Vice-President* (1804). The electors shall cast separate ballots for president and vice-president. If no person has a majority, the House of Representatives chooses the president from the three highest candidates. Each state casts a single vote in this election. The Senate follows a similar procedure to choose the vice-president when no candidate has a majority of the electoral votes.

ARTICLE XII. The electors shall meet in their respective States, and vote by ballot for President and Vice President, one of whom, at least, shall not be an inhabitant of the same State with themselves; they shall name in their ballots the person voted for as President, and in distinct ballots the person voted for as Vice President; and they shall make distinct lists of all persons voted for as President, and of all persons voted for as Vice President, and of the number of votes for each, which list they shall sign and certify, and transmit sealed to the seat of the government of the United States, directed to the President of the Senate; the President of the Senate shall, in the presence of the Senate and House of Representatives, open all the certificates, and the votes shall then be counted: the person having the greatest number of votes for President shall be the President, if such number be a majority of the whole number of electors appointed; and if no person have such majority, then from the persons having the highest numbers, not exceeding three, on the list of those voted for as President, the House of Representatives shall choose immediately by ballot the President. But in choosing the President, the vote shall be taken by States, the representation from each State having one vote; a quorum for this purpose shall consist of a member or members from two thirds of the States, and a majority of all the States shall be necessary to a choice. And if the House of Representatives shall not choose a President whenever the right of choice shall devolve upon them, before the fourth day of March next following, then the Vice President shall act as President, as in the case of the death or other constitutional disability of the President.

The person having the greatest number of votes as Vice President shall be the Vice President, if such number be a majority of the whole number of electors appointed; and if no person have a majority, then from the two highest numbers on the list the Senate shall choose the Vice President: a quorum for that purpose shall consist of two thirds of the whole number of Senators, and a majority of the whole number shall be necessary to a choice.

But no person constitutionally ineligible to the office of President shall be eligible to that of Vice President of the United States.

ARTICLE XIII. Section 1. Neither slavery nor involuntary servitude, except as a punishment for crime whereof the party shall have been duly convicted, shall exist within the United States, or any place subject to their jurisdiction.

Section 2. Congress shall have power to enforce this article by appropriate legislation.

ARTICLE XIV. Section 1. All persons born or naturalized in the United States, and subject to the jurisdiction thereof, are citizens of the United States and of the State wherein they reside. No State shall make or enforce any law which shall abridge the privileges or immunities of citizens of the United States; nor shall any State deprive any person of life, liberty, or property, without due process of law, nor deny to any person within its jurisdiction the equal protection of the laws.

Section 2. Representatives shall be apportioned among the several States according to their respective numbers, counting the whole number of persons in each State, excluding Indians not taxed. But when the right to vote at any election for the choice of electors for President and Vice President of the United States, representatives in Congress, the executive and judicial officers of a State, or the members of the legislature thereof, is denied to any of the male inhabitants of such State, being twenty-one years of age, and citizens of the United States, or in any way abridged, except for participation in rebellion or other crime, the basis of representation

ARTICLE XIII. *End of Slavery* (1865). Slavery or forced service is forbidden, except as punishment for a crime.

ARTICLE XIV. *Equal Rights for All Americans* (1868). All persons born or naturalized (granted citizenship) in the United States are citizens of the United States and of the state where they live. No state can take away their rights as citizens; deprive them of life, liberty, or property without due process of law; or deny them the equal protection of the laws.

The number of representatives from a state depends on the number of inhabitants it has. (This ends the three-fifths rule, in Section 2 of Article I). If a state denies the vote to citizens over twenty-one years of age, except for rebellion or crimes, the number of its representatives is to be reduced.

Anyone who took an oath, as a federal or state official, to support the Constitution and then supported a rebellion (the Confederacy) is forbidden to hold federal or state office. Congress may restore such rights by a two-thirds vote of both houses.

The debts of the United States in ending the rebellion (the Civil War) are legal. But debts arising from the rebellion against the United States and payments for the loss or emancipation of slaves are illegal. They may not be paid by the federal government or any state.

ARTICLE XV. *Right to Vote for Former Slaves* (1870). Citizens of the United States may not be denied the right to vote because of their race or color or because they were once slaves.

ARTICLE XVI. *Income Tax* (1913). Congress may collect taxes on incomes without regard to a state's population.

therein shall be reduced in the proportion which the number of such male citizens shall bear to the whole number of male citizens twenty-one years of age in such State.

Section 3. No person shall be a senator or representative in Congress, or elector of President and Vice President, or hold any office, civil or military, under the United States, or under any State, who having previously taken an oath, as a member of Congress, or as an officer of the United States, or as a member of any State legislature, or as an executive or judicial officer of any State to support the Constitution of the United States shall have engaged in insurrection or rebellion against the same, or given aid or comfort to the enemies thereof. But Congress may by a vote of two-thirds of each house remove such disability.

Section 4. The validity of the public debt of the United States, authorized by law, including debts incurred for payment of pensions and bounties for services in suppressing insurrection or rebellion, shall not be questioned. But neither the United States nor any State shall assume or pay any debt or obligation incurred in aid of insurrection or rebellion against the United States, or any claim for the loss or emancipation of any slave; but all such debts, obligations, and claims shall be held illegal and void.

Section 5. The Congress shall have power to enforce, by appropriate legislation the provisions of this article.

ARTICLE XV. Section 1. The right of citizens of the United States to vote shall not be denied or abridged by the United States or by any State on account of race, color, or previous condition of servitude.

Section 2. The Congress shall have power to enforce this article by appropriate legislation.

ARTICLE XVI. The Congress shall have power to lay and collect taxes on incomes, from whatever source derived, without apportionment among the several States, and without regard to any census or enumeration.

ARTICLE XVII. The Senate of the United States shall be composed of two Senators from each State, elected by the people thereof, for six years; and each Senator shall have one vote. The electors in each State shall have the qualifications requisite for electors of the most numerous branch of the State legislatures.

When vacancies happen in the representation of any State in the Senate, the executive authority of such State shall issue writs of election to fill such vacancies: *Provided,* That the legislature of any State may empower the executive thereof to make temporary appointments until the people fill the vacancies by election as the legislature may direct.

This amendment shall not be so construed as to affect the election or term of any Senator chosen before it becomes valid as part of the Constitution.

ARTICLE XVIII. Section 1. After one year from the ratification of this article the manufacture, sale, or transportation of intoxicating liquors within, the importation thereof into, or the exportation thereof from the United States and all territory subject to the jurisdiction thereof for beverage purposes is hereby prohibited.

Section 2. The Congress and the several States shall have concurrent power to enforce this article by appropriate legislation.

Section 3. This article shall be inoperative unless it shall have been ratified as an amendment to the Constitution by the legislatures of the several States, as provided in the Constitution, within seven years from the date of the submission hereof to the States by the Congress.

ARTICLE XIX. The right of citizens of the United States to vote shall not be denied or abridged by the United States or by any

ARTICLE XVII. *Direct Election of Senators* (1913). Senators are to be elected by the voters in each state—that is, by people eligible to vote for the lower house of the state legislature.

When a seat in the Senate becomes vacant, the governor of the state may appoint a senator to fill it. This person is to hold office either for the rest of the senator's term or until the next election, as the state legislature decides.

ARTICLE XVIII. *Prohibition* (1919). It is forbidden to make, sell, and transport intoxicating liquors within the United States, to import them, or to export them.

Congress and the states may pass laws to enforce this prohibition.

A seven-year limit is set for ratifying this amendment. (Several later amendments also included such a provision.)

ARTICLE XIX. *Voting for Women* (1920). A citizen of the United States may not be denied the right to vote on account of sex.

ARTICLE XX. *End of the "Lame Ducks"* (1933). The president and vice-president take office on January 20 (instead of March 4). The newly elected Congress meets on January 3, three months after Election Day. (It used to meet in December, more than a year after the election! During that year, the old Congress continued to meet and pass laws, even though it contained many "lame ducks," members of Congress who had lost the election.)

If the president-elect dies before the inauguration, the vice-president becomes president. If neither is available, Congress will choose someone to act as president.

State on account of sex.

Congress shall have power to enforce this article by appropriate legislation.

ARTICLE XX. Section 1. The terms of the President and Vice President shall end at noon on the 20th day of January, and the terms of Senators and Representatives at noon on the 3rd day of January, of the years in which such terms would have ended if this article had not been ratified; and the terms of their successors shall then begin.

Section 2. The Congress shall assemble at least once in every year, and such meeting shall begin at noon on the 3d day of January, unless they shall by law appoint a different day.

Section 3. If, at the time fixed for the beginning of the term of the President, the President elect shall have died, the Vice President elect shall become President. If a President shall not have been chosen before the time fixed for the beginning of his term, or if the President elect shall have failed to qualify, then the Vice President elect shall act as President until a President shall have qualified; and the Congress may by law provide for the case wherein neither a President elect nor a Vice President elect shall have qualified, declaring who shall then act as President, or the manner in which one who is to act shall be selected, and such person shall act accordingly until a President or Vice President shall have qualified.

Section 4. The Congress may by law provide for the case of the death of any of the persons from whom the House of Representatives may choose a President whenever the right of choice shall have devolved upon them, and for the case of the death of any of the persons from whom the Senate may choose a Vice President whenever the right of choice shall have devolved upon them.

Section 5. Sections 1 and 2 shall take effect on the 15th day of October following the ratification of this article.

Section 6. This article shall be inoperative unless it shall have been ratified as an amendment to the Constitution by the legislatures of three-fourths of the several States within seven years from the date of its submission.

ARTICLE XXI. Section 1. The eighteenth article of amendment to the Constitution of the United States is hereby repealed.

Section 2. The transportation or importation into any State, Territory, or possession of the United States for delivery or use therein of intoxicating liquors, in violation of the laws thereof, is hereby prohibited.

Section 3. This article shall be inoperative unless it shall have been ratified as an amendment to the Constitution by conventions in the several States, as provided in the Constitution, within seven years from the date of the submission hereof to the States by the Congress.

ARTICLE XXII. Section 1. No person shall be elected to the office of the President more than twice, and no person who has held the office of President, or acted as President, for more than two years of a term to which some other person was elected President shall be elected to the office of the President more than once. But this Article shall not apply to any person holding the office of President when this Article was proposed by the Congress, and shall not prevent any person who may be holding the office of President, or acting as President, during the term within which this Article becomes operative from holding the office of President or acting as President during the remainder of such term.

ARTICLE XXIII. Section 1. The District constituting the seat of Government of the United States shall appoint in such manner as the Congress may direct: A number of electors of President and Vice President equal to the whole number of Senators and Representatives in Congress to which the

ARTICLE XXI. *Repeal of Prohibition* (1933). The Eighteenth Amendment is repealed (ended).

Bringing intoxicating liquor into any state, territory, or possession where it is prohibited is illegal. (This is to protect those parts of the country that still have their own prohibition laws.)

ARTICLE XXII. *Two Terms for President* (1951). A person may be elected president for only two terms; or for only one term if the person has served as president for more than two years. (This happens when the president dies and the vice-president takes the elected president's place in the first two years of the term.)

ARTICLE XXIII. *Voting in the District of Columbia* (1961). The District of Columbia is to choose electors for president and vice-president. The number of electors is to be the same as if it were a state, except that it may not have more electors than the state with the least population.

ARTICLE XXIV. *Against the Poll Tax* (1964). No citizen of the United States may be denied the right to vote for presidential electors or members of Congress because he or she has failed to pay a poll tax or any other tax.

ARTICLE XXV. *Presidential Disability and Succession* (1967). If the president is removed from office, dies, or resigns, the vice-president becomes president.

When there is no vice-president, the president will nominate a vice-president, with the consent of more than half the votes of both houses of Congress.

If the president tells Congress in writing that the president is unable to perform the presidential duties, then the vice-president will take over as acting president.

Whenever the vice-president and a majority of the president's cabinet, or another body chosen by Congress, decide that the president cannot

District would be entitled if it were a State, but in no event more than the least populous State; they shall be in addition to those appointed by the States, but they shall be considered, for the purposes of the election of President and Vice President, to be electors appointed by a State; and they shall meet in the District and perform such duties as provided by the twelfth article of amendment.

Section 2. The Congress shall have power to enforce this article by appropriate legislation.

ARTICLE XXIV. Section 1. The right of citizens of the United States to vote in any primary or other election for President or Vice President, for electors for President or Vice President, or for Senator or Representative in Congress, shall not be denied or abridged by the United States or any State by reason of failure to pay any poll tax or other tax.

Section 2. The Congress shall have the power to enforce this article by appropriate legislation.

ARTICLE XXV. Section 1. In case of the removal of the President from office or his death or resignation, the Vice President shall become President.

Section 2. Whenever there is a vacancy in the office of the Vice President, the President shall nominate a Vice President who shall take the office upon confirmation by a majority vote of both houses of Congress.

Section 3. Whenever the President transmits to the President pro tempore of the Senate and the Speaker of the House of Representatives his written declaration that he is unable to discharge the powers and duties of his office, and until he transmits to them a written declaration to the contrary, such powers and duties shall be discharged by the Vice President as Acting President.

Section 4. Whenever the Vice President and a majority of either the principal officers of the executive departments, or of such other body as Congress may by law provide, transmit to the President pro tempore of the Senate and the Speaker of the House of Representatives their written declaration that the President is unable to discharge the powers and duties of his office, the Vice President shall immediately assume the powers and duties of the office as Acting President.

Thereafter, when the President transmits to the President pro tempore of the Senate and the Speaker of the House of Representatives his written declaration that no inability exists, he shall resume the powers and duties of his office unless the Vice President and a majority of either the principal officers of the executive department, or of such other body as Congress may by law provide, transmit within four days to the President pro tempore of the Senate and the Speaker of the House of Representatives their written declaration that the President is unable to discharge the powers and duties of his office. Thereupon Congress shall decide the issue, assembling within 48 hours for that purpose if not in session. If the Congress, within 21 days after receipt of the latter written declaration, or, if Congress is not in session, within 21 days after Congress is required to assemble, determines by two-thirds vote of both houses that the President is unable to discharge the powers and duties of his office, the Vice President shall continue to discharge the same as Acting President; otherwise, the President shall resume the powers and duties of his office.

ARTICLE XXVI. Section 1. The right of citizens of the United States, who are 18 years of age or older, to vote shall not be denied or abridged by the United States or by any state on account of age.

Section 2. The Congress shall have power to enforce this article by appropriate legislation.

discharge presidential duties, the vice-president will take over as acting president.

The president may begin working again after telling Congress of the ability to do so. If the vice-president and a majority of the president's cabinet or the body chosen by Congress disagree with the president, Congress will decide the issue. If it decides by a two-thirds vote that the president is unable to take up presidential duties, the vice-president will continue acting as president. Otherwise the president will return to office.

ARTICLE XXVII. No law, varying the compensation for the services of the Senators and Representatives, shall take effect, until an election of Representatives shall have intervened.

ARTICLE XXVII. *Congressional pay* (1992). No law can change congressional pay before the next election of Representatives.

ARTICLE XXVI. *Voting Age Lowered to 18* (1971). Eighteen is the legal voting age for citizens in local, state, and federal elections.

PRESIDENTS OF THE UNITED STATES

President	Term of Office	Political Party	Home State	Earlier Occupation
1. George Washington	1789–1797	None	VA	Planter
2. John Adams	1797–1801	Fed.	MA	Lawyer
3. Thomas Jefferson	1801–1809	Dem.–Rep.	VA	Lawyer
4. James Madison	1809–1817	Dem.–Rep.	VA	Lawyer
5. James Monroe	1817–1825	Dem.–Rep.	VA	Lawyer
6. John Quincy Adams	1825–1829	Nat.–Rep.	MA	Lawyer
7. Andrew Jackson	1829–1837	Dem.	TN	Lawyer, Army officer
8. Martin Van Buren	1837–1841	Dem.	NY	Lawyer
9. William H. Harrison	1841	Whig	OH	Army officer
10. John Tyler	1841–1845	Whig	VA	Lawyer
11. James K. Polk	1845–1849	Dem.	TN	Lawyer
12. Zachary Taylor	1849–1850	Whig	LA	Army officer
13. Millard Fillmore	1850–1853	Whig	NY	Lawyer
14. Franklin Pierce	1853–1857	Dem.	NH	Lawyer
15. James Buchanan	1857–1861	Dem.	PA	Lawyer
16. Abraham Lincoln	1861–1865	Rep.	IL	Lawyer
17. Andrew Johnson	1865–1869	Rep.	TN	Tailor
18. Ulysses S. Grant	1869–1877	Rep.	IL	Army officer
19. Rutherford B. Hayes	1877–1881	Rep.	OH	Lawyer
20. James A. Garfield	1881	Rep.	OH	Teacher, Lawyer
21. Chester A. Arthur	1881–1885	Rep.	NY	Lawyer
22. Grover Cleveland	1885–1889	Dem.	NY	Lawyer
23. Benjamin Harrison	1889–1893	Rep.	IN	Lawyer
24. Grover Cleveland	1893–1897	Dem.	NY	Lawyer
25. William B. McKinley	1897–1901	Rep.	OH	Lawyer
26. Theodore Roosevelt	1901–1909	Rep.	NY	Rancher, Writer
27. William Howard Taft	1909–1913	Rep.	OH	Lawyer
28. Woodrow Wilson	1913–1921	Dem.	NJ	Lawyer, Teacher
29. Warren G. Harding	1921–1923	Rep.	OH	Journalist
30. Calvin Coolidge	1923–1929	Rep.	MA	Lawyer
31. Herbert C. Hoover	1929–1933	Rep.	CA	Engineer
32. Franklin D. Roosevelt	1933–1945	Dem.	NY	Lawyer
33. Harry S. Truman	1945–1953	Dem.	MO	Merchant
34. Dwight D. Eisenhower	1953–1961	Rep.	NY, PA	Army officer
35. John F. Kennedy	1961–1963	Dem.	MA	Writer, Teacher
36. Lyndon B. Johnson	1963–1969	Dem.	TX	Teacher
37. Richard M. Nixon	1969–1974	Rep.	NY, CA	Lawyer
38. Gerald R. Ford	1974–1977	Rep.	MI	Lawyer
39. Jimmy (James Earl) Carter	1977–1981	Dem.	GA	Farmer
40. Ronald W. Reagan	1981–1989	Rep.	CA	Actor
41. George Bush	1989-1993	Rep.	ME	Businessman
42. Bill (William J.) Clinton	1993-	Dem.	AR	Lawyer

GLOSSARY

A

absolute monarchy—The type of government whereby a ruler has a great deal of power, which he or she has inherited.

accept—To receive with consent.

advise—To give information to; to tell what to do.

adviser—The one who offers advice, who suggests what can be done.

aerospace—Concerned with the designing and making of missiles and other means of traveling within and beyond the earth's atmosphere.

agencies—Groups that have the power to act for others, as committees acting for the president or Congress.

alien—A person who lives in a country he or she is not a citizen of.

alliances—The agreements between nations to cooperate in special ways.

ambassadors—The representatives from one government to another.

amend—To change.

amendments—Proposed changes.

appeal—To plea.

aristocracy—A type of government ruled by a small group of people with inherited positions or titles.

Articles of Confederation—The first plan for the American government after the Revolution.

assault—A violent attack.

assessed value—The value of property for tax purposes.

assessor—An official who determines the value of all property for tax purposes.

authority—The right to make the final decisions. The right to have the final say.

automation—The use of machines to do jobs people once did.

B

bail—A sum of money deposited by someone accused of a crime as guarantee that he or she will appear for trial.

balanced budget—A situation in which income equals expenses.

blacklist—A list of people considered undesirable.

boycott—The withholding of business in order to win a point of view.

budget—A list of expected income and expenses.

bureaucracy—The body of officials and administrators in a government; government through offices.

bureaus—Offices that carry out special duties.

burglary—Act of breaking into and entering a building to commit a crime.

business cycle—A change from boom to depression in the business activity of a country.

C

cabinet—The group of persons appointed by the heads of governments to advise them.

campaign—To take part in a plan or method used to win an election or reach a goal.

candidates—The people who seek public office.

captains—The people within a precinct who encourage members of their party to vote on election day.

capital—The resources or wealth owned or used in a business by a firm or corporation.

capitalism—An economic system based on private property and competition.

career—An occupation or job that a person takes as his or her life's work.

caucus—A meeting of party leaders at a local level.

ceremonial—Formal.

charter—The written laws under which people live—a constitution.

checks and balances—A system in which each branch of the government keeps the other branches from becoming too powerful.

427

chief executive—The head of the executive branch of government.

circuit—Moving around.

circulation—The movement of something through a system; money passing from one person to others as in trade.

citizenship—The status of being a native or naturalized person of a country.

city council—A group of people who make city laws.

city manager—The person chosen by the city council to run the city.

civil—Having to do with citizens.

civil service—Government jobs for those who pass a test.

collective—Of a group rather than of separate individuals.

collective bargaining—The act of employers meeting with employees to discuss differences.

commander in chief of the armed forces—A role of the president.

commissioners—The officials that head a county.

commission type—The form of city government whereby voters elect commissioners to run their city.

committees—Small groups of senators or representatives gathered to study specific bills.

competition—The act of trying against others for a prize or profit.

compromise—To work out an agreement.

concurrent—Existing together side by side.

conditions—The ways people or things are.

confederation—A league.

conference—Of or concerning a meeting of people or committees to settle differences.

conference committee—A meeting of members of the House and Senate to decide on the wording of a bill.

consent—Agreement on an action or opinion; approval.

Constitution—The plan of government for the United States.

convention—A formal meeting of members or delegates.

coroner—A person who investigates deaths whose cause is unclear.

corporation—A group of people given a charter from the state or federal government allowing it to conduct business. A corporation can have many owners but is treated in the eyes of the law as one person.

county—Next highest unit of government after a town.

county clerk—Person who keeps records of court cases.

county supervisors—Officials that head a county.

crime rate—A comparison between the number of crimes and the population.

criminal—A person who is involved with crime.

critical—Dangerous, with great risk.

cultural—Having to do with the customs, or practices, of a people.

cycle—An event that is repeated at particular times.

D

damages—A sum of money; the estimated cost of injury or harm done.

deduct—To take away.

deficit—The amount by which expenses are greater than income.

defendant—The accused in a trial.

delinquents—Those not doing what is required by law.

democratic republic—A form of government whereby voters elect whomever they wish to represent them.

demonstrate—To protest or march to show concern for an issue.

depression—A period of falling prices and profits, low wages, and unemployment.

deposit—To put in a safe place.

devices—Machines or things made for particular purposes.

dictator—A person who has absolute power in the government.

dictatorship—A form of government whereby one person who has not inherited power has absolute control.

direct primary elections—The elections that decide a party's official candidate.

discount—A payment of interest in advance of receiving a loan.

discrimination—The unfair treatment of a class, person, or group.

disputes—Arguments, differences of opinion.

428

district—A portion of a country, state, or city marked off for a special purpose.

district attorney—An official who represents a specific district in criminal cases.

diversity—Variety.

duplication—The act of doing double work or the same thing as another.

E

efficient—Very able; doing things without waste.

elastic clause—Refers to part of Article I of the Constitution, which has been loosely interpreted to give the government much power.

electoral college—All the electors.

electoral votes—The votes cast by electors, who are those elected to choose a president.

electors—The people who elect.

embarrass—To make a person feel uncomfortable, uneasy.

empathy—Deep sympathy; feeling another person's emotions as if they were one's own.

employees—The persons who work for another.

employers—The people or businesses that hire people to work for them.

entanglements—Acts or things that cause tangles.

enterprise—An important, difficult, or dangerous undertaking.

environment—Natural surroundings.

erosion—The process of wearing away.

excessive—Extreme; higher than might be expected.

excise tax—A type of tax on the making, sale, or use of goods made and used within a country.

executive—Having the power and duty of carrying out the laws.

exhausts—Fumes; used steam, gasoline, and so forth, that escapes from engines.

experiment—A test, an operation to discover something unknown.

F

federation—A group of several organizations; a union by agreement.

federal—Of or concerning a plan of government in which states recognize the power of a central government, but have powers of their own.

felony—A serious crime.

filibuster—The act of preventing passage of a bill by talking it to death.

fined—Told to pay a sum of money.

foreign—Having to do with other countries; coming from outside one's own country.

free enterprise—An economic and political idea that holds that businesses and people should be free to think and act as they wish without government intervention.

G

graduated—Arranged in degrees or amounts.

grants-in-aid—Money from the federal government that must be used as the federal government says.

grand jury—A jury that examines the accusations against a person or corporation. If the evidence warrants, it makes formal charges on which the accused persons are later tried.

H

hearing—A preliminary examination of the evidence by a judge to determine if a trial is necessary; a chance to be heard.

historians—Those who write or make a study of history.

home rule—Form of government whereby local voters run local government.

human rights—The rights that Americans believe all nations should respect.

I

identity—One's understanding of who one is.

immigrants—People who come from other countries to settle permanently.

impeachment—A method by which high government officials can be removed from office.

implied—Unstated, suggested.

income—The money that comes in; receipts; returns.

incorporated village—An area that has been granted certain rights by the state.

indictment—A formal charge by a grand jury.

indistinguishable—Appearing to be the same; not having clear differences.

industrial—Used in industry; referring to industry.

industry—Manufacturing products for business.

inflation—A period when there is a lot of money, few goods, and high prices.

influence—To use power to get others to agree with you; to have power over.

inherits—To receive a gift from someone who has died.

interdependence—The situation in which two or more things need each other to survive or succeed.

interest—Amount charged for borrowing money.

interfere—To meddle in the affairs of others.

interprets—Explains.

introduced—Brought forward.

isolation—The act of complete separation, of being alone.

J

judges—The officials who hear criminal and civil cases.

judicial—Having to do with a court of law or the administration of justice.

justice—Fair treatment.

justice of the peace—The lowest state court.

justices—Judges who sit on the Supreme Court.

juveniles—Young people, not yet adults.

L

labor—Workers.

land—A natural resource.

league—An organization of states that act together.

legislative—Having the duty and power of making laws.

levy—To order to be paid or to collect.

liberty—The freedom to act as one chooses.

limited government—A form of organized authority that is not all-powerful.

limited monarchy—A form of government whereby the monarch is not all powerful.

lobby—A hall or waiting room at the entrance to a building or meeting room.

lobbyists—Trained experts sent to Washington by various groups to influence members of the House and Senate.

lockout—A situation in which an employer refuses to allow employees to work in order to force them to agree to his or her terms.

M

Magna Carta—"Great Charter" that limited the power of the English king after 1215.

majority—A number greater than half the total.

major council—A type of city government where the mayor is the chief executive.

migrant—Someone who moves from one place to another.

minority—A number less than half the total.

misdemeanor—A minor crime.

monarch—A royal ruler such as a king or queen.

monarchy—A type of government having a hereditary ruler.

municipal—Of a city or town.

N

national committee—A group whose members are chosen by the party in each state—this committee is most active during presidential elections.

national government—The government of the whole nation; sometimes called the federal government.

naturalized—Having to do with being admitted to citizenship.

natural resources—Valuable things found in the natural environment.

neutral—Not taking sides in a dispute.

nominate—To name a candidate for an office.

O

oligarchy—A form of government in which a small group of people rules.

P

parish—A county in Louisiana.

par—Average, normal; equality.

parity—The quality or state of being equal.

Parliament—The governing body in England.

parole—To free a prisoner before the sentence is finished. The paroled person is under supervision until the end of the time he or she was sentenced to serve.

party platform—An official statement of a party's ideas.

permanent—Lasting, cannot be changed.

personal—Of or coming from a particular person; private.

personal liberties—The freedoms given to every citizen.

personal security—A situation in which an individual is free from danger—every citizen has the right to a safe life.

personnel—A body of persons; the people who work together in one place or for one group.

petition—A formal way (usually written) of asking a government official for something.

plaintiff—The person making the complaint in a trial.

policy—A plan, a way of acting toward others.

political machine—An organized political team.

political parties—The organizations of citizens who aim to elect their candidates to government offices.

political patronage—The distribution of jobs, contracts, and so forth, by a government official as rewards to his or her supporters.

political system—A plan for government.

politicians—The people who hold a public office; those who take part in the work of a political party.

politics—The management of political affairs; anything to do with government.

polluting—Making dirty.

pollution—Dirt, something impure.

poll watchers—The members of different parties who make sure that the laws concerning elections are observed at the polls.

popular sovereignty—When authority for government action comes from the people.

precinct—The space within a boundary; a part of a district of a city, town, village.

preliminary—Coming before the main action.

presides—Runs a meeting.

pressure groups—Groups organized to try and win votes from Congress.

prestige—Standing, reputation, or influence based on what is known of one's abilities, deeds, friends, and so forth.

primary—A special election to choose a political party's candidates, who will later run in a regular election.

private property—The things that an individual owns.

probation—A sentence from a court that is held off, on the promise of good behavior.

profit—The gain from a business.

Progressives—The people favoring progress; members of the Progressive party.

propaganda—The spreading of an idea in order to shape people's opinion.

property rights—The rights of every citizen to own property.

proposed—Suggested, offered.

proprietary colony—A piece of land owned by a private person.

publicity—Information given to the public; public attention.

purposely—With deliberate intent.

Q

qualifications—Those things needed to make a person fit to hold an office.

qualified—Permitted by law or rules.

R

ratify—To approve.

recession—A period in which there is growing unemployment and falling profits, wages, and production.

recognition—An official act by which one country admits that another country exists.

reforms—Improvements, removal of evils or defects.

register—In a store, a machine that shows the amount of the sale.

registered—Enrolled, entered, signed in.

regulate—To control by use of rules.

regulatory—Having to do with regulating or controlling.

reject—To refuse, deny, turn down.

repealed—Done away with; withdrawn.

representative democracy—A form of government whereby people elect representatives to govern.

republic—A nation where citizens elect representatives to manage the government.

reserve—To keep back, save.

reservoirs—The places where water is stored, reserves of water.

residency—Having to do with your official place of residence; where you live.

resources—A supply of something that can be used when needed, as coal, lumber, water.

revenue—Government income.

revenue sharing—A plan by which the federal government returns money to the states. The states may use this money as they want to.

royal—Of kings and queens.

S

sale—The act of exchanging goods for money; the amount sold.

sales taxes—A tax on items that people buy, often luxuries.

security—Freedom from danger, risk; safety.

segregation—The separation of a group.

selectmen—Officials that head the town government.

seniority—The practice of choosing the person

with the longest time on the committee as chairperson.

sensational—Concerning something that makes a person strongly interested; outstanding, exciting.

separation of powers—The system of dividing power between the different government branches.

session—The period of time during which sittings or meetings of a court, council, or law-making body take place.

share—A part.

shareholders—The owners of shares in a corporation.

sheriff—The official who supervises the county jail and calls people to jury duty.

snipers—The people who shoot at others from a hiding place.

snob—One who acts as though others were inferior.

soil bank—Land planted with grass for a few years.

sovereignty—The highest power of or over a nation.

specialize—To follow a special line of work.

state—A body of people occupying a definite area and organized under a national government.

subcommittee—A group formed within a committee in the House or Senate to carefully examine a few bills.

suburbs—The smaller towns and cities around a large city.

suffrage—The right to vote.

supervision—The act of directing or watching over someone's behavior.

supply-side economics—The policy and theory of cutting taxes to promote business growth.

surplus—More of something than is needed.

survey—An examination made by gathering information.

T

tariff—A tax on goods coming into the country.

technology—The methods and equipment used to do work.

telethons—Special fund-raising programs on television.

terrorist—Person who uses violence to send political messages.

theory—An idea used to explain an event, something that is happening.

totalitarian—A type of government whereby a ruler or rulers control the daily lives of all citizens.

town—The next unit of government above a village.

town clerk—The official who records births, marriages, deaths, and election results, and issues licenses.

township—Land around and outside of incorporated villages.

traits—Features, qualities, characteristics of a person.

treaties—Contracts or agreements between two or more countries.

trial—The examination of a case in court.

trustee—One who holds property for another and does business for that person or group.

U

unconstitutional—Not allowed by the Constitution.

undemocratic republic—A type of government whereby representatives must be titled or wealthy or chosen undemocratically.

unincorporated village—A village not yet granted certain rights by its state.

V

vacancy—An empty space; a position with no one to fill it.

vaccinations—Acts of giving medicine to prevent disease.

verdict—A decision by a jury.

veto—To refuse to sign a bill.

village—The smallest unit of government.

violation—The act of breaking or failing to keep a law.

void—Having no legal force.

volunteers—Those who do something by their own free will.

W

ward committee—A group within a political party whose members are elected from their precinct.

watchdogs—A group that guards against unfair practices.

welfare—The condition of happiness, success, and comfort.

world leader—A person known throughout the world.

INDEX

V

Vaccinations, 182, 183
Vermont, 260
Veterans pensions, 175
Veto
    governor's, 184
    mayor's 205
    president's, 116
    in Security Council, 368
Vice–presidency, 122, 147, 359
Vietnam, 102, 145, 268, 349, 360, 377
Vietnam War, 102, 349, 360
Villages, 197–200, 205
Virginia, 77, 184
Virgin Islands, 3
Voting, 41–44, 72
Voting Rights Act, 58

W

Wages and Hours Act, 287
Wallace, George C., 102, 103
War of 1812, 83, 341
"War on Poverty," 321, 322
War Powers Act, 145
Wars, 153
    declaration, 110
    Korean, 48, 360, 370, 377
    Vietnam, 102, 349, 360, 377
    War of 1812, 83, 341
    World War I, 296, 343, 358, 366
    World War II, 56, 58, 64, 153, 343–44, 347, 348, 350, 366, 377
Washington (state), 185
Washington D.C., 57
    protest marches, 139–40
Washington, George, 25, 26, 31, 77, 83, 153, 341, 362, 394
Water, 333
    pollution, 329–31
Welfare payments, 321
West Germany, 272, 295
White–collar crime, 227
White House, 58, 145
    staff, 154
Wilson, Woodrow, 102, 163, 185, 343
Wisconsin, 102
Women's rights movement, 43, 58–59, 235
World Court. *See* International Court of Justice
World Health Organization (WHO), 369
World population, 375–76
World War I, 296, 343, 358, 366
World War II, 56, 58, 64, 153, 343–44, 347, 349, 350, 366, 377

Z

Zimbabwe, 350. *See also* Rhodesia
Zoning laws, 205